CONSUMER BEHAVIOR

INSTRUCTOR'S RESOURCE MANUAL
John R. Brook, Jr.
Houston Baptist University

CONSUMER BEHAVIOR
Eighth Edition

Leon G. Schiffman
Leslie Lazar Kanuk

PEARSON
Prentice
Hall

Upper Saddle River, New Jersey 07458

Editor-in-Chief: Jeff Shelstad
Acquisitions Editor: Bruce Kaplan
Assistant Editor: Melissa Pellerano
Manager, Print Production: Christy Mahon
Production Editor & Buyer: Wanda Rockwell
Printer/Binder: Technical Communication Services

10 9 8 7 6 5 4 3 2 1
ISBN 0-13-142022-4

CONTENTS

Preface

PREFACE

HOW TO USE:

The 8th Edition of Schiffman/Kanuk's *Consumer Behavior* textbook has a complete set of supplemental learning and teaching aids. The *Instructor's Resource Manual* plays a central role in organizing this package. This manual has been designed so the instructor can plan lectures, demonstrations, discussions, visual presentations, and written assignments in a coordinated and efficient manner.

All 16 chapters of the textbook have been carefully reviewed in order to develop the most logical and helpful manual for you, the instructor. The primary features and instructions on how to use the *Instructor's Resource Manual* are described below.

LEARNING OBJECTIVES

Each chapter of the *Instructor's Resource Manual* contains a list of important learning objectives. These Learning Objectives are listed at the beginning of each chapter of the *Instructor's Resource Manual*. In addition, each Learning Objective (by number) is tied to the specific section(s) of the textbook (to which it pertains) in the Chapter Outline section of the *Instructor's Resource Manual*. You will find this to be helpful in assuring that all primary learning objectives have been covered in the course of the chapter lecture.

SUMMARY (Chapter Overview)

Each chapter of the textbook is summarized in the Summary. This section provides the instructor with a repeat of the information included at the end of each chapter. This material is especially helpful in planning chapter sequence presentation and any desired chapter combinations. In addition, this section may help the instructor plan introductory lecture remarks.

CHAPTER OUTLINE

This section is the core of the *Instructor's Resource Manual*. This teaching outline is a thorough outline (specifically tied to the actual phrases and definitions used in the textbook) of the material included in the textbook chapters. This outline includes major and minor headings from the textbook. The instructor will notice special information sections that appear periodically in the body of the outline. This material is indicated with **bold type** and **bold asterisks (*****)**. The purpose of the information block is to indicate to the instructor where key material appears in the textbook and when to use teaching aids. These information blocks may contain the following items of information:

Key Terms (term is identified); **Learning Objective** (learning objective is listed by number); **Discussion Questions** (discussion question is listed by number); **Exercises** (application exercise is listed by number); **chapter Figures** (listed by number); and **chapter Tables** (listed by number). It is recommended that the instructor carefully review the Chapter Outline prior to preparing a chapter lecture. This review will help in coordinating the learning activities that are available with the textbook and in making advance discussion assignments for students.

In addition, the instructor will find it useful to use the additional features found in the *Instructor's Resource Manual* when reviewing the Chapter Outline. Additional features (see descriptions below) include: (a) **S.T.A.R. (Self-Training and Reinforcement) Projects** (useful in-class and out-of-class assignments to reinforce learning concepts), and (b) **Cases** (text authors provide insight into how to solve the end-of-chapter cases). **Video Library Notes** may be found on the Prentice Hall Web site for the Schiffman and Kanuk text).

KEY TERMS

All Key Terms listed at the end of each chapter have been identified in the Chapter Outline section (see **bold asterisks ******* boxes) of the *Instructor's Resource Manual*.

DISCUSSION QUESTIONS

Discussion Questions and associated comments appear in this section. The questions appear in the textbook (assignments can be made from textbook chapters). However, the comments (answers) only appear in the *Instructor's Resource Manual*. Note that proper placement of the Discussion Questions is up to the instructor, although placement suggestions do appear in the **bold asterisks (*****)** boxes of the Chapter Outline section.

EXERCISES

Exercise questions and/or statements appear in the textbook (assignments can be made from textbook chapters). However, the *Instructor's Discussion* comments only appear in the *Instructor's Resource Manual*. Note that proper placement of Exercise questions is up to the instructor, although placement suggestions do appear in the **bold asterisks (*****)** boxes of the Chapter Outline section.

TABLES AND FIGURES

All chapter Tables and Figures have been matched to the appropriate sections of the Chapter Outline for the convenience of the instructor. See the **bold asterisks (*****)** boxes of the Chapter Outline section.

S.T.A.R. (Self-Training and Reinforcement) PROJECTS

This special student projects section is divided into three distinct parts: (a) *Ethical Issues in Consumer Behavior*, (b) *Small Group Projects*, and (c) *Using the Internet to Study Consumer Behavior*. The S.T.A.R. Projects do not appear in the text. The S.T.A.R. questions are written so the instructor can provide them for student use. *Instructor's Discussion* comments are intended for the instructor rather than for the individual student. *Ethical Issues in Consumer Behavior* projects are intended to give the students additional training in business ethics issues that might occur in the study of consumer behavior. *Small Group Projects* aid small groups in perfecting small group interaction, group problem solving, and developing group approaches to consumer behavior projects. *Using the Internet to Study Consumer Behavior* does just that—uses the Web to study consumer behavior (these projects are primarily for individuals). All Web addresses used in the various projects were valid at the time of this manual's preparation; however, please re-check accuracy before administering these questions to the students as Web addresses change frequently. These projects make excellent homework or out-of-class assignments.

All of the above projects have been classroom tested by this author to ensure applicability and usefulness in the classroom. These sections have been written so they may be given directly to the student without requiring the instructor to re-write them. Also, please modify these assignments to fit your individual needs or preferences. Have fun with these assignments, my students do.

CASES (Author's Comments)

Case comments appear in a special section of this *Instructor's Resource Manual* found at the end of each chapter's presentation. These case comments were written by the authors of the textbook to match the cases that appear in the special case section of the text. Use of these materials will greatly aid your students' learning experience.

VIDEOS

A Video Library has been prepared by Prentice Hall to be used with this text. Video Notes will help the instructor use this Video Library. The Video Library and associated Video Notes can be found by referencing the Prentice Hall Web site for this text (see www.prenhall.com). The instructor may use the Videos at any time. However, please preview the Videos prior to usage so you will be familiar with content and learning objectives. See Video Notes for further information.

<u>Final Note:</u>

Should you have any questions about, or difficulties with, the material contained in this *Instructor's Resource Manual*, please feel free to contact this author at the phone number or electronic address listed below so I may assist you:

Phone number: 281-649-3315
Fax Number: 281-649-3436
rustybroks@aol.com

John R. Brooks, Jr., DBA
Prince-Chavanne Professor of
Christian Business Ethics
Houston Baptist University

CHAPTER 1

Introduction: The Impact of the Digital Revolution on Consumer Behavior

LEARNING OBJECTIVES

After studying this chapter students should be able to:
1. Understand the impact of the digital revolution on general consumer behavior.
2. Define consumer behavior.
3. Identify the two major approaches to the study of consumer behavior.
4. Understand the development of the marketing concept.
5. Understand the role of consumer research in the study of consumer behavior.
6. Understand how segmentation, targeting, and positioning are used in the study of consumer behavior.
7. Define customer value, satisfaction, and retention.
8. Discuss the role of ethics in marketing.
9. Describe the societal marketing concept.
10. Briefly discuss the three interlocking stages of consumer decision-making.

CHAPTER SUMMARY

The study of consumer behavior enables marketers to understand and predict consumer behavior in the marketplace; it is concerned not only with what consumers buy but also with why, when, where, and how they buy it. Consumer research is the methodology used to study consumer behavior; it takes place at every phase of the consumption process: before the purchase, during the purchase, and after the purchase.

Consumer behavior is interdisciplinary; that is, it is based on concepts and theories about people that have been developed by scientists in such diverse disciplines as psychology, sociology, social psychology, cultural anthropology, and economics.

Consumer behavior has become an integral part of strategic market planning. The belief that ethics and social responsibility should also be integral components of every marketing decision is embodied in a revised marketing concept—the societal marketing concept—that calls on marketers to fulfill the needs of their target markets in ways that improve society as a whole.

CHAPTER OUTLINE

INTRODUCTION

1. As demonstrated in the movie *Minority Report*, consumers can now purchase highly personalized versions of many products.

2. For example, on Nike's Web site, buyers can now choose from many models of sneakers in different price ranges, customize the chosen shoe using several colors and features, put a personalized ID on each shoe, pay for the product, and have it shipped directly to them.
3. The age of one-to-one marketing has arrived.
4. The *digital revolution* of the marketplace allows much greater customization of products, services, and promotional messages than older marketing tools.
5. Businesses are able to build and maintain relationships with customers in ways never conceived before.
6. Digital technologies enable marketers to collect and analyze increasingly complex data on consumers' buying patterns and personal characteristics.

> *****Use Key Term digital revolution Here*****

7. Over a period of a decade of so, the digital revolution has introduced several drastic changes into the business environment.
   a) Consumers have more power than ever before.
   b) Consumers have access to more information then ever before.
   c) Marketers can offer more services and products than ever before.
   d) The exchange between marketers and customers is increasingly interactive and instantaneous.
   e) Marketers can gather more information about consumers more quickly and easily.
   f) Impact reaches beyond the PC-based connection to the Web.
8. Some suggest that because virtual competition eliminates distance and location-based benefits and, because it is increasingly dominated by intelligent merchant/brokerage agents that steer consumers toward the lowest possible price for a chosen product, online competition is likely to resemble perfect competition.
   a) Some agree with this observation; others do not.
   b) Will branding and competitive differentiation become meaningless?

> *****Use Learning Objective #1 Here; Use Discussion Question #1 Here*****

THE DEFINITION AND SCOPE OF CONSUMER BEHAVIOR

1. *Consumer behavior* is defined as the behavior that consumers display in searching for, purchasing, using, evaluating, and disposing of products and services that they expect will satisfy their needs.

> *****Use Key Term consumer behavior Here; Use Learning Objective #2 Here*****

   a) Consumer behavior focuses on how individuals make decisions to spend their available resources on consumption related items.
   b) We are all consumers. We all consume on a regular basis.

    c) To succeed, businesses need to know everything they can about consumers.
       i) They need to understand the personal and group influences that affect consumer decisions and how these decisions are made.
2. The term *consumer behavior* is often used to describe two different kinds of consuming entities: the personal consumer and the organizational consumer.
    a) The *personal consumer* buys goods and services for his or her own use, for the use of the household, or as a gift for a friend.
       i) Products are bought for final use by individuals (referred to as *end users* or *ultimate consumers*).
    b) The *organizational consumer*—includes profit and not-for-profit businesses, government agencies, and institutions, all of which must buy products, equipment, and services in order to run their organizations.
3. Despite the importance of both categories of consumers, individuals and organizations, this book will focus on the individual consumer, who purchases for his or her own personal use or for household use.
    a) End-use consumption is perhaps the most pervasive of all types of consumer behavior.

*****Use Learning Objective #3 Here; Use Discussion Question #2 Here*****

DEVELOPMENT OF THE MARKETING CONCEPT AND THE DISCIPLINE OF CONSUMER BEHAVIOR

1. The field of consumer behavior is rooted in the ***marketing concept***, a business orientation that evolved in the 1950s through several alternative approaches toward doing business referred to, respectively, as the *production concept*, the *product concept*, and the *selling concept*.

*****Use Key Term marketing concept Here*****

2. The *production concept* is characterized as the concept used by Henry Ford in the early 1900s.
    a) Ford produced a car for $850 in an era when only the wealthy could afford a car.
    b) The assembly line concept allowed him to reduce the price to $360.
    c) Because of Ford's products, Americans developed the nation's extensive highway system and, eventually, suburbs and their adjacent shopping malls.
    d) The production concept assumes that consumers are mostly interested in product availability at low prices.
       i) Implicit marketing objectives are cheap, efficient production, and intensive distribution systems.
       ii) This concept makes sense when consumers are more interested in obtaining the product than they are in specific features.
3. The *product concept* assumes that consumers will buy the product that offers them the highest quality, the best performance, and the most features.

a) A product orientation leads the company to strive constantly to improve the quality of its product and to add new features that are technically feasible without finding out first whether or not consumers really want these features.

b) This concept leads to "marketing myopia," that is, a focus on the product rather than on the consumer needs it presumes to satisfy.

    i) Railroads are often used as an example of marketing myopia.

    ii) A more modern example might be the PDA.

4. The *selling concept* is a natural extension of the production and product concepts. In this concept, marketing's primary focus is selling the product(s) that it has unilaterally decided to produce.

a) A hard sell approach is often used to persuade consumers to buy something (even if they don't really want it).

b) A negative of this concept is that consumers may not return for repeat sales because they may not have wanted the product to begin with.

c) This approach is typically used by the marketers of unsought goods (such as life insurance).

*****Use Learning Objective #4 Here; Use Discussion Question #2 Here; Use Exercise #3 Here*****

The Marketing Concept

1. The field of consumer behavior is rooted in a marketing strategy that evolved in the late 1950s.

2. Instead of trying to persuade customers to buy what the firm had already produced, marketing-oriented firms found that it was a lot easier to produce only products they had first confirmed, through research, that consumers wanted.

a) This consumer-oriented concept came to be known as the *marketing concept*.

b) Consumer needs and wants became the firm's primary focus.

3. The key assumption:

a) To be successful, a company must determine the needs and wants of specific target markets, and deliver the desired satisfactions better the competition.

4. The marketing concept is based on the premise that a marketer should make what it can sell, instead of trying to sell what it has made.

a) The older selling concept focused on the needs of the seller.

b) The marketing concept focuses on the needs of the buyer.

*****Use Learning Objective #4 Here; Use Discussion Question #2 Here; Use Exercise #3 Here; Use Table 1-1 Here*****

Implementing the Marketing Concept

1. The widespread adoption of the marketing concept by American business fed the need to study consumer behavior.

2. They discovered that consumers were highly complex individuals, subject to a variety of psychological and social needs quite apart from their survival needs.
   a) The needs and priorities of different consumer segments differed dramatically, and in order to design new products and marketing strategies that would fulfill consumer needs, they had to study consumers and their consumption behavior in depth.
3. The strategic tools that are used to implement the marketing concept include *segmentation, targeting, positioning,* and the *marketing mix.*

*****Use Learning Objective #4 Here*****

The Role of Consumer Research

1. *Consumer research* describes the process and tools used to study consumer behavior.
2. Broadly speaking, there are two theoretical perspectives that guide the development of consumer research methodology:
   a) The *positivist* approach—tends to be objective and empirical, to seek causes for behavior, and to conduct research studies that are generalized to larger populations.
      i) Consumer research designed to provide data to be used for strategic managerial decisions falls into this category of research.
   b) The *interpretivist* approach—tends to be qualitative and based on small samples.
      i) Interpretivists seek to find common patterns of operative values, meanings, and behavior across consumption situations.

*****Use Key Term** consumer research *Here; Use Learning Objective #5 Here; Use Discussion Question #3 Here*****

Segmentation, Targeting, and Positioning

1. The focus of the marketing concept is consumer needs.
2. Three elements form a strategic framework for bringing marketing efforts to consumers:
   a) *Market segmentation*—the process of dividing a market into subsets of consumers with common needs or characteristics.
   b) *Market targeting*—selecting one or more of the segments identified for the company to pursue.
   c) *Positioning*—developing a distinct image for the product or service in the mind of the consumer, an image that will differentiate the offering from competing ones and squarely communicate to consumers that the particular product or service will fulfill their needs better than competing brands.
      i) Key principles include:
         • Communicating the benefits that the product will provide rather than the product's features.
         • Developing a unique selling proposition—a distinctive benefit or point of difference.

*****Use Key Terms market segmentation, market targeting, and positioning *Here;*
Use Learning Objective #6 Here; Use Discussion Question #3 Here*****

The Marketing Mix

1. The **marketing mix** consists of a company's service and/or product offerings to consumers and the methods and tools it selects to accomplish the exchange.
2. Four basic elements include:
   a) The *product*—features, designs, brands, packaging, etc.
   b) The *price*—list price (including discounts, allowances, and payment methods).
   c) The *place*—distribution of the product or service.
   d) *Promotion*—advertising, sales promotion, public relations, and sales efforts designed to build awareness of, and demand for the product or service.

*****Use Key Term **marketing mix** *Here;* Use Discussion Question #3 Here; Use Table 1-2 Here*****

CUSTOMER VALUE, SATISFACTION, AND RETENTION

1. Since the 1950s many companies have successfully adopted the marketing concept.
2. The marketplace is now increasingly competitive.
3. Savvy marketers today realize that in order to outperform competitors they must achieve full profit potential from each and every consumer.
   a) An exchange with a consumer is part of a *customer relationship*, not just a *transaction*.
4. Three drivers of successful relationships between marketers and consumers are:
   a) *Customer value.*
   b) High levels of *customer satisfaction.*
   c) Building a structure of *customer retention.*

*****Use Learning Objective #7 Here; Use Exercise #1 Here*****

Providing Customer Value

1. *Customer value* is defined as the ratio between the customer's perceived benefits (economic, functional, and psychological) and the resources (monetary, time, effort, psychological) used to obtain those benefits.
   a) Perceived value is relative and subjective.
   b) Developing a value proposition is the core of successful positioning.

*****Use Key Term **customer value** *Here;* Use Learning Objective #7 Here; Use Exercise #1 Here*****

Customer Satisfaction

1. *Customer satisfaction* is the individual's perception of the performance of the product or service in relation to his or her expectations.
   a) The concept of customer satisfaction is a function of customer expectations.
2. With respect to customer satisfaction there might be several types of customers:
   a) *Loyalists*—completely satisfied customers who keep purchasing.
   b) *Apostles*—whose experiences exceed their expectations and who provide very positive word of mouth about the company to others.
   c) *Defectors*—who feel neutral or merely satisfied and are likely to stop doing business with the company.
   d) *Terrorists*—who have had negative experiences with the company and who spread negative word of mouth.
   e) *Hostages*—who are unhappy customers who stay with the company because of no choice (or other reasons).
   f) *Mercenaries*—very satisfied customers but who have no real loyalty to the company and may defect.

*****Use Key Term customer satisfaction Here; Use Learning Objective #7 Here; Use Exercise #1 Here*****

Customer Retention

1. The overall objective of providing value to customers continuously and more effectively than the competition is to have highly satisfied customers.
2. *Customer retention* makes it in the best interest of customers to stay with the company rather than switch to another firm.
3. Studies have shown that:
   a) Loyal customers buy more products.
   b) Loyal customers are less price sensitive and pay less attention to competitor's advertising.
   c) Servicing existing customers is cheaper.
   d) Loyal customers spread positive word of mouth and refer other customers.
4. *One-to-one marketing* offers more value through customer intimacy and keeping customers returning to the company.
   a) Marketers seek to build selective relationships.
   b) Customer profitability-focused marketing tracks costs and revenues of individual customers and then categorizes them into tiers based on consumption behaviors that are specific to the company's offerings. Examples include:
      i) Platinum tier
      ii) Gold tier
      iii) Iron tier
      iv) Lead tier

*****Use Key Term **customer retention** *Here; Use Learning Objective #7 Here; Use Discussion Question #5 Here; Use Exercise #1 Here; Use Table 1-3 and 1-4 Here*****

MARKETING ETHICS AND SOCIAL RESPONSIBILITY

1. The *societal marketing concept* requires that all marketers adhere to principles of social responsibility in the marketing of their goods and services.
2. A restructured definition of the marketing concept (to reflect social responsibility) would be to fulfill the needs of the target audience in ways that improve society as a whole, while fulfilling the objectives of the organization.
   a) A serious deterrent to the societal marketing concept is a short-term orientation toward increased market share and quick profits.

*****Use Key Term **societal marketing concept** *Here; Use Learning Objective #9 Here; Use Exercise #2 Here*****

3. To avoid exploiting consumers, marketers should develop a code of ethics—many have accomplished this task.
4. It is better to self-regulate than to be regulated by government.
5. *Marketing ethics* and social responsibility are important components of organizational effectiveness.

*****Use Key Term **marketing ethics** *Here; Use Learning Objective #8 Here*****

CONSUMER BEHAVIOR AND DECISION MAKING ARE INTERDISCIPLINARY

1. Consumer behavior was a relatively new field of study in the mid-to-late 1960s.
2. Marketing theorists borrowed heavily from concepts developed in other scientific disciplines:
   a) Psychology—the study of the individual.
   b) Sociology—the study of groups.
   c) Social psychology—the study of how an individual operates in groups.
   d) Anthropology—the influence of society on the individual.
   e) Economics to form the basis of this new marketing discipline.
3. Many early theories concerning consumer behavior were based on economic theory, the idea that individuals act rationally to maximize their benefits (satisfactions) in the purchase of goods and services.
4. Later research discovered that consumers are just as likely to purchase impulsively, and to be influenced not only by family, friends, advertisers and role models, but by mood, situation, and emotion.

*****Use Discussion Question #4 Here*****

A Simplified Model of Consumer Decision-Making

1. The process of **consumer decision-making** can be viewed as three distinct but interlocking stages: the *input stage*, the *process stage*, and the *output stage*.
2. The *input stage* influences the consumer's recognition of a product need and consists of two major sources of information:
    a) The firm's marketing efforts (the product itself, its price, promotion, and where it is sold).
    b) The external sociological influences on the consumer (family, friends, neighbors, other informal and noncommercial sources, social class, cultural and subcultural memberships.)
3. The *process stage* focuses on how consumers make decisions.
    a) The psychological factors inherent in each individual (motivation, perception, learning, personality, attitude) affect how the external inputs influence the consumer's recognition of a need, prepurchase search for information, and evaluation of alternatives.
    b) The experience gained through evaluation of alternatives, in turn, affects the consumer's existing psychological attributes.
4. The *output stage* of the consumer decision-making model consists of two closely-related post decision activities:
    a) Purchase behavior, which can be a trial purchase or a repeat purchase.
    b) The postpurchase evaluation of the product feeds directly into the consumer's experience in the process stage of the model.

*****Consumer decision-making is examined in greater depth in Chapter 16*****

*****Use Key Term **consumer decision-making** *Here; Use Learning Objective #10 Here; Use Discussion Question #4 Here; Use Figure 1-1 Here*****

PLAN OF THIS BOOK

The book is divided into four parts, as follows:
1. Part I gives an Introduction to the Study of Consumer Behavior.
2. Part II discusses the Consumer as an Individual.
3. Part III examines Consumers in Their Social and Cultural Settings.
4. Part IV synthesizes all of the variables discussed earlier into the Consumer Decision-Making Process.

Part 1

1. Chapter 1 introduces the reader to the study of consumer behavior as an interdisciplinary science, the reasons for the development of consumer behavior as an

academic discipline and an applied science, and it introduces a simplified model of consumer decision-making.

2. Chapter 2 examines the methodology of consumer research, including the assumptions underlying qualitative and quantitative research approaches.
3. Chapter 3 discusses the process of market segmentation, including the demographic, sociocultural, and psychographic bases for segmenting markets.

Part 2

1. Chapter 4 discusses how individuals are motivated.
2. Chapter 5 examines the impact of individual personality characteristics on consumer behavior.
3. Chapter 6 explores consumer perception.
4. Chapter 7 examines how consumers learn.
5. Chapter 8 discusses consumer attitudes.
6. Chapter 9 concludes Part 2 with an examination of the communications process and consumer persuasion.

Part 3

1. Chapter 10 focuses on consumers as members of society, subject to varying external influences on their buying behavior, such as their group and family memberships.
2. Chapter 11 looks at social class.
3. Chapters 12 and 13 examine the broad cultural and specific subcultural groups to which they belong.
4. The importance of cross-cultural consumer research to international marketing is explored in Chapter 14.

Part 4

1. Chapter 15 discusses the consumer's reactions to innovation and change and describes the process by which new products are adopted and become diffused throughout society.
2. Chapter 16 is an in-depth discussion of consumer decision-making that shows how all the psychological and sociocultural variables discussed in Parts 2 and 3 influence the consumer's decision-making process.

DISCUSSION QUESTIONS

1. Describe the impact of the digital revolution on marketing and on consumer behavior.

Today, the digital revolution of the marketplace allows much greater customization of products, services, and promotion messages than older marketing tools. By doing so, it enables marketers to build and maintain relationships with customers. These relationships are greater and more efficient than ever before. Digital technologies enable marketers to collect and analyze increasingly complex data on consumers' buying patterns and personal characteristics. On the other hand, the same technologies enable consumers to find more information about products and services, including prices, more easily, efficiently, and, for the most part, from the comfort of their own homes.

The digital revolution has introduced several drastic changes into the business environment:

- Consumers have more power than ever before
- Consumers have access to more information then ever before
- Marketers can offer more services and products than ever before
- The exchange between marketers and customers is increasingly interactive and instantaneous
- Marketers can gather more information about consumers more quickly and easily
- Impact reaches beyond the PC-based connection to the Web

2. Describe the interrelationship between the consumer behavior discipline and the marketing concept.

The term *consumer behavior* refers to the behavior that consumers display in searching for, purchasing, using, evaluating and disposing of products and services that they expect will satisfy their needs. The study of consumer behavior is the study of how individuals make consumption-related decisions. The key assumption underlying the *marketing concept* is that a company must determine the needs and wants of specific target markets, and deliver the desired satisfaction better than the competition. The marketing concept is based on the premise that a marketer should make what they can sell, instead of trying to sell what they have made. Thus, a company which adopts the marketing concept must continuously research and monitor its customers' and potential clients' needs and consumption-related behavior in order to develop, effectively promote, and deliver products and services which satisfy clients needs better than the competition.

3. Describe the interrelationship between consumer research, market segmentation and targeting, and the development of the marketing mix.

Consumer research describes the process and tools used to study consumer behavior. Broadly speaking, there are two theoretical perspectives that guide the development of consumer research methodology: the positivist approach (objective and empirical causal research) and the interpretivist approach (qualitative and based on small samples).

The focus of the marketing concept is consumer needs. Three elements for creating a strategic framework for discovering and analyzing those needs are market segmentation, market targeting, and positioning. *Market segmentation* is the process

11

of dividing a market into subsets of consumers with common needs or characteristics. Because most companies have limited resources, few companies can pursue all of the segments identified for the company to pursue. *Market targeting* is selecting one or more of the segments identified for the company to pursue. Because many companies have adopted the marketing concept, the marketplace is filled with many products and services claiming to satisfy consumer needs. *Positioning* is developing a distinct image for the product or service in the mind of the consumer, an image that will differentiate the offering from competing ones and squarely communicate to consumers that the particular product or service will fulfill their needs better than competing brands. The *marketing mix* consists of a company's service and/or product offerings to consumers and the methods and tools it selects to accomplish the exchange. Product, price, place, and promotion are the elements that make up this mix.

4. **Discuss the role of social and behavioral sciences in developing the consumer decision-making model.**

Consumer behavior was a relatively new field of study in the mid- to late-1960s. Because it had no history or body of research of its own, marketing theorists borrowed heavily from concepts developed in other scientific disciplines. These disciplines were psychology (the study of the individual), sociology (the study of groups), social psychology (the study of how an individual operates in groups), anthropology (the influence of society on the individual), and economics. Many early theories concerning consumer behavior were based on economic theory on the notion that individuals act rationally to maximize their benefits (satisfactions) in the purchase of goods and services. Later research discovered that consumers are just as likely to purchase impulsively and to be influenced not only by family, friends, advertisers, and role models, but also by mood, situation, and emotion. All of these factors combine to form a comprehensive model of consumer behavior that reflects both the cognitive and emotional aspects of consumer decision-making.

5. **Apply each of the two models depicted in Table 1-4 (i.e., traditional marketing and value and retention marketing) to the marketing of cellular phone services. You may want to incorporate into your answer the experiences that you and your peers' have had in selecting cellular communication providers.**

Students are free to create with this discussion question. Students should, however, observe the differences between the two approaches outlined in Table 1-4. While using the traditional marketing concept is a useful and correct approach (see features), it does not incorporate modern technology the way the value and retention concept does. Interactivity is also important to the value and retention model.

One way to make this exercise fun is to bring ads from cellular phone services to class. Ask students if they can identify the approaches being used. Next, ask them to change the approach observed to the other approach using information found in Table

1-4. This will aid students in learning the advantages and disadvantages of both concepts.

EXERCISES

1. **You are the marketing manager of Citibank's Online Banking Division. How would apply the concepts of providing value and customer satisfaction and retention to designing and marketing effective online banking?**

Instructor's Discussion

In order to answer this question, students should refer to Table 1-4 (to get ideas on value and retention-focused marketing). They should especially take notice of the use of information technology, databases, interactive communications, and usage of satisfaction surveys. Students might also wish to be aware of the introductory remarks to the chapter on the digital revolution and how this revolution might apply to the exercise. Note that *customer value* is defined as being the ratio between the customer's perceived benefits (economic, functional, and psychological) and the resources (monetary, time, effort, and psychological) used to obtain those benefits. Perceived value is relative and subjective. Citibank would need to develop a *value proposition* (unique selling proposition) for its service. What ideas do students have for doing this?

Customer satisfaction is the individual's perception of the performance of the product or service in relation to his or her expectations. Consumers often differ drastically with respect to the degree of satisfaction obtained. What are the factors that would ensure customer satisfaction with online banking (security, speed, accuracy, etc.)?

Lastly, students should carefully analyze customer retention. What types of customers would the bank most like to have? How could the bank retain these customers with their online banking service?

2. **Locate two examples (e.g., advertisements, articles, etc.) depicting practices that are consistent with the societal marketing concept and two examples of business practices that contradict this concept. Explain your choices.**

Instructor's Discussion

The *societal marketing concept* is described as being one where the marketer is required to adhere to the principles of social responsibility in the marketing of their goods and services; that is, they should endeavor to satisfy the needs and wants of their target markets in ways that preserve and enhance the well-being of consumers and society as a whole. Thus, the restructured definition of the marketing concept calls on marketers to fulfill the needs of the target audience in ways that improve society as a whole, while fulfilling the objectives of the organization. A serious deterrent to widespread implementation of the societal marketing concept is the short-term orientation embraced by most business executives in their drive for increased market share and quick profits.

Students should be clear as to why examples fit the pro and con approaches. Open the discussion with a clear definition of what the societal marketing concept is (see above). Next, match this concept to the supplied advertisements or articles. Conclude the discussion with comments on the applicability of the concept to modern business.

3. **Apply each of the concepts featured in the section describing the development of the marketing concept to manufacturing and marketing automobiles.**

Instructor's Discussion

The concepts to be reviewed are the production concept (assumes that the consumer is mostly interested in product availability at low prices), the product concept (assumes that consumers will buy the product that offers them the highest quality, the best performance, and the most features), the selling concept (assumes that consumers are unlikely to buy the product unless they are aggressively persuaded to do so), and the marketing concept (assumes that for a company to be successful it must determine the wants and needs of specific target markets and deliver the desired satisfactions better than the competition). Note that if the discussion is to be extended to the societal marketing concept review material is found in Exercise 2 above.

Before students make their application have them read Table 1-1 for additional business views toward the concepts. As an additional thought question, have students analyze Henry Ford's famous statement, "consumer's can have any color of car they wish as long as it is black."

S.T.A.R. PROJECTS

Ethical Issues in Consumer Behavior

S.T.A.R. Project #1
H&R Block is the 500-pound gorilla of individual income tax preparation. The company has a significant presence in the U.S. market (especially during the spring tax season). H&R Block has always been an aggressive competitor in this highly competitive market. A trade organization for accountants believes that H&R Block became too aggressive when it ran an ad campaign that showed a consumer running in a dark alley confronted with neon signs flashing "Prestige CPA," "Taxes Here," and "Tax Consortium." The consumer appears confused and frightened. At the end of the alley a solution to the fear and confusion appeared in the form of a warm and friendly H&R Block sign that promised that consumers do not have to pay until they are completely satisfied. Non-Block CPA professionals question whether H&R Block has fairly represented their businesses and consumer policies.

a. Is this form of advertising ethical? Why or why not?

b. With respect to what you have learned about ethics in the chapter, what suggestions do you have for H&R Block?

Instructor's Discussion

The H&R Block case is a good example of aggressive marketing that might exceed acceptable limits. The ad is much different than the H&R Block approach used on their Web site (see www.hrblock.com). Could a code of ethics help H&R Block? Possibly. CPA professionals do not see themselves as neon sign merchants nor do they believe that the average citizen has complaints with their preparation practices or guarantees. When does innuendo and appearance become unethical? This should be an interesting issue for the students to discuss. It will also be a good way to introduce the concept of a code of ethics. (See the exercise below for more work on a code of ethics.)

S.T.A.R. Project #2

Many consumers trust their medical supply needs to Johnson & Johnson. Johnson & Johnson is very clear as to its mission and commitment to the health and safety of its customers. The company is often cited as an example of how to do things right with respect to relations with customers and the public. Johnson & Johnson has gone so far as to construct a company credo that it features on its Web site (see www.jnj.com View Our Credo).

a. Assume that you have just been hired as a customer relations expert by Johnson & Johnson to answer a growing number of complaints that JNJ products are over-priced and have lost their sense of value for the consumer. The complainants cite lower priced private labels and store brands as illustrations of frustrations with JNJ. As one consumer states, "A band aid is just a band aid after all!" What would be your response?

b. How could you use the Johnson & Johnson Credo to aid you in your response?

Instructor's Discussion

First, all students should read the JNJ Credo. The Credo itself can be the discussion in this question. Next, students must carefully think about the scenario that has been presented. How could the company use its commitment to quality as an answer? How could the company comment without disparaging the competition? How can the company focus on value (see Table 1-4 for additional information). Take the two to three best responses and read them in class. An additional aid is to download the JNJ Credo and prepare it as a handout. What does the JNJ Credo say about the company's commitment to ethical behavior?

Small Group Projects

S.T.A.R. Project #3
Who designed the chicken sandwich? According to information provided on the Chick-fil-A Web site (www.chick-fil-a.com) it was Chick-fil-A founder Truett Cathy. Mr. Cathy is also known for his unique approach to the fast food business. This unique approach has at its center an appreciation of family values (the restaurants are closed on Sundays and all children's toys emphasize values rather than gimmicks or cartoon characters). After visiting the company Web site, your group's assignment is to list the ways that Chick-fil-A provides customer value, satisfaction, and retention for its customers. Once this is done, decide which of the two concepts displayed in Table 1-4 most appropriately describe the marketing approach of this company. Be sure to justify your decision.

Instructor's Discussion

The student group should not have a problem listing the ways that Chick-fil-A provides customer value and satisfaction. Retention may take longer. By making the attempt, however, students will appreciate the chapter comments more fully. After the list is complete, the second assignment sounds easy. Students should, however, observe that Chick-fil-A matches both of the two concepts rather well. The astute student will see that Chick-fil-A may still have some way to go with respect to technological application to the business, databases, and customer segmentation. Just because a company emphasizes value does not mean that it fulfills the right-hand side of Table 1-4. Does any other fast food company do a better job? Probably not.

S.T.A.R. Project #4
Nike is not just for males. This shoe giant, as can be seen by Case One and the opening comments to the chapter, has made great strides in market segmentation, customization, and customer relationship development. The result is that Nike is also a premier female shoe company. Your group assignment is split your team and analyze Nike. To do this, one team should review the www.nike.com Web site and analyze its contents based on its appeals to the male market segment (i.e., styles, language, colors, celebrity endorsers, games, customer relationships, etc.). The second team should analyze the Nike Goddess Web site at www.nikegoddess.com. As with Team One, Team Two should analyze the Web site based on its appeals to the female segment (i.e., styles, language, colors, celebrity endorsers, games, customer relationships, etc.). The two teams should now match their findings and write a summary report. What has Nike learned about market segments and market targets? How do the two Web sites assist Nike in its marketing efforts?

Instructor's Discussion

This exercise gives two small groups within a larger group the chance to explore Nike's marketing efforts to two distinct market segments. Case One and the opening comments to the chapter supply additional information about the company. If you would like to add additional comparison criteria, feel free to do so. Be sure to ask students what they have learned about consumer behavior from the Nike Web sites. This exercise will also give groups a chance to learn to work with each other and will pave the way for future group participation projects.

Using the Internet to Study Consumer Behavior

S.T.A.R. Project #5
1. What is your favorite flavor of Lifesaver's candy? The five traditional flavors are about to change and the Web surfer will aid in the change process. Lifesaver's has designed its Web site to be one that is fun and interactive. The company promises that it will be a primary avenue for customer contact and involvement. Choosing new flavors of Lifesaver's candy is only the first step in this direction. Visit the Lifesaver's Web site at www.candystand.com and review the opening page. Observe the activities available for the viewer. Next, note the shopping opportunities and links to other Web sites.

    a. What can you tell about the probable market segment that visits this Web site?
    b. How is the company using the marketing concept to interact with its customers via this Web site?
    c. What other advertisers (links) would you suggest for this Web site? Why?

Instructor's Discussion

This Web site is a great one to visit in class. It is bright, colorful, full of interactive games, and usually has some form of contest. Picking the Lifesaver color is a good example. Students should certainly be able to identify the market segment. How would this segment know to visit this site? At one time, word-of-mouth was about the only way a young customer would have known. Today, Lifesaver's features the address in many of its commercials. Have students examine the summary of the marketing concept focus found in Table 1-4 for quick answers to part "b." List these on the board if necessary. Once the market segment is identified (is it male or female—how could you tell?), students should be able to list various synergies with other companies (links).

S.T.A.R. Project #6
Who has the best cell phone service nationwide according to customer satisfaction ratings? If you guessed "Can you hear me now?" Verizon Wireless, you were right. Verizon is not only committed to providing excellent service to its customers but it has also made a significant commitment to community service and corporate sponsorship (see www.verizon.com and then links to Verizon in the Community and Verizon Sponsorships). After examining the section in the chapter on Marketing Ethics and Social Responsibility, review the definition of the societal marketing concept and answer the following questions about Verizon.
    a. What evidence do you find on the Verizon Web site that it is following the societal marketing concept?
    b. How would an adherence to this concept aid Verizon in its competitive environment?

c. What evidence do you find that Verizon is providing customer value and satisfaction to its market? How would this affect consumer behavior?

Instructor's Discussion

The students will find a clear discussion of Verizon's social efforts by following the links suggested. The students should then match this data to the definition provided in the chapter. Clearly, Verizon is making strides toward the societal marketing concept. Ask students how they think Verizon chooses its sponsorships? How would the societal marketing concept affect these choices? If Verizon is attempting to connect with consumers, community involvement is a worthy endeavor. Depending on when you check the Web site, the company usually provides updated data on customer value and satisfaction. In the highly competitive world of wireless communication, value and satisfaction are to be treasured. At this point in time, Verizon seems to have a good model for connecting with consumers.

CASES

Case One: Digitization Equals Customization

Question 1—Answer:

The customization strategies discussed in the case are refinements of the marketing concept, which calls for companies to identify and focus on consumer needs in developing, promoting, and selling their products and services. The new digital technologies enable marketers to maintain ongoing, *individual* dialogues with their customers, in which they learn about and respond to a customer's *personal* preferences. Instead of targeting a group of customers identified through market segmentation as sharing a common need or preference, these strategies focus on one-to-one marketing, producing and marketing a product precisely suited to satisfy one individual's needs.

Question 2—Answer:

Market segmentation and product customization can be viewed as different points on a *continuum* of fulfilling customers' needs. The instructor may use the sites listed in the question to illustrate that point. For example, discuss the differences between selling scores of Nike models at a store where athletic shoes are organized according to distinct needs and activities such as running, playing different sports etc., (i.e., market segmentation) and offering individually-customized versions of several shoe models online (i.e., Nike's present version of one-to-one marketing/product customization). Examples of products that do not lend themselves to customization and where effective market segmentation is still the key to success include many nondurable, mass-distributed consumer goods where several producers compete for relatively stable market segments (e.g., canned soft drinks, personal care products, and household care items).

Case Two: The Growth of "Personal TV"

Answer:

Free television is possible because advertisers pay for the content by paying for commercials placed in TV broadcasts, expecting viewers to watch the commercials. Thus, if technology provides viewers with an effective and easy way to avoid viewing commercials while still watching the content, this model of advertising may become obsolete. The demise of the present advertising/content model, however, at least in the short run, is unlikely. Consider the following:

1. Digital Video Recorders, such as TiVo and ReplayTV, may actually encourage viewers to watch more TV because they make finding and recording programs specifically tailored to the viewers' interests easier. If so, advertisers and broadcasters should view these devices as opportunities and focus on innovative ways of placing advertising within the TV broadcasts. For example:

   a. Creating TV shows without commercials where the advertising messages are incorporated into the show (e.g., singers on a set dominated by a logo or building comedy routines around a product. (See Bill Carter, "Skipping Ads? TV Gets Ready to Fight Back," *The New York Times Online*, January 10, 2003.)

   b. Advertisers may turn the new technology to their advantage. For example, Coca Cola has paid for advertising shown on the screen of ReplayTV when viewers pause programs. (See Amy Harmon, "Digital TV Recorders Give Advertisers Pause," *The New York Times Online*, May 29, 2002.)

   c. Advertisers may start demanding new ways of measuring audiences that account for the audiences that use DVR to watch broadcasts (and, presumably, skip commercials) rather than watching these broadcasts when they are actually shown.

2. TiVo and ReplayTV charge for the services listing the broadcasts. Major electronics companies, however, are adding DVD/DVR devices to their product lines where the listings are downloaded directly from the cable services and viewers do not have to pay for the listings. These products are not a threat to broadcasters because they do not include elaborate "skip" features. (See David Pogue, "TiVo Rivals Add DVD to the Mix," *The New York Times Online*, November,14, 2002.)

3. TiVo and ReplayTV have the potential to gather a lot of data about viewers' interests and preferences. Sophisticated marketers should form alliances with these services and devise ways to use this data to develop better programs focused specifically on viewers' interests. Viewers may be more willing to view advertising placed within such programs.

CHAPTER 2

Consumer Research

LEARNING OBJECTIVES

After studying this chapter students should be able to:
1. Compare the differences between customer research and marketing research.
2. Describe the differences between quantitative research and qualitative research.
3. Understand the use of positivist and interpretivist research.
4. Describe the steps in the consumer research process.
5. Explain the difference between primary and secondary research.
6. Discuss the differences between qualitative and quantitative research designs and why you would choose one over the other.
7. Discuss the differences between qualitative and quantitative data collection instruments or methods.
8. Identify the various probability and nonprobability sampling methods.

CHAPTER SUMMARY

The field of consumer research developed as an extension of the field of marketing research to enable marketers to predict how consumers would react in the marketplace and to understand the reasons they made the purchase decisions they did. Consumer research undertaken from a managerial perspective to improve strategic marketing decisions is known as *positivism*. Positivist research is quantitative and empirical, and tries to identify cause-and-effect relationships in buying situations. It is often supplemented with qualitative research.

Qualitative research is more concerned with probing deep within the consumer's psyche to understand the motivations, feelings and emotions that drive consumer behavior. Qualitative research findings cannot be projected to larger populations, but are used primarily to provide new ideas and insights for the development of positioning strategies. *Interpretivism*, a qualitative research perspective, is generally more concerned with understanding the act of consuming itself rather than the act of buying (i.e., consumer decision-making). Interpretivists view consumer behavior as a subset of human behavior, and increased understanding as a key to eliminating some of the ills associated with destructive consumer behavior.

Each theoretical research perspective is based on its own specific assumptions and uses its own research methodologies. Positivists generally use probability studies that can be generalized to larger populations. Interpretivists tend to view consumption experiences as unique situations that occur at specific moments in time; therefore they cannot be generalized to larger populations. The two theoretical research orientations are highly complementary and used together provide a deeper and more insightful understanding of consumer behavior than either approach used alone.

The consumer research process—whether quantitative or qualitative in approach—generally consists of six steps: defining objectives, collecting secondary data, developing a research design, collecting primary data, analyzing the data, and preparing a report of the findings. The researcher must make every effort to ensure that the research findings are *reliable* (that a replication of the study would provide the same results) and *valid* (that they answer the specific questions for which the study was originally undertaken).

CHAPTER OUTLINE

INTRODUCTION

1. The field of consumer research developed as an extension of the field of marketing research.
2. Studying consumer behavior enables marketers to predict how consumers will react to promotional messages and to understand why they make the purchase decisions they do.
3. Recently, marketers began to realize that customer research is a unique subset of marketing research, which merits the utilization of specialized research methods that collect customer data and also enhance the company's relationship with its customers.

*****Use Learning Objective #1 Here; Use Table 2-1 Here*****

CONSUMER RESEARCH PARADIGMS

1. The early consumer researchers gave little thought to the impact of mood, emotion, or situation on consumer decisions. They believed that marketing was simply applied economics.
2. Despite their assumptions that consumers were logical problem solvers who engaged in careful thought processes (i.e., information processing) to arrive at their consumption decisions, researchers soon realized that consumers were not always consciously aware of why they made the decisions they did.
3. In 1939, a Viennese psychoanalyst named Ernest Dichter began to use Freudian psychoanalytic techniques to uncover the hidden motivations of consumers.
4. By the late 1950s, his research methodology (called *motivational research*), which was essentially qualitative in approach, was widely adopted by consumer researchers.
5. As a result of Dichter's work and subsequent research designed to search deep within the consumer's psyche, consumer researchers today use two different types of research methodology to study consumer behavior—*quantitative research* and *qualitative research.*

*****Use Key Terms motivational research, quantitative research and qualitative research Here; Use Learning Objective #2 Here*****

Quantitative Research

1. Quantitative research is descriptive in nature, and is used by researchers to understand the effects of various promotional inputs on the consumer, thus enabling marketers to "predict" consumer behavior.
2. This research approach is known as *positivism*, and consumer researchers primarily concerned with predicting consumer behavior are known as *positivists*.
3. The research methods used in positivist research are borrowed primarily from the natural sciences and consist of experiments, survey techniques, and observation.
4. The findings are descriptive, empirical, and if collected randomly can be generalized to larger populations.

*****Use Key Term positivism Here; Use Learning Objectives #2 and #3 Here; Use Discussion Question #2 Here*****

Qualitative Research

1. Qualitative research methods consist of depth interviews, focus groups, metaphor analysis, collage research, and projective techniques.
2. These techniques are administered by a highly trained interviewer/analyst who also analyzes the findings—thus, they tend to be somewhat subjective.
3. Because sample sizes are necessarily small, findings cannot be generalized to larger populations.
4. A number of academicians view consumer behavior as a subset of human behavior.
5. Interest in understanding consumer experiences has led to the term *interpretivism*; the researchers who adopt this paradigm are known as *interpretivists*.
   a) Interpretivists engage in qualitative research.
   b) Among the research methodologies they use are ethnography, semiotics, and depth interviews.
   c) Qualitative research is also related to cultural anthropology and the study of symbols.
   d) Broadly speaking, the findings of qualitative research cannot be generalized to large populations. This form of research, however, is still meaningful.

*****Use Key Term interpretivism Here; Use Learning Objectives #2 and #3 Here; Use Discussion Question #2 Here; Use Table 2-2 Here*****

Combining Qualitative and Quantitative Research Findings

1. Some marketers use a combination of quantitative and qualitative research.
2. They use qualitative research findings to discover new ideas and to develop promotional strategy, and quantitative research findings to predict consumer reactions to various promotional inputs.
3. Sometimes ideas stemming from qualitative research are tested empirically.
4. Marketers have discovered that rather than conflicting, these two research paradigms are really complementary in nature.

THE CONSUMER RESEARCH PROCESS

1. The major steps in the consumer research process are:
   a) Defining the objectives of the research.
   b) Collecting and evaluating secondary data.
   c) Designing a primary research study.
   d) Collecting primary data.
   e) Analyzing the data.
   f) Preparing a report on the findings.

Developing Research Objectives

1. The first step in the consumer research process is to carefully define the objectives of the study.
2. It is important for the marketing manager and the researcher to agree at the outset on the purposes and objectives of the study to ensure that the research design is appropriate.
   a) A carefully thought-out statement of objectives helps to define the type and level of information needed.
3. If the purpose of the study is to come up with new ideas for products or promotional campaigns, then a qualitative study is usually undertaken.
4. Qualitative studies entail the interviewing of small numbers of respondents by trained professionals, who also do the analysis.
5. Because of the small number of respondents, the findings of the research are not usually projectable to the marketplace.
6. Quantitative studies are used to find out how many people in the population (what percentage) use certain products and how frequently they use them.
   a) An *exploratory study* may be used to identify the critical issues to include in the data collection instrument (e.g., questionnaire).

Collecting Secondary Data

1. Secondary information is any data originally generated for some purpose other than the present research objectives.
2. Locating secondary data is called *secondary research*. Original research performed by individual researchers or organizations to meet specific objectives is called *primary research.*
   a) Secondary research may provide sufficient insight so that primary research is not necessary.

23

    b)   There are numerous sources of secondary data.
    c)   Government agencies, private population data firms—such as A.C. Nielsen, marketing research companies, and advertising agencies.
    d)   Retailers and nonprofit organizations often have relevant demographic information.

> *****Use Key Terms* **secondary research and primary research** *Here; Use Table 2-3 Here*****

3. If more detailed information on purchasing patterns or product usage is needed, or if psychological or sociocultural consumer information is sought, then primary data must be collected.
4. Research to secure such information is more costly and more time-consuming than secondary research but is likely to yield a more accurate picture than studies based on secondary data alone.

> *****Use Learning Objective #5 Here; Use Discussion Question #3 Here*****

Syndicated Data

1. Because it is often very costly to collect primary data, many companies routinely purchase syndicated data on consumption patterns.

> *****Use Discussion Question #4 Here*****

Customer Profitability and Lifetime Value Data

2. The "80/20 rule" states that generally, a relatively small percentage of all customers (e.g., 20 percent) account for a disproportionately large portion of the company's sales and profits (e.g., 80 percent).
    a)   Companies today are developing systems that target highly profitable customers.
    b)   Such systems focus on internal secondary data.
    c)   Based on these data, savvy marketers compute ***customer lifetime value*** (CLV) profiles for various customer segments.

> *****Use Key Term* **customer lifetime value** *Here; Use Learning Objective #4 Here; Use Figure 2-2 Here*****

Designing Primary Research

1. The design of a research study is based on the purposes of the study.
2. If descriptive information is needed, then a quantitative study is likely to be undertaken; if the purpose is to get new ideas, then a qualitative study is undertaken.
3. Each approach is likely to differ in terms of the method of data collection, sample design, and type of data collection instrument used.

<u>Quantitative Research Designs</u>

1. Three forms of basic designs are useful—observation, experimentation, or survey.
2. *Observational Research*—consumers are watched during the process of buying and using products.
3. Observational researchers gain a better understanding of what a product symbolizes to a consumer and greater insight into the bond between people and product.
   a) *Mechanical observation* is using a mechanical or electronic device to record customer behavior or response to a particular marketing stimulus.
   b) Observations are increasing by companies because of the necessity of collecting data on customers. Privacy is always an issue.
   c) Marketers also use physiological observation devices that monitor respondents' patterns of information processing (e.g., eye tracking and brain activity).

*****Use Learning Objectives #6 Here; Use Discussion Question #5 Here; Use Experiment*
    *#1 and #2 (if not previously used) Here; Use Figure 2-3 Here*****

4. *Experimentation*—it is possible to test the relative sales appeal of many types of variables such as package designs, prices, promotional offers, or copy.
   a) In such experiments (called *causal research*), only one variable is manipulated at a time (the independent variable), although all other elements are kept constant.
   b) A controlled **experimentation** of this type ensures that any difference in outcome (the dependent variable) is due to different treatments of the variable under study and not to extraneous factors.
   c) Experiments are also conducted in laboratories with the use of special instrumentation, such as eye cameras that study the eye movement of subjects as they view competitive advertisements.
   d) A major application of causal research is *test marketing* in which, prior to launching a new product, elements such as package, price, and promotion are manipulated in a controlled setting in order to predict sales or gauge the possible responses to the product.
   e) Today some researchers employ *virtual reality methods* where researchers are able to create a setting wherein they can observe or track how long a consumer is engaged with the product (e.g., examines the package).

*****Use Key Term* **experimentation** *Here; Use Learning Objective #6 Here; Use Discussion*
    *Question #5 Here*****

5. *Surveys*—**surveys** ask consumers about their purchase preferences in person, by mail, or by telephone.

*****Use Key Term* **surveys** *Here; Use Table 2-4 Here; Use Discussion Question #7*
    *Here*****

a) Personal interview surveys most often take place in the home or in retail shopping areas. One of the common forms today is the *mall intercept*.

b) Telephone surveys are also used to collect consumer data; however, evenings and weekends are often the only times to reach the working homemaker, who tends to be less responsive to calls that interrupt dinner, television viewing, or general relaxation.

c) Mail surveys are conducted by sending questionnaires directly to individuals at their homes.

d) Online surveys are sometimes conducted on the Internet. Respondents are directed to the marketer's (or the researcher's) Web sites by computer ads or home pages; thus the samples tend to be self-selected and therefore the results cannot be projected to the larger population questions.

e) Researchers who conduct computer polling believe that the anonymity of the Net encourages respondents to be more forthright and honest than they would be if asked the same questions in person or by mail.

*****Use Learning Objectives #4 and #6 Here; Use Discussion Questions #1, #5, and #7 Here*****

Quantitative Research Data Collection Instruments

1. Data collection instruments are developed as part of a study's total research design to systematize the collection of data and to ensure that all respondents are asked the same questions in the same order.

2. Data collection instruments include questionnaires, personal inventories, attitude scales, and, for qualitative data, discussion guides.

3. Data collection instruments are usually pretested and "debugged" to assure validity and reliability of the research study.

4. A study is said to have **validity** if it does, in fact, collect the appropriate data needed to answer the questions or objectives stated in the first (objectives) stage of the research process.

5. A study is said to have **reliability** if the same questions, asked of a similar sample, produce the same findings.

   a) Often a sample is systematically divided in two, and each half is given the same questionnaire to complete. If the results from each half are similar, the questionnaire is said to have *split-half reliability*.

*****Use Key Terms **validity and reliability** Here; Use Learning Objective #7 Here*****

---

6. *Questionnaires*—for quantitative research, the primary data collection instrument is the questionnaire, which can be sent through the mail to selected respondents for self-administration or can be administered by field representatives in person or by telephone.

   a) The questionnaire itself can be *disguised* or *undisguised* as to its true purpose.

   b) *Open-ended questions* require answers to be in the respondent's own words. Open-ended questions yield more insightful information but are more difficult to code and analyze.

c) *Closed-ended questions* require that the respondent merely check the appropriate answer from a list of options. Closed-end questions are relatively simple to tabulate and analyze, but the answers are limited to the alternative responses provided.

d) Great care must be given to wording questions to avoid biasing the responses.

e) The sequence of questions is also important.

f) The format of the questionnaire and the wording and sequence of the questions affect the validity of responses and, in the case of mail questionnaires, the number (rate) of responses received.

*****Use Learning Objective #7 Here; Use Experiment #3 Here*****

---

7. *Attitude scales*—researchers often present respondents with a list of products or product attributes for which they are asked to indicate their relative feelings or evaluations.

a) The instruments most frequently used to capture this evaluative data are called **attitude scales**.

b) The most frequently used attitude scales are Likert scales, semantic differential scales, behavior intention scales, and rank-order scales.

c) *Likert scales* ask the respondent to check or write the number corresponding to their level of "agreement" or "disagreement" to statements.

d) *Semantic differential scales* ask the respondent to evaluate a concept, etc., on the basis of each attribute by checking the point on the continuum that best reflects their feelings.

e) *Behavior intention scales* measure the likelihood that consumers will act in a certain way in the future, such as buying the product again or recommending it to a friend.

f) *Rank-order scales* ask the respondent to rank items in order of preference in terms of some criterion, such as quality or value for the money.

*****Use Key Term attitude scale Here; Use Learning Objectives #4 and #7 Here; Use Experiment #3 (if not previously used) Here; Use Figure 2-4 Here*****

Qualitative Research Designs and Data Collection Methods

1. In selecting the appropriate research format for a qualitative study, the researcher has to take into consideration the purpose of the study and the types of data needed.

a) Although the research methods used may differ in composition, they all have roots in psychoanalytic and clinical aspects of psychology, and they stress open-ended and free-response types of questions to stimulate responses to reveal their innermost thoughts and beliefs.

2. The choice of data collection techniques for qualitative studies include depth interviews, focus groups, projective techniques, and metaphor analysis.

*****Use Learning Objective #6 and #7 Here; Use Experiment #1 (if not previously used) Here*****

---

3. *Depth Interviews*—A **depth interview** is a lengthy, nonstructured interview between a respondent and a highly trained interviewer.

a) Respondents are encouraged to talk freely about their activities, attitudes, and interests, in addition to the product category or brand under study.

b) Some marketers prefer the individual depth interview because they feel that respondents are free of group pressure, are less likely to give socially acceptable responses, are more likely to remain attentive, and more likely to reveal private thoughts.

*****Use Key Term **depth interview** *Here; Use Learning Objective #7 Here; Use Discussion Question #6 Here*****

4. *Focus Groups—focus groups* consist of eight to ten respondents who meet with a moderator/analyst for a group discussion.
   a) Respondents are encouraged to discuss their interests, attitudes, reactions, motives, lifestyles, feelings about the product, usage experience, etc.
   b) A researcher can easily conduct two or three focus groups in one day.
   c) Some marketers prefer focus groups because it takes them less time overall to complete the study, and the group concept yields a greater number of new ideas and insights.

*****Use Key Term **focus group** *Here; Use Learning Objective #7 Here; Use Discussion Question #6 Here; Use Figure 2-5 Here*****

5. *Projective Techniques—*projective techniques are designed to tap the underlying motives of individuals despite their unconscious rationalizations or efforts at conscious concealment.
   a) The respondent is asked to complete, describe, or explain the meaning of various stimuli.
   b) The theory behind projective tests is that the respondents' inner feelings influence how they perceive ambiguous stimuli.
   c) The stories they tell or the sentences they complete are actually projections of their inner thoughts.
   d) The basic assumption underlying projective techniques is that respondents are unaware that they are exposing their own feelings.

*****Use Learning Objective #7 Here*****

6. *Metaphor Analysis—*a new stream of consumer research suggests that most communication is nonverbal, and that people do not think in words, but in images.
   a) If consumers' thought processes consist of a series of images, or pictures in their mind, then it is likely that many respondents cannot adequately convey their feelings and attitudes about the research subject (e.g., a product or brand) through the use of words alone.
   b) In metaphor analysis, respondents are given magazines, scissors, paste, and paper, and asked to cut out pictures from magazines that represent their "feelings" about the product category under study; then to organize these clippings into a "meaningful" collage, which is then explicated with the help of the researcher.
   c) The Zaltman Metaphor Elicitation Technique (ZMET) combines collage research and metaphor analysis to bring to the surface the mental models and the major themes or

28

constructs that drive consumer thinking and behavior. Part of the construct elicitation process calls for the respondent to identify how any two of three stimuli presented are similar to each other but different from the third stimulus.

*****Use Learning Objectives #4 and #7 Here*****

Customer Satisfaction Management

1. Gauging the level of customer satisfaction and its determinates is critical for every company.
2. *Customer satisfaction management* includes quantitative and qualitative measures, as well as a variety of contact methods with customers.

*****Use Key Term customer satisfaction management Here; Use Learning Objective #4 Here; Use Discussion Question #9 Here; Use Table 2-5 Here*****

Sampling and Data Collection

1. An integral component of a research design is the sampling plan.
2. The sampling plan addresses three questions.
    a) Whom to survey (the sampling unit).
    b) How many to survey (the sample size).
    c) How to select (the sampling procedure).
3. Interviewing the correct target market or potential target market is basic to the validity of the study.
4. The size of the sample is dependent both on the size of the budget and on the degree of confidence that the marketer wants to place in the findings.
5. If the researcher wants the findings to be projectable to the total population, then a *probability sample* should be chosen; if it is sufficient to have the findings "representative" of the population, then a *nonprobability sample* can be selected.
6. Qualitative studies usually require highly trained social scientists to collect data.
    a) A quantitative study generally uses a field staff that is either recruited and trained directly by the researcher or contracted from a company that specializes in conducting field interviews.

*****Use Key Terms probability sample and nonprobability sample Here; Use Learning Objective #8 Here; Use Discussion Question #8 Here; Use Table 2-6 Here*****

Data Analysis and Reporting Research Findings

1. In qualitative research, the moderator or test administrator usually analyzes the responses received.
2. In quantitative research, the researcher supervises the analysis.
3. Open-ended responses are first coded and quantified (i.e., converted into numerical scores); then all of the responses are tabulated and analyzed.

4. In both qualitative and quantitative research, the research report includes a brief executive summary of the findings.
5. Depending on the assignment from marketing management, the research report may or may not include recommendations for marketing action.
6. The body of the report includes a full description of the methodology used and, for quantitative research, also includes tables and graphics to support the findings.
    a) A sample of the questionnaire is usually included in the appendix to enable management to evaluate the objectivity of the findings.

*****Use Learning Objective #4 Here*****

Conducting a Research Study

1. In designing a research study, researchers adapt the research process described in the previous sections to the special needs of the study.
2. Consider the following example: an online dating service.
    a) First task—collect secondary data.
    b) Then, together with the marketing manager, the researcher would specify the parameters (i.e., define the sampling unit) of the population to be studied.
    c) A qualitative study, (e.g., focus groups) might be undertaken first to gather information about the target population's attitudes and concerns about meeting people online, their special interests, and the specific services and precautions they would like an online dating service to provide.
    d) This phase of the research should result in tentative generalizations about the specific age group(s) to target and the services to offer.
    e) The marketing manager then might instruct the researcher to conduct a quantitative study to confirm and attach "hard" numbers (percentages) to the findings that emerged from the focus groups.
    f) The first-phase study should have provided sufficient insights to develop a research design and to launch directly into a large-scale survey.
    g) If, however, there is still doubt about any element of the research design, such as question wording or format, they might decide first to do a small-scale exploratory study.
    h) After refining the questionnaire and any other needed elements of the research design, they would launch a full-scale quantitative survey, using a probability sample that would allow them to project the findings to the total population of singles (as originally defined).
    i) The analysis should cluster prospective consumers into segments based on relevant sociocultural or lifestyle characteristics and on media habits, attitudes, perceptions, and geodemographic characteristics.

*****Use Learning Objective #4 Here*****

DISCUSSION QUESTIONS

1. **Have you ever been selected as a respondent in a marketing research survey? If yes, how were you contacted? Why do you think you, in particular, were selected? Did you know or could you guess the purpose of the survey? Do you know the name of the company or brand involved in the survey?**

This is an excellent way to introduce the topic of consumer research to the class. Students are likely to describe instances where they were stopped at malls, called on the phone, received mail questionnaires, and filled out surveys done by their universities. The instructor should inquire whether the students/respondents were "screened" before the beginning of the actual interviews, and use the students' descriptions to illustrate the sampling designs described in the text.

2. **Identify a purchase you have made that was motivated primarily by your desire to obtain a "feeling" or an "experience." Would the positivist or interpretivist research paradigm be a more appropriate approach to study your consumption behavior? Explain your answer.**

This exercise is designed to compare the positivist and interpretivist approaches to consumer research (see Table 2-2). To begin the discussion remind students of the basic definitions of the two terms in question.

First, cover *positivism*. Consider that quantitative research is descriptive in nature and is used by researchers to understand the effects of various promotional inputs on the consumer, thus enabling marketers to "predict" consumer behavior. This research approach is known as *positivism*, and consumer researchers primarily concerned with predicting consumer behavior are known as *positivists*. The research methods used in positivist research are borrowed primarily from the natural sciences and consist of experiments, survey techniques, and observation. The findings are descriptive, empirical, and, if collected randomly (i.e., using a probability sample), can be generated to larger populations. Because the data collected are quantitative, they lend themselves to sophisticated statistical analysis.

Second, cover *interpretivism*. Some researchers are more interested in the act of *consumption* rather than in the act of *buying* (i.e., decision making). They view consumer behavior as a subset of human behavior, and increased understanding as a key to reducing negative aspects of consumer behavior (such as shoplifting). Interest in understanding consumer experiences has led to the term *interpretivism*, and researchers who adopt this paradigm are known as *interpretivists*. Interpretivists engage in qualitative research. Among the research methodologies they use are depth interviews, projective techniques, and other methods borrowed from cultural anthropology to study the meanings of cultural practices and symbols. Broadly speaking, the findings of qualitative research cannot be generalized to large populations.

3. **What is the difference between primary and secondary research? Under what circumstances might the availability of secondary data make primary research unnecessary? What are some common sources of secondary data?**

Secondary information is any data originally generated for some purpose other than the present research objectives. It includes findings based on research done by outside organizations, data generated in-house for earlier studies, and even customer information collected by the firm's sales or credit departments. Locating secondary information is called *secondary research*. Such data sometimes provides sufficient insight into the problem at hand to eliminate the need for primary research. Most often, it provides clues and direction for the design of primary research. Major sources of secondary data are discussed in Table 2-4.

Primary research is original research performed by individual researchers or organizations to meet specific objectives. If detailed information on purchasing patterns or product usage is needed or if psychological or sociocultural consumer information is sought, then primary data must be collected. Research to secure such information is more costly and more time consuming than secondary research but is likely to yield a more accurate picture than studies based on secondary data alone.

Major sources of secondary data are discussed in Table 2-2.

4. **Visit the Web sites of A.C. Nielsen Research. Which of the Nielsen's syndicated data services would you use to develop a customer lifetime value and profitability analysis for a product or service of your choice?**

The students are free to choose from a variety of Nielsen services to answer the question. Their choice will be predicated on assumptions that they make. To make a more informed choice have the students consider (and review) the following information about *syndicated data services* and the terms *customer lifetime value* and *profitability analysis*.

First, because it is often very costly to collect primary data, many companies routinely purchase syndicated data on consumption patterns. Syndicated data is data of interest to a large number of users that are collected periodically and complied and analyzed according to a standard procedure and then the data is sold to interested buyers. As noted in the chapter and Nielsen Web site, Nielsen reports on the number of U.S. households tuned to national TV broadcasts, who is watching national TV programs, and on who is viewing local TV programs. (See Table 2-3 for more information on secondary data sources.)

Second, customer lifetime value and profitability analysis stems from the so-called "80/20 rule" that states generally, a relatively small percentage of all customers' account for a disproportionately large portion of the company's sales and profits. With the increased focus on building and maintaining long-term relationships with customers, many companies are developing systems that will identify highly profitable customers as quickly as possible and target these customers with special offers to buy even more of the company's products and services. Such systems are developed from internal data. Savvy marketers now compute customer lifetime value (CLV) profiles for various customer segments. (See Figure 2-2 for an example.)

5. **A manufacturer of powdered fruit drinks would like to investigate the effects of food color and label information on consumers' perceptions of flavor and product preferences. Would you advise the manufacturer to use observational research, experimentation, or a survey? Explain your choice.**

Students will be able to make a case for any of the three choices (with a little creativity). Whichever choice is made, students should justify the chosen alternative. To summarize each of the quantitative research designs, see the following brief summary (for more detail see section in the chapter):

- Observation research—one of the best ways to gain in-depth understanding of the relationship between people and products by watching them in the process of buying and using products. Mechanical observation is also possible.
- Experimentation—it is possible to test the relative sales appeal of many types of variables such as package designs, prices, promotional offers, or copy themes through experiments designed to identify cause and effect. In such experiments, only some variables are manipulated, while all other elements are kept constant. Major methods are test marketing and virtual reality methods.
- Survey research—asking consumers about their purchase preferences and consumption experiences. This can be done in person, by mail, by telephone, or online. (See Table 2-4 for advantages and disadvantages of the various survey formats.)

6. **Why might a researcher prefer to use focus groups rather than depth interviews? When might depth interviews be preferable?**

Focus groups consist of eight to ten respondents who meet with a moderator/analyst for a group discussion. Respondents are encouraged to discuss their interests, attitudes, reactions, motives, lifestyles, feelings about the product, usage experience, etc. A researcher can easily conduct two or three focus groups in one day. Some marketers prefer focus groups because it takes them less time overall to complete the study, and the group concept yields a greater number of new ideas and insights. (See Figure 2-5 for additional information on focus groups.)

A *depth interview* is a lengthy, nonstructured interview between a respondent and a highly trained interviewer. Respondents are encouraged to talk freely about their activities, attitudes, and interests, in addition to the product category or brand under study. Some marketers prefer the individual depth interview because they feel that respondents are free of group pressure, are less likely to give socially acceptable responses, are more likely to remain attentive, and reveal private thoughts.

7. **Compare the advantages and disadvantages of mail, telephone, personal, and online surveys.**

    For a complete listing of advantages and disadvantages see Table 2-4. A quick (and brief) summary of the highlights is presented below (see able for greater detail). The following score best with respect to the factors of:
    - Cost—mail and online
    - Speed—online
    - Response rate—personal interview
    - Geographic flexibility—mail and online
    - Interviewer bias—telephone (moderate)
    - Interviewer supervision—telephone
    - Quality of response—personal interview and online

8. **How would the interpretation of survey results change if the researcher used a probability sample rather than a nonprobability sample? Explain your answer.**

    Table 2-6 summarizes the features of various types of probability and nonprobability designs. In general, however, if the researcher wants the findings to be projectable to the total population, then a probability sample should be chosen. If it is sufficient to have the findings "representative" of the population, then a nonprobability sample can be selected.

9. **Why is customer satisfaction measurement an important part of marketing research? Apply one of the methods in Table 2-5 to measure your fellow students' satisfaction with the services provided by the registrar at your university.**

    Students are to choose one of the six customer satisfaction data collection methods indicated in Table 2-5. Any of these instruments can be used.

    Gauging the level of customer satisfaction and its determinants is critical for every company. Marketers can use such data to retain customers, sell more products and services, improve the quality and value of their offerings, and operate more effectively and efficiently. *Customer satisfaction measurement* includes quantitative and qualitative measures, as well as a variety of contact methods with customers.

EXERCISES

1. **Neutrogena is a manufacturer of personal care products for young adults. The company would like to extend its facial cleansers product line. Design a (a) qualitative and (b) quantitative research design for the company focused on this objective.**

<u>Instructor's Discussion</u>

A good place to begin this assignment is to have students briefly review exactly what qualitative and quantitative research designs are. Notice that, in addition to material found in the chapter, students can refer to Discussion Question #2 for insight and review.

Even though students can be basically familiar with what quantitative and qualitative research designs are, they may not be prepared (especially a this point in the course or if they have no prior experience with marketing research) to design an instrument. Try limiting the research experience (to begin with) to attitude scales shown in Figure 2-4. If students will read each of the six forms, they should be able to use one of the scales to begin their research experience. Once this is accomplished, springboard to other venues from this basic research effort. Small groups work well in this area.

2. **A real-life customer tracking model is featured in Figure 2-3. Develop a similar model for tracking customers' visits to one of Disney's theme parks.**

<u>Instructor's Discussion</u>

Before beginning this exercise, have students reread the section in the chapter on Observational Research including the section on *mechanical observation*. From this review, students will understand the material found in Figure 2-3. Next, quickly review that the observational method is excellent for observing the customer in their natural environment. How would this apply to the Disney experience? If the students want to expand to the mechanical observation, a TellUs kiosk (a small kiosk with a mechanism for recording impressions about the theme park) might be something that would prove to be useful. Allow students to be creative with their approach. Be sure, however, that the students understand how that cost sometimes tempers and limits research approaches.

3. **Develop a questionnaire to measure students' attitudes toward the instructor in this course.**
   (a) Prepare five statements to be measured on a Likert scale.
   (b) Prepare five semantic differential scales to measure these attitudes. Can the same dimensions be measured by using either scaling technique? Explain your answer.

<u>Instructor's Discussion</u>

A *Likert scale* and a *semantic differential scale* are shown in Figure 2-4. Clearly, the same dimensions can be measured by using either scaling method. The instructor may use the actual student evaluation form used by the university to illustrate how Likert scales and semantic differential scales can be used interchangeably.

A useful extension of this exercise is to have students pick the best three examples from the class (no matter which scale is used) and actually administer the examples to the class. Be forewarned that sometimes answers can be rather pointed and personal. Follow the actual questioning process with a debriefing of the students to enhance their learning experience. The instructor may ask students which factors have influenced their own responses to student evaluations of instructors which they filled out in the past and which influenced responses on the three administered in this class. For example, how is one's response related to getting back an exam grade on the same day the evaluations are administered? Is the response tempered by knowing that it will be made public?

S.T.A.R. PROJECTS

Ethical Issues in Consumer Behavior

S.T.A.R. Project #1

Acme Steel has employed you as a statistical analyst for almost ten years. In your job, you tracked steel prices, created customer profiles, maintained data on contract negotiations, provided data necessary for labor negotiations, researched information on new markets and joint ventures, and developed a unique system for cataloging competitors' strengths and weaknesses. Your skill in obtaining primary and secondary research is not only known in Acme but in the steel industry as a whole. The U.S. steel industry, however, is not doing well in the highly competitive global marketplace. A German steel firm is expanding into the United States and is currently negotiating to buy Bethlehem Steel. A recruiting firm has contacted you with a very attractive offer—the German firm wants you. Simply put, you could double your salary, receive a secure retirement and stock option package, and have a substantial position with a global industry leader that has not had a layoff in ten years. The offer sounds very attractive when you consider the situation at your own company and in the U.S. market in general. There is one catch, however. You must be willing to bring all your knowledge of Acme and its processes to your new firm. Though bringing actual data would be irresponsible, probably illegal, and very difficult, your new firm does expect you to bring your models, ability to analyze data, and knowledge of Acme customers, labor situations, and company weaknesses with you. Acme would most certainly ask you to sign a nondisclosure document, however, this would be difficult if not impossible to enforce. How should you meet your opportunity?

    a. Considering the descriptions in the first part of this story, what type of information would you feel comfortable in taking with you to the new firm? Explain.

    b. From an ethics standpoint, how can companies control or be secure with employees that are in position to gather and obtain information such as that described in the story?

    c. How do you feel about the dilemma created in this story? Comment.

Instructor's Discussion

There is nothing easy about the dilemma posed in this exercise. Students should see the opportunity and security that the new position might bring. Students should, however, also see the responsibility that is owed to company that has been the source of livelihood for several years. A good direction to go with respect to giving guidance on the thorny path that lies ahead is to have students review the *American Marketing Association's* Web site at www.ama.org (an alternative Web site is www.marketingpower.com) where marketing research ethics and general ethics in marketing are explored.

Have a lively discussion with the class on the responsibility of those that collect information and how those individuals must be ever vigilant in their responsibility.

S.T.A.R. Project #2
Advertising Age is an excellent marketing and advertising publication for summarizing current and contemporary issues that impact a firm and its promotion environment. On a weekly basis the publication examines contemporary advertising practices and ethical issues that are faced by advertising professionals. The *Advertising Age* Web site summarizes high impact articles and issues (see www.adage.com). Issues relating to tobacco advertising, promotion to underage consumers, antimarketing groups, sensitive promotions found on the Internet (such as pornography), racial discrimination in advertising, and gender advertising are explored and reviewed on an ongoing basis. Check out the Web site and complete the following assignments with respect to ethics in promotion and advertising.
   a. Find a customer research issue on the Web site. Briefly comment on what the issue is and how an ethics-orientation might be necessary with respect to the issue. Note: if the issue is not clearly oriented toward ethics, notice how it might be.
   b. Pick an issue described on the Web site. Propose an interpretivist or positivist approach for investigating the issue further. If ethical issues were to become part of your research effort, would this necessitate and change your designated approach? Explain why or why not.

Instructor's Discussion

This exercise is an excellent one for familiarizing the students with the *Advertising Age* Web site. This Web site is very useful in providing up-to-date research and statistics on consumers and promotion/advertising issues. The site also has excellent links to other well-known Web sites. Occasionally, the Web site also has downloads that make excellent in-class demonstrations. For example, for about two months after the annual Super Bowl, all the Super Bowl ads can be downloaded and then shown in class. Obviously, taste and ethical issues can be discussed from any ads of this nature. The publication and its Web site are not shy about covering controversial issues and in recent years the publication (Web site) has been a leader in attempting to bring an ethical focus to the field of advertising and associated data collection practices associated with the field. This is an assignment that can be completed at home by students. Because the number of "lead stories" is limited (thereby limiting student choice), it is interesting to see how students approach the same story or article from different perspectives.

Small Group Projects

S.T.A.R. Project #3

As announced by Sprint, its PCS Vision is "clearly a whole new way to look at wireless." PCS Vision gives the cell phone user the ability to access messaging, visual pictures, the Web, and games all from the convenience of their cell phone. Full-color digital images seem to be the real strength of this service. Similar services have been available in Japan for a year or more; however, Sprint is considered to be the initiator in the U. S. market. Sprint believes that its PCS Vision service gives customers the freedom to share information that is unmatched in contemporary wireless communication.

    a. Divide the class into research and consumer groups. Within the research groups, each group is to assume the roll of a focus group organization whose task it is to gather information from cell phone users (the consumer groups). Ideally, each research group should have three to five students and be paired with a consumer group of five to seven students. The research groups should read the section on "focus groups" to prepare for their assignment. The consumer group should go to www.sprint.com and review material about PCS Vision. Each focus group interview should last approximately 30 minutes.

    b. The research groups should prepare short questions that would review cell phone use, impressions of the PCS Vision service, likes and dislikes of existing services, and other questions that might enable PCS Vision to woo consumers from competing services.

    c. Once completed, each type of group should prepare a short report outlining what was learned about consumer behavior and focus groups.

Instructor's Discussion

Be sure each student group follows its assigned task as either a research organization or consumer group. Familiarization with the material in the chapter on *focus groups* and visitation of the Sprint Web site is essential. Other directions or adjustments are at the discretion of the instructor and can be modified to fit time parameters. Students will find the Sprint Web site to be user-friendly and informative about the PCS Vision service. This project is a good quick introduction to the focus group experience.

S.T.A.R. Project #4

One of the most difficult tasks for any researcher or research organization is where to find reliable secondary information on consumers and consumer behavior. One interesting Web site that assists in this process is Statistics.com (www.statistics.com). Statistics.com offers courses, software, job information, books, tutorial services, and expert advice on proper use of statistical methods. Of more interest to consumer researchers is the Statistics Data Sources service found on the Web site. With such broad areas from agriculture to education to opinion surveys, Statistics.com provides valuable links to pinpointed statistical databases and sources of information.

    a. Go to Statistics.com. Choose one of the Statistics Data Sources mentioned and determine what type of secondary information could be obtained. Would this information be valuable to the consumer researcher. Evaluate the search task (was it easy or

difficult?).
    b. Go to the Opinion Surveys link. Describe the types of information that can be found by using this link. If possible, participate in one of the opinion surveys listed on the link. Comment on your group's experience.

Instructor's Discussion

This project is a good one to use as an icebreaker to get groups acquainted with members. The tasks described are not difficult but do yield information that can be processed by group members. An add-on to this project is to assign each group a question about one of the research methods covered in the chapter and see what they can discover about the method using the Stat Methods "Ask an Expert" feature. Lastly, each group should comment on the amount of secondary information that could be obtained using Web sites such as this. This project will help groups to familiarize themselves with the power of using the Internet in their consumer research endeavors.

Using the Internet to Study Consumer Behavior

S.T.A.R. Project #5
In the spring of 2003, Mattel launched its *ello Creation System* for young girls. The theme for this new category of toys is "create whatever you can image!" This is rather a broad statement. However, Mattel believes its *ello Creation System* will give young girls the ability to create anything from funky characters, room accessories, jewelry, houses, and much more. The purpose of the system is to spark female imagination and creativity. The system, according to Mattel, is designed to be open-ended and creative to match the ways little girls play. In other words, girls can build it, change it, and rearrange it using the *ello Creation System*. Sound like fun? Investigate and see.
    a. Using the Mattel Web site (www.mattel.com), investigate the *ello Creation System*. Using information described in the chapter, propose a qualitative and a quantitative approach for researching the consumer for which this system is designed. How could your information (once it was obtained) help Mattel in marketing the system?
    b. Assuming that the *ello Creation System* was sold to young girls, propose a method of determining customer satisfaction using one of the methods outlined in Table 2-5.

Instructor's Discussion

The students will find the *ello Creation System* to be highly creative and innovative. Mattel, better known for its Barbie and Hot Wheels lines, is spending big money to ensure the success of this new line. Industry sources say that the *ello Creation System* is an alternative to video games (popular with most boys in this age range). Will the system be intriguing and stimulate purchase? Students should be able to gain insight as to the answer to this question by accomplishing the tasks outlined by the project. Save time to present the most creative results to the class as a whole. Finish the discussion by asking students to think about how the original testing of this line might have been done. If the instructor contacts Mattel, the response is often very informative with respect to this issue.

S.T.A.R. Project #6

Consumer researchers DeeDee Gordon and Sharon Lee are the founders of one of the hottest research companies in today's marketplace. Look-Look has found a way to tap into the wildly creative universe of teens. Few contemporary companies have done as well as Look-Look in exploring this dynamic and rapidly changing market. Look-Look combines research savvy with creative Web and real-time investigations to produce some of the most timely information available today on this highly profitable market segment. Look-Look gives its target research market a 24/7 look by giving a voice to the youth culture through online respondents, field reporters (armed with digital cameras), and trend spotters (this group examines every small youth trend as it develops). Currently, there are over 10,000 young people who communicate with Look-Look (and their clients) about what is going on in the teen world. The teen world is huge! Look-Look is betting that it will see this world as it is happening and changing—and so will its clients.

   a. First, familiarize yourself with the Look-Look method by investigating the company's Web site at www.look-look.com. What topics are covered by Look-Look as it explores the teen world? How might a researcher use this information to make predictions?
   b. Go to the Respondents section of the Look-Look Web site and participate in the Look-Look research experience. Critique this experience.
   c. Evaluate the "living research" offered by this company in light of what you have learned in the chapter about consumer and market research.

Instructor's Discussion

Students will really enjoy the Look-Look Web site. It is highly informative. The topics covered by Look-Look research are fashion, entertainment, technology, activities, eating and drinking, health and beauty, mindset, city guide, and the Lookout. Many of these items (the results of research done by the company) can be viewed in the classroom via the Web site. The company makes its money by charging clients for the "real information" separately. The client fee is high ($50,000 and up) but most clients agree that the information is well worth the cost. Look-Look reporters go where the average researcher cannot—teen clubs, locker and restrooms, mall hangouts, riding in cars, changing booths in clothing stores, and street corners where it is happening. Armed with digital cameras, the reporters record images (sent in their original forms to Look-Look), language, thoughts, likes and dislikes, and other preferences on a daily basis. The reporters are highly creative. Imagine the power of being able to know today that a new hair style or tattoo is hot and being able to deliver that information to an advertiser in the same day. That is the power of Look-Look. Take a look; you will enjoy the experience.

CASES

Case One: Using Secondary Data in Targeting Consumers

Question 1—Answer:

This is a practical exercise designed to illustrate how different magazines are used to target consumers.

Question 2—Answer:

It is impractical and unnecessary for marketers to develop their own databases of magazines' audience characteristics. MRI's data on magazines' readers' profiles can be used in class as an example of high quality, well-organized, and user-friendly secondary, syndicated data. The class discussion of this question should focus on the advantages and limitations of using secondary data that are discussed within the chapter.

Case Two: Privacy Issues in Consumer Research

Question 1—Answer:

The answers to this question will vary. Instructors may focus the discussion on the need to develop clear guidelines for companies on this matter (and, possibly, even enforce them through laws).

Question 2—Answer:

It is apparent that many consumers are ready to sacrifice a lot of privacy for shopping online and via other electronic means. As we use electronic devices, there are electronic records of everything we do. For example, EZ Passes record our driving patterns; movie tickets or books ordered online reveal a lot about our preferences, as do movies we order on-demand or belonging to a video club; registering in order to use a free online guide for movies, restaurants, and other services enable marketers to match consumer demographics to their information retrieval patterns; and this list goes on and on.

Companies want to target consumers more effectively and are likely to develop progressively better ways to combine data about consumers from multiple sources and create more and more precise consumer profiles. Thus, as many more consumers use electronic means to shop, the prospects for maintaining privacy are rather bleak.

The best ways to create balance between consumers' desires to maintain privacy and also shop conveniently are clear policies stating the extent to which data collected about consumers will be used by the company collecting the information as well as other parties to whom this data may be sold.

41

CHAPTER 3

Market Segmentation

LEARNING OBJECTIVES

After studying this chapter students should be able to:
1. Define market segmentation.
2. Explain how and why market segmentation is used.
3. Identify the nine major categories of consumer characteristics used to segment markets.
4. Enumerate the variables within the nine segment bases.
5. Describe an AIO inventory and cite its use.
6. Discuss the family life cycle concept.
7. Explain the concept of geodemographic segmentation.
8. Discuss the value of VALS research for the marketer.
9. Categorize the criteria for targeting a market segment.
10. Explain the use of concentrated, differentiated, and countersegmentation when implementing a segmentations strategy.

CHAPTER SUMMARY

Market segmentation and diversity are complementary concepts. Without a diverse marketplace, composed of many different peoples with different backgrounds, countries of origin, interests, needs, and wants, there really would be little reason to segment markets.

Before the widespread adoption of the marketing concept, mass marketing (offering the same product or marketing mix to everyone) was the marketing strategy most widely used. Market segmentation followed as a more logical way to meet consumer needs. *Segmentation* is defined as the process of dividing a potential market into distinct subsets of consumers with a common need or characteristic and selecting one or more segments to target with a specially designed marketing mix. Besides aiding in the development of new products, segmentation studies assist in the redesign and repositioning of existing products, in the creation of promotional appeals, and the selection of advertising media.

Because segmentation strategies benefit both marketers and consumers, they have received wide support from both sides of the marketplace. Market segmentation now is widely used by manufacturers, by retailers, and by the nonprofit sector.

Nine major classes of consumer characteristics serve as the most common bases for market segmentation. These include geographic factors, demographic factors, psychological factors, psychographic characteristics, sociocultural variables, use-related characteristics, use-situation factors, benefits sought, and hybrid forms of segmentation (e.g., psychographic-demographic profiles, such as VALS, and geodemographic factors, such as PRIZM). Important criteria for targeting market segments include identification, sufficiency, stability, and accessibility. Once an organization has identified promising target markets, it must decide whether to pursue several segments (differentiated marketing) or just one segment (concentrated marketing). It then develops a positioning strategy for each targeted segment. In certain instances, a company might decide to follow a countersegmentation strategy and recombine two or more segments into one large segment.

CHAPTER OUTLINE

INTRODUCTION

1. Diversity in the American marketplace, as well as diversity in the global marketplace, makes market segmentation an attractive, viable, and potentially highly profitable strategy.
2. Successful segmentation requires a large enough population with sufficient money to spend, who have sufficient diversity to be capable of being divided into sizable segments on the basis of demographic, psychological, or other strategic variables.
   a) These conditions currently exist in the United States, Canada, Western Europe, Japan, Australia, and other industrialized nations.
3. When marketers provide a range of product or service choices to meet diverse consumer interests, consumers are better satisfied, and their overall happiness, satisfaction, and quality of life are ultimately enhanced.

WHAT IS MARKET SEGMENTATION?

1. *Market segmentation* is the process of dividing a potential market into distinct subsets of consumers with common needs or characteristics and selecting one or more segments to target with a distinct marketing mix.
2. Prior to the development of market segmentation, *mass marketing* was the prevailing method. The same product and marketing mix were offered to all consumers.

> *****Use Key Terms** market segmentation and mass marketing *Here; Use Learning*
>   *Objective #1 Here*****

3. If all consumers were alike, if they all had the same needs, wants, and desires, and the same background, education, and experience, mass (undifferentiated) marketing would be a logical strategy.
   a) Primary advantage is that it costs less.
   b) Some companies, primarily those that deal in agricultural products or very basic manufactured goods, successfully follow a mass marketing strategy.
   c) Other marketers, however, see major drawbacks in an undifferentiated marketing approach.
   d) This strategy often means that sell the same to everyone—this can lead to selling to no one.

4. The strategy of segmentation allows producers to avoid head-on competition in the marketplace by differentiating their offerings, not only on the basis of price, but also through styling, packaging, promotional appeal, method of distribution, and superior service.
   a) Marketers have found that the costs of consumer segmentation are usually more than offset by increased sales.
5. Market segmentation is just the first step in a three-phase marketing strategy.
   a) After segmenting the market into homogeneous clusters, the marketer then must select one or more segments to target.
   b) To accomplish this the marketer must decide on a specific marketing mix—that is, a specific product, price, channel and/or promotional appeal for each distinct segment.
   c) The third step is *positioning* the product so that it is perceived by each target market as satisfying that market's needs better than other competitive offerings.

*****Use Key Term positioning *Here; Use Discussion Question #1 and #2 Here******

Who Uses Market Segmentation?

1. Both sides of the market place benefit from market segmentation.
   a) Consumers receive products targeted to their specific needs.
   b) Marketers are able to offer more differentiated products, increasing profits, market share, etc.
   c) Retailers, industrial manufacturers, hotels, and the media have all benefited from market segmentation.
2. Retailers benefit from market segmentation. One company, such as Gap, is able to deliver their goods through a diversity of stores, Gap, Super Gap, Gap Shoe, etc., depending on the segment and product line.
3. Hotels target their different changes to different segments.
4. Industrial, not-for-profit, and even the media also use market segmentation.
5. More and more businesses today are using database marketing programs to find out who their best customers are, and these firms will then divide their customer base into segments. An example would be:
   a) LoLows—low current share, low consumption customers.
   b) HiLows—high current share, low-consumption customers.
   c) LowHighs—low current share, high-consumption customers.
   d) HiHighs—high current share, high-consumption customers.

*****Use Learning Objective #2 Here; Use Table 3-1 Here*****

How Market Segmentation Operates

1. Segmentation studies are designed to discover the needs and wants of specific groups of consumers.
   a) This permits the development and offering of specialized goods and services.
2. Segmentation studies permit repositioning of existing products. *Repositioning* is accomplished by changing the promotional appeal, the distribution strategy, or the price of the product.

3. Segmentation research can also be used to identify the most appropriate media in which to place advertisements.

*****Use Key Term* repositioning *Here; Use Learning Objective #2 Here*****

BASES FOR SEGMENTATION

1. The first step in developing a segmentation strategy is to select the most appropriate base(s) on which to segment the market.
2. There are *nine major categories* of consumer characteristics on which to base market segmentation.
    a) They include geographic factors, demographic factors, psychological factors, psychographic (lifestyle) characteristics, sociocultural variables, use-related characteristics, use-situation factors, benefits sought, and hybrid segmentation forms, such as demographic/psychographic profiles, geodemographic factors, and values and lifestyles.
    b) Hybrid segmentation formats each use a combination of several segmentation bases to create rich and comprehensive profiles of particular consumer segments (e.g., a specific age range, income, lifestyle, and profession).

*****Use Learning Objective #3 and #4 Here; Use Table 3-2 Here*****

Geographic Segmentation

1. In *geographic segmentation*, the market is divided by location.
    a) The theory behind geographic segmentation is that people who live in the same area have similar needs and wants, and these needs and wants differ from those of people living in other areas.
    b) Climate is sometimes a factor in consumption differences.
2. It can be argued that merchandise catalogues, cross-national toll free telephone numbers, worldwide satellite television transmission, global communication networks, as well as the Internet have erased all regional boundaries and, therefore, that geographic segmentation should be replaced by a single global marketing strategy.
3. Other marketers have, for a number of years, been moving in the opposite direction and developing highly regionalized marketing strategies.
    a) Working closely with regional retailers often produces *micromarketing strategies* and these strategies have generally won strong consumer support.
4. Marketers have observed divergent consumer purchasing patterns among urban, suburban, and rural areas.
    a) It is relatively easy to find geographically based differences for many products.
5. Geographic segments can be easily reached through the local media, including newspapers, TV, and radio, and through regional editions of magazines.

*****Use Key Terms* geographic segmentation and micromarketing strategies *Here;*
*Use Learning Objective #3 and #4 Here; Use Discussion Question #9 Here*****

Demographic Segmentation

1. *Demographic segmentation* is the process of segmenting the market based on demographic characteristics.
2. Demography refers to the vital and measurable statistics of a population. Age, sex, marital status, income, occupation, and education, are most often used as the basis for demographic market segmentation.
3. Demographics help to *locate* a target market. It is the most accessible and cost effective way to identify a target market. These characteristics are easy to measure.
4. Demographic variables reveal trends, such as shifts in age, gender, and income distributions that signal business opportunities to alert marketers.

> *****Use Key Term demographic segmentation Here; Use Discussion Question #3, #7, and #9 Here*****

Age

1. Because product needs often vary with consumer age, age is a very useful demographic variable for marketers.
   a) Chronological age implies a number of underlying forces.
      i) Age effects—occurrences due to age.
      ii) Cohort affects—occurrences due to being born at a certain time in a similar environment.

> *****Use Learning Objective #3 and #4 Here; Use Table 3-3 and 3-4 Here; Use Experiment #2 Here*****

Sex

1. Gender is frequently cited as a distinguishing segmentation variable.
2. More recently, some believe that gender is no longer an accurate way to distinguish consumers in some product categories as sex roles blur.
   a) Much of the change comes due to two-income households.
   b) The increase in male homemakers is another gender-related trend.
3. Recent research has shown that men and women differ in terms of the way they look at their Internet usage.

> *****Use Learning Objective #3 and #4 Here; Use Table 3-5 Here*****

Marital Status

1. Traditionally the family has been the focus of most marketing efforts. The household continues to be a relevant consuming unit.
2. Marketers are also interested in the demographic and media profiles of the household decision makers.

3. There are benefits to targeting specific marital status groups.
    a) Singles consume differently than marrieds
    b) Both consume differently than divorced.

*****Use Learning Objective #3 and #4 Here*****

Income, Education, and Occupation

1. It is difficult to segment a market on income alone. It only indicates the ability to pay.
2. Marketers tend to group income with other variables to get a more complete and accurate profile.
3. Income, education, and occupation tend to be closely related. There is almost a cause-effect relationship.

*****Use Learning Objective #3 and #4 Here; Use Table 3-5 Here; Use Discussion Questions #3, #7, and #9 Here*****

Psychological Segmentation

1. *Psychological segmentation* (characteristics) refers to the inner or intrinsic qualities of the individual consumer as a basis for segmentation.
2. Consumers can be segmented in terms of their needs and motivation, personality, perceptions, learning, level of involvement, and attitudes.

*****Use Key Term psychological segmentation Here; Use Learning Objectives #3 and #4 Here; Use Discussion Question #9 Here*****

Psychographic Segmentation

1. *Psychographic segmentation* (segmenting based on personality and attitude measures) is closely aligned with psychological research, especially personality and attitude measurement.
2. Commonly referred to as *lifestyle analysis*, psychographic segmentation has proven to be a valuable marketing tool to help identify promising consumer segments that are likely to be responsive to specific marketing messages.
3. Psychographic profiles of consumer segments can be thought of as being composed of a composite of consumers' measured activities, interests, and opinions (i.e., *AIOs*).
4. In their most common form, AIO-psychographic studies use a battery of statements (a *psychographic inventory*) designed to identify relevant aspects of a consumer's personality, buying motives, interests, attitudes, beliefs, and values.
5. The results of psychographic segmentation efforts are frequently reflected in firms' marketing messages.

*****Use Key Terms **psychographic segmentation, AIOs,** and **psychographic inventory**
Here; Use Learning Objectives #3, #4, and #5 Here; Use Table 3-6 and 3-7 Here; Use
Figure 3-1 Here; Use Discussion Questions #3, #7, and #9 Here; Use Exercises #2,
#3, #4, and #5 Here*****

Sociocultural Segmentation

1. Sociocultural segmentation studies sociological and anthropological group characteristics, as opposed to individual characteristics.
   a) *Sociocultural variables* provide further bases for market segmentation.
2. Consumer markets have been subdivided into segments on the basis of stages in the family life cycle, social class, core cultural values, subcultural memberships, and cross-cultural affiliation.

*****Use Key Term **sociocultural variables** Here; Use Learning Objectives #3 and #4 Here;
Use Discussion Question #9 Here*****

Family Life Cycle

1. Family life cycle is based on the premise that many families pass through similar phases in their formation, growth, and final dissolution.
2. It is a composite variable based explicitly on marital and family status and implicitly includes relative age, income, and employment status.
3. The traditional stages are bachelorhood, honeymooners, parenthood, postparenthood, and dissolution.

*****Use Learning Objectives #3, #4, and #6 Here*****

Social Class

1. Status (social class) is usually measured by a weighted index of several demographic variables, such as education, occupation, and income.
2. *Social class* implies a hierarchy whereby individuals in the same class generally have the same degree of status, although members of other classes have either higher or lower status.
   a) Studies have shown that consumers in different social classes vary in terms of values, product preferences, and buying habits.

*****Use Learning Objectives #3 and #4 Here*****

Culture and Subculture

1. Cultural segmentation is useful for both domestic and international marketing.
2. It is useful because members of the same culture tend to share the same values, beliefs, and customs.

a) Subgroups exist within the larger culture based on demographics such as race, religion, ethnicity, age, or lifestyle characteristics.
3. Culturally distinct segments may be prospects for the same product but may be targeted more effectively with different promotional appeals.

*****Use Learning Objective #3 and #4 Here*****

Cross-Cultural or Global Marketing Segmentation

1. A true global marketplace has developed.
2. Certain segments (such as teens) seem to demand the same products worldwide.
   a) Global advertising campaigns often transcend international borders.

*****Use Learning Objectives #3 and #4 Here; Use Discussion Question #9 Here*****

Use-Related Segmentation

1. *Use-related segmentation* categorizes consumers in terms of product-service, or brand usage characteristics such as usage rate, awareness status, and degree of brand loyalty.
2. *Rate of usage* segmentation differentiates among heavy users, medium users, light users, and nonusers of a specific product, service, or brand.
   a) Generally, a small group of heavy users often account for a disproportionately high percentage of product use and are often targeted by marketers.

*****Use Key Term use-related segmentation Here; Use Learning Objectives #3 and #4 Here; Discussion Question #4 Here*****

3. *Awareness status* encompasses the notion of buyer readiness, consumer awareness, or interest level.
   a) Marketers need to determine whether potential customers are aware of the product, interested in the product, or need to be informed about the product.

*****Use Discussion Question #4 Here; Use Figure 3-2 Here*****

4. *Brand loyalty* identifies those customers who continually purchase the same brands, as opposed to those consumers who continually switch brands.
   a) Marketers often try to identify the characteristics of their brand-loyal consumers so that they can direct their promotional efforts to people with similar characteristics in the larger population.
   b) Other marketers target consumers who show no brand loyalty (i.e., "brand switchers"), in the belief that such people represent greater market potential than consumers who are loyal to competing brands.
   c) Increasingly, marketers stimulate and reward brand loyalty by offering special benefits to consistent or frequent customers.

*****Use Learning Objectives #3 and #4 Here; Use Discussion Questions #5 and #9 Here; Use Figure 3-3 Here*****

Usage Situation Segmentation

1. The occasion or *usage situation* often determines what consumers will purchase or consume.
   a) Some marketers try to install the idea of suitability for a particular occasion.
   b) Many products are promoted for special usage occasions.

*****Use Learning Objectives #3 and #4 Here; Use Discussion Questions #5 and #9 Here; Use Figure 3-4 Here*****

Benefits Segmentation

1. Marketers and advertisers seek to isolate one particular benefit that they should communicate to the consumer.
2. Examples of benefits that are commonly used include: financial security (Prudential Financial), reduced calories (Amstel Light), comfort (Bausch & Lomb disposable contact lenses), good health (Egg Beaters egg substitute), proper fit (Wrangler women's jeans), and backache relief (Advil).
3. Changes in lifestyle play a major role in determining the key product benefits to promote.
4. *Benefit segmentation* can be used to position various brands within the same product line.

*****Use Key Term benefit segmentation Here; Use Learning Objective #3 and #4 Here; Use Discussion Questions #6 and #9 Here; Use Figure 3-5 Here; Use Exercise #1 (if not previously used) Here*****

Hybrid Segmentation Approaches

1. Marketers commonly segment markets by combining many segmentation bases, rather than relying on a single base. This is called *hybrid segmentation*.
2. Hybrid bases include psychographic/demographic profiles, geodemographics, VALS, and Yankelovich's Mindbase Segmentation.

*****Use Key Term hybrid segmentation Here; Use Learning Objective #3 and #7 Here; Use Discussion Question #9 Here*****

Psychographic/Demographic Profiles

1. These profiles are highly complementary approaches that work best when used together.
2. Demographic/psychographic profiling has been widely used in the development of advertising campaigns to answer three questions: "Whom should we target? . . . . What should we say? . . . .Where should we say it?"
3. Advertisers are increasingly designing ads that depict, in words and/or pictures, the essence of a particular target-market lifestyle or segment that they want to cater to.

50

*****Use Learning Objective #3 and #4 Here; Use Table 3-8 and 3-9 Here; Use Figure 3-6 Here*****

Geodemographic Segmentation

1. This hybrid segmentation scheme is based on the idea that people who live close to one another are likely to have similar financial means, tastes, preferences, lifestyles, etc.
2. This is useful when an advertiser's best prospects can be isolated in terms of where they live.

*****Use Learning Objective #3, #4, and #7 Here; Use Table 3-10 Here; Use Figure 3-6 Here*****

SRI Consulting's Values and Lifestyle System (VALS)

1. *VALS* draws on Maslow's needs hierarchy. It was originally designed to explain the dynamics of social change but was picked up by marketers.
2. Later editions of VALS focused on explaining consumer purchase behavior and divided the American population into eight distinctive subgroups or segments.
3. The major groupings are defined in terms of three major *self-orientations* and a new definition of resources:
   a) The *principle-oriented*—consumers whose choices are motivated by their beliefs, rather than by desires for approval.
   b) The *status-oriented*—consumers whose choices are guided by the actions, approval, and opinions of others.
   c) The *action-oriented*—consumers who are motivated by a desire for social or physical activity, variety, and risk taking.
4. Each of these three major self-orientations has distinct attitudes, lifestyles, and decision-making styles.
5. *Resources* refer to the range of psychological, physical, demographic, and material means and capacities consumers have to draw upon.

*****Use Key Term VALS Here; Use Learning Objective #3, #7, and #8 Here; Use Discussion Question #8 Here; Use Exercise #3 (if not previously used) Here; Use Figure 3-7, and 3-8 Here; Use Table 3-11 Here*****

Yankelovich Mindbase Segmentation

1. A new segmentation methodology, Monitor Mindbase, was recently developed to focus on households.
2. Yankelovich researchers used their annual Monitor Survey of American Values and Attitudes to identify the eight major groups and 32 subsegments that serve as the basis for Mindbase.

*****Use Learning Objective #3 and #4 Here; Use Discussion Question #9 Here; Use Table 3-12 and 3-13 Here*****

51

CRITERIA FOR EFFECTIVE TARGETING OF MARKET SEGMENTS

1. After consumer segments have been identified and clustered, the next challenge for the marketer is to select one or more segments to target with an appropriate marketing mix.
2. To be an effective target, a market segment should be:
   a) Identifiable.
   b) Sufficient (in terms of size).
   c) Stable or growing.
   d) Accessible (reachable) in terms of both media and cost.

*****Use Learning Objective #9 Here; Use Discussion Question #10 Here*****

Identification

1. To divide the market into separate segments on the basis of a series of *common* or *shared* needs or characteristics that are relevant to the product or service, a marketer must be able to identify these relevant characteristics.
2. Some segmentation variables such as *geography* (location) or *demographics* (age, gender, etc.) are relatively easy to identify. Others are not.

*****Use Learning Objective #9 Here; Use Discussion Question #10 Here*****

Sufficiency

1. For a market segment to be a worthwhile target it must consist of a sufficient number of people to warrant tailoring a product or promotional campaign to its specific needs or interests.
2. Secondary data is often used to determine sufficiency.

*****Use Learning Objective #9 Here; Use Discussion Question #10 Here*****

Stability

1. Most marketers prefer to target consumer segments that are relatively stable in terms of demographic and psychological factors and needs that are likely to grow larger over time.

*****Use Learning Objective #9 Here; Use Discussion Question #10 Here*****

Accessibility

1. Accessibility means that marketers must be able to reach the market segments they want to target in an economical way.
2. One way this can be accomplished is via the Internet.

*****Use Learning Objective #9 Here; Use Discussion Question #10 Here*****

IMPLEMENTING SEGMENTATION STRATEGIES

1. Firms that use market segmentation can pursue a *concentrated* marketing strategy or a *differentiated* marketing strategy.
2. In certain instances, they might use a **countersegmentation** strategy.

*****Use Key Term countersegmentation Here; Use Learning Objective #10 Here*****

Concentrated versus Differentiated Marketing

1. Once an organization has identified its most promising market segment, it must then decide whether to target several segments or just one. The premise behind market segmentation is that each targeted segment receives a specially designed marketing mix.
2. **Differentiated marketing** is when the marketer targets several segments using individual marketing mixes.
   a) This strategy is highly appropriate for financially strong companies that are well established in a product category and competitive with other firms that are also strong in the category.
3. *Concentrated marketing* is when the marketer targets only one segment with a unique marketing mix.
   a) This strategy is better for small firms or firms new to the field.

***** Use Key Term differentiated marketing Here; Use Learning Objective #10 Here*****

Countersegmentation

1. Sometimes companies find that it is beneficial to recombine some segments into a new single segment that could be targeted with an individually tailored product or promotional campaign.
2. When a company seeks to discover a more generic need or consumer characteristic that would apply to members of two or more segments and recombine those segments into a larger single segment that could be targeted with an individually tailored product or promotional message, this is called a *countersegmentation strategy*.

*****Use Learning Objective #10 Here*****

DISCUSSION QUESTIONS

1. What is market segmentation? How is the practice of market segmentation related to the marketing concept?

Market segmentation is the process of dividing a potential market into distinct subsets of consumers with common needs or characteristics and selecting one or more segments to target with a distinct marketing mix. Before the widespread adoption of the marketing concept, most companies practiced mass marketing that is, offering the same product and marketing mix to all consumers. The marketing concept states that a company must determine the needs and wants of specific market segments and satisfy them better than competition. Thus, companies who adopt the marketing concept must segment their markets and develop products or services targeting different consumer groups. For example, Marriott operates Fairfield Inns (short stay) and Residence Inns (apartment-like accommodations for extended stays) for the value- or budget-oriented traveler, Courtyard for the price-conscious businessperson, Marriott Hotel for full-service business travelers, Marriott Resorts for leisure and vacation guests, and Marriott Senior Living environments for elderly people.

2. **How are market segmentation, targeting, and positioning interrelated? Illustrate how these three concepts can be used to develop a marketing strategy for a product of your choice.**

Market segmentation consists of subdividing the market into homogeneous clusters, and it is the first step in a three-phase market strategy. After segmenting the market, the marketer must select one or more segments to target (*targeting*) with a specific marketing mix. The third step is to position (*positioning*) the product so that it is perceived by the target market to satisfy its needs better than other competitive offerings. For example, a toothpaste manufacturer can segment the market according to the benefits that consumers look for in the product. The firm may select one segment, such as those consumers who are primarily concerned with plaque prevention, as its target market. Then, the company must position the product so that it is perceived as providing better plaque prevention than other toothpaste brands on the market.

3. **Discuss the advantages and disadvantages of using demographics as a basis for segmentation. Can demographics and psychographics be used together to segment markets? Illustrate your answer with a specific example.**

Demographic information is the most accessible and cost effective way to identify a target market. Demographics are easier to measure than other segmentation variables. Most secondary data (e.g., census data) are expressed in demographic terms and most media develop demographic profiles of their audiences. Also, demographic trends reveal shifts in age and income that signal business opportunities for marketers. Demographics, however, tend to be one-dimensional because it provides information on the potential for usage but not on why a particular brand is used or exactly who uses it. Thus, demographics help locate a target market, although psychological and sociocultural characteristics help describe who its members are, how they think, feel, and behave. (See Table 3-2 and 3-3 for examples of how these segmentation strategies can be used.)

4. **Many marketers have found that a relatively small group of heavy users account for a disproportionately large amount of the total product consumed. What are the advantages and disadvantages of targeting these heavy users?**

Heavy users represent the most profit potential. For example, research shows that between 25 and 35 percent of beer drinkers account for more than 70 percent of all beer consumed. Therefore, many companies target heavy users, rather than try to increase the consumption among light and medium users of their products. If too many companies target the heavy users, however, these markets will become saturated. Marketers must therefore take note of gaps in targeting light and medium users, and pursue these consumer groups more aggressively.

5. **Under which circumstances and for what types of products should a marketer segment the market on the basis of (a) awareness status, (b) brand loyalty, and (c) use-situation?**

Summary of circumstances and products are as follows (note that opinions on these issues may vary):

a) *Awareness status* is most appropriate for segmenting the market for a new product. For example, if most potential consumers are unaware of the product, the marketer should design an awareness-building promotional campaign. Later on, when most potential buyers become aware of the product, the advertising should be designed to get consumers to desire and actually buy the product.

b) *Brand loyalty* can be used in segmentation in several ways. For example, a marketer of instant coffee should: 1) Study the characteristics of its "hard core" loyal customers and support their loyalty with special deals and promotions. The company should also target consumers with similar characteristics within the larger population. 2) The marketer should also study consumers who are loyal to two or three brands of coffee, including its own brand. These brands should be those that are similar to its own brand because such data will show the firm the brands that are its closest competitors. 3) By studying consumers who show no loyalty to any brand, the company may decide whether such customers are worth attracting and how to do so.

c) *Use-situation analysis* can help marketers to increase product usage. For example, candy, flower, and greeting cards marketers aggressively promote their products around Mother's Day and Father's Day. Recently, camera film marketers started to promote their products for these occasions by encouraging consumers to take pictures of their parents on these holidays.

6. **Some marketers consider benefit segmentation as the segmentation approach most consistent with the marketing concept. Do you agree or disagree with this view? Why?**

Benefit segmentation is built upon the premise that consumers are basically purchasing needs, wants, and satisfactions. Thus, it is entirely consistent with the marketing concept. *Benefit segmentation* allows marketers to position various brands within the same product category by stressing those benefits/desired satisfactions appropriate to each segment served. For example, in the toothpaste market, Close-up is marketed by using a social appeal that stresses bright teeth and is targeted to young people; Aim is targeted to parents as a good tasting toothpaste that will encourage children to brush longer; Viadent is targeted to adults as a means to remove tartar (cosmetic benefit) and plaque (health benefit).

7. Club Med is a prominent company in the vacation and travel industry. Describe how the company can use demographics and psychographics to identify TV shows and magazines in which to place its advertisements.

Club Med's catalog describes the company's resorts and includes a chart that specifies which ones are particularly suited for families with babies, families with young children, couples, honeymooners, and singles. Obviously, the company relies on demographics in segmenting its market. Within each of the demographic groups listed above, the company should identify additional socioeconomic factors (i.e., income, education, occupation) of consumers to whom a Club Med vacation "away from it all" may appeal. The company should identify the psychographics of consumers in the different segments, combine demographics and psychographics, and create several profiles of its likely customers. Then, Club Med should identify TV shows and magazines that have "audience profiles" matching its customers' profiles, and place its advertisements in such media.

8. How can a marketer for a chain of health clubs use the VALS segmentation profiles to develop an advertising campaign? Which segments should be targeted? How should the health club be positioned to each of these segments?

The VALS segments are described in Figure 3-17, Figure 3-8, and Table 3-11. The best prospects (note that opinions on the following may vary) for health clubs appear to be the *Actualizers* and *Achievers* because members of these groups are interested in growth, control of their lives, self-discovery, and self-expression. Many of them are probably already involved in some form of physical activity; however, a health club that is positioned as, say, "for people who are in the best shape they have ever been in but still aren't satisfied" will appeal to them. The health club should be portrayed as a mechanism which will help these people control an additional aspect of their lives—their health and physical well-being— through exercise. Normally, the *Experiencers* and *Makers* are not good prospects for a health club because they are interested in outdoor sports and recreation. If, however, seasonal weather prevents such endeavors, the health club could be presented as an alternative. The *Believers* are probably too set in their ways to join a health club, and the *Strivers* and *Strugglers* do not have the financial resources to join one. The *Fulfilled* represent a good target market because they are mature, educated, and financially secure individuals who might want to broaden their horizons. To them, the health club should be positioned as a new, highly fulfilling, and beneficial experience; value should be stressed in the promotion because these consumers are practical and concerned with the functionality of their purchases.

9. **For each of the following products, identify the segmentation base that you consider to be the best one for targeting consumers: (a) coffee, (b) soups, (c) home exercise equipment, (d) portable telephones, and (e) nonfat frozen yogurt. Explain your choices.**

A summary of answers or options is listed below (note that opinions on this issue may vary):

a) Coffee—demographics (size and composition of family); geographic factors (regional taste differences); benefit segmentation (health concerns, taste); user behavior (usage situation, time pressure and rate of usage).

b) Soups—demographics (size and composition of family); geographic factors (regional taste differences); usage situation (e.g., family dining versus entertaining); brand loyalty; rate of usage (e.g., suggesting new uses through recipes on the package).

c) Home exercise equipment - a combination of demographics and psychographics.

d) Portable phones - occupation and income.

e) Nonfat frozen yogurt—geographic factors; benefit segmentation; usage rate (i.e., identifying the psychographics and demographics of heavy users).

10. **Apply the criteria for effective segmentation to marketing a product of your choice to college students.**

The four criteria for effective targeting of market segments are: 1) identification, 2) sufficiency, 3) stability, and 4) accessibility. Marketing credit cards to college students provides a good illustration of utilizing the four criteria. Thus, a bank offering its credit card to students has apparently identified a common need for the service among students, determined that there is a sufficient number of consumers in this segment to make it profitable for the company, that the segment is stable (i.e., not fickle, eager to buy, and able to spend), and that it is accessible (i.e., can be reached in an economical way).

EXERCISES

1. **Select a product and brand that you use frequently and list the benefits you receive from using it. Without disclosing your list, ask a fellow student who uses a different brand in this product category (preferably, a friend of the opposite sex) to make a similar list for his or her brand. Compare the two lists and identify the implications for using benefit segmentation to market the two brands.**

Instructor's Discussion

This exercise is designed to illustrate the variability of the benefits that consumers seek in the same product and that knowledge of desired benefits can be used to position different brands within the same product category. This project can also be done between small teams or groups. If time is a problem, select the individuals or small groups that seem to have performed the exercise the best and have the students present results to class as a whole.

2. **Does your lifestyle differ significantly from your parents' lifestyle? If so, how are the two lifestyles different? What factors cause these differences?**

Instructor's Discussion

This is an interesting way to illustrate similarities and differences between the activities, interests, and opinions of two distinct groups, as the factors that determine one's lifestyle. With respect to presenting or discussing the results (if time is a problem), select the individuals that seem to have performed the exercise the best and have the students present results to class as a whole. Be sure to probe students as to mechanisms used to determine their parents (and their own) lifestyles. How could marketers use this information?

3. **Do you anticipate any major changes in your lifestyle in the next five years? If so, into which VALS segment are you likely to belong five years from now? Explain.**

Instructor's Discussion

This question matches nicely with Exercise Question #2 above. Students responses to this assignment are likely to illustrate that as one obtains additional resources, one's self-orientation is likely to change. An interesting discussion develops when students who are likely to obtain similar financial resources following graduation, characterize their future lifestyles differently. How could marketers use this information?

4. **The owners of a local health-food restaurant have asked you to prepare a psychographic profile of families living in the community surrounding the restaurant's location. Construct a ten-question psychographic inventory appropriate for segmenting families on the basis of their dining-out preferences.**

Instructor's Discussion

The psychographic items developed by the students can fall into any of a large number of dining-out and meal-related categories (price consciousness, food venturesomeness, social dimensions of eating, home-orientation, etc.). The instructor should maintain an inventory of student responses to this question and use them to demonstrate good and bad psychographic statements when this exercise is discussed.

5. **Find three print advertisements that you believe are targeted at a particular psychographic segment. How effective do you think each ad is in terms of achieving its objective? Why?**

Instructor's Discussion

Students can easily find numerous ads that are based on psychographics. Their responses will illustrate that markets of many well-known brands utilize psychographic segmentation.

S.T.A.R. PROJECTS

Ethical Issues in Consumer Behavior

S.T.A.R. Project #1

One of the best and easiest ways to segment a market is on the basis of age. As marketers have discovered, however, this is a form of segmentation that can become a very sticky proposition. Consider the number of marketing efforts directed toward the elderly. In this case, marketers must be aware that, even though they are dealing with experienced consumers, this segment is considered to be susceptible to deceptive marketing practices. A dilemma exists. How to aggressively market to a segment that often has substantial income without taking advantage of the segment's vulnerability? Visit the American Association of Retired Persons (AARP) Web site at www.aarp.org for information and guidance in accomplishing the following assignment:

a). Construct a list of five (5) ethical taboos that a marketer should avoid when marketing to this market segment. Explain the taboos.

b). Find an illustration of a company that you believe markets to the elderly in an ethical manner. Discuss why you picked the company and why you consider its practices to be ethical.

Instructor's Discussion

Students will be able to observe a variety of issues that impact and affect the elderly market segment via the AARP Web site. To begin a discussion of taboos, consider the following propositions—thou shall not steal, thou shall not harm, thou shall inform, thou shall not deceive, and thou shall not pressure. From this simple list, students should be able to create and construct a list of ethical don'ts. Be sure the students consider the Internet when constructing their list.

Students are free to select any company they wish for excellent elderly business practices. A good illustration to begin with would be McDonald's. This company often designates special discounts and coffee times for seniors.

S.T.A.R. Project #2

Few subjects are as controversial in the United States today as gun control. Given the violence in our society, the number of incidents in which guns were weapons of destruction, and the growing void between those that demand the right to own guns and those that want all guns destroyed, the National Rifle Association is at the center of a whirlwind of controversy. The NRA (see www.nra.org) has been singled out as an organization that is either a defender of the Constitution or evil (depending on one's point of view). Ethical situation—assuming that you have been given the task of evaluating a request from the NRA to sponsor a local civic event in your area (for example, a 10K run benefiting cancer patients), conduct the following activities:

a). What evidence do you find on the NRA Web site that it is concerned about public welfare?

b). What evidence do you find on the Web site that the NRA is an effective marketer?

c). What ethical issues might be present should the NRA request to sponsor your civic event be granted? How would you deal with these issues?

d). What market segments would be impacted by your evaluation of the NRA request?

e). What would you personally do in this illustration? Explain why?

<u>Instructor's Discussion</u>

This is a controversial assignment that is designed to get students to think about an issue from several perspectives. Certainly the amount of violence (and the use of guns with respect to this violence) will temper decisions and comments in this area. If students learn to deal with difficult issues now, however, they will be better prepared to address difficult issues in the future. No one can disagree that this organization is an effective marketer to a select group of people. Students can learn about this particular market segment by examining the opening page of the Web site and the various folders present. The ethical dilemma is more difficult to deal with. The NRA has deep pockets and many civic projects might need this support. Some will feel uncomfortable is accepting the support. Is acceptance any different, however, than accepting support from cigarette, alcohol, or other controversial product manufacturers? That is the real issue to be discussed. Please fell free to change this assignment to fit circumstances and preferences. Please be forewarned that this assignment may not be for everyone.

Small Group Projects

S.T.A.R. Project #3
One of the hardest assignments for a marketing manager is how to reinvigorate a brand that has been around for a long time. Time-tested brands have met the needs of their consumers but often forget to keep pace with changes in the marketplace and new market segments that are constantly forming. One such time-tested brand is Rit Dye (see www.ritdye.com). Your group's assignment is to learn about Rit Dye and propose a new segmentation strategy for the organization that would boost sales. Consider existing segments and look for new ones. Be sure justify your ideas. Visit the company's Web site to learn about the ABCs of dyeing, the art of dyeing, and how to send a virtual dye. Write a short report about your experience and your segmentation strategy for the company.

<u>Instructor's Discussion</u>

Rit Dye has been an excellent marketer through the years and has provided products that have met a real need. When, however, is the last time you dyed something? That is the crux of Rit Dye's problem. Have students examine how the brand is used today and how its use might be expanded in the future. Notice the segments on the Web page devoted to tie dyeing (yes, the same tie dyeing that was done in the Flower Power '60s). This might give students a clue as to potential segments for the future.

S.T.A.R. Project #4
Given the business challenges of the last few years, companies must always look for new ways to retain customers and enhance the value experience brought to them. One company that has specialized in this art is Carnival Cruise Lines. Carnival has learned how to target potential customers, provide fun and excitement for current customers, and bring loyal customers back again and again. Personal attention, e-mail reminders, and an interactive Web site have aided the

company in building and maintaining relationships with customers. Your group's assignment is to construct a segmentation profile of Carnival's first time customers, current customers, and past customers. Though information specifics will be beyond your grasp, general information about these groups can be obtained via the company's Web site (see www.carnival.com).Your profiles should consider age, income, lifestyle, and other variables found in Table 3-2 in the chapter. Be creative (or contact a travel agent). Present your profiles to the class. How did your group's profiles match those of other groups? Based on your profiles, comment on any new perceived opportunities for Carnival based on your segmentation work.

Instructor's Discussion

The Carnival Web site provides a wealth of information about itself and its customers. Some of the information is straightforward and some must be presumed. Students are encouraged to create with this exercise. The experience will aid them understanding how to use Table 3-2 and construct segmentation profiles. This exercise can also be a springboard to the lifestyle information presented in the chapter.

Using the Internet to Study Consumer Behavior

S.T.A.R. Project #5

According to recent reports, Linux is kicking some tails at Microsoft and Sun. This aggressive uprising on the part of Linux has been in the works for some time. The Linux geeks believe they have a better (and cheaper) way to compute and reach the Internet. From a humble beginning, Linux has moved into corporate computing, desktop computing, simulation, digital animation, number-crunching, and consumer electronics with surprising speed. The company used legal rulings against Microsoft as a barrier against the industry giant's forecasted retaliation. The strategy seems to have worked. Companies such as IBM, Intel, Dell, and Red Hat have been lining up to embrace the Linux system and method. Where will the Linux penguin appear next?

a). Visit the Linux Web site at www.linux.com. Using information that you find or links provided, write a short paragraph that outlines what you perceive to be the Linux advantage.

b). Following comments in (a) above, write a short paragraph about Linux's segmentation strategy as you perceive it.

c). Summarize what you perceive to be Linux's chances for success in the future. Justify your statements.

Instructor's Discussion

Few areas get the current generation of student's attention faster than the battles being waged between Internet service providers, cell phone companies, and software systems manufacturers. In this vein, the Linux-Microsoft conflict is an interesting one. For additional information before proceeding with the exercise see "The Linux Uprising," *BusinessWeek,* March 3, 2003 or other updated articles via the *BusinessWeek* Web site. Students should be able to answer all the exercise's questions with a little creativity by utilizing the information supplied by the company Web site or additional contemporary information in this rapidly changing field. This exercise should give them experience in constructing segmentation strategy. If there are Microsoft, Sun, or Linux loyalists in class, a debate (not an argument) is a good idea.

S.T.A.R. Project #6

Do you have a pen that remembers everything you write as you write it? Would like to have such an interesting device? Logitech (see www.logitech.com/what's new/hot products) has developed what they believe is the handwriting tool for the digital world. Using the Logitech IO Personalized Digital Pen, everything you write can be saved, organized, and shared. At about $200, the pen incorporates a tiny camera that records the pattern of dots you create when you write on specially designed paper. When you put the pen in its specially designed dock, the information contained in the pen can be transferred to your PC. The image of what you wrote (the "digital ink") can then be pasted into many applications. Writing may not be such a drag after all.

    a). Visit the Logitech Web site to learn more about the IO Personalized Digital Pen.
    b). What market segments might be interested in such a device?
    c). Which of the Mindbase segments mentioned in Table 3-12 might be a good segment(s) for Logitech to pursue first?
    d). After examining the segments that you have constructed or seen in Table 3-12, apply the four characteristics of an effective market target described in the chapter. Comment on which segment(s) now appear to be attractive.

Instructor's Discussion

Logitech has many great innovations as can be seen via their Web site. The IO Personalized Digital Pen is one of these. Be sure that students understand that this pen would not be for everyone (especially at $200). More importantly, the pen must use special paper. At this time, a three-pack of special 160-page notebooks is priced at $24.99. If IO and its system catches on, the prices of the pen and paper would most likely drop. What other companies would view the IO system as a threat? Palm-based technology might for one. This exercise should give students experience with the Mindbase system (you can use other categories if you so choose) and the effective market-targeting list.

CASES

Case One: Muscle Car for Middle Age

The introduction of this model is an attempt by Mercury to go after a different demographic segment of the automobile market—younger consumers. But given the features of the car, it is likely that students might propose a form of "hybrid segmentation"—that combines age and lifestyle or psychographic factors (i.e., "fantasy car enthusiasts"). In order for Mercury to remain a viable brand, it must attract owners that are significantly younger and have a different set of lifestyle-related "needs" that they are trying to satisfy than the typical Mercury automobile buyer (i.e., who are on average 69 years of age for Mercury Grand Marquis). It would seem that the new Marauder model is targeted to the aging Baby Boomer—perhaps in his 50s—who wants Camaro-like performance without the cramped interior or harsh ride.

Case Two: Is There Such a Thing as Women's Toothpaste?

Student responses may vary. The Figure presenting the SRI VALS segments indicate that Actualizers are receptive to new products, *Achievers* are attracted to premium products, whereas Experiencers follow fashion and fads and buy on impulse. So any of these segments might contain potential product purchasers.

CHAPTER 4

Consumer Motivation

LEARNING OBJECTIVES

After studying this chapter students should be able to:
1. Explain motivation.
2. Define the terms *needs* and *goals* in the context of consumer behavior.
3. Understand positive and negative motivation.
4. Discuss the difference between rational and emotional motives.
5. Understand the dynamic nature of motivation.
6. Explain the various defense mechanisms people use to manage their frustration.
7. Identify the four types of arousal stimulus.
8. Explain need systems, specifically, identify the components of Maslow's need theory, and offer a critique of needs theory.
9. Define a trio of needs theory.
10. Define validity and reliability in terms of researching consumer behavior.
11. Discuss motivational research, past and present, and its limitations.

CHAPTER SUMMARY

Motivation is the driving force within individuals that impels them to action. This driving force is produced by a state of uncomfortable tension, which exists as the result of an unsatisfied need. All individuals have needs, wants, and desires. The individual's subconscious drive to reduce need-induced tension results in behavior that he or she anticipates will satisfy needs and thus bring about a more comfortable internal state.

All behavior is goal oriented. Goals are the sought-after results of motivated behavior. The form or direction that behavior takes—the goal that is selected—is a result of thinking processes (cognition) and previous learning. There are two types of goals: generic goals and product-specific goals. A generic goal is a general category of goal that may fulfill a certain need; a product-specific goal is a specifically branded or labeled product that the individual sees as a way to fulfill a need. Product-specific needs are sometimes referred to as wants.

Innate needs—those an individual is born with—are physiological (biogenic) in nature; they include all the factors required to sustain physical life (e.g., food, water, clothing, shelter, and sex). Acquired needs—those an individual develops after birth—are primarily psychological (psychogenic): they include love, acceptance, esteem, and self-fulfillment. For any given need, there are many different and appropriate goals. The specific goal selected depends on the individual's experiences, physical capacity, prevailing cultural norms and values, and the goal's accessibility in the physical and social environment.

Needs and goals are interdependent, and change in response to the individual's physical condition, environment, interaction with other people, and experiences. As needs become satisfied, new, higher-order needs emerge that must be fulfilled.

Failure to achieve a goal often results in feelings of frustration. Individuals react to frustration in two ways: "fight" or "flight." They may cope by finding a way around the obstacle that prohibits goal attainment or by adopting a substitute goal (fight); or they may adopt a defense mechanism that enables them to protect their self-esteem (flight). Defense mechanisms include aggression, regression, rationalization, withdrawal, projection, autism, identification, and repression.

Motives cannot easily be inferred from consumer behavior. People with different needs may seek fulfillment through selection of the same goals: people with the same needs may seek fulfillment through different goals. Although some psychologists have suggested that individuals have different need priorities, others believe that most human beings experience the same basic needs, to which they assign a similar priority ranking. Maslow's hierarchy of needs theory proposes five levels of prepotent human needs: physiological needs, safety needs, social needs, egoistic needs, and self-actualization needs. Other needs widely integrated into consumer advertising include the needs for power, affiliation, and achievement.

There are three commonly used methods for identifying and "measuring" human motives: observation and inference, subjective reports, and qualitative research (including projective techniques.) None of these methods is completely reliable by itself. Therefore, researchers often use a combination of two or three techniques in tandem to assess the presence or strength of consumer motives. Motivational research is qualitative research designed to delve below the consumer's level of conscious awareness. Despite some shortcomings, motivational research has proved to be of great value to marketers concerned with developing new ideas and new copy appeals.

CHAPTER OUTLINE

INTRODUCTION

1. Human needs—consumer needs are the basis of all modern marketing.
    a) Needs are the essence of the marketing concept.
    b) The key to a company's survival, profitability, and growth in a highly competitive marketing environment is its ability to identify and satisfy unfulfilled consumer needs better and sooner than the competition.
2. Marketers do not create needs, though in some instances they may make consumers more keenly aware of unfelt needs.
    a) Successful marketers define their markets in terms of the needs they presume to satisfy, not in terms of the products they sell. This is a market-oriented, rather than a production-oriented, approach to marketing.
    b) A marketing orientation focuses on the needs of the buyer; a production orientation focuses on the needs of the seller.

c) The marketing concept implies that the manufacturer will make only what it knows people will buy; a production orientation implies that the manufacturer will try to sell what it decides to make.

3. Marketers who base their offerings on recognition of consumers' needs find a ready market for their products.

*****Use Table 4-1 Here*****

MOTIVATION AS A PSYCHOLOGICAL FORCE

1. *Motivation* can be described as the driving force within individuals that impels them to action. This driving force is produced by a state of tension, which exists as the result of an unfilled need.
2. The specific courses of action that consumers pursue and their specific goals are selected on the basis of their thinking process and previous learning.

*****Use Key Term motivation Here; Use Learning Objective #1 Here; Use Figure 4-1 Here*****

Needs

1. Every individual has needs; some are innate, others are acquired.
2. *Innate needs* are physiological or *biogenic*, and include food, water, air, clothing, shelter, and sex.
   a) These needs (innate) are considered *primary needs* or motives.
3. *Acquired needs* are needs that we learn in response to our culture or environment and include the need for self-esteem, prestige, affection, power, and learning.
   a) These needs are generally psychological (i.e., *psychogenic* or acquired) and are considered to be secondary needs or motives.
   b) They result from the individual's subjective psychological state and from relationships with others.

*****Use Key Terms innate needs, biogenic needs, primary needs, acquired needs, and psychogenic needs Here; Use Learning Objective #2 Here; Use Discussion Question #1, #2, #3, and #4 Here*****

Goals

1. Goals are the sought after results of motivated behavior. All behavior is goal oriented.
2. *Generic goals* are the general classes or categories of goals that consumers select to fulfill their needs.
3. *Product-specific goals* are the products they select to fulfill their needs.
4. Individuals set goals on the basis of their personal values and they select means (or behaviors) that they believe will help them achieve their desired goals.

*****Use Key Terms generic goals and product-specific goals *Here; Use Figure 4-1, 4-2 (A, B, and C), and 4-3 Here; Use Learning Objective #2 Here; Use Discussion Question #4 Here*****

The Selection of Goals

1. Goal selection by individuals depends on:
   a) Their personal experiences.
   b) Physical capacity.
   c) Prevailing cultural norms and values.
   d) The goal's accessibility in the physical and social environment.
2. An individual's own perception of himself, or self-image, also serves to influence the specific goals selected.
3. The products a person owns, would like to own, or would not like to own, are often perceived in terms of how closely they reflect the person's self-image.
   a) A product that is perceived as matching a consumer's self-image has a greater probability of being selected than one that does not.

*****Use Discussion Question #5 Here; Use Figure 4-4 Here*****

Interdependence of Needs and Goals

1. Needs and goals are interdependent—neither exists without the other.
2. People are often not as aware of their needs as they are of their goals.
3. Individuals are usually more aware of their physiological needs than they are of their psychological needs.

*****Use Discussion Question #4 and #5 Here*****

Positive and Negative Motivation

1. Motivation can be positive or negative in direction.
   a) We may feel a driving force toward some object or condition, or a driving force away from some object or condition.
2. Some psychologists refer to positive motivation as needs, wants, or drives.
   a) They may refer to negative motivation as negative drives, fears, and aversions.
3. Some distinguish between needs and wants by calling wants product-specific needs.
   a) Although *positive* and *negative motivational forces* seem to differ dramatically in terms of physical (and sometimes emotional) activity, they are basically similar in that both serve to initiate and sustain human behavior.
   b) There is no uniformly accepted distinction among needs, wants, and desires.

*****Use Key Terms **positive and negative motivational forces** *Here; Use Learning Objective #3 Here*****

4. Goals can be positive or negative.
5. A positive goal is one toward which behavior is directed, and thus is often referred to as an *approach object*.
6. A negative goal is one from which behavior is directed away, and thus is sometimes referred to as an *avoidance object*.
7. People become motivationally aroused by a threat to, or the elimination of, a behavioral freedom
    a) This motivational state is called *psychological reactance* and is usually manifested by a negative consumer response.

*****Use Key Terms* approach object, avoidance object, and psychological reactance *Here; Use Figure 4-5 (A and B) Here; Use Learning Objective #3 Here*****

Rational versus Emotional Motives

1. Some consumer behaviorists distinguish between so-called *rational motives* and *emotional motives.*
2. They use the term *rationality* in the traditional economic sense, which assumes that consumers behave rationally when they carefully consider all alternatives and choose those that give them the greatest utility.
3. In a marketing context, the term rationality implies that consumers select goals based on totally objective criteria, such as size, weight, price, or miles per gallon. Emotional motives imply the selection of goals according to personal or subjective criteria (e.g., pride, fear, affection, status).

*****Use Key Terms* rational motives and emotional motives *Here; Use Learning Objective #4 Here*****

4. The assumption underlying this distinction is that subjective or emotional criteria do not maximize utility or satisfaction.
    a) It is reasonable, however, to assume that consumers always attempt to select alternatives that, in their view, serve to maximize their satisfaction.
5. Consumer researchers who subscribe to the *positivist* research perspective tend to view all consumer behavior as rationally motivated, and they try to isolate the causes of such behavior so that they can predict, and thus influence, future behavior.
6. *Experientialists* are often interested in studying the hedonistic pleasures that certain consumption behaviors provide, such as fun, fantasy, or sensuality. They study consumers in order to gain insights and understanding of the behaviors they have in various unique circumstances.

*****Use Learning Objective #4 Here*****

THE DYNAMIC NATURE OF MOTIVATION

1. Needs and goals are constantly growing and changing.
   a) They don't cease because existing needs are never completely satisfied.
   b) Newer, higher-level needs replace fulfilled needs.

*****Use Learning Objective #5 Here; Use Figure 4-6 Here*****

Needs Are Never Fully Satisfied

1. Most human needs are not fully or permanently satisfied.
2. Temporary goal achievement does not adequately satisfy the need.

*****Use Learning Objective #5 Here; Use Discussion Question #6 Here*****

New Needs Emerge as Old Needs Are Satisfied

1. Some motivational theorists believe that a hierarchy of needs exists, and that new, higher-order needs emerge as lower-order needs are fulfilled.
2. Marketers should to be attuned for changing needs.

*****Use Learning Objective #5 Here; Use Figure 4-7 Here*****

Success and Failure Influence Goals

1. Researchers have concluded that individuals who successfully achieve their goals usually set new and higher goals for themselves. Individuals raise their *levels of aspiration*.
2. The nature and persistence of an individual's behavior often is influenced by expectations of success or failure in reaching certain goals.
3. The effects of success or failure on goal selection have implications for marketers.
   a) Advertisements should not promise more than the product can deliver.
   b) Creating unrealistic expectations can backfire on the marketer.

*****Use Key Term levels of aspiration Here; Use Learning Objective #5 Here; Use Discussion Question #6 Here*****

Substitute Goals

1. When an individual cannot attain a specific goal or type of goal that he or she anticipates will satisfy certain needs, behavior may be directed to a *substitute goal*.
2. Although the substitute goal may not be as satisfactory as the primary goal, it may be sufficient to dispel uncomfortable tension.

***** Use Key Term substitute goal Here; Use Learning Objective #5 Here*****

<u>Frustration</u>

1. Failure to achieve a goal often results in feelings of frustration. Individuals react differently to frustrating situations.
2. Some people are adaptive and manage to cope by finding their way around the obstacle or, if that fails, by selecting a substitute goal.
3. Some people are less adaptive and may regard their inability to achieve a goal as a personal failure and experience feelings of anxiety.

*****Use Learning Objective #6 Here*****

<u>Defense Mechanisms</u>

1. People who cannot cope with frustration often mentally redefine the frustrating situation in order to protect their self-image and defend their self-esteem. These reactions are known as *defense mechanisms*.
2. Reaction to the frustration of not being able to reach goal attainment can take many forms, such as aggression, rationalization, regression, withdrawal, projection, autism, identification, and repression.
3. Marketers often consider the protection of self-esteem by consumers when selecting advertising appeals. The ads (appeals) often portray a person resolving a particular frustration through the use of the advertised product.

*****Use Key Term defense mechanisms Here; Use Learning Objective #6 Here; Use Table 4-2 Here; Use Exercise #2 Here*****

Multiplicity of Needs

1. Consumer behavior often fulfills more than one need.
2. Specific goals are often selected because they fill several needs.
   a) A *prepotent need* is a triggering mechanism for need fulfillment.

*****Use Key Term prepotent need Here*****

<u>Needs and Goals Vary Among Individuals</u>

1. It is difficult to infer motives from behavior.
2. People with different needs may seek fulfillment through selection of the same goals, although people with the same needs may seek fulfillment through different goals.

Arousal of Motives

1. Specific needs of an individual are dormant much of the time.
   a) The arousal of any particular set of needs at a specific point in time may be caused by internal stimuli found in the individual's physiological condition, emotional or cognitive processes, or by stimuli in the outside environment.

*****Use Learning Objective #7 Here; Use Discussion Question #6 Here*****

Physiological Arousal

1. Bodily needs, at any one specific moment in time, are rooted in an individual's physiological condition at that moment.
2. Most physiological cues are involuntary; however, they arouse related needs that cause uncomfortable tensions until they are satisfied.

*****Use Learning Objective #7 Here; Use Discussion Question #6 Here*****

Emotional Arousal

1. Sometimes thinking or daydreaming results in the arousal or stimulation of latent needs.
   a) These thoughts tend to arouse dormant needs, which may produce uncomfortable tensions that "push" them into goal-oriented behavior.

*****Use Learning Objective #7 Here; Use Discussion Question #6 Here*****

Cognitive Arousal

1. Sometimes random thoughts or personal achievement can lead to a cognitive awareness of needs.

*****Use Learning Objective #7 Here; Use Discussion Question #6 Here; Use Figure 4-8 Here*****

Environmental Arousal

1. The set of needs activated at a particular time is often determined by specific cues in the environment.
2. When people live in a complex and highly varied environment, they experience many opportunities for need arousal. Conversely, when people live in a poor or deprived environment, fewer needs are activated.
3. The *behaviorist* school considers motivation to be a mechanical process; behavior is seen as the response to a stimulus, and elements of conscious thought are ignored.
4. The *cognitive* school believes that all behavior is directed at goal achievement.

a) Needs and past experiences are reasoned, categorized, and transformed into attitudes and beliefs that act as predispositions to behavior.

***** *Use Learning Objective #7 Here; Use Discussion Question #6 Here* *****

TYPES AND SYSTEMS OF NEEDS

1. Most lists of human needs tend to be diverse in content as well as in length.
   a) Although there is little disagreement about specific physiological needs, there is considerable disagreement about specific psychological (i.e., psychogenic) needs.
2. In 1938, the psychologist Henry Murray prepared a detailed list of 28 psychogenic needs that have served as the basic constructs for a number of widely used personality tests.
   a) Murray's basic needs include many motives that are assumed to play an important role in consumer behavior, such as acquisition, achievement, recognition, and exhibition.

***** *Use Learning Objective #8 Here; Use Table 4-3 Here* *****

Hierarchy of Needs

1. Dr. Abraham Maslow formulated a widely accepted theory of human motivation. Maslow's theory postulates five basis levels of human needs, which rank in order of importance from low-level (biogenic) needs to higher-level (psychogenic) needs.
2. *Maslow's hierarchy of needs* theory suggests that individuals seek to satisfy lower-level needs before higher-level needs emerge.

***** *Use Key Term* **Maslow's hierarchy of needs** *Here; Use Learning Objective #8 Here; Use Figure 4-9 Here; Use Discussion Question #7 Here* *****

Physiological Needs

1. Physiological needs are those things that are required to sustain biological life; food, water, air, shelter, clothing, and sex.
2. Dominant when chronically unsatisfied.

***** *Use Learning Objective #8 Here; Use Figure 4-9 Here* *****

Safety Needs

1. Safety needs are concerned with much more than physical safety. They include order, stability, routine, familiarity, control over one's life and environment, and certainty. Health is also a safety concern.

***** *Use Learning Objective #8 Here; Use Figure 4-9 Here* *****

Social Needs

1. Social needs relate to such things as love, affection, belonging, and acceptance.

*****Use Learning Objective #8 Here; Use Figure 4-9 Here*****

Egoistic Needs

1. Egoistic needs can take an inward or outward orientation.
2. Inwardly-directed ego needs reflect an individual's need for self-acceptance, for self-esteem, for success, for independence, for personal satisfaction with a job well done.
3. Outwardly-directed ego needs include the needs for prestige, for reputation, for status, for recognition from others.

*****Use Learning Objective #8 Here; Use Figure 4-9 and 4-10 Here*****

Need for Self-Actualization

1. Need for self-actualization refers to an individual's desire to fulfill his or her potential to become everything he or she is capable of becoming.

*****Use Learning Objective #8 Here; Use Figure 4-9 and 4-11 Here*****

An Evaluation of the Need Hierarchy and Marketing Applications

1. The major problem with Maslow's theory is that it cannot be tested empirically; there is no easy way to measure precisely how satisfied one need is before the next higher need becomes operative.
2. Maslow's hierarchy offers a useful, comprehensive framework for marketers trying to develop appropriate advertising appeals for their products.
3. The hierarchy enables marketers to focus their advertising appeals on a need level that is likely to be shared by a large segment of the prospective audience.
4. The hierarchy facilitates product positioning or repositioning.

*****Use Learning Objective #8 Here; Use Discussion Question #7 Here; Use Exercise #1 Here*****

Segmentation and Promotional Applications

1. Needs hierarchy is often the basis for market segmentation with specific advertising appeals directed to one or more need-segment levels.

*****Use Figure 4-13 Here*****

Positioning Applications

1. The key to positioning is to find a niche that is not occupied by a competing product or brand.
   a) This application of the needs hierarchy relies on the notion that no need is ever fully satisfied, that it always continues to be somewhat motivating.

A Trio of Needs Theory

1. Some psychologists believe in the existence of a trio of basic needs: the needs for power, for affiliation, and for achievement.

***** *Use Learning Objective #9 Here; Use Exercise #3 Here* *****

Power

1. The power need relates to an individual's desire to control his or her environment.
2. Many individuals experience increased self-esteem when they exercise power over objects or people.

***** *Use Learning Objective #9 Here; Use Exercise #3 Here; Use Figure 4-12 Here* *****

Affiliation

1. The affiliation need suggests that behavior is highly influenced by the desire for friendship, for acceptance, and for belonging.
2. People with high affiliation needs tend to be socially dependent on others.

***** *Use Learning Objective #9 Here; Use Exercise #3 Here; Use Figure 4-13 Here* *****

Achievement

1. Individuals with a strong need for achievement often regard personal accomplishment as an end in itself.
2. The achievement need is closely related to both the egoistic need and the self-actualization need.
   a) People with a high need for achievement tend to be more self-confident, enjoy taking calculated risks, actively research their environments, and value feedback.
   b) Monetary rewards provide an important type of feedback as to how they are doing.
3. People with high achievement needs prefer situations in which they can take personal responsibility for finding solutions.
4. Individuals with specific psychological needs tend to be receptive to advertising appeals directed at those needs. They also tend to be receptive to certain kinds of products.
5. Knowledge of motivational theory provides marketers with additional bases on which to segment their markets.

*****Use Learning Objective #9 Here; Use Exercise #3 Here; Use Figure 4-14 Here*****

THE MEASUREMENT OF MOTIVES

1. How are motives identified? How are they measured? How do researchers know which motives are responsible for certain kinds of behavior?
   a) These are difficult questions to answer because motives are hypothetical constructs—that is, they cannot be seen or touched, handled, smelled, or otherwise tangibly observed. For this reason, no single measurement method can be considered a reliable index.
   b) Instead, researchers usually rely on a combination of various qualitative research techniques to try to establish the presence and/or the strength of various motives.
2. Some psychologists are concerned that most measurement techniques do not meet the crucial test criteria of *validity* and *reliability*.
3. The findings of qualitative research methods are highly dependent on the analyst; they focus not only on the data themselves but also on what the analyst thinks they imply. Therefore, many consumer behaviorists are reluctant to rely on one technique alone.
   a) By using, however, a combination of assessments (called *triangulation*) based on behavioral data (observation), subjective data (self reports) and qualitative data (projective tests, collage research, etc.), consumer researchers feel more confident.
4. Though some marketers are concerned that qualitative research does not produce hard numbers that objectively "prove" the point under investigation, others are convinced that qualitative studies are more revealing than quantitative studies.

*****Use Learning Objective #10 Here; Use Discussion Question #8 Here*****

Motivational Research

1. *Motivational research* is a term generally used to refer to qualitative research designed to uncover the consumer's subconscious or hidden motivation.

*****Use Key Term motivational research Here; Use Learning Objective #11 Here*****

The Developer of Motivational Research

1. Psychoanalytic theory of personality, developed by Freud, provided the basis for the development of motivational research.
2. The theory is built on the premise that unconscious needs or drives, especially biological and sexual drives, are at the heart of human motivation and personality.
3. Dr. Dichter adapted Freud's psychoanalytic techniques to the study of consumer buying habits.
   a) Previous to Dr. Dichter, marketing research focused on what consumers did rather than why they did it.

75

4. By the early 1960s, drawbacks to motivational research were noted.
   a) Because of the intensive nature of qualitative research, samples necessarily were small; thus, there was concern about generalizing findings to the total market.
   b) Also, marketers soon realized that the analysis of projective tests and depth interviews was highly subjective. The same data given to three different analysts could produce three different reports.
5. Other consumer theorists noted additional inconsistencies in applying Freudian theory to the study of consumer behavior.
6. There are a number of research techniques that can be used to delve into the consumer's unconscious or hidden motivations.

*****Use Learning Objective #11 Here; Use Table 4-4 and 4-5 Here*****

Evaluation of Motivational Research

1. Despite these criticisms, motivational research is still regarded as an important tool by marketers who want to gain deeper insights into the *whys* of consumer behavior than conventional marketing research techniques can yield.
2. Motivational research's principal use today is in the development of new ideas for promotional campaigns, ideas that can penetrate the consumer's conscious awareness by appealing to unrecognized needs.
3. Motivational research also provides marketers with a basic orientation for new product categories, and enables them to explore consumer reactions to ideas and advertising copy at an early stage to avoid costly errors.
4. Despite the drawbacks of motivational research, there is new and compelling evidence that the unconscious is the site of a far larger portion of mental life than even Freud envisioned.
   a) Research studies show that the unconscious mind may understand and respond to nonverbal symbols, form emotional responses, and guide actions largely independent of conscious awareness.

*****Use Learning Objective #11 Here*****

DISCUSSION QUESTIONS

1. a. "Marketers don't create needs; needs pre-exist marketers." Discuss this statement.
   b. Can marketing efforts change consumers' needs? Why or why not?

   a. Marketers do not create needs, though in some instances they may make consumers more keenly aware of unfelt needs. The tact that many new products take illustrates that marketers often do not recognize or understand consumer needs and that they cannot create a need for products. On the other hand, there are countless examples of products that have succeeded in the marketplace because they fulfill consumer needs.

   b. Marketing efforts are generally not designed to change consumer needs but to create or trigger "wants" for products/services that consumers would then purchase to satisfy needs that already exist. Market-oriented companies use consumer research to uncover relevant needs, translate them into "wants" by designing appropriate products and services, and position their offerings as satisfying needs and wants better than competitors' products/services.

2. **Consumers have both innate and acquired needs. Give examples of each kind of need and show how the same purchase can serve to fulfill either or both kinds of needs.**

Innate needs are physiological in nature (e.g., food, water, air, clothing, shelter, sex). *Acquired needs* are generally psychological in nature (e.g., esteem, prestige, affection, power, and the like). The purchase of a house satisfies the individual's innate need for shelter, but the type of house he or she buys, its interior and exterior design, and location are likely to reflect acquired needs. For example, an individual may seek a place where large groups of people can be entertained (fulfilling social needs) and want to live in an exclusive community to impress friends (fulfilling ego needs).

3. **Specify both innate and acquired needs that would be useful bases for developing promotional strategies for:**
   a. **global positioning systems**
   b. **Harley Davidson motorcycles**
   c. **recruiting college seniors to work for a high-technology company.**

   a. Global positioning systems in cars: physical safety and survival, self-esteem, affection toward one's family and friends—social needs—and even ego needs—by using the latest technology available.
   b. Harley Davidson motorcycles: power needs—control of one's environment—and ego needs—impress one's friends.
   c. Recruiting college seniors to work for a high tech company: achievement—personal accomplishment—and self-actualization—realizing one's full potential.

4. **Why are consumers' needs and goals constantly changing? What factors influence the formation of new goals?**

Needs and goals are constantly growing and changing in response to an individual's physical condition, environment, interactions with others, and experiences. As individuals attain their goals, they develop new ones. If they do not attain their goals, they continue to strive for old goals, or they develop substitute goals. Some of the reasons why need-driven human activity never ceases include the following: 1) existing needs are never completely satisfied; they continually impel activity designed to attain or maintain satisfaction; 2) as needs become satisfied, new and higher-order needs emerge to be fulfilled; and 3) people who achieve their goals set new and higher goals for themselves.

5. **How can marketers use consumers' failures to achieve goals in developing promotional appeals for specific products and services? Give examples.**

Failure to achieve a goal often results in feelings of frustration, and individuals react differently to frustrating situations. Some people are adaptive and cope with frustrating situations by finding their way around the obstacle or, if this fails, by selecting a substitute goal. People who cannot cope with frustration adopt defense mechanisms to protect their egos from feelings of failure when they do not attain their goals. The eight defense mechanisms are: aggression, rationalization, regression, withdrawal, projection, autism, identification, and repression (for more information see Table 4-2).

6. **Most human needs are dormant much of the time. What factors cause their arousal? Give examples of ads for audio/video equipment that are designed to arouse latent consumer needs.**

The arousal of any particular set of needs at a specific point in time may be caused by physiological/internal stimuli (e.g., a drop in blood sugar level, or stomach contractions trigger awareness of hunger need), emotional processes (e.g., daydreaming results in arousal or stimulation of latent needs), cognitive process, or environmental cues (e.g., fast-food commercials may arouse the need for food).

7. **For each of the situations listed in Question 3, select one level from Maslow's hierarchy of human needs that can be used to segment the market and position the product (or the company). Explain your choices. What are the advantages and disadvantages of using Maslow's hierarchy in segmentation and positioning applications?**

a) Global positioning systems—physiological needs. b) Harley Davidson motorcycle—ego needs. c) Recruiting college seniors to work for a company in the energy field—self actualization.

Maslow's needs hierarchy received wide acceptance in many social disciplines because it appears to reflect the assumed or inferred motivations of many people in our society. The five levels of need postulated by the hierarchy are sufficiently generic to encompass most lists of individual needs. Some critics, however, maintain that Maslow's concepts are too general. To say that hunger and self-esteem are similar, in that both are needs, is to obscure the urgent, involuntary nature of the former and the largely conscious, voluntary nature of the latter. The major problem with the theory is that it cannot be tested empirically; there is no way to measure precisely how satisfied one need must be before the next higher need becomes operative. The need hierarchy also appears to be very closely bound to our contemporary American culture. Despite these criticisms, Maslow's hierarchy is a useful tool for understanding consumer motivations and is readily adaptable to marketing strategy. Offer the students several current examples, one for each level of the hierarchy.

8.a. How do researchers identify and "measure" human motives? Give examples.

This is a difficult question to answer because motives are hypothetical constructs—that is, they cannot be seen or touched, handled, smelled, or otherwise tangibly observed. For this reason, no single measurement method can be considered a reliable index. Instead, researchers usually rely on a combination of various qualitative research techniques to try to establish the presence and/or the strength of various motives.

b. Does motivational research differ from qualitative research? Discuss.

Motivational research is a term generally used to refer to qualitative research designed to uncover the consumer's subconscious or hidden motivation. Psychoanalytic theory of personality, developed by Freud, provided the basis for the development of motivational research. The theory is built on the premise that unconscious needs or drives, especially biological and sexual drives, are at the heart of human motivation and personality.

c. What are the strengths and weaknesses of motivational research?

Because of the intensive nature of qualitative research, samples necessarily were small; thus, there was concern about generalizing findings to the total market. Also, marketers soon realized that the analysis of projective tests and depth interviews was highly subjective. The same data given to three different analysts could produce three different reports. Other consumer theorists noted additional inconsistencies in applying Freudian theory to the study of consumer behavior. Despite these criticisms, motivational research is still regarded as an important tool by marketers who want to gain deeper insights into the whys of consumer behavior than conventional marketing research techniques can yield. Motivational research's principal use today is in the development of new ideas for promotional campaigns, ideas that can penetrate the consumer's conscious awareness by appealing to unrecognized needs. Motivational research also provides marketers with a basic orientation for new product categories, and enables them to explore consumer reactions to ideas and advertising copy at an early stage to avoid costly errors.

EXERCISES

1. **You are a member of an advertising team assembled to develop a promotional campaign for a new digital camera. Develop three headlines for this campaign, each based on one of the levels in Maslow's need hierarchy.**

Instructor's Discussion

Here are four examples of appeals, one for each level. Students' slogans will vary. 1) Appeal to safety and security needs by stressing the product's durability and dependability and its use in recording digital pictures that are important to those needs (such as a home inventor for insurance purposes). 2) Appeal to social needs by showing that the consumer's peers highly approve the selection of the camera and how memories can be recorded from social situations. 3) Appeal to ego needs by featuring peers who are impressed by the purchase. 4)

Appeal to self-actualization by showing how the camera enables the consumer using it to continuously improve his/her social or business performance.

2. **Find an advertisement that depicts a defense mechanism. Present it in class and evaluate its effectiveness.**

Instructor's Discussion

Have students clearly identify the defense mechanism first. Then have them explain how the ad taps that defense mechanism and how effective it is. For example, a "slice-of-life" commercial may show a young man faced with the problem of convincing a girl he likes to accept a date with him. A friend advises him to change his toothpaste, his shampoo, or whatever, to the advertised product; when he does, he gets the girl and his problem is solved.

3. **Explain briefly the needs for power, affiliation, and achievement. Find three advertisements for different products that are designed to appeal to these needs.**

Instructor's Discussion

Power needs relate to an individual's desire to control his or her environment, both animate and inanimate. An automobile ad that stresses speed capability utilizes this notion. *Affiliation needs* refer to the human need for friendship, for acceptance, for belonging. Advertisements for personal care products often suggest that use of the advertised product will improve the user's social life—thus fulfilling the need for affiliation. *Achievement needs* refer to those individuals who regard personal accomplishments as an end in itself. Such individuals are often good prospects for do-it-yourself products and for such advertising appeals as "we try harder."

S.T.A.R. PROJECTS

Ethical Issues in Consumer Behavior

S.T.A.R. Project #1
The Advertising Council is a nonprofit organization made up of volunteers from the advertising industry whose goal and mission is to provide quality promotion for those needy causes that could not afford such high-powered services on their own. Issues impacting health, the welfare of our country, women's issues, social causes like drug use prevention, and environmental concerns have been the forte of the Ad Council in recent years. For all the good work that the council does, some question whether the Ad Council has become more left-wing than right-wing in their politics (and campaign messages) in recent years. Does a political spin to the promotions created by the Ad Council harm its credibility?
   a. Review the Ad Council's Web page at www.adcouncil.org.
   b. Review the issues, campaigns, organizations, and non-profit resources created and used by the Ad Council. Do you think the Ad Council seems to have a political agenda? If so, is this correct or incorrect ethical behavior for such an organization?

c. How does the Ad Council attempt to impact consumer motivation? Find one illustration from the Ad Council Web page to illustrate your thoughts.

Instructor's Discussion

The Ad Council is a great place to see great advertising. In fact, the organization often wins the coveted CLIO award in advertising. The point of this exercise is to not only introduce the student to the Ad Council and its work but to get the student to think about how an organization such as this can impact consumer motivation, behavior, and even purchasing. The Ad Council sponsors many worthy causes, however, because the Council is made up of many talented members, all of the members do not necessarily think alike or approach problems from the same direction. The students should be able to find at least one controversial ad (please preview these before discussion in class as some are just that—controversial (such as planned parenthood). This is where the ethical discussion can begin with respect to public responsibility, noble intent, and the politics of issues. A very big part of consumer motivation is moving a consumer toward a particular point of view. Ethical behavior is part of that process.

S.T.A.R. Project #2

After you have read the opening vignette to the chapter on Revlon, see if you can guess who might be Revlon's archrival. If you said L'Oréal, you were correct. L'Oréal matches Revlon in almost all competitive categories. Examine the L'Oréal Web site at www.loreal.com for more information on this cosmetic industry giant. Having done this, consider the following imaginary scenario: as a marketing manager for Revlon, you have just discovered that L'Oréal is using the frustration dynamic of motivation to persuade young teenage girls to switch from Revlon products to those of L'Oréal. L'Oréal ads show two teen girls discussing their difficulties in finding dates to a prom. One girl having seen that her friend has just applied Revlon nail polish and lipstick, says "Maybe the reason you can't get a date is that you are using your mother's nail polish and lipstick—it's just too old fashion!"
   a. Considering the information above, how might L'Oréal be using the frustration dynamic of motivation to woo Revlon users?
   b. What defense mechanisms might be at work in the above scenario if the first girl defends her choice of nail polish and lipstick?
   c. Do you see any ethical problems with the approach used by L'Oréal? Explain.

Instructor's Discussion

First, the students will find a wealth of consumer information on the L'Oréal Web site. This information can be useful for constructing other projects or exercises on needs and motivation. Advise students to carefully read the section on *frustration, defense mechanisms,* and Table 4-2 before attempting the answers to the questions posed by the imaginary scenario. Notice that frustration often occurs when one fails to achieve a goal. In the scenario, if the goal was to get a prom date, the girls might be frustrated. Girl One might be ready to blame almost anything other than herself. Girl Two might easily label Revlon as an old fashion product that might be a reason for inattention from males. Girl One, depending on her like or dislike for her nail polish and lipstick, might revert to one of the defense mechanisms displayed in Table 4-2. Though there might be several applications, one defense mechanism could be aggression where Girl One answers Girl Two's tacky comment with an even tackier rebuttal comment of her own. Lastly, in the imaginary scenario, L'Oréal has commented no sin, however, labeling a competitive product as old fashioned may not be fair (additionally, it might offend older users). As one might say, all is fair game in the fashion and cosmetic industry—or is it?

Small Group Projects

S.T.A.R. Project #3
According to all published reports, the United States is an overweight nation. Slim-Fast (see www.slim-fast.com) believes that it has an answer to America's weight problem. Your group's assignment is to visit the Slim-Fast Web site, review the information, then turn to Table 4-2 in the chapter, consider the defense mechanisms cited in the table that someone that is overweight might use, and then devise a plan for Slim-Fast to penetrate the overweight consumer's defense barriers. There will be several pertinent facts on the Web site that your group can use in constructing its plan. Be sure to clearly identify which defense mechanisms must be overcome and how your plan will address these mechanisms. Lastly, evaluate your own effort and share your plan with the class.

Instructor's Discussion

This is a sensitive issue for some so handle it delicately. Students, as they brainstorm, will find several features on the Slim-Fast Web site that will help them to accomplish the assignment. First, students will see products (and associated benefits), healthy dining guides, recipes, success stories for support and encouragement, chat rooms, etc. Students can choose their own menu for assistance, however, choices should be justified. Next, students should choose from among the defense mechanisms outlined by Table 4-2 (these answers may be different for each group). The plan devised should be a combination of problem identification and solution. The table and the Web site provide most of the ingredients for completing the task. It will be interesting to see how each group approaches the problem.

S.T.A.R. Project #4
It is often difficult to decide whether to choose rational or emotional motives when promoting a product or service. Rational motives and the information directed toward these motives can often be supported with facts. Facts can be boring, however, and stifle action. Emotional motives and information can be exciting and energizing but sensationalism is often a shallow long-term strategy. Which approach is best? There is no clear answer. Your group's task is to see which approach might be best in the following scenario: your group has just been hired by Mother's Against Drunk Driving (MADD—www.madd.org) to develop a new promotional campaign to increase awareness of the national problem of drinking while driving and the consequences of those actions. One group from MADD encourages you to use facts; one group encourages you to use graphic scenes from highway accidents to make your point. Your group must come up with a new and fresh approach. Pick a motivational direction for MADD, describe your approach, and justify why your group selected the direction. Briefly outline your promotional suggestions.

Students will find both rational and emotional information (motivations) on the MADD Web site. Obviously, the problem of drunk driving is of national concern. Have student's debate the correct way to address the problem. By examining the pros and cons of the two approaches (rational versus emotional), students should be better prepared to recognize the two approaches when they see them. Examining these two approaches is a good first step in designing motivational-oriented promotions.

Using the Internet to Study Consumer Behavior

S.T.A.R. Project #5

With the resurgence of the Volkswagen Beetle, VW is once again a competitive automotive force in the teen and youth market. The VW Web site (www.vw.com) provides exciting graphics and links to other youth-oriented interests (the Sundance Film Festival and Radio VW, for example). Volkswagen was one of the first automotive companies to see the power of the Internet and one of the first to promote colorful interactivity as a way of stimulating interest in its products and sales on the showroom floor.

    a. Using the Build Your VW feature, build your own dream VW.

    b. Once your have built your VW, analyze what needs you filled. To aid you with this analysis, use the categories found in Table 4-3 (Murray's List of Psychogenic Needs) and Figure 4-9 (Maslow's Hierarchy of Needs). Be sure to cite specific needs from both of these sources.

    c. Lastly, what need does the interactivity present on the VW Web site address in you?

This Web site is just plain fun for students. To see some really wild cars, have students e-mail their picks to you and show them in class. This is a great way to engage the entire class in a discussion of needs from Table 4-3 and Figure 4-9. It is also great fun to try and guess who belongs to what car. There is no right or wrong answer here, however, this exercise should give students the opportunity to create (a need for many) and show off what they have accomplished (a need for others).

S.T.A.R. Project #6

You have just been hired as the marketing manager for Wine.com (see www.wine.com). You are concerned that with all the recent publicity about the harmful effects of alcohol, global terrorism, and overeating, your Web site, after many years of success, may begin to falter. Wine consumption in America has been growing for a number of years. Your Web site has been at the forefront of this growth. Sales of wine products, information about wine consumption, wine growing regions, and an excellent browsing feature (review of wines) are all noted features of your Web site. Your problem is how to maintain the arousal of motives in the consuming public that has made wine drinking so popular in recent years. Consider the problem.

    a. Considering that the arousal of any particular set of needs at a specific moment in time may be caused by internal stimuli, which of the following arousals would be most important for Wine.com to address in solving the problems mentioned above—

physiological, emotional, cognitive, or environmental? Explain and comment.

b. Find two examples on the Web site that indicates how Wine.com is addressing the arousal problem (or opportunity) that you have identified in "a" above.

Instructor's Discussion

Wine drinker or not, Wine.com is a highly informative Web site and one that is rich in marketing efforts and illustrations. Students should refer to the Arousal of Motives section in the chapter, where they will find pertinent information about physiological, emotional, cognitive, and environmental arousal. Any of these areas can be picked as an answer to part "a" of the question, however, the answer should then be justified or explained. For example, wine consumption might aid digestion (physiological arousal/needs), be part of a romantic setting (emotional), cause the person to think about happy times and camaraderie (cognitive), or consider the other foods or dinning treats associated with wine consumption (environmental).

Consider how any of these might enhance the motivation to purchase and consume wine. Examples for part "b" can be found for almost anything on the Web site because it is rather extensive.

CASES

Case One: The Product Collection at New Product Works

Question 1—Answer:

The products in this link of the Web site are changed periodically. The discussion of this question can be an interesting introduction to this chapter.

Question 2—Answer:

This is probably the most interesting portion of the site. The instructor should illustrate how product failures are often a result of failing to understand different dimensions of consumer behavior not limited to needs and motivation only. For example:

1. Kimberly Clark's "Avert"—a tissue coated with substances designed to kill cold-causing viruses when flu or cold-infected users sneezed or blew their noses into it—failed because the claim was not believable and the name frightened consumers. Also, the benefit the product delivers is not really directed toward the users themselves but to those who happen to be near them when they sneeze or cough.

2. Wheaties "Dunk-A-Ball" cereal encouraged kids to play with their food in a messy way. It completely ignored the needs of the parents.

3. By the nature of its name, Clairol's "Look of Buttermilk" shampoo did not convey a clear and desirable benefit to consumers.

Case Two: Need-Focused Definition of Business

Answers:

The questions for this case are designed to illustrate that need-oriented definitions of business are far more strategically insightful than product-oriented definitions. Instructors may want to use other companies of their choice instead of the companies listed in the case (perhaps even the companies listed in Table 4-1).

Here is an illustration of the concepts in the case using the Merck company:

Merck's Mission:

The mission of Merck is to provide society with superior products and services by developing innovations and solutions that improve the quality of life and satisfy customer needs, and to provide employees with meaningful work and advancement opportunities, and investors with a superior rate of return. (http://www.merck.com/about/mission.html).

The mission is centered on providing products and solutions that improve quality of life and satisfy consumer needs. It does not refer to "medications" or "pharmaceuticals" because such products are generally perceived as cures for illnesses and medical conditions. In not including these words, Merck's mission encompasses their efforts to develop new products that enhance the quality of life, and positions Merck as a broader entity than "just" a drug manufacturer.

In class discussions, instructors may go to Merck's Web site and see which products are designed to relieve physical ailments and which are designed to enhance the quality of one's life. Clearly, such determinations are somewhat subjective, but they can be used to illustrate how Merck strives to satisfy some of the needs discussed in the chapter.

On a side note, another aspect that makes Merck's mission statement very good is the clear identification of the company's main constituencies—customers, employees, and investors.

CHAPTER 5

Personality and Consumer Behavior

LEARNING OBJECTIVES

After studying this chapter students should be able to:
1. Define personality.
2. Describe the nature and development of personality.
3. Outline Freudian personality theory and the corresponding stages of development.
4. Discuss neo-Freudian personality theory and trait theory.
5. Discuss the relationship of personality and consumer diversity.
6. Enumerate cognitive personality factors, consumption, and possession traits.
7. Trace the shift from consumer materialism to compulsive consumption.
8. Explain consumer ethnocentrism.
9. Describe the elements of brand personality.
10. Discuss the concepts of self and self-image.
11. Identify the four forms of self-image plus two other versions of self-image.
12. Describe virtual personality or self.

SUMMARY

Personality can be described as the psychological characteristics that both determine and reflect how a person responds to his or her environment. Although personality tends to be consistent and enduring, it may change abruptly in response to major life events, as well as gradually over time.

Three theories of personality are prominent in the study of consumer behavior: psychoanalytic theory, neo-Freudian theory, and trait theory. Freud's psychoanalytic theory provides the foundation for the study of motivational research, which operates on the premise that human drives are largely unconscious in nature and serve to motivate many consumer actions. Neo-Freudian theory tends to emphasize the fundamental role of social relationships in the formation and development of personality. Alfred Adler viewed human beings as seeking to overcome feelings of inferiority. Harry Stack Sullivan believed that people attempt to establish significant and rewarding relationships with others. Karen Horney saw individuals as trying to overcome feelings of anxiety and categorized them as compliant, aggressive, or detached.

Trait theory is a major departure from the qualitative or subjective approach to personality measurement. It postulates that individuals possess innate psychological traits (e.g., innovativeness, novelty seeking, need for cognition, materialism) to a greater or lesser degree, and that these traits can be measured by specially designed scales or inventories. Because they are simple to use and to score and can be self-administered, personality inventories are the preferred method for many researchers in the assessment of consumer personality. Product and brand personalities represent real opportunities for marketers to take advantage of consumers' connections to various brands they offer. Brands often have personalities—some include "human-like" traits and even gender. These brand personalities help shape consumer responses, preferences, and loyalties.

Each individual has a perceived self-image (or multiple self-images) as a certain kind of person with certain traits, habits, possessions, relationships, and ways of behaving. Consumers frequently attempt to preserve, enhance, alter, or extend their self-images by purchasing products or services and shopping at stores believed to be consistent with the relevant self-image and by avoiding products and stores that are not. With the growth of the Internet, there appear to be emerging virtual selves or virtual personalities. Consumer experiences with chat rooms sometimes provide an opportunity to explore new or alternative identities.

CHAPTER OUTLINE

INTRODUCTION

1. Marketers have long tried to appeal to consumers in terms of their personality characteristics.
   a) Marketers have intuitively felt that what consumers purchase, and when and how they consume, are likely to be influenced by personality factors.
2. Advertising and marketing people have frequently depicted or targeted specific consumer personalities in their advertising messages.

WHAT IS PERSONALITY?

1. *Personality* is defined as those inner psychological characteristics that both determine and reflect how a person responds to his or her environment.
2. The emphasis in this definition is on *inner characteristics*—those specific qualities, attributes, traits, factors, and mannerisms that distinguish one individual from other individuals.
3. The identification of specific personality characteristics associated with consumer behavior has proven to be highly useful in the development of a firm's market segmentation strategies.

> *****Use Key Term personality Here; Use Learning Objective #1 Here; Use Discussion Question #1 Here*****

The Nature of Personality

1. In the study of personality, three distinct properties are of central importance:
   a) Personality reflects individual differences.
   b) Personality is consistent and enduring.
   c) Personality can change.

> *****Use Learning Objective #1 Here*****

Personality Reflects Individual Differences

1. An individual's personality is a unique combination of factors; no two individuals are exactly alike.
2. Personality is a useful concept because it enables us to categorize consumers into different groups on the basis of a single trait or a few traits.

*****Use Learning Objective #2 Here; Use Discussion Question #1 Here*****

Personality is Consistent and Enduring

1. Marketers learn which personality characteristics influence specific consumer responses and attempt to appeal to relevant traits inherent in their target group of consumers.
2. Even though an individual's personality may be consistent, consumption behavior often varies considerably because of psychological, sociocultural, and environmental factors that affect behavior.

*****Use Learning Objective #2 Here; Use Discussion Question #1 Here*****

Personality can Change

1. An individual's personality may be altered by major life events, such as the birth of a child, the death of a loved one, a divorce, or a major career change.
2. An individual's personality also changes as part of a gradual maturing process.
   a) Personality stereotypes may also change over time.
   b) There is a prediction, for example, that a *personality convergence* is occurring between men and women.

*****Use Learning Objective #2 Here; Use Discussion Question #1 Here; Use Exercise #1 Here*****

THEORIES OF PERSONALITY

1. There are three major theories of personality discussed in the chapter. They are:
   a) *Freudian theory.*
   b) *Neo-Freudian personality theory.*
   c) *Trait theory.*

*****Use Key Terms Freudian theory, neo-Freudian personality theory, and trait theory Here; Use Discussion Question #2 Here*****

Freudian Theory

1. Sigmund Freud's *psychoanalytic theory of personality* is the cornerstone of modern psychology.
2. This theory was built on the premise that *unconscious needs* or *drives*, especially biological and sexual drives, are at the heart of human motivation and personality.

> *****Use Key Term psychoanalytic theory of personality Here; Use Learning Objective #3 Here*****

Id, Superego, and Ego

1. The *Id* is the "warehouse" of primitive and impulsive drives, such as: thirst, hunger, and sex, for which the individual seeks immediate satisfaction without concern for the specific means of that satisfaction.
2. *Superego* is the individual's internal expression of society's moral and ethical codes of conduct.
   a) The superego's role is to see that the individual satisfies needs in a socially acceptable fashion.
   b) The superego is a kind of "brake" that restrains or inhibits the impulsive forces of the id.
3. *Ego* is the individual's conscious control which functions as an internal monitor that attempts to balance the impulsive demands of the id and the sociocultural constraints of the superego.
4. Freud emphasized that an individual's personality is formed as he or she passes through a number of distinct stages of infant and childhood development.
5. These distinct stages of infant and childhood development are: oral, anal, phallic, latent, and genital stages.
6. An adult's personality is determined by how well he or she deals with the crises that are experienced while passing through each of these stages.

> *****Use Learning Objective #3 Here; Use Figure 5-1 and 5-2 Here*****

Freudian Theory and Product Personality

1. Those stressing Freud's theories see that human drives are largely *unconscious*, and that consumers are primarily unaware of their true reasons for buying what they buy.
2. These researchers focus on consumer purchases and/or consumption situations, treating them as an extension of the consumer's personality.

> *****Use Learning Objective #3 Here; Use Discussion Question #2 Here; Use Table 5-1 Here; Use Exercise #2 Here*****

Neo-Freudian Personality Theory

1. Several of Freud's colleagues disagreed with his contention that personality is primarily instinctual and sexual in nature.
   a) They argued that *social relations* are fundamental to personality development.
2. Alfred Adler viewed human beings as seeking to attain various rational goals, which he called *style of life*, placing emphasis on the individual's efforts to overcome *feelings of inferiority*.
3. Harry Stack Sullivan stressed that people continuously attempt to establish significant and rewarding relationships with others, placing emphasis on efforts to reduce tensions.
4. Karen Horney focused on the impact of child-parent relationships, especially the individual's desire to conquer feelings of *anxiety*. She proposed three personality groups: compliant, aggressive, and detached.
   a) *Compliant individuals* are those who move toward others—they desire to be loved, wanted, and appreciated.
   b) *Aggressive individuals* move against others—they desire to excel and win admiration.
   c) *Detached individuals* move away from others—they desire independence, self-sufficiency, and freedom from obligations.
5. A personality test based on the above (the CAD) has been developed and tested.
   a) It reveals a number of tentative relationships between scores and product and brand usage patterns.
6. It is likely that many marketers have used some of these neo-Freudian theories intuitively.

*****Use Learning Objective #4 Here; Use Discussion Question #2 Here; Use Figure 5-3 Here*****

Trait Theory

1. Trait theory is a significant departure from the earlier *qualitative* measures that are typical of Freudian and neo-Freudian theory.
2. It is primarily quantitative or empirical, focusing on the measurement of personality in terms of specific psychological characteristics called *traits*.
   a) A *trait* is defined as any distinguishing, relatively enduring way in which one individual differs from another.
3. Selected *single-trait personality* tests increasingly are being developed specifically for use in consumer behavior studies. Types of traits measured include:
   a) **Consumer innovativeness**—how receptive a person is to new experiences.
   b) **Consumer materialism**—the degree of the consumer's attachment to "worldly possessions."
   c) **Consumer ethnocentrism**—the consumer's likelihood to accept or reject foreign-made products.
4. Researchers have learned to expect personality to be linked to how consumers *make their choices*, and to the purchase or consumption of a *broad product category* rather than a specific brand.

PERSONALITY AND UNDERSTANDING CONSUMER DIVERSITY

1. Marketers are interested in understanding how personality influences consumption behavior because such knowledge enables them to better understand consumers and to segment and target those consumers who are likely to respond positively to their product or service communications.

Consumer Innovativeness and Related Personality Traits

1. Marketing practitioners must learn all they can about *consumer innovators*—those who are likely to try new products. Those innovators are often crucial to the success of new products.
2. Personality traits have proved useful in differentiating between consumer innovators and noninnovators.
3. Personality traits to be discussed include:
   a) Consumer innovativeness.
   b) Dogmatism.
   c) Social character.
   d) Need for uniqueness.
   e) Optimum stimulation level.
   f) Variety-novelty seeking.

Consumer Innovativeness

1. How receptive are consumers to new products, new services, or new practices?
2. Recent consumer research indicates a positive relationship between innovative use of the Internet and buying online.

Dogmatism

1. *Dogmatism* is a personality trait that measures the degree of rigidity an individual displays toward the unfamiliar and toward information that is contrary to their established beliefs.
   a) Consumers low in dogmatism are more likely to prefer innovative products to established ones.

b) Consumers high in dogmatism are more accepting of authority-based ads for new products.

***** *Use Key Term **dogmatism** Here; Use Figure 5-4 Here*****

Social Character

1. Social character is a personality trait that ranges on a continuum from inner-directed to other-directed.
   a) **Inner-directed** consumers tend to rely on their own "inner" values or standards in evaluating new products and are innovators. They also prefer ads stressing product features and personal benefits.
   b) **Other-directed** consumers tend to look to others for direction and are not innovators. They prefer ads that feature social environment and social acceptance.

***** *Use Key Terms **inner-directedness** and **other-directedness** Here; Use Discussion Question #4 Here*****

Need for Uniqueness

1. We all know people who seek to be unique.
2. These people avoid conformity.

***** *Use Table 5-3 Here*****

Optimum Stimulation Level

1. Some people prefer a simple, uncluttered, and calm existence, although others seem to prefer an environment crammed with novel, complex, and unusual experiences.
2. Persons with **optimum stimulation levels (OSLs)** are willing to take risks, to try new products, to be innovative, to seek purchase-related information, and to accept new retail facilities.
3. The correspondence between an individual's OSL and their actual circumstances has a direct relationship to the amount of stimulation individual's desire.
   a) If the two are equivalent, they tend to be satisfied.
   b) If bored, they are understimulated, and vice versa.

***** *Use Key Term **optimum stimulation levels** Here*****

Variety-Novelty Seeking

1. This is similar to OSL.
   a) Primary types are **variety** or **novelty seeking**.
2. There appear to be many different types of variety seeking: *exploratory purchase behavior* (e.g., switching brands to experience new and possibly better alternatives), *vicarious*

exploration (e.g., where the consumer secures information about a new or different alternative and then contemplates or even daydreams about the option), and *use innovativeness* (e.g., where the consumer uses an already adopted product in a new or novel way).

    a) The third form of variety or novelty seeking—use innovativeness—is particularly relevant to technological.

3. Consumers with high variety seeking scores might also be attracted to brands that claim to have novel or multiple uses or applications.
4. Marketers, up to a point, benefit from thinking in terms of offering additional options to consumers seeking more product variety.

    a) Ultimately, marketers must walk the fine line between offering consumers too little and too much choice.

5. The stream of research examined here indicates that the consumer innovator differs from the non-innovator in terms of personality orientation.

> *****Use Key Terms **variety seeking and novelty seeking** *Here; Use Learning Objective #5 Here; Use Discussion Question #3 Here; Use Exercise #1 (if not previously used) Here*****

Cognitive Personality Factors

1. Market researchers want to understand how ***cognitive personality*** influences consumer behavior.
2. Two cognitive personality traits have been useful in understanding selected aspects of consumer behavior. They are:

    a) ***Need for cognition.***
    b) ***Visualizers versus verbalizers.***

> *****Use Key Terms **cognitive personality, need for cognition, and visualizers versus verbalizers** *Here; Use Discussion Question #5 Here*****

Need for Cognition

1. This is the measurement of a person's craving for or enjoyment of *thinking*.
2. Consumers who are *high* in NC (need for cognition) are more likely to be responsive to the part of an advertisement that is rich in product-related information of description.

    a) They are also more responsive to cool colors.

3. Consumers who are relatively *low* in NC are more likely to be attracted to the background or peripheral aspects of an ad.

    a) They spend more time on print content and have much stronger brand recall.

4. Need for cognition seems to play a role in an individual's use of the Internet.

> *****Use Discussion Question #5 Here*****

<u>Visualizers versus Verbalizers</u>

1. *Visualizers* are consumers who prefer visual information and products that stress the visual.
2. *Verbalizers* are consumers who prefer written or verbal information and products that stress the verbal.
3. This distinction helps marketers know whether to stress visual or written elements in their ads.

*****Use Learning Objective #5 and #6 Here; Use Discussion Question #5 Here; Use Exercise #1 (if not previously used) Here; Use Figure 5-5 and 5-6 Here*****

From Consumer Materialism to Compulsive Consumption

<u>Consumer Materialism</u>

1. *Materialism* is a trait of people who feel their possessions are essential to their identity.
2. They value acquiring and showing off possessions, they are self-centered and selfish, they seek lifestyles full of possessions, and their possessions do not give them greater happiness.

*****Use Learning Objective #7 Here; Use Exercise #3 Here; Use Table 5-4 Here*****

<u>Fixated Consumption Behavior</u>

1. Somewhere between being materialistic and being compulsive is being *fixated* with regard to consuming or possessing.
2. Like materialism, *fixated consumption behavior* is in the realm of normal and socially acceptable behavior.
3. Fixated consumers' characteristics:
    a) A deep (possibly: "passionate") interest in a particular object or product category.
    b) A willingness to go to considerable lengths to secure additional examples of the object or product category of interest.
    c) The dedication of a considerable amount of discretionary time and money to searching out the object or product.
4. This profile of the fixated consumer describes many collectors or hobbyists (e.g., coin, stamp, antique collectors, vintage wristwatch, or fountain pen collectors).

*****Use Learning Objective #7 Here*****

<u>Compulsive Consumption Behavior</u>

1. ***Compulsive consumption*** is in the realm of abnormal behavior.
2. Consumers who are compulsive have an addiction; in some respects, they are out of control, and their actions may have damaging consequences to them and those around them.

*****Use Key Term compulsive consumption *Here; Use Learning Objective #5, #6, and #7 Here; Use Table 5-5 Here*****

Consumer Ethnocentrism: Responses to Foreign-Made Products

1. To identify consumer segments receptive to foreign-made products, researchers have developed and tested the *consumer ethnocentrism* scale—CETSCALE.
   a) CETSCALE results identify consumers with a predisposition to reject or accept foreign-made products.
2. Consumers who are highly ethnocentric feel that it is wrong to purchase foreign-made products because it would hurt the domestic economy.
   a) Non-ethnocentric consumers tend to evaluate foreign-made products more objectively.
3. Marketers can appeal to ethnocentric consumers by stressing nationalistic themes in their promotional efforts.

*****Use Learning Objectives #5 and #8 Here; Use Discussion Question #6 Here; Use Table 5-6 and 5-7 Here*****

BRAND PERSONALITY

1. It appears that consumers tend to ascribe various descriptive "personality-like" traits or characteristics—the ingredients of *brand personalities*—to different brands in a wide variety of product categories.
2. A brand's personality can either be functional ("provides safety") or symbolic ("the athlete in all of us").

*****Use Learning Objective #9 Here*****

Brand Personification

1. A **brand personification** recasts consumers' perception of the attributes of a product or service into the form of a "human-like character."
2. It seems that consumers can express their inner feelings about products or brands in terms of association with a known personality.
3. Identifying consumers' current brand-personality link or creating one for new products are important marketing tasks.
4. There are five defining *dimensions* of a brand's personality ("sincerity," "excitement," "competence," "sophistication," and "ruggedness"), and fifteen *facets* of personality that flow out of the five dimensions (e.g., "down-to-earth," "daring," "reliable," "upper class," and "outdoors").

*****Use Key Term brand personification *Here; Use Learning Objective #9 Here; Use Exercise #2 (if not previously used) Here; Use Table 5-7 Here*****

Product Personality and Gender

1. A product personality or persona, frequently means that the product or brand has a "gender."
2. This assigning of a gender as part of personality description is fully consistent with the marketplace reality that products and services, in general, are viewed by consumers as having a "gender-being."
3. Armed with such knowledge of the perceived gender of a product or a specific brand, marketers are in a better position to select visual and copy-text for various marketing messages.

*****Use Learning Objective #9 Here*****

Product Personality and Geography

1. Marketers learned along time ago that certain products, in the minds of consumers, possess a strong geographical association.
2. Using the geographical association can create a geographic equity.
3. The real question is, "Does location (geography) add to the brand image and to the product's brand equity?"

*****Use Learning Objective #9 Here; Use Table 5-8 Here*****

Personality and Color

1. Consumers also tend to associate personality factors with specific colors.
   a) In some cases, various products, even brands, associate a specific color with personality-like connotations.
   b) It appears that blue appeals particularly to female consumers.
   c) Yellow is associated with "novelty," and black frequently connotes "sophistication."
   d) For this reason, brands wishing to create a sophisticated persona (e.g., Minute Maid juices or Pasta LaBella) or an upscale or premium image (e.g., Miller Beers' Miller Reserve) use labeling or packaging that is primarily black.
2. Many fast-food restaurants use combinations of bright colors, like red, yellow, and blue, for their roadside signs and interior designs.
   a) These colors have come to be associated with fast service and food being inexpensive.
3. In contrast, fine dining restaurants tend to use sophisticated colors like gray, white, shades of tan, or other soft, pale, or muted colors to reflect fine leisurely service.
4. Consumers' like or dislike for various colors can differ between countries.

*****Use Learning Objective #9 Here; Use Table 5-9 and 5-10 Here*****

SELF AND SELF-IMAGE

1. Self-images, or "perceptions of self," are very closely associated with personality in that individuals tend to buy products and services and patronize retailers with images or "personalities" that closely correspond to their own self-images.
2. Such concepts as one or multiple selves, self-image, and the notion of the **extended self** is explored by consumer behavior researchers.

*****Use Key Term* extended self *Here; Use Learning Objective #10 Here*****

One or Multiple Selves

1. Historically, individuals were thought to have a single self-image and focused on products accordingly.
   a) Research indicates a consumer is quite likely to be or act differently with different people and in different situations.
2. The idea that an individual embodies a number of different **multiple selves** suggest that marketers should target their products and services to consumers within the context of a particular self.
3. The healthy or normal person is likely to display a somewhat different personality in various situations or social **roles**.

*****Use Key Terms* multiple selves and roles *Here; Use Learning Objective #10 Here*****

The Makeup of the Self-Image

1. A person has a self-image of him/herself as a certain kind of person.
   a) The individual's self-image is unique, the outgrowth of that person's background and experience.
2. Products and brands have symbolic value for individuals, who evaluate them on the basis of their consistency with their personal pictures or images of themselves.
3. Products seem to match one or more of individual's self images; other products seem totally alien.
4. Four aspects of self-image are:
   a) *Actual self-image*—how consumers see themselves.
   b) *Ideal self-image*—how consumers would like to see themselves.
   c) *Social self-image*—how consumers feel others see them.
   d) *Ideal social self-image*—how consumers would like others to see them.
5. Some marketers have identified a fifth and sixth self-image.
   a) *Expected self-image*—how consumers expect to see themselves at some specified future time.
   b) *"Ought-to" self*—traits or characteristics that an individual believes it is his or her duty or obligation to possess.
   c) In different contexts consumers might select different self-images to guide behavior.
6. The concept of self-image has strategic implications for marketers.

7. Marketers can segment their markets on the basis of relevant consumer self-images and then position their products or stores as symbols for such self-images.

> *****Use Key Terms* **actual self-image, ideal self-image, ideal social self-image, expected self-image, and "ought-to" self** *Here; Use Learning Objective #10 and #11 Here; Use Discussion Question #7 Here; Use Figure 5-8 and 5-9 Here*****

The Extended Self

1. Consumers' possessions can be seen to "confirm" or "extend" their self-images.
2. The above suggests that much of human emotion can be connected to valued possessions.
3. Possessions can extend the self in a number of ways:
   a) *Actually*, by allowing the person to do things that otherwise would be very difficult or impossible to accomplish (e.g., problem-solving by using a computer).
   b) *Symbolically*, by making the person feel better or "bigger" (e.g., receiving an employee award for excellence).
   c) *By conferring status* or *rank* (e.g., status among collectors of rare works of art because of the ownership of a particular masterpiece).
   d) *By bestowing feelings of immortality*, by leaving valued possessions to young family members (this also has the potential of extending the recipients' "selves").
   e) *By endowing with magical powers* (e.g., a cameo pin inherited from one's aunt might be perceived as a magic amulet bestowing good luck when it is worn).

> *****Use Learning Objective #10 Here; Use Table 5-11 Here*****

Altering the Self

1. Consumers often wish to change themselves—to become a different or improved self.
2. It seems consumers are trying to express their individualism or uniqueness by creating and maintaining a new self.
3. Clothing, cosmetics, jewelry, grooming aids, and all kinds of accessories offer consumers the opportunity to modify their appearance and thereby to alter their selves.
4. Personal vanity and self-image are closely related.

> *****Use Learning Objective #10 Here; Use Table 5-12 Here; Use Figure 5-10 Here*****

VIRTUAL PERSONALITY OR SELF

1. There has been a tremendous growth in the use of online chat rooms.
2. People who are visiting chat rooms are able to carry on real time conversations about themselves and topics of mutual interest with people from all over the globe.
   a) The participants commonly never get to see each other.
   b) This creates an opportunity for chat room participants to try out new identifies or to change their identities while online.

3. In terms of personality, one can change from mild-mannered to aggressive, or from introvert to extravert.
4. The notion of a *virtual personality* or *virtual self* provides an individual with the opportunity to try on different personalities or different identities, much like going to the mall and trying on different outfits in a department or specialty store.
5. If the identity fits, or the personality can be enhanced, maybe we keep the new personality in favor of our old personality.
6. The Internet is redefining human identify, creating an "online self."

*****Use Key Terms* virtual personality and virtual self *Here; Use Learning Objective #12 Here*****

DISCUSSION QUESTIONS

1. **How would you explain the fact that, although no two individuals have identical personalities, personality is sometimes used in consumer research to identify distinct and sizable market segments?**

Because the inner characteristics that constitute an individual's personality are a unique combination of factors, no two individuals are exactly alike. Nevertheless, many individuals tend to be similar in terms of a single personality characteristic. For instance, many people can be described as "high" in sociability (the degree of interest they display in social or group activities), although others can be described as "low" in sociability. *Personality* is a useful concept because it enables us to categorize consumers into different groups on the basis of a single trait or a few traits. If each person were different in all respects, it would be impossible to group consumers into segments, and there would be little reason to develop standardized products and promotional campaigns. Marketers seek to identify those particular personality characteristics that are shared by those individuals who constitute a particular market segment.

2. **Contrast the major characteristics of the following personality theories: a) Freudian theory, b) neo-Freudian theory, and c) trait theory. In your answer, illustrate how each theory is applied to the understanding of consumer behavior.**

a) Freudian (or psychoanalytic) theory is based on the premise that subconscious needs, especially biological and sexual needs, are the center of human motivation and personality. Because of its clinical origin, this theory stresses measurement of personality through qualitative or subjective approaches (e.g., projective techniques). The major application of Freudian theory to consumer behavior is Ernest Dichter's work.

b) Neo-Freudian theory contends that social relationships are fundamental to the development of personality. For example, Adler proposed that overcoming feelings of inferiority is the major factor in human motivation, and Sullivan viewed reduction of anxiety as a key factor. The most systematic application of neo-Freudian theory in consumer research is the development of the CAD scale—a personality test based on

Karen Horney's proposition that individuals can be classified into three personality types: compliant, aggressive, and detached. These personality types and the research findings of studies that used the CAD scale are described in the text.

c) Trait theory, in contrast to Freudian and neo-Freudian theories, is quantitative in its orientation. It views personality as a set of enduring traits rather than the result of subconscious drives. These traits are usually expressed in numerical scores obtained on self-administered paper-and-pencil tests. Single trait personality tests have been particularly successful in adding to the understanding of consumer behavior, and such tests are increasingly being developed for use in consumer research. Personality traits have been linked to many consumption behaviors including purchase patterns of various products (but seldom to consumption of specific brands), store choices, purchasing foreign made products, and to differentiating between innovators and non-innovators.

3. Describe personality trait theory. Give five examples of how personality traits can be used in consumer research.

Trait theory constitutes a major departure from the qualitative measures that typify the Freudian and neo-Freudian movements (e.g., personal observation, self-reported experiences, dream analysis, projective techniques). *Trait theory* is primarily quantitative or empirical; it focuses on the measurement of personality in terms of specific psychological characteristics, called traits, "any distinguishing, relatively enduring way in which one individual differs from another." Selected single-trait personality tests (which measure just one trait, such as self-confidence) are increasingly being developed specifically for use in consumer behavior studies. These tailor-made personality tests measure such traits as consumer innovativeness, consumer susceptibility to interpersonal influence, materialism, and consumer ethnocentrism.

Examples:
- The Consumer Innovativeness Scale can be used to study how receptive consumers are to new products or services.
- Consumer researchers recently developed a scale that measures consumers' susceptibility to interpersonal influence.
- In testing a new materialism scale, researchers found that materialistic people, value acquiring and showing off possessions, are self-centered, etc.
- In an effort to distinguish between consumer segments that are likely to be receptive to foreign-made products and those that are not, researchers have developed and tested the consumer ethnocentrism scale.
- Need for cognition measures the person's craving for, or enjoyment of, thinking.

4. How can a marketer of cameras use research findings that indicate a target market consists primarily of inner-directed or other-directed consumers? Of consumers who are high (or low) on innovativeness?

Inner-directed and *other-directed* consumers have different preferences with respect to promotional messages. Because inner-directed people tend to depend on their own inner values in evaluating new products and services, they prefer advertisements that emphasize product features and personal benefits. As other-directed individuals turn to other people for

100

direction, they are most likely to prefer ads that feature a social environment or social acceptance. They would evaluate a product in terms of its potential for social approval. Therefore, a manufacturer of cameras who advertises to inner-directed consumers should stress the ability to take better pictures and the resulting personal satisfaction. An ad aimed at other-directed consumers should portray photographing others (e.g., photographing friends standing near a famous landmark) or showing friends pictures or slides taken during a trip. Consumers who are high on *innovativeness* are more receptive to new products than persons who are low on innovativeness. Thus, when introducing a new model or new product features, the cameras marketer should advertise to those who are high on innovativeness because they approach unfamiliar products with considerable openness and little anxiety.

5. **Describe the type of promotional message that would be most suitable for each of the following personality market segments and give an example of each: (a) highly dogmatic consumers, (b) inner-directed consumers, (c) consumers with high optimum stimulation levels, (d) consumers with a high need for cognition, and (e) consumers who are visualizers versus consumers who are verbalizers.**

a) Highly dogmatic consumers are likely to respond favorably to a new product when the advertising message is presented in an authoritarian manner (e.g., celebrity endorsement or expert testimonials).

b) Inner-directed consumers tend to use their own values and standards in evaluating a new product; therefore, ads aimed at them should depict the attainment of personal achievement and satisfaction.

c) Consumers with a high optimum stimulation level are more open to risk-taking, more likely to be innovative, try products with many novel features, and shop in new retail outlets. Consumers with high OSL are likely to respond favorably to promotional messages stressing more rather than less risk, novelty, or excitement.

d) Consumers with a high need for cognition are ones who often crave or enjoy thinking. They are likely to be responsive to ads that are rich in product-related information or description, and unresponsive to the auxiliary or contextual aspects of an advertisement.

e) Marketers should stress visual dimensions in attracting visualizers, consumers who prefer visual information, products that stress the visual, and detailed descriptions and explanations in targeting verbalizers (i.e., consumers who prefer written and verbal product information).

6. **Is there likely to be a difference in personality traits between individuals who readily purchase foreign-made products and those who prefer American-made products? How can marketers use the consumer ethnocentrism scale to segment consumers?**

The consumer ethnocentrism scale, called CETSCALE is designed to identify consumers with a predisposition to accept (or reject) foreign-made products. Consumers who are highly ethnocentric feel that it is inappropriate or wrong to purchase foreign-made products, and a domestic marketer can attract them by stressing ethnocentric themes in its advertising. Non-ethnocentric consumers tend to evaluate foreign-made products more objectively for their extrinsic characteristics rather than for where the products were manufactured.

7. **A marketer of health foods is attempting to segment a certain market on the basis of consumer self-image. Describe the four types of consumer self-image and discuss which one(s) would be most effective for the stated purpose.**

Four different self image constructs have been identified: (1) *actual self-image* (e.g., how the consumers in fact see themselves), (2) *ideal self-image* (e.g., how consumers would like to see themselves), (3) *social self-image* (e.g., how consumers feel others see them), and (4) *ideal social self-image* (e.g., how consumers would like others to see them). Other research has identified a fifth type of self-image, *expected self-image* (e.g., how consumers expect to see themselves at some specified future time) and a sixth self-image, the *ought-to self* (e.g., consists of traits or characteristics that an individual believes its is his or her duty or obligation to possess). The expected self-image is somewhere between the actual and ideal self-images. It is somewhat like a future-oriented combination of "what is" (the actual self-image) and what consumers would like "to be" (the ideal self-image). Moreover, because the expected self-image provides consumers with a realistic "opportunity" to change the "self," it is likely to be more valuable to marketers than the actual or ideal self-image as a guide for designing and promoting products. In targeting consumers of health foods, the marketer can use the expected self-image to attract consumers who would like to enhance the quality of their lifestyles through better nutrition, and ideal social self-image to appeal to consumers who are likely to adopt health foods due to peer influence and pressure.

EXERCISES

1. **How do your clothing preferences differ from those of your friends? What personality traits might explain why your preferences are different from those of other people?**

Instructor's Discussion

This discussion-based exercise should help students reflect on the impact of personality on common consumer choices and the challenges the use of personality-related segmentation criteria presented by marketers. Be sure that students examine the personality traits explored in the Personality and Understanding Consumer Diversity section of the chapter. Consider the following general traits and apply these to the exercise at hand: innovativeness, dogmatism, social character (e.g., inner- and other-directedness), the need for uniqueness, optimum stimulation level (OSL), sensation seeking, variety seeking, and novelty seeking. Students can also explore cognitive personality factors, consumer materialism, consumer compulsive behavior, and ethnocentrism.

2. **Find three print advertisements based on Freudian personality theory. Discuss how Freudian concepts are used in these ads. Do any of the ads personify a brand? If so, how?**

Instructor's Discussion

This discussion-based exercise should help students apply in concrete terms the elements of Freudian personality theory. Notice which of the ads might appeal to the id, ego, or super ego. Also explore the "product personality" examined in Table 5-1. How do the ads match to this table?

3. **Administer the nine items from the materialism scale (listed in Table 5-2) to two of your friends. In your view, are their consumption behaviors consistent with their scores on the scale? Why or why not?**

Instructor's Discussion

This exercise provides students with practical material to work with in their application of and understanding of consumer behavior and personality. Students may also wish to expand this exercise to include the Internet and e-commerce. Notice that the chapter suggests that recent consumer research indicates a positive relationship between innovative use of the Internet and buying online.

S.T.A.R. PROJECTS

Ethical Issues in Consumer Behavior

S.T.A.R. Project #1
The AdForum is a place where advertising agencies can display creative work. This intriguing Web site boasts that the viewer can find 23,500+ domestic and global ads with a click of the mouse. In addition, AdForum has up-to-the-minute news about the advertising world and how viewers, readers, and listeners respond to this world. Go to the AdForum Web site at www.adforum.org and find three (3) domestic or international examples of advertisements that display good ethical behavior with respect to focusing on personality as a creative advertising theme. These ads could show people making good choices, making ethical decisions, or be scenes where personality traits match to correct ethical choices or decisions.
    a. Describe or download the ads.
    b. Describe the situations found in the ads and comment on the ethics involved
    c. How do the situations relate to the personality variable in consumer behavior?

Instructor's Discussion

Typically, the AdForum Web site will have at least one cover story that will spark the student's interest with respect to ethics. With a little reading and appreciation of the material contained in the chapter, the student should be able to make a connection between the ethical situation involved in the advertisement and the personality variable. For example, in a recent commercial sponsored by the Partnership for a Drug Free America, a young teen is shown being pressured by peers to inhale cocaine—"a little bit won't hurt," say the friends. In a later scene, the teen's nose begins to bleed in school—"a little bit won't hurt!" This exercise will practice students on finding and recognizing ads that feature the personality theme and ads that have an ethical message or situation featured.

S.T.A.R. Project #2

Few of us would misidentify who said "What's Up Doc?" and "Tickle Me Elmo" is not usually mistaken as a directive to a friendly relative. Warner Bros. and Sesame Street Productions have a unique position in our society. They also have a unique responsibility in that their messages are seen and acted upon by thousands of children on a daily basis. To children, the characters from these two creative giants are real and not imaginary. The personalities of the characters are often emulated by youth. Go to the Warner Bros. (www.warnerbros.com {see Looney Tunes}) and Sesame Street (www.sesamestreet.com) Web sites and observe how cartoon personalities are developed.

   a. What ethical responsibilities do Warner Bros. and Sesame Street Productions shoulder?
   b. Examine the personalities of characters on each of the two Web sites. Give two examples of characters that exhibit human personality characteristics or traits. Explain.
   c. Discuss what you perceive to be correct and incorrect product endorsement by cartoon or puppet characters. Explain your thinking.

Instructor's Discussion

The students will find a wealth of information about cartoon and puppet characters on these two Web sites. Matching these characters to personality types will make an interesting in-class discussion. Discussing ethical ramifications is more difficult. Focus on part "c" to extend this discussion.

Small Group Projects

S.T.A.R. Project #3

Have you ever been to a SlamBall match? Probably not. Warner Bros. and TNN network, however, are betting that you soon will. What is SlamBall? Think about combining basketball, hockey, roller derby, and trampolines. Sound exciting? SlamBall is played four on four on a full court. Hockey-style rules make dribbling the SlamBall (similar to a basketball) somewhat difficult so innovations in ball control are encouraged. There are basket goals that may be approached from the front, side, or rear. The court is enclosed in plexi-walls to keep the ball in play. HotSpot trampolines extend play to heights of up to 17 feet above the game floor. At present there are six professional teams, however, this number is expected to grow as this new extreme sport catches on. For more information visit the SlamBall Web site at www.slamball.net.

   a. Using the personality traits discussed in the chapter, your group should profile the type of consumer that might be interested in SlamBall. Explain your group's rationale.
   b. Take the profile developed above and indicate how SlamBall might reach these consumers. Part of the group might examine the media, endorsements, publicity, or

104

other venues.

   c. Comment on what your group perceives to be the future of extreme sports like SlamBall. Explain your group's forecast and judgment.

<u>Instructor's Discussion</u>

Small teams or groups will enjoy learning about this new extreme sport. The Web site allows for some action downloads. At present the SlamBall league has six teams, however, this may grow. Students should focus on the personality of the extreme sports enthusiast by first considering what an extreme sport is. Next, the teams should consider how to reach these enthusiasts. What companies would most be interested in this personality group?

S.T.A.R. Project #4

How does a consumer achieve an optimum stimulation level? How do you? To explore this subject more carefully have your group visit the Sprite (www.sprite.com) and Kit-Cat (www.kit-cat.com) Web sites. The Sprite Web site is one of the hottest hip-hop sites going according to contemporary news media. Sprite Radio has become a mainstay for many teens. The Kit-Cat Web site puts a retro-spin on an old product and produces stimulation in an unusual way.

   a. After your team visits both Web sites, divide the group into two parts. Working separately, each team should list the OSL scores (devise your own scale) that would be given to both Web sites.

   b. Compare the two score lists. How could the looser enhance OSL?

<u>Instructor's Discussion</u>

The Sprite Web site is full of stimulation and the natural tendency is to give it the stimulation award quickly, however, the Kit-Cat clock has been around longer than Sprite. Therefore, Kit-Cat must be doing something right. Have the groups discuss their stimulation scales in class. What were the components? How were judgments made? Discuss differences.

Using the Internet to Study Consumer Behavior

S.T.A.R. Project #5

Are you a visualizer or a verbalizer? Crayola is betting that your visual side is the stronger of the two. Crayola has constructed a great Web site for your visual pleasure (see www.crayola.com). While on the Web site, the visitor can find many activities, ideas, create cards, learn about color, how crayons are made, and get helpful information to make a rainy day pass more quickly. One of the most interesting features is giving the consumer the ability to design his or her own color box of crayons. The color choices are endless.

   a. What visualizer techniques does Crayola use to enhance the need for visualization in consumers?

   b. What verbalizer skills are used on the Web site?

   c. Describe the colors you selected for your box of crayons. Why did you select the colors that you did? What does the color selection say about you and your personality?

Instructor's Discussion

This colorful Web site is a great example of the visualizing aspect of a consumer's personality. The students will find many areas of visual stimulation. For a unique discussion, have the class name the new Crayola color (a contest). This Web site is a great way to cover the aspect of color mentioned in the text. To extend the project, have students match their color preferences to the tables sited in the chapter.

S.T.A.R. Project #6

Are you a chocoholic? Are you compulsive (see Table 5-5)? For many Americans, the one sin that is permissible is consuming chocolate. Hershey's (www.hersheys.com) and Godiva (www.godiva.com) are more than ready to feed this insatiable taste for chocolate. As explained on their Web sites, the history of chocolate and chocolate consumption (obsession) is long and pleasurable. Think about chocolate while you answer the questions below.

   a. What are your feelings toward chocolate? Would you describe these feelings as compulsive? Explain.

   b. Did you find anything on the two Web sites that would indicate that some people have problems with eating too much chocolate? Should the companies address these compulsions?

   c. Design your own chocolate t-shirt by visiting www.hersheyshappiness.com. What was the message on your shirt? What does this message say about personality and compulsions?

Instructor's Discussion

This is a fun assignment and good way to address the difficult subject of compulsion. By talking about chocolate, the instructor can work in a discussion of the more difficult compulsions described in the chapter. The t-shirt assignment is also one that can say something about one's personality and compulsions. If all else fails, give the class some Hershey's Kisses and enjoy.

CASES

Case One: Four-On-The-Floor

This question has a lot of possibilities, and student answers may take a number of different tacks. Some of the traits that students might specifically include in their responses are: *detached individuals* (i.e., those who move *away* from others—seeking self-reliance, self-sufficiency, and individualism), and *high inner-directedness* (i.e., those who tend to rely on their own "inner" values or standards in evaluating product choices). Two other traits that students might explore are: a need for cognition, and venturesomeness.

Case Two: Product Testing on the Internet

Because student answers will probably vary, some of the personality traits mentioned with some frequency should be *high consumer innovativeness* or *venturesomeness* (i.e., those particularly receptive to new product or experiences), *high optimum stimulation level* (i.e., consumers who

106

tend to prefer an environment crammed with novel, complex, and unusual experiences), and *high variety-novelty seeking* (i.e., consumers who like to change what they do and use, and are open to new products or experiences that provide such opportunities).

CHAPTER 6

Consumer Perception

LEARNING OBJECTIVES

After studying this chapter students should be able to:
1. Define perception and its key elements.
2. Differentiate between absolute threshold and differential threshold.
3. Explain the marketing applications of just noticeable difference (j.n.d.).
4. Review the concept of subliminal perception and the reality of its use.
5. Discuss the dynamics of perception in terms of its three main aspects—selection, organization, and interpretation.
6. Discuss the various forms of selective perception.
7. Explain the concept of Gestalt psychology.
8. Discuss the various forms of perceptual distortion.
9. Understand the implications of consumer imagery by positioning and repositioning products.
10. Understand the positioning of services.
11. Explain the impact of price on consumer perception of products, service, and quality.
12. Discuss the terms *retail store image* and *manufacturer's image*.
13. Describe consumers' perception of risk and key risk reduction strategies.

SUMMARY

Perception is the process by which individuals select, organize, and interpret stimuli into a meaningful and coherent picture of the world. Perception has strategy implications for marketers because consumers make decisions based on what they perceive rather than on the basis of objective reality.

The lowest level at which an individual can perceive a specific stimulus is that person's absolute threshold. The minimal difference that can be perceived between two stimuli is called the differential threshold or just noticeable difference (j.n.d.). Most stimuli are perceived by consumers above the level of their conscious awareness; however, weak stimuli can be perceived below the level of conscious awareness (i.e., subliminally). Research refutes the notion that subliminal stimuli influence consumer-buying decisions.

Consumers' selection of stimuli from the environment is based on the interaction of their expectations and motives with the stimulus itself. The principles of selective perception include the following concepts: selective exposure, selective attention, perceptual defense, and perceptual blocking. People usually perceive things they need or want, and block the perception of unnecessary, unfavorable, or painful stimuli.

Consumers organize their perceptions into unified wholes according to the principles of Gestalt psychology: figure and ground, grouping, and closure. The interpretation of stimuli is highly subjective and is based on what the consumer expects to see in light of previous experience, on the number of plausible explanations he or she can envision, on motives and interests at the time of perception, and on the clarity of the stimulus itself. Influences that tend to distort objective interpretation include physical appearances, stereotypes, halo effects, irrelevant cues, first impressions, and the tendency to jump to conclusions.

Just as individuals have perceived images of themselves, they also have perceived images of products and brands. The perceived image of a product or service (how it is positioned) is probably more important to its ultimate success than are its actual physical characteristics. Products and services that are perceived distinctly and favorably have a much better chance of being purchased than products or services with unclear or unfavorable images.

Compared with manufacturing firms, service marketers face several unique problems in positioning and promoting their offerings because services are intangible, variable, perishable, and are simultaneously produced and consumed. Regardless of how well positioned a product or service appears to be, the marketer may be forced to reposition it in response to market events, such as new competitor strategies or changing consumer preferences.

Consumers often judge the quality of a product or service on the basis of a variety of informational cues; some are intrinsic to the product (such as color, size, flavor, and aroma), whereas others are extrinsic (e.g., price, store image, brand image, and service environment). In the absence of direct experience or other information, consumers often rely on price as an indicator of quality. How a consumer perceives a price—as high, low, or fair—has a strong influence on purchase intentions and satisfactions. Consumers often rely on both internal and external reference prices when assessing the fairness of a price.

Consumer imagery also includes perceived images of retail stores that influence the perceived quality of products they carry, as well as decisions as to where to shop. Manufacturers who enjoy a favorable image generally find their new products are accepted more readily than those of manufacturers with less favorable images.

Consumers often perceive risk in making product selections because of uncertainty as to the consequences of their product decisions. The most frequent types of risk that consumers perceive are functional risk, physical risk, financial risk, social risk, psychological risk, and time risk. Consumer strategies for reducing perceived risk include increased information search, brand loyalty, buying a well-known brand, buying from a reputable retailer, buying the most expensive brand, and seeking reassurance in the form of money-back guarantees, warranties, and prepurchase trial. The concept of perceived risk has important implications for marketers, who can facilitate the acceptance of new products by incorporating risk-reduction strategies in their new-product promotional campaigns.

CHAPTER OUTLINE

INTRODUCTION

1. Individuals act and react on the basis of their perceptions, not on the basis of objective reality.
    a) Therefore, consumers' perceptions are more important to a marketer than their knowledge of objective reality, because people make decisions based on their perceptions.
2. In this chapter we examine the psychological and physiological bases of human perception and the principles that control that perception and the interpretation of what we see.
    a) Understanding this information enables marketers to develop more effective advertisements.

ELEMENTS OF PERCEPTION

1. *Perception* is the process by which an individual selects, organizes, and interprets stimuli into a meaningful and coherent picture of the world.

> *****Use Key Term perception *Here; Use Learning Objective #1 Here*****

Sensation

1. *Sensation* is the immediate and direct response of the sensory organs to stimuli (an advertisement, a package, and a brand name).
2. A *stimulus* is any unit of input to any of the senses.
3. *Sensory receptors* are the human organs (i.e., the eyes, ears, nose, mouth, and skin) that receive sensory inputs, sight, sound, smell, taste, or touch.
4. Human sensitivity refers to the experience of sensation.
    a) Sensitivity to stimuli varies with the quality of an individual's sensory receptors and the amount or intensity of the stimuli to which he/she is exposed.
    b) Sensation itself depends on energy change, the difference of input.
    c) Thus, a constant environment, whether very busy and noisy or relatively quiet, would provide little sensation because of the lack of change, the consistent level of stimulation.
5. As sensory input *decreases*, the ability to detect changes *increases*.
    a) This ability of the human organism to accommodate itself to varying levels of sensitivity as external conditions vary not only protects us from damaging, disruptive, or irrelevant bombardment when the input level is high but has important implications for marketers.

> *****Use Key Terms sensation and sensory receptors *Here; Use Learning Objective #1 Here*****

The Absolute Threshold

1. The lowest level at which an individual can experience a sensation is called the ***absolute threshold***.
   a) The point at which a person can detect the difference between "something" and "nothing" is that person's absolute threshold for the stimulus.
   b) For example, the distance at which a driver can note a specific billboard on a highway is that individual's absolute threshold.
   c) Under conditions of constant stimulation, such as driving through a "corridor" of billboards, the absolute threshold increases (that is, the senses tend to become increasingly dulled).
2. Adaptation refers specifically to "getting used to" certain sensations, becoming accustomed to a certain level of stimulation.
   a) ***Sensory adaptation*** is a problem that causes many advertisers to change their advertising campaigns regularly.

*****Use Key Terms* absolute threshold and sensory adaptation *Here; Use Discussion Question #1 Here*****

---

3. Marketers try to increase sensory input in order to cut through the daily clutter consumers experience in the consumption of advertising.
   a) Some increase sensory input in an effort to cut through the advertising "clutter."
4. Other advertisers try to attract attention by decreasing sensory input.
   a) Some advertisers use silence (the absence of music or other audio effects) to generate attention.
   b) Some marketers seek unusual media in which to place their advertisements in an effort to gain attention.
   c) Some use scent researchers to enhance their products with a unique smell.
5. Package designers try to determine consumers' absolute thresholds to make sure that their new product designs will stand out from competitors' packages on retailers' shelves.

*****Use Learning Objective #1 and #2 Here; Use Discussion Question #1 and #2 Here; Use Figure 6-1 Here*****

The Differential Threshold

1. The minimal difference that can be detected between two stimuli is called the ***difference threshold*** or the ***j.n.d. (just noticeable difference)***.
2. A 19th century German scientist named Ernst Weber discovered that the j.n.d. between two stimuli was not an absolute amount, but an amount relative to the intensity of the first stimulus.
3. ***Weber's law*** states that the stronger the initial stimulus, the greater the additional intensity needed for the second stimulus to be perceived as different.
   a) Also, an additional level of stimulus, equivalent to the j.n.d., must be added for the majority of people to perceive a difference between the resulting stimulus and the initial stimulus.

111

b) Weber's law holds for all senses and almost all levels of intensity.

c) Retailers use the principle in reducing prices.

d) Markdowns must amount to at least twenty percent to be noticed by shoppers.

***

*****Use Key Terms **difference threshold, j.n.d. (just noticeable difference), and Weber's law** *Here; Use Learning Objective #1, #2, and #3 Here; Use Discussion Question #2 and #3 Here*****

***

Marketing Applications of the J.N.D.

1. Manufacturers and marketers endeavor to determine the relevant j.n.d. for their products so that:
    a) Negative changes—reductions or increases in product size, or reduced quality—are not readily discernible to the public.
    b) So that product improvements are readily discernible to the consumer without being wastefully extravagant.

2. Marketers use the j.n.d. to determine the amount of change or updating they should make in their products to avoid losing the readily recognized aspects of their products

3. To better compete in a global marketplace that has been radically altered by computer technology, many companies are updating their corporate logos to convey the notion that they are timely and fast-paced and at the top of their respective product class.
    a) Many feature some element that conveys motion—streaking, slashing, and orbiting.

4. Although some companies make minor changes (below the j.n.d.) to promote continuity, others have deliberately changed their traditional block lettering and dark colors in favor of script typefaces, bright colors, and hints of animation—taking their cues from pop icons like MTV.

5. Marketers want to meet or exceed the consumers' differential threshold so that they readily perceive the improvements made in the original product.

***

*****Use Learning Objective #1 and #3 Here; Use Discussion Question #2 and #3 Here; Use Figure 6-2, 6-3, and 6-4 Here*****

***

Subliminal Perception

1. People are also stimulated below their level of conscious awareness—they can perceive stimuli without being consciously aware of it.

2. The threshold for conscious awareness appears to be higher than the absolute threshold for effective perception.

3. Stimuli below the "limen" of conscious awareness, too weak or brief to be consciously seen or heard, may be strong enough to be perceived by one or more receptor cells.
    a) This is *subliminal perception*.

4. In the late 1950s there was a stir when consumers were being exposed to subliminal advertising messages they were not aware of receiving.
    a) Messages were supposedly persuading people to buy goods and services without their being aware of it.

112

b)   The effectiveness of the concept was tested at a drive-in theater by flashing the words "eat popcorn" and "drink coke" on the screen during the movie, so quickly that the audience was not aware of it.

c)   In a six-week test, popcorn sales increased 58 percent and coke sales 18 percent.

d)   No scientific controls were used, and results were never replicated.

*****Use Key Term subliminal perception Here; Use Learning Objective #4 Here; Use Table 6-1 Here*****

Evaluating the Effectiveness of Subliminal Persuasion

1. There is no evidence that subliminal advertising works.
2. Current research is based on two approaches.
    a)   The first theory is that constant repetition of very weak stimuli will have incremental effects.
    b)   A second approach is based on sexual stimulation through sexual embeds.
3. There is some indication that subliminal advertising may help modify antisocial behavior by calling for generalized behavior change.
4. In summary, although there is some evidence that subliminal stimuli may influence affective reactions, there is no evidence that subliminal stimulation can influence consumption motives or actions.
5. A recent review of the evidence on subliminal persuasion indicates that the only way for subliminal techniques to have a significant persuasive effect would be through long-term repeated exposure under a limited set of circumstances, which would not be economically feasible or practical within an advertising context.
6. As to sexual embeds, most researchers are of the opinion that "What you see is what you get."
    a)   That pretty much sums up the whole notion of perception: individuals see what they want to see (e.g., what they are motivated to see) and what they expect to see.
7. Several studies concerned with public beliefs about subliminal advertising found that a large percentage of Americans know what subliminal advertising is, they believe that it is used by advertisers, and that it is effective in persuading consumers to buy.
8. To correct misperceptions among the public, the advertising community occasionally sponsors ads that ridicule the notion that subliminal techniques are effective or that they are used in advertising applications.
9. Because of the absence of any evidence that subliminal persuasion really works, no state or federal laws have been enacted to restrict the use of subliminal advertising.
10. The Federal Communications Commission has adopted the position that "covert messages by their very nature are against the public interest."
    a)   Clearly, that position covers both paid (commercial) subliminal advertisements and unpaid (public service) subliminal messages.

*****Use Learning Objective #4 Here; Use Discussion Question #4 Here; Use Figure 6-5 Here*****

DYNAMICS OF PERCEPTION

1. Human beings are constantly bombarded with stimuli during every minute and every hour of every day.
2. Perception is not a function of sensory input alone, rather, perception is the result of two different kinds of inputs that interact to form the personal pictures—the perceptions—that each individual experiences.
   a) *Physical stimuli* from the outside environment, and internal stimuli based on expectations, motives, and learning are based on *previous experiences*.
3. Because each person is a unique individual, with unique experiences, needs, wants, desires, and expectations, it follows that each individual's perceptions are also unique.
4. There are three aspects to perception—*selection*, *organization*, and *interpretation of stimuli*.
   a) Individuals are very selective as to which stimuli they "recognize."
   b) They subconsciously organize the stimuli they do recognize according to widely held psychological principles.
   c) And they interpret such stimuli (i.e., they give meaning to them) subjectively in accordance with their needs, expectations, and experiences.

> *****Use Key Term** selection, organization, and interpretation of stimuli *Here; Use*
> *Learning Objective #5 Here; Use Discussion Question #5 Here*****

Perceptual Selection

1. Consumers subconsciously exercise selectivity as to the stimuli they perceive.
2. Which stimuli get selected depends on two major factors in addition to the nature of the stimulus itself:
   a) Consumers' *previous experience* as it affects their expectations.
   b) Their *motives* at the time (their needs, desires, interests, and so on).
3. Each of these factors can serve to increase or decrease the probability that a stimulus will be perceived.

> *****Use Learning Objective #5 Here; Use Discussion Question #6 Here*****

The Nature of the Stimulus

1. Marketing stimulus contains an enormous number of variables. Examples include:
   a) Nature of the product.
   b) Its physical attributes.
   c) The package design.
   d) The brand name.
   e) The advertisements and commercials.
   f) The position of a print ad or commercial.
   g) The editorial environment.
2. *Contrast* is one of the most attention-compelling attributes of a stimulus.
   a) Advertisers use extreme attention-getting devices to get maximum contrast and penetrate the consumer's perceptual screen.

    b)   Advertisers use color contrasts, size, etc., to create stopping power and gain attention.

3. Packaging is also differentiated sufficiently to ensure rapid consumer perception.
4. Sometimes advertisers capitalize on the lack of contrast.
5. A technique that has been used effectively in TV commercials is to position the commercial so close to the storyline of a program that viewers are unaware they are watching an ad until they are well into it.
    a)   The Federal Trade Commission has strictly limited the use of this technique in children's programming.
6. Advertisers are also running print ads (called *advertorials)* that closely resemble editorial material, making it increasingly difficult for readers to tell them apart.
7. Advertisers are producing 30-minute commercials (called *infomercials)* that appear to the average viewer as documentaries.

*****Use Learning Objective #5 Here; Use Exercise #1 Here; Use Figure 6-6 Here*****

Expectations

1. People see what they expect to see.
2. What they expect to see is usually based on familiarity, previous experience, or preconditioned set **expectations**.
3. Stimuli that conflict sharply with expectations often receive more attention than those that conform to expectations.
4. For years, certain advertisers have used blatant sexuality in advertisements for products to which sex was not relevant in the belief that such advertisements would attract a high degree of attention.
5. Ads with irrelevant sexuality often defeat the marketer's objectives, because readers tend to remember the sexual aspects of the ad, not the product or brand advertised.

*****Use Key Term expectations Here; Use Learning Objective #5 Here; Use Figure 6-7 Here*****

Motives

1. People tend to perceive things they need or want.
    a)   The stronger the need, the greater the tendency to ignore unrelated stimuli in the environment.
2. An individual's perceptual process attunes itself more closely to those elements of the environment that are important to that person.
3. Marketing managers recognize the efficiency of targeting their products to the perceived needs of consumers.

*****Use Learning Objective #5 Here*****

Selective Perception

1. The consumer's "selection" of stimuli *(selective perception)* from the environment is based on the interaction of expectations and motives with the stimulus itself.
2. *Selective exposure*—consumers actively seek out messages they find pleasant or with which they are sympathetic.
   a) Consumers actively avoid painful or threatening messages.
3. *Selective attention*—consumers have a heightened awareness of the stimuli that meet their needs or interests.
   a) Consumers have a lower awareness of stimuli irrelevant to their needs.
   b) People vary in terms of the kind of information in which they are interested and the form of message and type of medium they prefer.
4. *Perceptual defense*—threatening or otherwise damaging stimuli are less likely to be perceived than are neutral stimuli. Individuals unconsciously may distort information that is not consistent with their needs, values, and beliefs.
5. *Perceptual blocking*—consumers screen out enormous amounts of advertising by simply "tuning out."

*****Use Key Terms selective perception, perceptual defense, and perceptual blocking Here; Use Learning Objective #5 and #6 Here; Use Exercise #2 Here*****

Perceptual Organization

1. People do not experience the numerous stimuli they select from the environment as separate and discrete sensations.
   a) People tend to organize stimuli into groups and perceive them as unified wholes.
2. *Gestalt psychology (Gestalt,* in German, means pattern or configuration) is the name of the school of psychology that first developed the basic principles of perceptual organization.
3. Three of the most basic principles of perceptual organization are *figure and ground*, *grouping*, and *closure*.

*****Use Key Term Gestalt psychology Here; Use Learning Objective #5 and #7 Here*****

Figure and Ground

1. Stimuli that contrast with their environment are more likely to be noticed.
2. The simplest example is the contrast between a *figure and the ground* on which it is placed.
   a) The figure is usually perceived clearly.
   b) The ground is usually perceived as indefinite, hazy, and continuous.
3. The figure is more clearly perceived because it appears to be dominant—the ground appears to be subordinate and less important.
4. Advertisers have to plan their advertisements carefully to make sure that the stimulus they want noted is seen as figure and not as ground.
5. Marketers sometimes run advertisements that confuse the consumer because there is no clear indication of which is figure and which is ground.

*****Use Key Term **figure-and-ground** Here; Use Learning Objective #5 Here; Use Discussion Question #6 Here; Use Figure 6-8 Here*****

Grouping

1. Individuals tend to group stimuli in "chunks" rather than as discrete bits of information.
2. *Grouping* can be used advantageously by marketers to imply certain desired meanings in connection with their products.
   a) Most of us remember things like a social security number because it can be broken into three "chunks."

*****Use Key Term **grouping** Here; Use Learning Objective #5 Here*****

Closure

1. Individuals have a need for *closure*.
   a) As a result, people organize a perception so they see a complete picture.
   b) If the pattern of stimuli to which they are exposed is incomplete, they tend to perceive it as complete—they fill in the missing pieces.
2. The very act of completion serves to involve the consumer more deeply in the message.

*****Use Key Term **closure** Here; Use Learning Objective #5 Here; Use Figure 6-9 Here*****

Perceptual Interpretation

1. The interpretation of stimuli is uniquely individual because it is based on what individuals expect to see in light of their previous experience.
2. Stimuli are often highly ambiguous.
   a) When stimuli are highly ambiguous, individuals usually interpret them in such a way that they serve to fulfill personal needs, wishes, and interests.
3. How close a person's interpretations are to reality depends on the clarity of the stimulus, the past experiences of the perceiver, and his or her motives and interests at the time of perception.

*****Use Learning Objective #5 Here*****

Perceptual Distortion

1. With respect to *perceptual distortion*, individuals are subject to a number of influences that tend to distort their perceptions.
2. *Physical Appearances*—people tend to attribute the qualities they associate with certain people to others who may resemble them.
   a) Attractive models are more persuasive and have a more positive influence on consumer attitudes and behavior than do average-looking models.

117

3. *Stereotypes*—individuals tend to carry "pictures" in their minds of the meaning of various kinds of stimuli.
4. *First Impressions*—these tend to be lasting but formed while the perceiver does not know which stimuli are relevant, important, or predictive.
5. *Jumping to Conclusions*—many people tend to jump to conclusions before examining all the relevant evidence—hearing the beginning of an ad and drawing the incorrect conclusion.
6. *Halo Effect*—describes situations where the evaluation of a single object or person on a multitude of dimensions is based on the evaluation of just one or a few dimensions.
    a) Consumers often evaluate an entire product line on the basis of the one product within the product line.
    b) *Licensing* also is based on the halo effect—associating products with a well-known celebrity or designer name.

*****Use Key Term* **perceptual distortion** *Here; Use Learning Objective #5 and #8 Here; Use Discussion Question #7 Here; Use Figure 6-10 Here*****

CONSUMER IMAGERY

1. Consumers attempt to preserve or enhance their self-images by buying products they believe agree with that self-image and avoiding products that do not agree. This is called ***consumer imagery***.
2. Consumers tend to shop in stores that have images that agree with their own self-images.

*****Use Key Term* **consumer imagery** *Here; Use Learning Objective #9 Here*****

Product Positioning

1. Positioning strategy (***product positioning***) is the essence of the marketing mix.
    a) ***Positioning*** conveys the concept or meaning of the product or service, in terms of how it fulfills a consumer need.
    b) The marketer must create a distinctive product image in the mind of the consumer.
2. How a product is positioned in the mind of the consumer is more important to the product's success than are the product's actual characteristics.
3. Marketers try to differentiate their products by stressing attributes they claim will fulfill the consumer's needs better than competing brands.
4. The result of a successful positioning strategy is a distinctive brand image on which consumers rely to make choices.
5. A positive brand image is associated with consumer loyalty, consumer beliefs about positive brand value, and a willingness to search for the brand.
6. A positive brand image also serves to promote consumer interest in future brand promotions, and inoculates against competitors' marketing activities.

*****Use Key Terms* **product positioning and positioning** *Here; Use Figure 6-11 Here; Use Learning Objective #9 Here*****

7. Major positioning strategies include:
   a) *Umbrella positioning*—creating an overall image of the company around which a lot of products can be featured individually.
   b) *Positioning against the competition.*
   c) *Positioning based on a specific benefit*—effective depictions of a core **product benefit** often include memorable imagery.
   d) *Finding an "unowned" position*—finding a niche unfilled by other companies.
   e) *Filling several positions*—because unfilled gaps or "unowned" perceptual positions present opportunities for competitors, sophisticated marketers create several distinct offerings, often in the form of different brands, to fill several identified niches.

> *****Use Key Term* **product benefit** *Here; Use Figure 6-12 Here; Use Learning Objective #9 Here; Use Exercise #3 and #4 Here*****

Product Repositioning

1. Regardless of how well positioned a product appears to be the marketer may be forced to reposition *(product repositioning)* it in response to market events, such as a competitor cutting into the brand's market share.
2. Rather than trying to meet the lower prices of high-quality private label competition, some premium brand marketers have repositioned their brands to justify their higher prices, playing up brand attributes that had previously been ignored.
3. Another reason to reposition a product or service is to satisfy changing consumer preferences.

> *****Use Key Term* **product repositioning** *Here; Use Learning Objective #9 Here; Use Discussion Question #8 Here; Use Figure 6-13 Here*****

Perceptual Mapping

1. *Perceptual mapping* allows marketers to determine how their products appear to consumers in relation to competitive brands on one or more relevant characteristics.
2. Perceptual mapping enables the marketer to see gaps in the positioning of all brands in the product class and to identify areas in which consumer needs are not being adequately met.

> *****Use Key Term* **perceptual mapping** *Here; Use Learning Objective #9 Here; Use Exercise #5 Here; Use Figure 6-14 Here*****

Positioning of Services

1. Compared with manufacturing firms, service marketers face several unique problems in positioning and promoting their offerings.
2. Services are intangible, image becomes a key factor in differentiating a service from its competition.
   a) The marketing objective is to enable the consumer to link a specific image with a specific brand name.
3. Many service marketers have developed strategies to provide customers with visual images and tangible reminders of their service offerings.
   a) Examples would include painted delivery vehicles, restaurant matchbooks, packaged hotel soaps and shampoos, and a variety of other specialty items.
4. Sometimes companies market several versions of their service to different market segments by using a differentiated positioning strategy.
5. The design of the service environment is an important aspect of service positioning strategy and sharply influences consumer impressions and consumer and employee behavior.
6. The physical environment is particularly important in creating a favorable impression for such services as banks, retail stores, and professional offices, because there are so few objective criteria by which consumers can judge the quality of the services they receive.
7. The service environment conveys the image of the service provider with whom the service is so closely linked.
8. One study of service environments identified five environmental variables most important to bank customers.
   a) Privacy—both visually and verbally, with enclosed offices, transaction privacy, etc.
   b) Efficiency/convenience—transaction areas that are easy to find, directional signs, etc.
   c) Ambient background conditions—temperature, lighting, noise, and music.
   d) Social conditions—the physical appearance of other people in the bank environment, such as bank customers and bank personnel.
   e) Aesthetics—e.g., color, style, use of materials, and artwork.

*****Use Learning Objective #10 Here*****

Perceived Price

1. How a consumer perceives a price (*perceived price*)—as high, as low, as fair—has a strong influence on both purchase intentions and purchase satisfaction.
2. Perception of price fairness—customers pay attention to the prices paid by other customers (e.g., senior citizens, frequent fliers, affinity club members).
   a) Customers perceive differential pricing strategies used by some marketers as unfair to those not eligible for the special prices.
   b) Perceptions of price unfairness affect consumers' perceptions of product value, and ultimately, their willingness to patronize a store or a service.

*****Use Key Term perceived price *Here; Use Table 6-2 Here*****

Reference Prices

1. A *reference price* is any price that a consumer uses as a basis for comparison in judging another price.
2. Reference prices can be external or internal.
3. An advertiser generally uses a higher *external reference price* ("sold elsewhere at...") in an ad in which a lower sales price is being offered, to persuade the consumer that the product advertised is a really good buy.
4. *Internal reference prices* are those prices (or price ranges) retrieved by the consumer from memory.
   a) Internal reference points are thought to play a major role in consumers' evaluations and perceptions of value of an advertised (i.e., external) price deal, as well as in the believability of any advertised reference price.
5. *Acquisition-transaction utility* theory—acquisition utility represents the perceived economic gain or loss associated with a purchase, and is a function of product utility and purchase price.
   a) *Transaction utility* concerns the perceived pleasure or displeasure associated with the financial aspect of the purchase and is determined by the difference between the internal reference price and the purchase price.
6. Several studies have investigated the effects on consumer price perceptions of three types of advertised reference prices: plausible low, plausible high, and implausible high.
   a) *Plausible low prices* are well within the range of acceptable market prices.
   b) *Plausible high* is near the outer limits of the range but not beyond the realm of believability.
   c) *Implausible high* is well above the consumer's perceived range of acceptable market prices.
7. As long as an advertised reference price is within a given consumer's acceptable price range, it is considered plausible and is assimilated.
   a) If the advertised reference point is outside the range of acceptable prices (i.e., implausible), it will be *contrasted* and thus will not be perceived as a valid reference point.

*****Use Key Terms reference prices and acquisition-transaction utility Here; Use Learning Objective #11 Here*****

Tensile and Objective Price Claims

1. The semantic cues (i.e., specific wording) of the phrase used to communicate the price-related information may affect consumers' price perceptions.
2. *Acquisition-transaction utility* (e.g., "save 10 to 40 percent," "save up to 60 percent," "save 20 percent or more") are used to promote a range of price discounts for a product line, an entire department, or sometimes an entire store.
3. *Objective price claims* provide a single discount level (e.g., "save 25 percent").
4. Tensile and objective price claims have a potentially greater effect on consumer shopping and on store traffic than a reference price advertisement that promotes a single product because of the broader range of merchandise covered by them.

121

a) Consumer evaluations and shopping intentions are least favorable for advertisements stating the minimum discount level ("save 10 percent or more").

b) Ads that state a maximum discount level ("save up to 40 percent") either equal or exceed the effectiveness of ads stating a discount range ("save 10 to 40 percent").

5. Consumer reactions to *tensile price claims* are affected by the *width* of the discount range.

a) Studies found that, for *broader* discount ranges, tensile claims stating the maximum level of savings have more positive effects than those stating the minimum level or the entire savings range.

b) For more *narrow* discount ranges, tensile claims stating the maximum level of savings appear to be no more effective than claims stating the minimum level or the entire savings ranges.

6. Consumers are less sensitive to price when using credit cards than when they use cash.

a) In a similar vein, a recent study reported that consumers tend to be less sensitive to price when they shop online rather than when they shop in stores.

*****Use Key Terms objective price claims and tensile price claims Here; Use Learning Objective #11 Here*****

Perceived Quality

1. Consumers often judge the quality of a product (*perceived quality*) on the basis of a variety of informational cues.

a) *Intrinsic cues* are physical characteristics of the product itself, such as size, color, flavor, or aroma.

b) *Extrinsic cues* are such things as price, store image, service environment, brand image, and promotional message.

*****Use Key Terms perceived quality, intrinsic cues, and extrinsic cues Here; Use Discussion Question #9 and #10 Here*****

Perceived Quality of Products

1. *Intrinsic cues* are concerned with physical characteristics of the product itself, size, color, flavor, etc.

a) Consumers like to think they base quality evaluations on intrinsic cues, but in reality, they are often unable to identify that product in a taste test.

b) In the absence of actual experience with a product, consumers often evaluate quality on the basis of extrinsic cues, price, brand image, store image, etc.

2. Many consumers use *country-of-origin* stereotypes to evaluate products.

*****Use Learning Objective #11 Here; Use Discussion Question #9 and #10 Here*****

Perceived Quality of Services

1. It is more difficult for consumers to evaluate the quality of services than the quality of products.
2. Service characteristics include—intangibility, variability, perishability, simultaneously produced, and consumed.
3. Consumers are unable to compare services side-by-side as they do products, so consumers rely on surrogate or extrinsic cues when purchasing services.
4. Marketers try to standardize their services in order to provide consistency of quality.
5. Service is consumed as it is being produced.
    a) As a result, defective services are difficult to correct.
6. Researchers have concluded that the service quality that a customer perceives is a function of the magnitude and direction of the gap between *expected service* and the customer's *assessment of the service actually delivered.*
7. SERVQUAL, measures the gap between customers' expectations of services and their perceptions of the actual service.
    a) These perceptions are based on the dimensions of; tangibles, reliability, responsiveness, assurance, and empathy.
    b) Two dimensions used to measure service quality are *outcome* dimensions—the reliable delivery of the core service—and *process* dimensions—how the core service is delivered.
8. *Transaction satisfaction index* is one tool researchers have used to try to integrate the concepts of product quality and service quality.
9. Conceptual Model of Transaction Satisfaction—the model suggests that the consumer's overall satisfaction with the transaction is based on evaluation of service quality, product quality, and price.

*****Use Learning Objective #11 Here; Use Discussion Question #9 and #10 Here; Use Table 6-3 and 6-4 Here; Use Figure 6-15 and 6-16 Here*****

Price/Quality Relationship

1. Perceived product value has been described as a trade-off between the product's perceived benefits (or quality) and perceived sacrifice required to acquire it.
2. A number of research studies support the view that consumers rely on price as an indicator of product quality.
    a) Other studies suggest consumers are actually relying on a well-known brand name as a quality indicator.
3. Because price is so often considered to be an indicator of quality, some products deliberately emphasize a high price to underscore their claims of quality.
4. Marketers have used the *price/quality relationship* to position their products as the top-quality offering in their product category.
    a) There is a positive price/quality relationship.
    b) Consumers use price as a surrogate indicator of quality if they have little information or little confidence in their ability to make a choice.

*****Use Key Term **price/quality relationship** *Here; Use Learning Objective #11 Here; Use Figure 6-17 Here*****

Retail Store Image

1. Retail stores have their own images that influence the perception of the quality of the products they carry.
2. Studies show consumers perceive stores with small discounts on a large number of products as having lower-priced items than stores that offer large discounts on a small number of products.
3. One study showed that frequent advertising that presents large numbers of price specials reinforces consumer beliefs about the competitiveness of a store's prices.
    a) The downside of constant advertising of sale prices can be an unwanted change in store image.
4. The width of product assortment also affects retail store image.
5. The type of product the consumer wishes to buy influences his or her selection of retail outlet, conversely, the consumer's evaluation of a product often is influenced by the knowledge of where it was bought.
6. Most studies of the effects of extrinsic cues on perceived product quality have focused on just one variable—either price or store image.
    a) When a second extrinsic cue is available (e.g., price and store image), however, perceived quality is sometimes a function of the interaction of both cues on the consumer.

*****Use Learning Objective #12 Here*****

Manufacturer's Image

1. Consumer imagery extends beyond perceived price and store image to the producers themselves.
2. Manufacturers who enjoy a favorable image generally find that their new products are accepted more readily than those of manufacturers who have a less favorable or even a "neutral" image.
3. Researchers have found that consumers generally have favorable perceptions of pioneer brands (the first in a product category), even after follower brands become available.
    a) They also found a positive correlation between pioneer brand image and an individual's ideal self-image, which suggests that positive perceptions toward pioneer brands lead to positive purchase.
4. Some major marketers introduce new products under the guise of supposedly smaller, pioneering (and presumably more forward-thinking) companies.
    a) The goal of this so-called *stealth* (or faux) *parentage* is to persuade consumers (particularly young consumers) that the new brands are produced by independent, nonconformist free spirits, rather than by giant corporate entities such as their parents might patronize.
5. Companies sometimes use stealth parentage when they enter a product category totally unrelated to the one with which their corporate name has become synonymous.

6. Today, companies are using advertising, exhibits, and sponsorship of community events to enhance their images.

****Use Learning Objective #12 Here*****

Perceived Risk

1. *Perceived risk* is the uncertainty that consumers face when they cannot foresee the consequences of their purchase decision.
2. The degree of risk that consumers perceive and their own tolerance for risk taking are factors that influence their purchase strategies.
3. Consumers are influenced by risks that they perceive, whether or not such risks actually exist.
   a) Risk that is not perceived will not influence consumer behavior.
4. Types of risk include: *functional risk, physical risk, financial risk, social risk, psychological risk,* and *time risk.*

****Use Key Term* perceived risk *Here; Use Learning Objective #13 Here; Use Table 6-5 Here*****

Perception of Risk Varies

1. The amount of risk perceived depends on the specific consumer.
2. *High-risk perceivers* are **narrow categorizers** because they limit their choices.
3. *Low-risk perceivers* are **broad categorizers** because they make their choice from a wide range of alternatives.
4. Individual perception of risk varies by product category.
   a) Consumers are likely to perceive a higher degree of risk in the purchase of a high definition television set (e.g., functional risk, financial risk, time risk) than in the purchase of an automobile.
5. Researchers have identified *product-specific* perceived risk.
   a) One study found that consumers perceive service decisions to be riskier than product decisions, particularly in terms of social risk, physical risk, and psychological risks.
6. Perception of the degree of risk is also affected by the shopping situation.

****Use Key Terms* narrow categorizers and broad categorizers *Here; Use Learning Objective #13 Here*****

How Consumers Handle Risk

1. *Consumers seek information* about products and product categories by word-of-mouth.
   a) They spend more time considering their decision the higher the perceived risk.
2. *Consumers are brand loyal.*
   a) Consumers avoid risk by staying with a brand they know and are satisfied with.
   b) High-risk perceivers are the most brand loyal.

3. *Consumers select by brand image.*
   a) When consumers lack experience with a product, they trust a well-known brand.
   b) Consumers believe well-known brands are better and are worth buying for assured quality.
4. *Consumers rely on store image.*
   a) If consumers have no other information about a product, they judge it based on the store.
   b) Store image imparts the implication of product testing and assurance of service.
5. *Consumers buy the most expensive model.*
   a) When in doubt, consumers equate price with quality.
6. *Consumers seek reassurance.*
   a) Consumers, uncertain about a product choice, seek reassurance through guarantees, tryouts, money-back offers, etc.
7. The concept of perceived risk has major implications for the introduction of new products.
   a) Because high-risk perceivers are less likely to purchase new or innovative products than low-risk perceivers, it is important for marketers to provide such consumers with persuasive risk-reduction strategies.

*****Use Learning Objective #13 Here*****

DISCUSSION QUESTIONS

1. How does sensory adaptation affect advertising effectiveness? How can marketers overcome sensory adaptation?

Adaptation refers specifically to "getting used to" certain sensations, becoming accustomed to a certain level of stimulation. Marketers try to increase sensory input in order to cut through the daily clutter consumers experience in the consumption of advertising by using media different than expected. Some marketers seek unusual media, shopping carts, movies, fragrance samples in magazines, etc.

2. Discuss the differences between the absolute threshold and the differential threshold. Which is more important to marketers? Explain your answer.

The lowest level at which an individual can experience a *sensation* (e.g., the immediate and direct response of the sensory organs to stimuli) is called the *absolute threshold*. To illustrate, the distance at which a driver can note a specific billboard on a highway is that individual's absolute threshold. Other people riding in the car (because of vision or position in the car) could have different absolute thresholds for this event. The minimal difference that can be detected between two similar stimuli is called the *differential threshold*, or the *just noticeable difference* (the j.n.d.). This matches to Weber's Law. According to Weber's Law, an additional level of stimulus equivalent to the j.n.d. must be added for the majority of people to perceive a difference between the resulting stimulus and the initial stimulus. The differential threshold seems to have more importance for marketers. For example, when it comes to product improvements, marketers very much want to meet or exceed the customer's differential threshold.

3. **For each of these products—energy bars and expensive face moisturizers—describe how marketers can apply their knowledge of differential threshold to packaging, pricing, and promotional claims during periods of (a) rising ingredient and materials costs and (b) increasing competition.**

To repeat the information found in Question 2, the *differential threshold* is the minimal difference that can be detected between two stimuli. It is also called j.n.d. (just noticeable difference). Weber's law states that the stronger the initial stimulus, the greater the additional intensity needed for the second stimulus to be perceived as different. Also, an additional level of stimulus, equivalent to the j.n.d., must be added for the majority of people to perceive a difference between the resulting stimulus and the initial stimulus.

In the (a) case, manufacturers and marketers endeavor to determine the relevant j.n.d. for their products so that negative changes—reductions or increases in product size, or reduced quality—are not readily discernible to the public and so that product improvements are readily discernible to the consumer without being wastefully extravagant. In the (b) case, marketers use the j.n.d. to determine the amount of change or updating they should make in their products to avoid losing the readily recognized aspects of their products. For example, the subtle incremental changes in "Betty Crocker" (see Figure 6-2) and changes in Campbell Soup labeling could produce changes and better meet competition. Marketers want to meet the consumers' differential threshold so that they readily perceive the improvements made in the original product. This could create a competitive differential advantage.

4. **Does subliminal advertising work? Support your view.**

Students may argue both sides of the issue. They should note the following key information. The purpose of the concept is to stimulate people below their level of conscious awareness—they can perceive stimuli without being consciously aware of it. It can be briefly presented visual stimuli, accelerated speech in low-volume auditory messages, or embedded or hidden imagery or words. Embeds are disguised stimuli not readily recognized by readers. A series of highly imaginative laboratory experiments gave some support to the notion of subliminal awareness, but no evidence was found that consumers could be persuaded to act in response to such messages. Auditory subliminal stimuli seem to have even less effect than visual. Nevertheless a whole industry based on audio-perception has grown up, using subliminal sound to try to teach while you sleep, and using music to influence you while shopping. There is no evidence that subliminal advertising works. Because no evidence exists as to its real effects, there are currently no federal or state laws addressing its use. The FCC has issued a statement against its use, however.

5. **How do advertisers use contrast to make sure that their ads are noticed? Would the lack of contrast between the advertisement and the medium in which it appears help or hinder the effectiveness of the ad? What are the ethical considerations in employing such strategies?**

Stimuli that contrast with their environment are more likely to be noticed. The simplest example is the contrast between a *figure and the ground* on which it is placed. The figure is usually perceived clearly. The ground is usually perceived as indefinite, hazy, and continuous. Perceptual organization is affected by consumer expectations. A *reversible figure-ground pattern* will result in different perceptions based on consumers' experiences. The lack of contrast can be effective because individuals have a need for closure. As a result, people organize a perception so they see a complete picture. If the pattern of stimuli to which they are exposed is incomplete, they tend to perceive it as complete (i.e., they fill in the missing pieces). *Tension* is created by incomplete messages resulting in better consumer retention. Incomplete advertising messages "beg" for completion by consumer. The very act of completion serves to involve the consumer more deeply in the message. The ethical question will be an interesting debate. Be sure you're clear where you stand before the students start. They will tend to polarize, either anything is okay or it is all manipulation.

6. **What are the implications of figure-ground relationship for print ads and for online ads? How can the figure-ground construct help or interfere with the communication of advertising messages?**

Stimuli that contrast with their environment are more likely to be noticed. The simplest visual illustration consists of a figure on a ground (i.e., background). In print and in online ads, the figure should appear well defined, solid, in the forefront and in contrast to its ground so that consumers can perceive it clearly. Therefore, advertisers must plan their advertisements carefully to make sure the stimulus they want noted is seen as figure and not as ground. The musical background must not overwhelm the jingle; the background of an advertisement must not detract from the product. Some print advertisers often silhouette their products against a white background to make sure that the features they want noted are clearly perceived. Others use reverse lettering (white letters on a black background) to achieve contrast. Marketers must make sure that their ads clearly indicate which is figure and which is ground in order to prevent consumer confusion and avoid the problem of figure-ground reversal.

7. **Find two ads depicting two different types of perceptual distortions. Discuss your choices.**

Though students are free to choose examples of perceptual distortion, it will be best to refresh their memories about the concept. Have them look for the influences suggested by the chapter. For example, look for distortion because of physical appearances, stereotypes, first impressions, jumping to conclusions, or the halo effect.

8. **Why are marketers sometimes "forced" to reposition their products or services? Illustrate your answers with examples.**

The image that a product or service has in the mind of the consumer—that is, how it is positioned—is probably more important to its ultimate success than are its actual characteristics. Marketers try to position their brands so that they are perceived by the consumer to fit a distinctive niche in the marketplace—a niche occupied by no other product. They try to differentiate their products by stressing attributes they claim will fulfill the consumer's needs better than competing brands. They strive to create a product image consistent with the relevant self-image and needs of the targeted consumer segment. The result of a successful positioning strategy is a distinctive brand image of which consumers rely in making product choices. In today's highly competitive environment, a distinctive product image is most important. As products become more complex and the marketplace more crowded, consumers rely more on the product's image than on its actual attributes in making purchase decisions. The technique of perceptual mapping helps marketers to determine just how their products and services appear to consumers in relation to competitive brands on one or more relevant characteristics. It enables them to see gaps in the positioning of all brands in the product or service class, and to identify areas in which consumers' needs are not adequately met. Thus, marketers may either create new brands to satisfy unmet needs, or through promotional messages reposition existing brands by stressing those product attributes that are likely to satisfy unfilled consumer needs.

9. **(a) Why is it more difficult for consumers to evaluate the quality of services than the quality of products? (b) Apply two of the concepts used to explain consumers' evaluations of service quality to your evaluation of this course up to this point in the semester.**

(a) Because of certain distinctive characteristics of services: their intangibility, their variability, the fact that services are simultaneously produced and consumed, and their perishability, services are difficult to evaluate with respect to quality. To overcome the fact that consumers are unable to compare services side-by-side as they do with products, consumers rely on surrogate cues (i.e., extrinsic cues) to evaluate service quality.

(b) Students are free use whatever criteria they wish for the comparison, however, explanation as to methodology and conclusions should be required.

10. **Discuss the roles of extrinsic cues and intrinsic cues in the perceived quality of: (a) wines, (b) restaurants, (c) plasma TV monitors, and (d) graduate education.**

(a) Both the extrinsic and intrinsic cues affect the perception of product quality for wines. Intrinsic cues, such as taste, color, smell, and vintage year are important indicators of quality to knowledgeable consumers. Many consumers, however, cannot evaluate subtle variations of taste, and may not know how to judge color, smell, and vintage; these consumers often rely on such extrinsic cues as price, where the wine was made (i.e., high-priced, French wine would imply good quality), the appearance of the bottle, or the image of the store which carries the wine (i.e., brands carried exclusively by wine specialty stores are perceived as being of higher quality than wines sold at regular liquor stores) to evaluate the product.

Parts (b), (c), and (d) will have similar responses. Allow students to be creative. Note for them, however, that the decisions made at this point will have impact with respect to advertising, promotion, and marketing decisions.

A good way to conclude this question is have students bring in ads from the different areas and have the class discuss which form of cues are being used.

EXERCISES

1. **Find three examples of print advertisements that use some of the stimulus factors discussed in the chapter to gain attention. For each example, evaluate the effectiveness of the stimulus factors used.**

Instructor's Discussion

Factors which students are likely to bring up include size of ads, the position of the ad, the color and shelf position of the package, and the contrast between the stimulus and its physical environment. The professor should ask students to identify the utilization of the principles of perceptual organization, that is, figure and ground grouping and closure, in the ads or packages selected.

2. **Define selective perception. Thinking back, relate one or two elements of this concept to your own attention patterns in viewing print advertisements and TV commercials.**

Instructor's Discussion

Consumers select stimuli from the environment based on the interaction of expectations and motives with the stimulus itself. This selection process gives rise to four important concepts concerning perception:

- Selective exposure—consumers actively seek out messages that they find pleasant or with which they are sympathetic, and they actively avoid painful or threatening ones.
- Selective attention—consumers exercise a great deal of selectivity in terms of the attention they give to commercial stimuli.
- Perceptual defense—consumers subconsciously screen out stimuli that they find psychologically threatening, even though exposure has already taken place.
- Perceptual blocking—consumers protect themselves from being bombarded with stimuli by simply "tuning out"—blocking such stimuli form conscious awareness.

3. **Find an ad or example in another form (e.g., an article) illustrating two of the positioning approaches discussed in the chapter. Evaluate the effectiveness of each ad or example selected.**

Instructor's Discussion

The positioning strategy of a product is designed to create a perception of a product. The positioning appeal may be based on a total image rather than an attribute that is unique to the product (e.g., Compaq is positioned as "the high quality computer"), or it can center on a single, important attribute (e.g., Gateway is the friendly computer company that will design a computer especially for you). For more details and examples see the chapter.

4. **Select a company that produces several versions of the same product under the same or different brands (one that is not discussed in this chapter). Visit the firm's Web site and prepare a list of the product items and the positioning strategy for each of the products. (You may use the chapter's discussions of Anheuser-Busch, Tylenol, and Proctor & Gamble as a guide to the type of company to choose).**

Instructor's Discussion

A good place for students to begin this exercise might be the computer, automobile, cereal, or gasoline industries. The Web sites for these industries are usually very clear as to product mix and positions.

5. **Construct a two-dimensional perceptual map of your college using the two attributes that were most influential in your selection. Then mark the position of your school on the diagram relative to that of another school you considered. Discuss the implications of this perceptual may for the student recruitment function of the university that you did not choose.**

Instructor's Discussion

A good place to begin the discussion of this exercise is to have students review Figure 6-14 that shows a method of perceptually mapping a magazine. If students still seem to be stumped, have them construct a perceptual map of a few restaurants. This will get them in practice for the actual assignment.

S.TA.R. PROJECTS

Ethical Issues in Consumer Behavior

S.T.A.R. Project #1
The conclusion on the part of most scholars and researchers is that subliminal perception (advertising) does not work. The field continues to intrigue and interest communicators, however. As can be seen in Table 6-1, the history of the subject stretches back some fifty years.

Your task is to evaluate the ethics of subliminal persuasion. During your evaluation consider the positive and negative effects of the phenomenon. For example, on the one hand, persuading below the conscious thinking level might induce purchases that normally would not be made—poor ethics. On the other hand, teaching a smoker or alcoholic to give up his or her bad habit with subliminal auditory tapes might give the person a new lease on life—good ethics. Write a short paper that takes a position on the subject from an ethical standpoint. Be sure to support your conclusions. Remember, every position has two points of view.

Instructor's Discussion

Students should be encouraged to read the material in the chapter before beginning this assignment. It is essential that Table 6-1 be reviewed. Students should also be encouraged to do an Internet search on the subject. Obviously, two points of view can be supported. Making judgments in this area is extremely difficult. Once students have completed the assignment, put the papers into two groups (pro and con) and have a mini-debate. The results are often informative and thought provoking.

S.T.A.R. Project #2
As indicated in the chapter, "the consumer's selection of stimuli from the environment is based on the interaction of expectations and motives with the stimulus itself." Assume that you are the marketing manager for a large suburban toy and game store. In an effort to stimulate sales, your marketing team has employed an outside consultant. After a careful study of the store's marketing and merchandising practices, the consultant has observed that although children still demand toys their parents are becoming increasingly resistant to marketing efforts and are increasing their perceptual defenses against such efforts. The consult has recommended that your store move the marketing efforts toward the child segment (e.g., skipping the parent) by placing merchandise lower to the floor, using larger price signs, associating more products with animated characters from television and the movies, and introducing "kiddie" shopping carts so children can have their own carts with which to shop. Although the ideas seem new and fresh, you wonder about the ethics of bypassing the parent and going directly toward the child with your marketing effort. Consider your feelings and write a one-page position paper that supports or rejects the consultant's advice.

Instructor's Discussion

In this case, the marketing manager is confronted with an interesting situation. When does making a sale out shadow ethical behavior? Does the consultant's report over step good ethics? Students should be able to generate good responses. It will be interesting to see the differences between the two points of view. A mini-debate can be held if time permits.

Small Group Projects

S.T.A.R. Project #3
Every child has had the experience of taking a lunch to school. For older generations this meant peanut butter and jelly or baloney sandwiches. For today's youth it is more likely to be Lunchables or some similar product. Kraft Foods has aggressively promoted Lunchables as a

healthy alternative to the "old time" sandwiches. Many mother do not agree, however, and continue to prepare lunches in the older fashion. Your group's assignment is to examine Lunchables (see www.lunchables.com) with respect to possible perceptual barriers that might be erected by non-users. For example, a mother might not use a Lunchable because she wants to give her child a lunch made with her own loving hands or nutrition may be a concern. Considering the influences (see chapter) that might enhance perceptual distortion and devise a plan for Kraft to overcome such a mother's objections. How might your plan be implemented through communication channels?

Instructor's Discussion

The group will find ample information on the Lunchables Web site on which to build their plan. Product variety, nutrition facts, and information can be used to overcome acceptance barriers. The main intent of the exercise, however, is to have students carefully examine the perceptual distortion influences (physical appearances, stereotypes, first impressions, jumping to conclusions, and the halo effect). Be sure eventual conclusions address these influences.

S.T.A.R. Project #4

According to the chapter, the halo effect "has been used to describe situations in which the evaluation of a single object or person on a multitude of dimensions is based on the evaluation of just one or a few dimensions." There is a feeling in the marketing world today that a secret to merchandising success is to find a product that already has a positive connotation and then build secondary products around this product (the halo effect). Your group's assignment is to explore the toy world and how its products have led to product line extensions in movies, videos, and other products. For example, Mattel's popular *Hot Wheels* cars are coming to life on the big and small screens. Your group should find other examples of this phenomenon and then relate your findings to the halo effect. Is this strategy a sound one? What are the advantages and disadvantages of such a strategy?

Instructor's Discussion

The halo effect is an interesting perceptual distortion influence. Additionally, as will be seen in Chapter 7, it is also the basis for many licensing efforts. Students can review Barbie, Hot Wheels, Play-Doh, and other popular children's products in order to complete this assignment. Is the strategy a sound one? The answer is "it depends." Some products are able to make the jump successfully and some are not. The reasons for success and failure match well to the information about perception presented in the text.

Using the Internet to Study Consumer Behavior

S.T.A.R. Project #5

It has been said that product positioning is more important to the ultimate success of a product than are its actual characteristics. A good illustration of this is the yo-yo. That's right, the yo-yo. For years the yo-yo was considered a child's toy and would not be taken seriously by any self-respecting teen. If Extreme Spin has its way, this will no longer be true. This company has designed a new generation of yo-yo type products that are designed to appeal a teen's need for excitement, risk, and daring. If the secret to effective positioning is that a product should occupy a unique position in the mind of the consumer, Extreme Spin (see www.extremespin.com) may have found the right answer.

  a. After visiting the Extreme Spin Web site, comment on what position the company seems to be occupying with its products.
  b. Which of the positioning strategies suggested in the chapter, is Extreme Spin using?
  c. What would you change about this company's positioning approach?

Instructor's Discussion

Extreme Spin is not your average yo-yo company. The company has honed in on the desires of Generation Y with its marketing appeals. What other yo-yo company features throwing knives on its Web site? Notice that the company calls these knives "juggling knives"—might be a good way to lose a finger or hand! Students should be able to match the positioning strategies used by the company to those suggested in the chapter. Some suggestions for improving the Web site with respect to positioning might be to include more pictures of the target market using the product.

S.T.A.R. Project #6

What better treat for a hot summer's day than a cool pitcher of Kool-Aid (especially cherry)? Kool-Aid has owned the pre-mix beverage market for years. As bottled waters, numerous soda products, and juices began to invade Kool-Aid's territory, however, the company began to consider product line extension and repositioning strategies. Complaints about Kool-Aid's dependence on a high amount of sugar for taste and its image as a little kid's drink were taken seriously. Recently, Kool-Aid developed a new product called Kool-Aid Jammers (a fruit juice Kool-Aid that comes in a clear pouch pack). Jammers have 100 percent Vitamin C and will be sold in a different section of the grocery store than the traditional Kool-Aid packets. Will Kool-Aid once again rule the summer drink market with its new product? You decide.

  a. Visit the Kool-Aid Web site at (www.kool-aid.com) and review the page for Kool-Aid Jammers. What did you learn about Kool-Aid's positioning strategies?
  b. Can this product be considered a repositioning for Kool-Aid? Why? Is this a good move for Kool-Aid?
  c. Do you think this product will be successful in reaching an older youth market? Explain.

Instructor's Discussion

This exercise will take the students to a highly visual and exciting Web site. The Web site is really designed for kids (with plenty of sounds attached). Will Kool-Aid's new product be a success? Will the repositioning strategy work? Students should be encouraged to examine how Kool-Aid became vulnerable and why they made the move toward a juice product. This exercise is a good quick illustration of how a well-known company can attempt to move into another market and at the same time reposition themselves against competition.

CASES

Case One: Purchasing Medicines Online

Question 1—Answer:

The students should recognize that consumers cannot foresee various aspects of the consequences of their purchase decisions. Usually, when a person "needs" to take a prescription medication, he or she needs it now, and often cannot wait for a shipping delay. Yet one way to lessen the high cost of prescription medicines today is by using a mail-order pharmacy, whether it is in the United States or Canada. So the consumer must weigh perceived cost savings versus the additional time (time risk as well as physical risk) it might take to fill the prescription rather than filling it at the local neighborhood pharmacy.

Question 2—Answer:

Online pharmacies have established an accreditation association, the North American Pharmacy Accreditation Commission (www.napac.org/Mission.asp). The group presently has 68 members, most of whom are Canadian. Members agree to follow the commission's strict code of service standards, and in return they get to use the group's seal of approval on their Web sites. As with other "seals of approval" (e.g., The Good Housekeeping Seal of Approval), this tactic should lessen consumers' perceived risk of purchasing prescription medicines online. To further reduce American consumers' perceived risk, Canadians pharmacies belonging to the North American Pharmacy Accreditation Commission might also guarantee delivery within the United States within a certain number of days (e.g., ten days) or they would pay a penalty by reducing the price of the ordered prescription by 25 percent.

Case Two: Repositioning and Revitalizing Classic Brands

Question 1—Answer:

The strategies illustrated in the case are totally consistent with the Product Life Cycle. All the products listed in the case are *mature* products. Because they are nondurables, it is generally not feasible to improve them by adding new features. Thus, the key to growth in these situations is to provide consumers with additional ways to use these products by altering their established images—that is, "repositioning" them in a way that extends into new uses for them. This strategy is particularly applicable to Rice Krispies and Arm & Hammer.

The case of Old Spice is a bit different. Consumers perceive Old Spice as an "old" brand strongly associated with aftershave lotion. Thus, the new products in the Old Spice line have more contemporary names in addition to the well-established Old Spice "umbrella" name. This example also illustrates the concept of *stimulus generalization* discussed in Chapter 7.

Question 2—Answer:

Marketers must always look for repositioning opportunities as their products mature in order to find additional uses for them and extend their product life cycles. Another reason for repositioning is the loss of a product's initial distinction because competitors pursuing the same target market position their products close to the product in question.

CHAPTER 7

Consumer Learning

LEARNING OBJECTIVES

After studying this chapter students should be able to:
1. Explain consumer learning theory and identify the necessary elements.
2. Discuss the elements of Classical Conditioning theory.
3. Identify the three strategic applications of Classical Conditioning.
4. Discuss the concept of licensing and its importance to marketing.
5. Review the elements of Instrumental Conditioning.
6. Discuss the strategic applications of Instrumental Conditioning.
7. Describe modeling (observational learning).
8. Explain and apply cognitive learning theory in a marketing situation.
9. Describe three ways information may be stored in memory.
10. Relate involvement theory to consumer behavior.
11. Describe the Elaboration Likelihood Model.
12. Outline measures of involvement.
13. Understand how consumer learning can be measured.
14. Discuss the concepts of brand loyalty and brand equity.

SUMMARY

Consumer learning is the process by which individuals acquire the purchase and consumption knowledge and experience they apply to future related behavior. Some learning is intentional; much learning is incidental. Basic elements that contribute to an understanding of learning are motivation, cues, response, and reinforcement.

There are two schools of thought as to how individuals learn—behavioral theories and cognitive theories. Behavioral theorists view learning as observable responses to stimuli; whereas cognitive theorists believe that learning is a function of mental processing.

Three types of behavioral learning theories are classical conditioning, instrumental conditioning, and observational (vicarious) learning. The principles of classical conditioning that provide theoretical underpinnings for many marketing applications include repetition, stimulus generalization, and stimulus discrimination. Neo-Pavlovian theories view traditional classical conditioning as cognitive associative learning rather than as reflexive action.

Instrumental learning theorists believe that learning occurs through a trial-and-error process in which positive outcomes (i.e., rewards) result in repeat behavior. Both positive and negative reinforcement can be used to encourage the desired behavior. Reinforcement schedules can be total (consistent) or partial (fixed ratio or random). The timing of repetitions influences how long the learned material is retained. Massed repetitions produce more initial learning than distributed repetitions; however, learning usually persists longer with distributed (i.e., spread out) reinforcement schedules.

Cognitive learning theory holds that the kind of learning most characteristic of humans is problem solving. Cognitive theorists are concerned with how information is processed by the human mind: how is it stored, retained, and retrieved. A simple model of the structure and operation of memory suggests the existence of three separate storage units: the sensory store, short-term store (or working memory), and long-term store. The processes of memory include rehearsal, encoding, storage, and retrieval.

Involvement theory proposes that people engage in limited information processing in situations of low importance or relevance to them and in extensive information processing in situations of high relevance. Hemispheral lateralization theory gave rise to the theory that television is a low-involvement medium that results in passive learning and that print and interactive media encourage more cognitive information processing.

Measures of consumer learning include recall and recognition tests, cognitive responses to advertising, and attitudinal and behavioral measures of brand loyalty in terms of the consumer's behavior or the consumer's attitude toward the brand. Brand equity refers to the inherent value a brand name has in the marketplace.

For marketers, the major reasons for understanding how consumers learn are to teach them that their brand is best and to develop brand loyalty.

CHAPTER OUTLINE

INTRODUCTION

1. Marketers are concerned with how individuals learn because they want to teach them, in their roles as consumers, about products, product attributes, and potential consumer benefits; about where to buy their products, how to use them, how to maintain them, even how to dispose of them.
2. Marketing strategies are based on communicating with the consumer.
   a) Marketers want their communications to be noted, believed, remembered, and recalled.
   b) For these reasons, they are interested in every aspect of the learning process.
3. There is no single, universal theory of how people learn.
4. There are two major schools of thought concerning the learning process: one consists of *behavioral learning theories*, the other of *cognitive learning theories*.
5. Cognitive theorists view learning as a function of purely mental processes, although behavioral theorists focus almost exclusively on observable behaviors (responses) that occur as the result of exposure to stimuli.

| *****Use Key Terms** behavioral learning theory and cognitive learning theory *Here***** |

CONSUMER LEARNING

1. Consumer learning can be thought of as *the process by which individuals acquire the purchase and consumption knowledge and experience that they apply to future related behavior.*
2. Several points in this definition are worth noting.
    a) First, consumer learning is a *process*; that is, it continually evolves and changes as a result of newly acquired *knowledge* or from actual *experience*.
    b) Both newly acquired knowledge and personal experience serve as *feedback* to the individual and provide the basis for *future behavior* in similar situations.
3. The role of experience in learning does not mean that all learning is deliberately sought. A great deal of learning is also *incidental*, acquired by accident or without much effort.
4. The term **learning** encompasses the total range of learning, from simple, almost reflexive responses to the learning of abstract concepts and complex problem solving.
    a) Most learning theorists recognize the existence of different types of learning and explain the differences through the use of distinctive models of learning.
5. Despite their different viewpoints, learning theorists in general agree that in order for learning to occur, certain basic elements must be present—motivation, cues, response, and reinforcement.

*****Use Key Term **learning** Here; Use Learning Objective #1 Here*****

Motivation

1. **Motivation** is based on needs and goals.
    a) The degree of relevance, or *involvement*, with the goal, is critical to how motivated the consumer is to search for information about a product.
2. Uncovering consumer motives is one of the prime tasks of marketers, who try to teach consumer segments why their product will best fulfill their needs.

*****Use Key Term **motivation** Here; Use Learning Objective #1 Here*****

Cues

1. If motives serve to stimulate learning, **cues** are the stimuli that give direction to the motives.
    a) In the marketplace, price, styling, packaging, advertising, and store displays all serve as cues to help consumers fulfill their needs.
2. Cues serve to direct consumer drives when they are consistent with their expectations.

*****Use Key Term **cues** Here; Use Learning Objective #1 Here*****

Response

1. How individuals react to a cue—how they behave—constitutes their **response**.
2. A response is not tied to a need in a one-to-one fashion.

3. A need or motive may evoke a whole variety of responses.
4. The response a consumer makes depends heavily on previous learning; that, in turn, depends on how related responses were reinforced previously.

*****Use Key Term response *Here; Use Learning Objective #1 Here*****

Reinforcement

1. *Reinforcement* increases the likelihood that a specific response will occur in the future as the result of particular cues or stimuli.

*****Use Key Term reinforcement *Here; Use Learning Objective #1 Here; Use Exercise #1 Here; Use Figure 7-1 Here*****

BEHAVIORAL LEARNING THEORIES

1. Behavioral learning theories are sometimes called *stimulus-response theories*.
   a) When a person responds in a predictable way to a known stimulus, he or she is said to have "learned."
2. Behavioral theories are most concerned with the *inputs* and *outcomes* of learning, not the *process*.
3. Two theories relevant to marketing are *classical conditioning* and *instrumental (or operant) conditioning*.

*****Use Key Terms stimulus-response theories, classical conditioning, and instrumental (or operant) conditioning *Here*****

Classical Conditioning

1. Early classical conditioning theorists regarded all organisms as passive recipients.
   a) *Conditioning* involved building automatic responses to stimuli.
2. Ivan Pavlov was the first to describe conditioning and to propose it as a general model of how learning occurs.
   a) For Pavlov, *conditioned learning* results when a stimulus that is paired with another stimulus elicits a known response and serves to produce the same response when used alone.
   b) He used dogs to demonstrate his theories.
   c) The dogs were hungry and highly motivated to eat.
   d) Pavlov sounded a bell and then immediately applied a meat paste to the dogs' tongues, which caused them to salivate.
   e) After a sufficient number of repetitions of the bell sound, followed almost immediately by the food, the bell alone caused the dogs to salivate.

3. In a consumer behavior context, an ***unconditioned stimulus*** might consist of a well-known brand symbol (e.g., the Microsoft "windows" icon) that implies technological superiority and trouble-free operation (the *unconditioned response*).
4. ***Conditioned stimuli*** might consist of new products bearing well-known symbols.

> *****Use Key Terms conditioned learning, unconditioned stimulus, and conditioned stimuli Here; Use Learning Objective #2 Here; Use Figure 7-1, 7-2A, and 7-2B Here*****

Cognitive Associative Learning

1. Recent conditioning theory views classical conditioning as the learning of associations among events that allows the organism to anticipate and "represent" its environment.
2. The relationship (i.e., contiguity) between the conditioned stimulus and the unconditioned stimulus (the bell and the meat paste) influenced the dogs' expectations, which in turn influenced their behavior (salivation).
3. Classical conditioning is seen as ***cognitive associative learning*** not the acquisition of new reflexes, but the acquisition of new knowledge about the world.
4. *Optimal conditioning*—that is, the creation of a strong association between the conditioned stimulus (CS) and the unconditioned stimulus (US)—requires forward conditioning; that is, the CS should precede the US, repeated pairings of the CS and the US, a CS and US that logically belong together, a CS that is novel and unfamiliar, and a US that is biologically or symbolically salient.
5. Under ***neo-Pavlovian conditioning***, the consumer can be viewed as an information seeker who uses logical and perceptual relations among events, along with his or her own preconceptions, to form a sophisticated representation of the world.

> *****Use Key Terms cognitive associative learning and neo-Pavlovian conditioning Here; Use Learning Objective #2 Here; Use Discussion Question #1 Here*****

Strategic Applications of Classical Conditioning

1. Three basic concepts derive from classical conditioning: *repetition, stimulus generalization,* and *stimulus discrimination.*
2. ***Repetition*** works by increasing the strength of the association and by slowing the process of forgetting.
   a) After a certain number of repetitions retention declines.
   b) This effect is known as ***advertising wearout*** and can be decreased by varying the advertising messages.
   c) Wearout may be avoided by varying the message through *cosmetic variation* or *substantive variation.*
3. Some don't agree about how much repetition is needed.
   a) The three-hit theory states that the optimum number of exposures to an ad is three.
      i) One to make the consumer aware of the product.
      ii) A second to show consumers the relevance of the product.
      iii) A third to remind them of its benefits.

4. The effectiveness of repetition is somewhat dependent upon the amount of competitive advertising to which the consumer is exposed.
   a) As exposure increases, the potential for *interference* increases.

*****Use Key Terms* **repetition, advertising wearout** *Here; Use Learning Objective #2 and*
*#3 Here; Use Figure 7-3 and 7-4 Here; Use Discussion Question #1 Here*****

---

5. According to classical conditioning theorists, learning depends not only on repetition, but also on the ability of individuals to generalize.
6. *Stimulus generalization* explains why imitative "me too" products succeed in the marketplace: consumers confuse them with the original product they have seen advertised.
   a) It also explains why manufacturers of private label brands try to make their packaging closely resemble the national brand leaders.

*****Use Key Term* **stimulus generalization** *Here; Use Learning Objective #2 and*
*#3 Here; Use Exercise #2 Here; Use Discussion Question #1 and #3 Here*****

---

7. The principle of stimulus generalization is applied by marketers to product line, form, and category extensions.
   a) In *product line extensions*, the marketer adds related products to an already established brand, knowing that the new product is more likely to be adopted when it is associated with a known and trusted brand name.
      i) Conversely, it is much more difficult to develop a totally new brand.
   b) Marketers offer *product form extensions* that include different sizes, different colors, and even different flavors.
   c) *Product category extensions* generally target new market segments.
      i) The success of this strategy depends on a number of factors.
      ii) For example, if the image of the parent brand is one of quality, consumers are more likely to bring positive associations to the new category extensions.

*****Use Key Terms* **product line extensions, product form extensions, and product**
category extensions *Here; Use Learning Objective #2 Here; Use Figure 7-5, 7-6, and*
*7-7 Here*****

---

8. *Family branding*—the practice of marketing a whole line of company products under the same brand name—is another strategy that capitalizes on the consumer's ability to generalize favorable brand associations from one product to the next.
9. Retail private branding often achieves the same effect as family branding.
   a) For example, Wal-Mart used to advertise that its stores carried only "brands you trust." Now, the name Wal-Mart itself has become a "brand" that consumers have confidence in, and the name confers brand value on Wal-Mart's store brands.

*****Use Key Term* **family branding** *Here; Use Learning Objective #2 Here; Use Discussion*
*Question #2 Here*****

---

10. *Licensing*—allowing a well-known brand name to be affixed to products of another manufacturer—is a marketing strategy that operates on the principle of *stimulus generalization.*

11. Corporations also license their names and trademarks, usually for some form of brand extension, where the name of the corporation is licensed to the maker of a related product and thereby enters a new product category.

12. Municipal and state governments have begun licensing their names to achieve new sources of revenue. The Vatican Library licenses its name for a variety of products from luggage to bed linens.

13. The increase in licensing has made counterfeiting a booming business, as counterfeiters add well-known licensor names to a variety, of products without benefit of control or quality control.

*****Use Key Term licensing Here; Use Learning Objective #2, #3, and #4 Here; Use Discussion Question #1 Here; Use Exercise #2 Here; Use Figure 7-8 Here*****

14. **Stimulus discrimination** is the opposite of stimulus generalization and results in the selection of specific stimulus from among similar stimuli.
   a) The consumer's ability to discriminate among similar stimuli is the basis of positioning strategy, which seeks to establish a unique image for a brand in the consumer's mind.

*****Use Key Term stimulus discrimination Here; Use Learning Objective #4 Here; Use Exercise #2 Here*****

15. The key to stimulus discrimination is effective *positioning*, a major competitive advantage.
   a) The image, or position, that a product or service has in the mind of the consumer is critical to its success.
   b) Unlike the imitator who hopes consumers will generalize their perceptions and attribute special characteristics of the market leader's products to their own products, market leaders want the consumer to discriminate among similar stimuli.

16. Most product differentiation strategies are designed to distinguish a product or brand from that of competitors on the basis of an attribute that is relevant, meaningful, and valuable to consumers.

17. It often is quite difficult to unseat a brand leader once stimulus discrimination has occurred.
   a) In general, the longer the period of learning—of associating a brand name with a specific product—the more likely the consumer is to discriminate, and the less likely to generalize the stimulus.

18. The principles of classical conditioning provide the theoretical underpinnings for many marketing applications.
   a) Repetition, stimulus generalization, and stimulus discrimination are all major applied concepts that help explain consumer behavior.

*****Use Key Term positioning Here; Use Learning Objective #2 and #4 Here; Use Exercise #2 Here; Use Discussion Questions #1 and #4 Here; Use Figure 7-9 Here*****

Instrumental Conditioning

1. Like classical conditioning, *instrumental conditioning* requires a link between a stimulus and a response.
   a) However, in instrumental conditioning, the stimulus that results in the most satisfactory response is the one that is learned.
2. Instrumental learning theorists believe that learning occurs through a trial-and-error process, with habits formed as a result of rewards received for certain responses or behaviors.
   a) Although classical conditioning is useful in explaining how consumers learn very simple kinds of behaviors, instrumental conditioning is more helpful in explaining complex, goal-directed activities.
3. According to American psychologist B. F. Skinner, most individual learning occurs in a controlled environment in which individuals are "rewarded" for choosing an appropriate behavior.
   a) In consumer behavior terms, instrumental conditioning suggests that consumers learn by means of a trial-and-error process in which some purchase behaviors result in more favorable outcomes (i.e., rewards) than other purchase behaviors.
   b) A favorable experience is instrumental in teaching the individual to repeat a specific behavior.
4. Like Pavlov, Skinner developed his model of learning by working with animals.
   a) In a marketing context, the consumer who tries several brands and styles of jeans before finding a style that fits her figure (positive reinforcement) has engaged in instrumental learning.

*****Use Key Term** instrumental conditioning *Here; Use Learning Objective #5 Here; Use Discussion Questions #1 and #3 Here; Use Figure 7-10 Here*****

Reinforcement of Behavior

1. Skinner distinguished two types of reinforcement (or reward) influence , which provided that the likelihood for a response would be repeated.
   a) The first type, *positive reinforcement*, consists of events that strengthen the likelihood of a specific response.
   b) *Negative reinforcement* is an unpleasant or negative outcome that also serves to encourage a specific behavior.
      i) Fear appeals in ad messages are examples of negative reinforcement.
   c) Either positive or negative reinforcement can be used to elicit a desired response.
   d) Negative reinforcement should not be confused with punishment, which is designed to discourage behavior.

*****Use Key Terms** positive reinforcement and negative reinforcement *Here; Use Learning Objective #5 Here*****

1. Forgetting and extinction—when a learned response is no longer reinforced, it diminishes to the point of extinction; that is, to the point at which the link between the stimulus and the expected reward is eliminated.

a) Forgetting is often related to the passage of time; this is known as the process of *decay*.

b) Marketers can overcome forgetting through repetition and can combat extinction through the deliberate enhancement of consumer satisfaction.

*****Use Learning Objective #5 Here; Use Discussion Question #1 Here*****

Strategic Applications of Instrumental Conditioning

1. The objective of all marketing efforts should be to maximize customer satisfaction.
2. Aside from the experience of using the product itself, consumers can receive reinforcement from other elements in the purchase situation, such as the environment in which the transaction or service takes place, the attention and service provided by employees, and the amenities provided.
   a) Some hotels provide reinforcement to guests in the form of small amenities.
   b) Most frequent shopper programs are based on enhancing positive reinforcement and encouraging continued patronage.
3. *Relationship marketing*—developing a close personalized relationship with customers—is another form of non-product reinforcement.

*****Use Learning Objective #5 and #6 Here; Use Discussion Question #1 Here*****

4. Reinforcement schedules—marketers have found that product quality must be consistently high and provide customer satisfaction with each use for desired consumer behavior to continue.
5. Marketers have identified three types of reinforcement schedules: total (or continuous) reinforcement, systematic (*fixed ratio*) reinforcement, and random (*variable ratio*) reinforcement.
6. Variable ratios tend to engender high rates of desired behavior and are somewhat resistant to extinction—perhaps because, for many consumers, hope springs eternal.

*****Use Learning Objective #5 and #6 Here*****

7. Shaping—the reinforcement of behaviors that must be performed by consumers before the desired behavior can be performed is called **shaping**.
   a) Shaping increases the probabilities that certain desired consumer behavior will occur.

*****Use Key Term shaping Here; Use Learning Objective #5 and #6 Here*****

8. Massed versus distributed learning—*timing* has an important influence on consumer learning.
   a) Question—should a learning schedule be spread out over a period of time (*distributed learning*), or should it be "bunched up" all at once (*massed learning*)?
   b) The question is an important one for advertisers planning a media schedule because massed advertising produces more initial learning, although a distributed schedule usually results in learning that persists longer.

145

c) When advertisers want an immediate impact (e.g., to introduce a new product or to counter a competitors blitz campaign), they generally use a massed schedule to hasten consumer learning.

d) When the goal is long-term repeat buying on a regular basis, however, a distributed schedule is preferable.

e) A distributed scheduler with ads repeated on a regular basis, usually results in more long-term learning and is relatively immune to extinction.

*****Use Discussion Questions #1, #3, and #4 Here; Use Learning Objective #5 and #6 Here*****

Modeling or Observational Learning

1. Learning theorists have noted that a considerable amount of learning takes place in the absence of direct reinforcement, either positive or negative, through a process psychologists call *modeling or observational learning* (also called *vicarious learning*).

2. They observe how others behave in response to certain situations (stimuli), the ensuing results (reinforcement) that occur, and they imitate (model) the positively-reinforced behavior when faced with similar situations.

a) Modeling is the process through which individuals learn behavior by observing the behavior of others and the consequences of such behavior.

b) Their role models are usually people they admire because of such traits as appearance, accomplishment, skill, and even social class.

c) Children learn much of their social behavior and consumer behavior by observing their older siblings or their parents.

3. Advertisers recognize the importance of observational learning in their selection of models, whether celebrities or unknowns.

4. Sometimes ads depict negative consequences for certain types of behavior.

a) This is particularly true of public policy ads, which may show the negative consequences of smoking, of driving too fast, or taking drugs.

*****Use Key Term modeling or observational learning (vicarious learning) Here; Use Discussion Question #4 Here; Use Learning Objective #7 Here; Use Figure 7-11 Here*****

COGNITIVE LEARING THEORY

1. Not all learning is the result of repeated trials.

a) Learning also takes place as the result of consumer thinking and problem solving.

2. *Cognitive learning* is based on mental activity.

3. Cognitive learning theory holds that the kind of learning most characteristic of human beings is problem solving, and it gives some control over their environment.

*****Use Key Term cognitive learning Here; Use Learning Objective #8 Here; Use Figure 7-12 Here*****

146

Information Processing

1. The human mind processes the information it receives as input much as a computer does.
   a) *Information processing* is related to both the consumer's cognitive ability and the complexity of the information to be processed.
2. Individuals differ in terms of their ability to form mental images and in their ability to recall information.
3. The more experience a consumer has with a product category, the greater his or her ability to make use of product information.

***** *Use Key Term* information processing *Here; Use Learning Objective #8 Here* *****

How Consumers Store, Retain, and Retrieve Information

1. The structure of memory—because information processing occurs in stages, it is believed that content is stored in the memory in separate storehouses for further processing; a sensory store, a short-term store, and a long-term store.
2. *Sensory store*—all data comes to us through our senses, however, our senses do not transmit information as whole images.
   a) The separate pieces of information are synchronized as a single image.
   b) This sensory store holds the image of a sensory input for just a second or two.
   c) This suggests that it's easy for marketers to get information into the consumer's sensory store, but hard to make a lasting impression.
3. *Short-term store*—if the data survives the sensory store, it is moved to the short-term store.
   a) This is our working memory.
   b) If *rehearsal*—the silent, mental repetition of material—takes place, then the data is transferred to the long-term store.
   c) If data is not rehearsed and transferred, it is lost in a few seconds.
4. *Long-term store*—once data is transferred to the long-term store it can last for days, weeks, or even years.

***** *Use Key Terms* sensory store, short-term store, and long-term store *Here; Use Discussion Question #5 Here; Use Learning Objective #9 Here; Use Figure 7-13 Here* *****

5. *Rehearsal* and encoding—the amount of information available for delivery from the short-term store to the long-term store depends on the amount of rehearsal an individual gives to it.
   a) *Encoding* is the process by which we select and assign a word or visual image to represent a perceived object.
   b) Learning visually takes less time than learning verbal information.
   c) How much consumers encode depends on their cognitive commitment to the intake of the information and their gender.
6. *Information overload* takes place when the consumer is presented with too much information.
   a) It appears to be a function of the amount of information and time frame of that information.

147

b) There are contradictory studies on what constitutes overload.
c) The difficulty is determining the point of "overload."

> *****Use Key Terms* rehearsal, encoding, and information overload *Here; Use Discussion Question #5 Here*****

7. Retention—information is constantly organized and reorganized as new links between chunks of information are forged.
   a) In fact, many information-processing theorists view the long-term store as a network consisting of nodes (i.e., concepts) with links among them.
   b) As individuals gain more knowledge they expand their network of relationships, and sometimes their search for additional information.
   c) This process is known as *activation*, which involves relating new data to old to make the material more meaningful.
   d) The total package of associations brought to mind when a cue is activated is called a *schema*.
   e) Research has found that older adults appear to be more reliant on schema-based information processing strategies than younger adults.
   f) Consumers' information search is often dependent upon how similar or dissimilar (discrepant) presented products are to product categories already stored in memory.
      i) Consumers recode what they have already encoded to include larger amounts of information (chunking).
   g) The degree of prior knowledge is an important consideration.
   h) Knowledgeable consumers can take in more complex chunks of information than those who are less knowledgeable in the product category.
   i) Information is stored in long-term memory in two ways: *episodically* (i.e., by the order in which it is acquired) and *semantically* (according to significant concepts).
   j) Many learning theorists believe that memories stored semantically are organized into frameworks by which we integrate new data with previous experience.
8. *Retrieval* is the process by which we recover information from long-term storage.
   a) A great deal of research is focused on how individuals retrieve information from memory.
   b) Studies show that consumers tend to remember the product's benefits, rather than its attributes.
   c) Motivated consumers are likely to spend time interpreting and elaborating on information they find relevant to their needs; and are likely to activate such relevant knowledge from long-term memory.
   d) Research findings suggest that incongruent (e.g. unexpected) elements pierce consumers' perceptual screens and improve the memorability of an ad when these elements are relevant to the advertising message.
   e) Incongruent elements that are not relevant to an ad also pierce the consumer's perceptual screen but provide no memorability for the product.
9. *Interference effects* are caused by confusion with competing ads and result in a failure to retrieve.

a) Advertisements for competing brands or for other products made by the same manufacturer can lower the consumer's ability to remember advertised brand information.
b) There are actually two kinds of interference.
   i) New learning can interfere with the retrieval of previously stored material.
   ii) Old learning can interfere with the recall of recently learned material.

*****Use Key Terms **retrieval and interference effects** *Here; Use Discussion Question #5 Here*****

Limited and Extensive Information Processing

1. For a long time, consumer researchers believed that all consumers passed through a complex series of mental and behavioral stages in arriving at a purchase decision *(extensive information processing)*.
   a) These stages ranged from awareness (exposure to information), to evaluation (preference, attitude formation), to behavior (purchase), to final evaluation (adoption or rejection). This same series of stages is often presented as the consumer adoption process.
2. Some theorists began to realize that there were some purchase situations that simply did not call for extensive information processing and evaluation; that sometimes consumers simply went from awareness of a need to a routine purchase, without a great deal of information search and mental evaluation *(limited information processing)*.
3. Purchases of minimal personal importance were called low-involvement purchases, and complex, search-oriented purchases were considered high-involvement purchases.

*****Use Key Terms **extensive and limited information processing** *Here; Use Discussion Question #4 Here; Use Learning Objective #8 Here; Use Table 7-1 Here*****

Involvement Theory

1. *Involvement theory* developed from research into *hemispherical lateralization* or split-brain theory.
   a) The premise is that the right and left hemispheres of the brain specialize in the kinds of information they process.
   b) The left hemisphere is responsible for cognitive activities such as reading, speaking, and attribution information processing.
   c) The right hemisphere of the brain is concerned with nonverbal, timeless, pictorial, and holistic information.

*****Use Key Terms **involvement theory** *Here; Use Learning Objective #10 Here; Use Figure 7-14 and 7-15 Here*****

<u>Involvement Theory and Media Strategy</u>

1. Individuals *passively* process and store right-brain information.
    a) Because it is largely pictorial, TV viewing is considered a right hemisphere activity.
    b) ***Passive learning*** was thought to occur through repeated exposures to low-involvement information.
        i) TV commercials were thought to produce change in consumer behavior before it changed consumer attitudes.
    c) The left hemisphere is associated with high-involvement information.
        i) Print media (newspapers and magazines) are considered left hemisphere or high-involvement activity.
2. Right-brain theory is consistent with classical conditioning and stresses the importance of the *visual component* of advertising.
    a) Recent research suggests that pictorial cues help recall and familiarity, although verbal cues trigger cognitive functions, encouraging evaluation.
    b) The right-brain processing theory stresses the importance of the visual component of advertising, including the creative use of symbols.
    c) Pictorial cues are more effective at generating recall and familiarity with the product, although verbal cues (which trigger left-brain processing) generate cognitive activity that encourages consumers to evaluate the advantages and disadvantages of the product.
3. There are limitations to split-brain theory.
    a) Research suggests the spheres of the brain do not always operate independently of each other, but work together to process information.
    b) There is evidence that both sides of the brain are capable of low- and high-involvement.
    c) It does seem the right side is more cognitively oriented and the left side more affectively oriented.

> *****Use Key Terms* **passive learning** *Here; Use Learning Objective #10 Here; Use Figure 7-15 Here; Use Discussion Question #6 Here*****

<u>Involvement Theory and Consumer Relevance</u>

1. A consumer's level of involvement depends on the degree of personal relevance that the product holds for the consumer.
    a) High-involvement purchases are those that are very important to the consumer in terms of perceived risk.
    b) Low-involvement purchases are purchases that are not very important to the consumer, hold little relevance, and little perceived risk.
2. Highly involved consumers find fewer brands acceptable (they are called ***narrow categorizers***); uninvolved consumers are likely to be receptive to a greater number of advertising messages regarding the purchase and will consider more brands (they are ***broad categorizers***).

> *****Use Key Terms* **narrow and broad categorizers** *Here; Use Learning Objective #10 Here*****

Central and Peripheral Routes to Persuasion

1. ***Central and peripheral routes to persuasion***—the central premise is that consumers are more likely to weigh information carefully about a product and to devote considerable cognitive effort to evaluating it when they are highly involved with the product category and vice versa.
    a) Use of the central route to persuasion is more effective in marketing for high-involvement purchases.
    b) The peripheral route to persuasion is more effective for low-involvement purchases.

> *****Use Key Terms* central and peripheral routes to persuasion *Here; Use Learning Objective #10 Here*****

2. The ***elaboration likelihood model (ELM)*** suggests that a person's level of involvement during message processing is the critical factor in determining the most effective route of persuasion.
    a) Thus, when involvement is high, consumers follow the central route and base their attitudes or choices on the message arguments.
    b) When involvement is low, they follow the peripheral route and rely more heavily on other message elements to form attitudes or make product choices.
3. The marketing implications of the elaboration likelihood model are clear:
    a) For high-involvement purchases, marketers should use arguments stressing the strong, solid, high-quality attributes of their products—thus using the central (i.e., highly cognitive) route.
    b) For low-involvement purchases, marketers should use the peripheral route to persuasion, focusing on the method of presentation rather than on the content of the message (e.g., through the use of celebrity spokespersons or highly visual and symbolic advertisements).

> *****Use Key Term* elaboration likelihood model (ELM) *Here; Use Learning Objective #11 Here; Use Figure 7-12 (previously used), 7-16, and 7-17 Here*****

Measures of Involvement

1. Researchers have defined and conceptualized involvement in a variety of ways including ego involvement, commitment, communication involvement, purchase importance, extent of information search, persons, products situations, and purchase decisions.
    a) Some studies have tried to differentiate between brand involvement and product involvement.
    b) Others differentiate between situational, enduring, and response involvement.
2. The lack of a clear definition about the essential components of involvement poses some measurement problems.
    a) Researchers who regard involvement as a cognitive state are concerned with the measurement of ego involvement, risk perception, and purchase importance.
    b) Researchers who focus on the behavioral aspects of involvement measure such factors as the search for and evaluation of product information.

c) Others argue that involvement should be measured by the degree of importance the product has to the buyer.

3. Because of the many different dimensions and conceptualizations of involvement, it makes sense to develop an *involvement profile*, rather than to measure a single involvement level.

*****Use Learning Objective #12 Here; Use Table 7-2 and 7-3 Here*****

Marketing Applications of Involvement

4. Involvement theory has a number of strategic applications for the marketer.
   a) The left-brain (cognitive processing)/right-brain (passive processing) paradigm seems to have strong implications for the content, length, and presentation of both print and television advertisements.
   b) By understanding the nature of low-involvement information processing, marketers can take steps to increase consumer involvement with their ads.

*****Use Discussion Question #4 Here*****

MEASURES OF CONSUMER LEARNING

1. Market share and the number of brand-loyal consumers are the dual goals of consumer learning.
   a) Brand-loyal customers provide the basis for a stable and growing market share.
   b) Brands with larger market shares have proportionately larger groups of loyal buyers.

*****Use Learning Objective #13 Here*****

Recognition and Recall Measures

1. *Recognition and recall tests* are conducted to determine whether consumers remember seeing an ad, the extent to which they have read it or seen it and can recall its content, their resulting attitudes toward the product and the brand, and their purchase intentions.
   a) Recognition tests are based on *aided recall*, although recall tests use *unaided recall*.
   b) In recognition tests, the consumer is shown an ad and asked whether he or she remembers seeing it and can remember any of its salient points.
   c) In recall tests, the consumer is asked whether he or she has read a specific magazine or watched a specific television show, and if so, can recall any ads or commercials seen, the product advertised, the brand, and any salient points about the product.

*****Use Key Terms recognition and recall tests Here; Use Learning Objective #13 Here; Use Discussion Question #9 Here; Use Figure 7-18 Here*****

Cognitive Responses to Advertising

1. *Comprehension* is a function of the message characteristics, the consumer's opportunity and ability to process the information, and the consumer's motivation (or level of involvement).
2. To ensure a high level of comprehension, many marketers conduct **copy testing** either *before* the advertising is actually run in media (called **pre-testing**) or *after it* appears (**post-testing**).
3. Pre-tests are used to determine which, if any, elements of an advertising message should be revised before major media expenses are incurred.
4. Post-tests are used to evaluate the effectiveness of an ad that has already run, and to identify which elements, if any, should be changed to improve the impact and memorability of future ads.

> *****Use Key Terms comprehension, copy testing, pretesting, and posttesting *Here; Use Learning Objective #13 Here*****

Attitudinal and Behavioral Measures of Brand Loyalty

1. *Brand loyalty* is the ultimate desired outcome of consumer learning.
   a) There is no single definition of this concept.
2. *Attitudinal measures* are concerned with consumers' overall feelings (i.e., evaluation) about the product and the brand, and their purchase intentions.
3. *Behavioral measures* are based on observable responses to promotional stimuli—purchase behavior, rather than attitude toward the product or brand.
4. A basic issue among researchers is whether to define brand loyalty in terms of consumer behavior or consumer attitudes.
   a) *Behavioral* scientists who favor the theory of instrumental conditioning believe that brand loyalty results from an initial product trial that is reinforced through satisfaction, leading to repeat purchase.
   b) *Cognitive* researchers, on the other hand, emphasize the role of mental processes in building brand loyalty.
      i) They believe that consumers engage in extensive problem-solving behavior involving brand and attribute comparisons, leading to a strong brand preference and repeat purchase behavior.
5. To cognitive learning theorists, behavioral definitions (e.g., frequency of purchase or proportion of total purchases) lack precision, because they do not distinguish the "real" brand-loyal buyer.
   a) Often consumers buy from a mix of brands within their acceptable range (i.e., their *evoked set*).
6. An integrated conceptual framework views consumer loyalty as the relationship between an individual's relative attitude toward an entity (brand, service, store, or vendor) and patronage behavior.
7. The consumer's relative attitude consists of two dimensions:
   a) The strength of the attitude.
   b) The degree of attitudinal differentiation among competing brands.
8. Some theorists suggest that brand loyalty is correlated with the consumer's degree of involvement:

153

a) High involvement leads to extensive information search and, ultimately, to brand loyalty.

b) Low involvement leads to exposure and brand awareness, and then possibly to brand habits.

9. As a customer's satisfaction with a product increases along with repeat purchases, the search for information about alternative brands decreases.

> *****Use Key Terms* **brand loyalty, attitudinal measures and behavioral measures, and evoked set** *Here; Use Learning Objective #13 and #14 Here; Use Table 7-1 (previously used) and Table 7-4 Here; Use Figure 7-19 and 7-20 Here*****

Brand Equity

1. *Brand equity* refers to the value inherent in a well-known brand name.

   a) From a consumer's perspective, brand equity is the added value bestowed on the product by the brand name.

   b) Brand equity facilitates the acceptance of new products and the allocation of preferred shelf space, and enhances perceived value, perceived quality, and premium pricing options.

   c) For many companies, their most valuable assets are their brand names.

   d) Well known brand names are known as *megabrands*.

2. Because a brand that has been promoted heavily in the past retains a cumulative level of name recognition, companies buy, sell, and rent (i.e., license) their brand names, knowing that it is easier to buy than to create a brand name with enduring strength.

3. Brand equity enables companies to charge a price premium—an additional amount over and above the price of an identical store brand.

4. A relatively new strategy among some marketers is *co-branding* (also called double branding).

   a) In co-branding, two brand names are featured on a single product.

   b) It uses another product's brand equity to enhance the primary brand's equity.

   c) Some experts believe that using a second brand's equity may imply that the host brand can no longer stand on its own.

   d) Others question whether a co-branded product causes consumer confusion as to who actually makes the product, and whether the host brand can survive if the second brand endorsement is taken away.

5. Brand equity is important to marketers because it leads to brand loyalty, which in turn leads to increased market share and greater profits.

   a) To marketers, the major function of learning theory is to teach consumers that their product is best, to encourage repeat purchase, and, to develop loyalty to the brand name.

> *****Use Key Terms* **brand equity, megabrands, and co-branding** *Here; Use Learning Objective #13 and #14 Here; Use Discussion Question #8 Here*****

154

DISCUSSION QUESTIONS

1. How can the principles of a) classical conditioning theory and b) instrumental conditioning theory be applied to the development of marketing strategies?

Classical conditioning is now seen as cognitive associative learning; not the acquisition of new reflexes, but the acquisition of new knowledge about the world. Marketers can use product line extensions, family branding, and licensing to capitalize on the principles of classical conditioning. The consumer may be viewed as an information seeker who uses logical and perceptual relations among events, along with his or her own preconceptions, to form a sophisticated representation of the world. Instrumental conditioning is the learning that results from exposure to relationships among events in the environment; such exposure creates expectations as to the structure of the environment. Therefore, marketers should portray logical relationships among events in their ads, thus creating realistic consumer expectations, which in turn will influence consumer behavior.

2. Describe in learning terms the conditions under which family branding is a good policy and those under which it is not.

The main advantage of family branding is that marketers can build on the good reputation of their existing products through stimulus generalization. This makes the introduction of new products under the old brand name that much easier. As illustrations of family branding and the different approaches to it, consider the following: the main reason that Kraft and P&G have different family branding policies is that Kraft's products are homogeneous (they are all food products) and P&G's products are not. Thus, it would not make sense for P&G to attempt to apply the same name to the whole variety of products it markets. Another reason for P&G's branding strategy is the company's penchant for bringing out different brands in a particular product category, such as detergents, in order to satisfy different market segments and broaden its market share.

3. Neutrogena, the cosmetic company, has introduced a new line of shaving products for men. How can the company use stimulus generalization to market these products? Is instrumental conditioning applicable to this marketing situation? If so, how?

According to classical conditioning theorists, learning depends not only on repetition, but also on the ability of individuals to generalize. Stimulus generalization explains why imitative "me too" products succeed in the marketplace: consumers confuse them with the original product they have seen advertised. In extending its product line, the marketer adds related products to an already established brand, knowing that the new product is more likely to be adopted when it is associated with a known and trusted brand name. Conversely, it is much more difficult to develop a totally new brand.

What might be the reward from using the new product (i.e., instrumental conditioning)? Because Neutrogena has a good reputation in skin care, the new shaving line can build on this reputation and add skin care value to the male segment. Like classical conditioning, instrumental conditioning requires a link between a stimulus and a response. In instrumental conditioning, however, the stimulus that results in the most satisfactory response is the one that is learned. Instrumental learning theorists believe that learning occurs through a trial-and-error process, with habits formed as a result of rewards received for certain responses or behaviors. Although classical conditioning is useful in explaining how consumers learn very simple kinds of behaviors, instrumental conditioning is more helpful in explaining complex, goal-directed activities. Therefore, for Neutrogena to use instrumental conditioning, they must provide consumers the opportunity to try the product and then like what they try.

4. **Which theory of learning (i.e., classical conditioning, instrumental conditioning, observational learning, or cognitive learning) best explains the following consumption behaviors: (a) buying a six-pack of Evian water, (b) preferring to purchase clothes at the Gap, (c) buying a digital camera for the first time, (d) buying a new car, and (e) switching from one cellular phone service to another? Explain your choices.**

Students' responses may vary based on their perceptions of these products. Classical conditioning, in a consumer behavior context, an unconditioned stimulus might consist of a well-known brand symbol that implies technological superiority and trouble-free operation (the unconditioned response). Instrumental conditioning, the stimulus that results in the most satisfactory response is the one that is learned. Instrumental learning theorists believe that learning occurs through a trial-and-error process, with habits formed as a result of rewards received for certain responses or behaviours. Observational learning occurs by modelling or observing what others do. Cognitive learning is based on mental activity. Cognitive learning theory holds that the kind of learning most characteristic of human beings is problem solving, and it gives some control over their environment. Have students justify and explain choices.

5.a. **Define the following memory structures: sensory store, short-term store (working memory), and long-term store. Discuss how each of these concepts can be used in the development of an advertising strategy.**

Sensory store—receives what the senses deliver but retains information for only a fraction of a second. For marketing, this means that although it is easy to expose consumers to information, it is difficult to make a lasting impression. Therefore, messages must be brief and attract attention.

Short-term store—the stage of memory where information which is rehearsed is transferred to real memory, and data which is not rehearsed is lost within less than one minute. Because the amount of time available for memorization is very limited, the message must encourage immediate rehearsal of materials to stimulate retention. Chucking information also stimulates rehearsal of information and its transfer to long-term memory.

Long-term store—a data bank which lasts up to many years with almost unlimited capacity. The data is organized through linking and clustering of information according to its meaningfulness. The marketers must provide a message that can be readily linked to information stored here. Also, the advertiser should remember that the consumer interprets new information in a manner consistent with data stored in the long-term memory.

b. How does information overload affect the consumer's ability to comprehend an ad and store it in his or her memory?

When consumers are presented with too much information (called *information overload),* they may encounter difficulty in encoding and storing it all. It has been argued that consumers can become cognitively overloaded if they are given a lot of information in a limited time. The result of this overload is confusion, resulting in poor purchase decisions. One study found that consumers make less effective choices when presented with too much information. Other studies have found that consumers can handle large amounts of information without experiencing overload. The apparent contradiction between these findings may be due to the absence of a precise definition as to how much information constitutes overload. Is it five items or fifteen items? One experiment, which concluded that consumers are confused and make poor choices as the result of information overload, provided consumers with 10 to 25 choice alternatives, and with information concerning 15 to 25 product attributes. Research is needed to determine at what point information overload sets in for various subsets of consumers.

6. Discuss the differences between low- and high-involvement media. How would you apply the knowledge of hemispheric lateralization to the development of TV commercials and print advertisements?

The research called *hemispheric lateralization*, or *split-brain theory*, suggests that the left brain is responsible for cognitive activities, such as reading, speaking and processing verbal information, and that the right brain processes nonverbal and pictorial information and forms holistic images. Because TV is primarily a pictorial medium, TV viewing is considered to be a right brain, passive and holistic processing of images viewed on the screen, and TV is regarded as a low-involvement medium. On the other hand, print media (i.e., newspapers and magazines) are high-involvement because exposure to them results in the left-brain's active processing of verbal data and, ultimately, in cognitive learning. Thus, TV commercials should be short, rich in visual symbolism and repeated frequently. Consumers process and learn TV advertising passively, and the major objective of TV ads should be to form consumer familiarity with the brand and package which will result in the object's recognition and purchase by consumers. The objective of print ads is to present detailed, rather than "overall image," information to generate cognitive evaluations of the advantages and disadvantages of the product. The text discussion of *central and peripheral routes to persuasion* provides additional insights into the advertising applications of the concept of hemispheric lateralization.

7. Why are both attitudinal and behavioral measures important in measuring brand loyalty?

Brand loyalty is the ultimate desired outcome of consumer learning. There is, however, no single definition of this concept. Marketers agree that brand loyalty consists of both attitudinal and actual behaviors toward a brand and that both must be measured. *Attitudinal measures* are concerned with consumers' overall feelings (i.e., evaluations) about the product and the brand and their purchase intentions. *Behavioral measures* are based on observable responses to promotional stimuli—repeat purchase behavior rather than attitude toward the product or brand.

8. What is the relationship between brand loyalty and brand equity? What roles do both *concepts play in the development of marketing strategies?*

As mentioned in Question 7, *brand loyalty* is the ultimate desired outcome of consumer learning. The term *brand equity* refers to the value inherent in a well-known brand name. The value stems from the consumer's perception of the brand's superiority and the social esteem that using it provides and the trust and identification with the brand. For many companies, their most valuable assets are their brand names. With respect to strategies, because of the escalation of new-product costs and the high rate of new-product failures, many companies prefer to leverage their brand equity through brand extensions rather than risk launching a new brand.

9. How can marketers use measures of recognition and recall to study the extent of consumer learning?

Recognition and *recall tests* are conducted to determine whether consumers remember seeing an ad, the extent to which they have read it or seen it and can recall its contents, their resulting attitudes toward the product and the brand, and their purchase intentions. Recognition tests are based on *aided recall*, whereas recall tests used *unaided recall*.

EXERCISES

1. Imagine you are the instructor in this course and that you are trying to increase students' participation in class discussions. How would you use reinforcement to achieve your objective?

Instructor's Discussion

From an *instrumental (operant) conditioning* viewpoint, a professor should use positive reinforcement and reward students for participation through praises, keeping count of the number of times students participate, and giving a grade for class participation. If these means are used, however, students will learn to expect external motivations/rewards and, if these reinforcers are discontinued, will stop participating. A better approach may be to require students to prepare answers to questions and exercises given to them in advance of the class and to present their responses in class. Thus, students will be intellectually challenged, will clearly know what is expected of them, and will prepare for class discussions in order to avoid embarrassment in front of the class when they present their answers (i.e., due to internal motivation rather than due to external reinforcement).

2. **Visit a supermarket. Can you identify any packages where the marketer's knowledge of stimulus generalization and stimulus discrimination was incorporated into the package design? Note these examples and present them in class.**

Because the average package on the supermarket shelf has about one-tenth of a second to make an impression, astute marketers usually try to differentiate their packages sufficiently to ensure rapid consumer recognition. Thus, national manufacturers create packages that provide unique sensory input, are heavily advertised, create instant recognition, and are distinctly different from other packages in the same product category (i.e., stimulus discrimination). On the other hand, a trip to the supermarket reveals that manufacturers of private and store brands often design packages that resemble those of national brands; they hope that consumers will generalize from the national brands that they are likely to instantly recognize to the lesser-known store and private brands.

S.T.A.R. PROJECTS

Ethical Issues in Consumer Behavior

S.T.A.R. Project #1
As indicated in the chapter, behavioral learning theories are sometimes referred to as stimulus-response theories because they are based on the premise that observable responses to specific external signal that learning has taken place. Behavioral theories are not so much concerned with the process of learning as they are with the inputs and outcomes of learning, that is, in the stimuli that consumers select from the environment and the observable behaviors that result. Which of the behavioral learning theories relate most closely conduct of good business ethics?
   a. Review each of the behavioral learning theories and briefly describe the theories that you perceive to be most closely associated with the ethical transmission of information for the purpose of learning.
   b. Create an example to illustrate your position in the above question.

Instructor's Discussion

As indicated previously, *Classical Conditioning* is now seen as cognitive associative learning; not the acquisition of new reflexes, but the acquisition of new knowledge about the world. Marketers can use product line extensions, family branding, and licensing to capitalize on the principles of classical conditioning. The consumer may be viewed as an information seeker who uses logical and perceptual relations among events, along with his or her own preconceptions, to form a sophisticated representation of the world. *Instrumental conditioning (operant)* is the learning that results from exposure to relationships among events in the environment; such exposure creates expectations as to the structure of the environment.

With respect to ethical behavior in business, either position can be defended. In the case of classical conditioning, however, good business ethics can be seen as a "knee-jerk" or automatic reaction. Repeated exposure to proper behavior would produce this response through conditioning. Symbols would be important in this form of learning. In the case of instrumental conditioning, business ethics is often presented as a system of rewards or punishments learned through trial and error. Experience is the guide.

S.T.A.R. Project #2

Modeling is the process through which individuals learn behavior by observing the behavior of others and the consequences of such behavior. Does this cause a problem with respect to ethical behavior? When can modeling step over the line with respect to business ethics? To learn more about the role that modeling plays with respect to business ethics complete the assignments below.

a. Evaluate the ad in Figure 7-11. Indicate two ways the modeling displayed in the ad might be positive with respect to business ethics and two ways it might be negative with respect to business ethics.

b. Bring an ad to class that appears to use modeling in an unethical manner. Explain the ad.

Instructor's Discussion

The ad in Figure 7-11 can be seen in several ways. First, from a positive view, the young man is learning proper hygiene (shaving) from the older man and the innuendo is that the older generation might pass down treasured items to the younger generation. From a negative view, however, the ad displays a very expensive watch and may create desires for something unattainable. Next, values based on material things might be questioned.

Students are encouraged to bring in their own ads that show questionable modeling based on business ethics. Be sure to ask for explanations.

Small Group Projects

S.T.A.R. Project #3

Your group's assignment is to learn about how Internet brokerage firms attempt to teach you about online trading. Have one part of your group analyze eTrade.com and the other part analyze Charles Schwab (www.charlesschwab.com). Each sub-group should construct a table that indicates how each of the Web sites attempts to enhance consumer learning. What behavioral learning theories does each Web site appear to be using? Gauge effectiveness of the effort. Share the information with one another.

Instructor's Discussion

As students explore the two Web sites, they will observe two different techniques for transmitting information to consumers. Though both are considered to be excellent online traders, they follow different paths. Both, however, probably use instrumental conditioning rather than classical conditioning to get their points across. Have the student groups debate their findings. Was there consensus among the groups? If not, try to resolve the findings.

S.T.A.R. Project #4

Family branding is the practice of marketing a whole line of company products under the same brand name. This strategy capitalizes on the consumer's ability to generalize favorable brand associations from one product to others. Your group assignment is to analyze two separate family branding giants—Kellogg's and C.W. Post cereals. Go to both of the company's Web sites and make a list of all the products that are under the respective corporate umbrellas. After reviewing the material in the chapter on family branding, evaluate which organization appears to be superior. How did your group determine this? What behavioral learning principles does each appear to be using? Provide supportive evidence.

Instructor's Discussion

Students will find the Kellogg's Web site (www.kelloggs.com) and C.W. Post (www.postcereals.com) to be rich information warehouses of information. Students will be somewhat surprised by the amount of brands housed by either of these two megabrands. If the class is large and more work in this area is needed also try General Foods.

The student group should be encouraged to be creative with its evaluation scheme. There is ample information in the chapter that can be used in the evaluation method construction. Be sure to compare the student methods as each group makes its presentation.

Using the Internet to Study Consumer Behavior

S.T.A.R. Project #5

Recognition and recall tests are conducted to determine whether consumers remember seeing an ad, the extent to which they have read it or seen it and can recall its content, their resulting attitudes toward the product and the brand, and their purchase intentions. A number of syndicated research services conduct recognition and recall tests. One such organization is the Starch Readership Service (see www.roper.com). This service evaluates the effectiveness of magazine advertisements. See Figure 7-18 for an example of an ad that has been "Starched."
   a. Go to the Starch Readership Service Web site and describe other services that Starch provides to marketers and advertisers.
   b. Which of these services (beyond the Readership Service) seems to most closely match the marketer or advertiser's desire to learn how consumers learn, recognize, and recall information?
   c. After reviewing the information about the Starch services found in the chapter and seen on their Web site, pick a magazine ad and devise your own method for measuring recognition and recall. How does your method match that of Starch? How does your method differ? Try administering your test method to five fellow students. Critique your results.

Instructor's Discussion

Students should benefit from the information found on the Starch (Roper) Web site. There are several Starch methods that will be of interest. Be sure that students explain why they believe the Starch tests fit with the queries in "b" above. Students, once they have carefully read the material

161

in the chapter and visited the Web site, will produce some interesting recognition and recall tests. Present the best of these in class. Ask two to three students to present the results of their magazine ad test. All can learn from this experience.

S.T.A.R. Project #6

As indicated in the chapter, the basis of co-branding (in which two brand names are featured on a single product) is to use another product's brand equity to enhance the primary brand's equity. Notice the synergy that occurs when Nabisco combines its name with Ocean Spray to form Cranberry Newton's. Your assignment is to go to the Web and find <u>three examples</u> where companies doing business on the Internet have formed co-branding opportunities. List the examples you have found and comment on what you perceive to be the strategies behind these moves. Lastly, suggest a co-branding opportunity among e-commerce companies that has yet to materialize. Comment on why your suggested opportunity would be a good one.

<u>Instructor's Discussion</u>

This assignment asks students to be creative with their search of the Internet. If they become stuck, suggest automotive companies, organizations such as NASCAR, non-profits such as the United Way, computer companies, soft drink companies, and music companies. Remember, Peter Pan peanut butter is great when pre-mixed (co-branded) with Welch's grape jelly.

CASES

Case One: Stimulus Generalization, Consumer Confusion and the Law

Question 1—Answer:

Arguments that support Ringling Bros. include the duration with which it has used its mark, the fact that it has spent enormous resources to support its mark, and the fact that the mark has succeeded in meaning something to most consumers. Its mark is fairly distinct and the competing mark is identical, but for a *single* letter. Strong arguments also support Utah, however. No reasonably prudent consumer would confuse a ski industry in the Wasatch mountain range with Barnum & Bailey's Circus. The two are simply not competing services, though both are generally classified as entertainment. No consumer is likely to be "tricked" into traveling to Utah to see a circus by hearing or seeing "The Greatest Snow on Earth." Utah's use of this slogan, though quite similar, is unlikely to harm Ringling's business, (i.e., it will not lose attendees to its circuses because Utah is advertising its ski industry with a similar phrase). Moreover, Utah's use of "The Greatest Snow on Earth" will not detract from the association of Ringling's mark with circuses and thus would not be expected to "dilute" its mark. Ringling lost the case and each party uses its mark today with no apparent consumer confusion.

Question 2—Answer:

Fundamentally, trademark laws enforce equity or fairness. It is unfair for one company to exploit the good will that another company has developed perhaps over decades of marketing the same product and after billions of dollars invested in distinguishing a particular product or service and maintaining consistency of quality. Consumers would not benefit from the absence of trademark laws because they would be unable to discern the "genuine" article from a counterfeit copy. Counterfeit goods and services would flood the market, as they now do in countries with weakly enforced trademark laws or none at all. Although some prices might fall, perceived quality would suffer greatly. Trademark laws thus protect both consumers and trademark owners. Generally, trademark owners seek to enforce trademark laws against infringers. Government entities, however, also bring actions against trademark infringers on behalf of the public and enforce criminal laws against the most blatant trademark infringement (counterfeiting).

Case Two: The Pitfalls of Reinforcement of Customer Behavior

Question 1—Answer:

The drawback to creating a reward system based entirely on measured past behavior is that such a system tends to follow a totally predictable and continuous schedule of reinforcement. Thus, in the long run, it may not be effective in generating more business from the customers who are being rewarded. In addition, it may generate customers "demanding" that they be rewarded if, for any chance, the reward is lessened or discontinued. So, in effect, constantly rewarded customers may constitute a continued expense for the company that is not matched by additional business from these customers. Such a situation defeats the very purpose of the reward system.

Question 2—Answer:

Companies should strive to develop more creative reward systems than those discussed in the case. For example, companies may develop "reward tiers" that are based on qualitative rather than quantitative data.

Too many companies focus primarily on the very profitable customers. It may be wise to create lesser rewards for "middle of the road" customers with the objective of increasing their loyalty to the company and, in time, moving them to the "top reward tier" category. To illustrate, a customer who, overall, spends less at a hotel-chain than is required to move to a certain "tier" but who uses the service during off-peak times can be moved to the upper "tier." Companies should develop more insightful ways to measure usage behavior and use it to create reward systems.

CHAPTER 8

Consumer Attitude Formation And Change

LEARNING OBJECTIVES

After studying this chapter students should be able to:
1. Describe attitude in terms of its four elements.
2. Discuss the structural models of attitude: tricomponent, multi-attribute, trying-to-consume, and attitude-toward-the-ad.
3. Describe the tricomponents of the tricomponent attitude model.
4. Compare the tricomponent attitude model and the multi-attribute attitude models.
5. Describe how attitudes are formed.
6. Describe how attitudes are learned.
7. Identify the sources of influence on attitude formation.
8. Outline and explain the five strategies for changing consumer attitudes.
9. Identify the elaboration Likelihood model (ELM).
10. Describe how behavior can precede or follow attitude formation from the perspective of cognitive dissonance theory, attribution theory, and self-perception theory.
11. Discuss how we test our attributions.

SUMMARY

An *attitude* is a learned predisposition to behave in a consistently favorable or unfavorable way with respect to a given object (e.g., a product category, a brand, a service, an advertisement, a Web site, or a retail establishment). Each property of this definition is critical to understanding why and how attitudes are relevant in consumer behavior and marketing.

Of considerable importance in understanding the role of attitudes in consumer behavior is an appreciation of the structure and composition of an attitude. Four broad categories of attitude models have received attention: the tricomponent attitude model, multi-attribute attitude models, trying-to-consume attitude model, and attitude-toward-the-ad model.

The tricomponent model of attitudes consists of three parts: a cognitive component, an affective component, and a conative component. The cognitive component captures a consumer's knowledge and perceptions (i.e., beliefs) about products and services. The affective component focuses on a consumer's emotions or feelings with respect to a particular product or service. Evaluative in nature, the affective component determines an individual's overall assessment of the attitude object in terms of some kind of favorableness rating. The conative component is concerned with the likelihood that a consumer will act in a specific fashion with respect to the attitude object. In marketing and consumer behavior, the conative component is frequently treated as an expression of the consumer's intention to buy.

164

Multiattribute attitude models (i.e., attitude-toward-object, attitude-toward-behavior, and the theory-of-reasoned-action models) have received much attention from consumer researchers. As a group, these models examine consumer beliefs about specific-product attributes (e.g., product or brand features or benefits). Recently, there has been an effort to better accommodate consumers' goals as expressed by their "trying to consume" (i.e., a goal the consumer is trying or planning to accomplish). The theory of trying is designed to account for the many cases in which the action or outcome is not certain. The attitude-toward-the-ad models examine the influence of advertisements on the consumer's attitudes toward the brand.

How consumer attitudes are formed and how they are changed are two closely related issues of considerable concern to marketing practitioners. When it comes to attitude formation, it is useful to remember that attitudes are learned and that different learning theories provide unique insights as to how attitudes initially may be formed. Attitude formation is facilitated by direct personal experience and influenced by the ideas and experiences of friends and family members and exposure to mass media. In addition, it is likely that an individual's personality plays a major role in attitude formation.

These same factors also have an impact on attitude change; that is, attitude changes are learned, and they are influenced by personal experiences and the information gained from various personal and impersonal sources. The consumer's own personality affects both the acceptance and the speed with which attitudes are likely to be altered.

Strategies of attitude change can be classified into six distinct categories: (1) changing the basic motivational function, (2) associating the attitude object with a specific group or event, (3) relating the attitude object to conflicting attitudes, (4) altering components of the multiattribute model, (5) changing beliefs about competitors' brands, and (6) the elaboration likelihood model. Each of these strategies provides the marketer with alternative ways of changing consumers' existing attitudes.

Most discussions of attitude formation and attitude change stress the traditional view that consumers develop attitudes before they act. This may not always, however, or even usually be true. Both cognitive dissonance theory and attribution theory provide alternative explanations of attitude formation and change that suggest that behavior might precede attitudes. Cognitive dissonance theory suggests that the conflicting thoughts, or dissonant information, that follow a purchase decision might propel consumers to change their attitudes to make them consonant with their actions. Attribution theory focuses on how people assign causality to events and how they form or alter attitudes as an outcome of assessing their own behavior, or the behavior of other people or things.

CHAPTER OUTLINE

INTRODUCTION

1. Consumers have a vast number of attitudes toward products, services, advertisements, direct mail, the Internet, and retail stores.
   a) Consequently, within consumer behavior there is a growing appreciation of the strategy value of attitude research.
2. At the heart of consumer behavior, *attitude research* has been used to study a wide range of strategic marketing questions; to determine whether consumers will accept a proposed new product idea, to gauge why a firm's target audience has not reacted more favorably to its new promotional theme, or to learn how target customers are likely to react to a proposed change in the firm's packaging design.

WHAT ARE ATTITUDES?

1. Researchers tend to assess attitudes by asking questions or making inferences from behavior.
2. An **attitude** is a learned predisposition to behave in a consistently favorable or unfavorable way with respect to a given object.

> *****Use Key Term** attitude *Here; Use Learning Objective #1 Here; Use Discussion Question #2 Here*****

The Attitude "Object"

1. *Object* refers to such things as: product, product category, brand, service, possessions, product use, advertisement price, or retailer.
   a) In attitude research we tend to be *object-specific*.

> *****Use Learning Objective #1 Here*****

Attitudes Are a Learned Predisposition

1. Attitudes are *learned*.
   a) They are formed as a result of direct experience with the product, information acquired from others, and exposure to mass media.
   b) Although attitudes may result in behaviors, they are, however, not synonymous with behavior.
2. As *learned predispositions*, attitudes have a motivational quality.

> *****Use Learning Objective #1 Here; Use Discussion Question #2 Here*****

Attitudes Have Consistency

1. Attitudes are relatively consistent with the behavior they reflect.
    a) Attitudes are not necessarily permanent; they do change.
    b) We should consider situational influences on consumer attitudes and behavior.

*****Use Learning Objective #1 Here*****

Attitudes Occur Within a Situation

1. Consumer attitudes occur within, and are affected by, the *situation*.
    a) By situation we mean events or circumstances that, at a particular time, influence the relationship between an attitude and a behavior.
2. Individuals can have a variety of attitudes toward a particular behavior, each tied to a specific situation.
    a) This can cause consumers to behave in ways seemingly inconsistent with their attitudes.
3. It is important when measuring attitudes that we consider the situation in which the behavior takes place, or the relationship between attitudes and behavior could be misinterpreted.

*****Use Learning Objective #1 Here; Use Discussion Question #1 Here; Use Figure 8-1 Here; Use Table 8-1 Here*****

STRUCTURAL MODELS OF ATTITUDES

1. Psychologists have developed a number of models in order to understand consumer attitudes.
    a) Each of these models provides a somewhat different perspective on the number of component parts of an attitude and how those parts are arranged or interrelated.

*****Use Learning Objective #2 Here*****

Tricomponent Attitude Model

1. According to the ***tricomponent attitude model***, attitudes consist of three major components: cognition, affect, and conation.

*****Use Learning Objective #3 Here; Use Figure 8-2*****

The Cognitive Component

1. *Cognitions* are previous knowledge or experiences with or about the object.
   a) This previous knowledge/experience allows the consumer to form perceptions or beliefs about the product.

*****Use Learning Objective #3 Here; Use Figure 8-3; Use Exercise #1 Here*****

The Affective Component

1. The *affective component* of an attitude consists of the consumer's *emotions* or *feelings*.
   a) Researchers frequently treat these emotions and feelings as *evaluative* in nature.
2. Affect-laden experiences manifest themselves as *emotionally charged states* (such as happiness or sadness).
   a) These states may enhance positive or negative experiences for the consumer.
3. Consumer researchers try to measure this element using global evaluative measures.

*****Use Learning Objective #3 Here; Use Table 8-2 and 8-3 Here; Use Exercise #1 Here*****

The Conative Component

1. *Conation*, the final component of the tricomponent attitude model, is concerned with the *likelihood* or *tendency* that an individual will undertake a specific action or behave in a particular way with regard to the attitude object.
   a) The conative component may include the actual behavior itself.
2. In marketing and consumer research, the conative component is frequently treated as an expression of the consumer's *intention to buy*.
   a) **Intention-to-buy scales** are used to assess the likelihood of a consumer purchasing a product or behaving in a certain way.

*****Use Key Term intention-to-buy scales Here; Use Learning Objective #2, #3, and #4 Here; Use Discussion Question #3 Here; Use Table 8-4 Here*****

Multi-Attribute Attitude Models

1. **Multi-attribute attitude models** examine attitudes in terms of selected product attributes or beliefs.

*****Use Key Term multi-attribute attitude models Here*****

The Attitude-Toward-Object Model

1. According to the ***attitude-toward-object model***, the consumer's attitude toward a product or specific brands of a product is a function of the presence (or absence) and evaluation of certain product-specific beliefs and/or attributes.
2. What consumers will purchase is a function of how much they know, what they feel are the important features for them, and their awareness as to whether particular brands possess (or lack) these valued attributes.

*****Use Key Term** attitude-toward-object model *Here; Use Figure 8-3 Here*****

The Attitude-Toward-Behavior Model

1. The ***attitude-toward-behavior model*** is the individual's attitude toward behaving or acting with respect to an object, rather than the attitude toward the object itself.
2. The appeal of this model is that it seems to correspond somewhat more closely to actual behavior than does the attitude-toward-object model.

*****Use Key Term** attitude-toward-behavior model *Here*****

Theory-of-Reasoned-Action Model

1. The ***theory-of-reasoned-action*** is a comprehensive integration of attitude components into a structure that is designed to lead to both better explanation and better predictions of behavior.
2. Like the basic tricomponent attitude model, the theory-of-reasoned-action model incorporates a *cognitive* component, an *affective* component, and a *conative* component; however, these are arranged in a pattern different from that of the tricomponent model.
3. To understand intention we also need to measure the *subjective norms* that influence an individual's *intention* to act.
   a) A *subjective norm* can be measured directly by assessing a consumer's feelings as to what relevant others (family, friends, roommates, co-workers) would think of the action being contemplated.
   b) Consumer researchers can get behind the subjective norm to the underlying factors that are likely to produce it.
   c) They accomplish this by assessing the normative beliefs that the individual attributes to relevant others, as well as the individual's *motivation to comply* with each of the relevant others.

*****Use Key Term** theory-of-reasoned-action *Here; Use Learning Objective #2 and #4 Here; Use Figure 8-4 Here; Use Exercise #3 Here*****

Theory of Trying-to-Consume

1. The ***theory of trying-to-consume*** is designed to account for the cases where the action or outcome is not certain but reflects the consumer's efforts to consume.
   a) Sometimes *personal impediments* or *environmental impediments* prevent the desired outcome.
2. Researchers have recently extended this inquiry by examining those situations where consumers do not try to consume—that is, *fail to try to consume.*
   a) In this case, consumers appear to fail see or are too ignorant of their options.
      i) Consumers appear to make a conscious effort not to consume.

> *****Use Key Term* theory of trying-to-consume *Here; Use Learning Objective #2 Here; Use Figure 8-5 and 8-6 Here; Use Discussion Question #4 Here*****

Attitude-Toward-the-Ad Models

1. As the ***attitude-toward-the-ad model*** depicts, the consumer forms various feelings (affects) and judgments (cognitions) as the result of exposure to an ad.
2. These feelings and judgments in turn affect the *consumer's attitude toward the ad* and *beliefs about the brand* acquired from exposure to the ad.
3. Finally, the consumer's attitude toward the ad and beliefs about the brand influence his or her attitude toward the brand.
4. It appears that for a novel product (e.g., "contact lenses for pets"), the consumer's attitude toward the ad has a *stronger* impact on brand attitude and purchase intention than for a familiar product (e.g., pet food).
5. This research points up the importance of considering the nature of the attitude object in assessing the potential impact of advertising exposure.
6. Consumer socialization has also shown itself to be an important determinant of a consumer's attitudes toward advertising.

> *****Use Key Term* attitude-toward-the-ad model *Here; Use Learning Objective #2 Here; Use Figure 8-6 Here; Use Exercise #2 and #3 Here*****

ATTITUDE FORMATION

1. How do people, especially young people, form their initial general attitudes toward "things"?
2. How do family members and friends, admired celebrities, mass media advertisements, even cultural memberships, influence the formation of their attitudes concerning consuming or not consuming each of these types of apparel items?
3. Why do some attitudes seem to persist indefinitely, while others change fairly often?
4. The answers to the above are of vital importance to marketers, for without knowing how attitudes are formed, they are unable to understand or to influence consumer attitudes or behavior.

How Attitudes Are Learned

1. When we speak of the formation of an attitude, we refer to the shift from having no attitude toward a given object to having some attitude toward it.
2. Consumers often purchase new products that are associated with a favorably viewed brand name.
   a) Their favorable attitude toward the brand name is frequently the result of repeated satisfaction with other products produced by the same company.
3. In terms of *classical conditioning*, an established brand name is an unconditioned stimulus that through past positive reinforcement resulted in a favorable brand attitude.
   a) A new product, yet to be linked to the established brand, would be the conditioned stimulus.
4. Research suggests that the "fit" between a parent brand (e.g., Oil of Olay) and a brand extension (e.g., Oil of Olay Daily Renewal Moisturizing Body Wash) is a function of two factors:
   a) The similarity between the pre-existing product categories already associated with the parent brand and the new extension.
   b) The "fit" or match between the images of the parent brand and the new extension.
5. Sometimes attitudes *follow* the purchase and consumption of a product.
6. In situations in which consumers seek to solve a problem or satisfy a need, they are likely to form attitudes (either positive or negative) about products on the basis of information exposure and their own cognition (knowledge and beliefs).
7. In general, the more information consumers have about a product or service, the more likely they are to form attitudes about it, either positive or negative.
8. Consumers are not always ready or willing to process product-related information.
9. Consumers often use only a limited amount of the information available to them.
10. Research suggests that only two or three important beliefs about a product dominate in the formation of attitudes and that less important beliefs provide little additional input.

*****Use Learning Objective #6 Here; Use Figure 8-7 Here*****

Sources of Influence on Attitude Formation

1. The formation of consumer attitudes is strongly influenced by *personal experience*, the *influence* of family and friends, *direct marketing*, and *mass media*.
2. The primary means by which attitudes toward goods and services are formed is through the consumer's direct experience in trying and evaluating them.
3. As we come in contact with others, especially family, close friends, and admired individuals (e.g., a respected teacher), we form attitudes that influence our lives.
   a) The family is an extremely important source of influence on the formation of attitudes.
4. Marketers are increasingly using highly focused direct marketing programs to target small consumer niches with products and services that fit their interests and lifestyles.
   a) Niche marketing is sometimes called *micromarketing*.

5. Direct marketing efforts have an excellent chance of favorably influencing target consumers' attitudes, because the products and services offered, and the promotional messages conveyed, are very carefully designed to address the individual segment's needs and concerns and, thus, are able to achieve a higher "hit rate" than mass marketing.

6. Mass media communications provide an important source of information that influences the formation of consumer attitudes.

*****Use Learning Objective #7 Here; Use Figure 8-8 Here; Use Exercise #2 Here*****

Personality Factors

1. Individuals with a high *need for cognition* (information) are likely to form positive attitudes in response to ads that are rich in product-related information.

2. Consumers who are relatively low in *need for cognition* (information) are more likely to form positive attitudes to ads that feature attractive models or well-known celebrities.

*****Use Exercise #3 Here*****

STRATEGIES OF ATTITUDE CHANGE

1. Attitude changes are *learned*; they are influenced by *personal experience* and *other sources of information*, and *personality* affects both the receptivity and the speed with which attitudes are likely to be altered.

2. Altering attitudes is a key strategy for marketers, especially when taking aim at market leaders.

3. Marketers have several *attitude-change strategies* from which to choose:
   a) Changing the consumer's basic motivational function.
   b) Associating the product with an admired group or event.
   c) Resolving two conflicting attitudes.
   d) Altering components of the multi-attribute model.
   e) Changing consumer beliefs about competitors' brands.

*****Use Learning Objective #8 Here; Use Discussion Question #5 Here*****

Changing the Basic Motivational Function

1. An effective strategy for changing consumer attitudes toward a product or brand is to make particular needs prominent.

2. One method for doing this is called the ***functional approach*** and can be classified into four functions.

<u>The Utilitarian Function</u>

1. ***Utilitarian function***—changing attitudes by showing that the product serves a useful purpose that the consumers did not previously consider.

<u>The Ego-Defensive Function</u>

1. ***Ego-defensive function***—offers reassurance to the consumer's self-concept.

<u>The Value-Expressive Function</u>

1. ***Value-expressive function***—anticipate and appeal to the consumer's values, lifestyle, and outlook.

<u>The Knowledge Function</u>

1. ***Knowledge function***—individuals generally have a strong need to know and understand the people and things with whom they come in contact.
   a) Most product and brand positioning are attempts to satisfy the consumer's need to know and to improve the consumer's attitudes toward the brand by emphasizing its advantages over competitive brands.

<u>Combining Several Functions</u>

1. Combining Several Functions—involves using more than one of the above because different consumers may like a product for different reasons.

*****Use Key Terms* functional approach, utilitarian function, ego-defensive function, value-expressive function, and knowledge function *Here; Use Learning Objective #8 Here; Use Discussion Question #5 Here; Use Exercise #4 Here; Use Figure 8-9, 8-10, 8-11, and 8-12 Here*****

Associating the Product with a Special Group, Event, or Cause

1. It is possible to alter attitudes toward products by pointing out their relationships to particular social groups, events, or causes.

*****Use Learning Objective #8 Here*****

Resolving Two Conflicting Attitudes

1. If consumers can be made to see that their attitude toward a brand is in conflict with another attitude, they may be induced to change their evaluation of the brand.

*****Use Learning Objective #8 Here; Use Figure 8-13 Here*****

Altering Components of the Multi-Attribute Model

1. Multi-attribute models provide marketers with insights as to how to bring about attitude change.

Changing the Relative Evaluation of Attributes

1. The market for many product categories is structured so that different consumer segments are attracted to brands that offer different features or beliefs.
2. In these market situations, marketers have an opportunity to persuade consumer's to "crossover," to shift their favorable attitude toward another version of the product. It serves to upgrade consumer beliefs about one product although downgrading another.

*****Use Discussion Objective #5 Here*****

Changing Brand Beliefs

1. This is the most common form of advertising appeal. .
2. Advertisers constantly remind us that their product has "more," or is "better," or "best" in terms of some important product attribute.
3. Within the context of brand beliefs, there are forces working to stop or slow down attitude change.
   a) Therefore, information suggesting a change in attitude needs to be compelling and repeated enough to overcome the natural resistance to letting go of established attitudes.

*****Use Discussion Question #5 and #7 Here; Use Figure 8-14 Here*****

Adding an Attribute

1. This cognitive strategy pivots on adding a previously ignored attribute, or *adding an attribute* that reflects an actual product or technological innovation.

*****Use Discussion Question #5 Here; Use Figure 8-15 Here*****

Changing the Overall Brand Rating

1. Another cognitive-oriented strategy is altering consumers' *overall assessment of the brand* by using global statements (making claims that set the product above all competitors).

*****Use Discussion Question #7 Here; Use Learning Objective #8 Here*****

Changing Beliefs About Competitors' Brands

1. This strategy involves changing consumer beliefs about *attributes of competitive brands*.
   a) One tool is comparative advertising.
   b) But comparative advertising can boomerang by giving visibility to competing brands.

*****Use Discussion Question #5 and #7 Here; Use Learning Objective #8 Here; Use Figure 8-16 Here*****

Elaboration Likelihood Model (ELM)

1. The *elaboration likelihood model (ELM)* involves a more global view that two different persuasive routes change attitudes.
   a) The *central route* is particularly relevant to attitude change when a consumer's motivation or ability to assess the attitude object is high; that is, attitude change occurs because the consumer actively seeks out information relevant to the attitude object itself.
      i) When consumers are willing to exert the effort to comprehend, learn, or evaluate the available information about the attitude object, learning and attitude change occur via the central route.
   b) In contrast, when a consumer's motivation or assessment skills are low (e.g., low-involvement), learning and attitude change tend to occur via the *peripheral route* without the consumer focusing on information relevant to the attitude object itself.
      i) In such cases, attitude change often is an outcome of secondary inducements (e.g., cents-off coupons, free samples, beautiful background scenery, great package, or the encouragement of a celebrity endorsement).
2. Current research indicates that even in low-involvement conditions (e.g., like exposure to most advertising), where both central and secondary inducements are initially equal in their ability to evoke similar attitudes, it is the central inducement that has the greatest "staying power"—that is over time it is more persistent.

*****Use Key Term elaboration likelihood model (ELM) Here; Use Discussion Question #6 Here; Use Learning Objective #9 Here; Use Figure 8-16 Here*****

BEHAVIOR CAN PRECEDE OR FOLLOW ATTITUDE FORMATION

Cognitive Dissonance Theory

1. According to *cognitive dissonance theory*, discomfort or dissonance occurs when a consumer holds confusing thoughts about a belief or an attitude object (either before or after the purchase).
2. *Postpurchase dissonance* occurs after the purchase.

175

a) The consumer is not happy with the purchase—so they adjust their attitudes to conform to their behavior.
b) Postpurchase dissonance is quite normal.
c) Attitude change is frequently an outcome of an action or behavior.
d) Dissonance propels consumers to reduce the unpleasant feelings created by the rival thoughts.

3. Tactics that consumers can use to reduce dissonance include reduction:
a) By rationalizing the decision as being wise.
b) By seeking out advertisements that support the original reason for choosing the product.
c) By trying to "sell" friends on the positive features of the brand.
d) By looking to known satisfied owners for reassurance.

4. Marketers can help reduce postpurchase uncertainty by aiming specific messages at reinforcing consumer decisions.

5. Beyond these dissonance-reducing tactics, marketers increasingly are developing affinity or relationship programs designed to reward good customers and to build customer loyalty and satisfaction.

*****Use Key Term cognitive dissonance theory Here; Use Discussion Question #9 Here; Use Learning Objective #10 Here; Use Figure 8-16 Here; Use Exercise #5 Here*****

Attribution Theory

1. *Attribution theory* attempts to explain how people assign causality to events on the basis of either their own behavior or the behavior of others.

*****Use Key Term attribution theory Here; Use Learning Objective #10 Here*****

Self-Perception Theory

6. *Self-perception theory* addresses individuals' inferences or judgments as to the cause of their own behavior.

7. In terms of consumer behavior, self-perception theory suggests that attitudes develop as consumers *look at and make judgments about their own behavior.*

8. *Internal and external attributions*—attitudes develop as consumers look at and make judgments about their own behavior. These judgments can be divided into internal, external, and defensive attributions.
a) *Internal attribution*—giving yourself credit for the outcomes—your ability, your skill, or your effort.
b) *External attribution*—the purchase was good because of factors beyond your control—luck, etc.

9. *Defensive attribution*—consumers are likely to accept credit personally for success, and to credit failure to others or to outside events.

a) For this reason, it is crucial that marketers offer uniformly high-quality products that allow consumers to perceive themselves as the reason for the success; that is, "I am competent."

> *****Use Key Terms **self-perception theory, internal and external attributions, and defensive attribution** *Here; Use Discussion Question #6 and #8 Here*****

---

10. *Foot-in-the-door technique*—the foot-in-the-door technique, is based on the premise that individuals look at their prior behavior (e.g., compliance with a minor request) and conclude that they are the kind of person who says "Yes" to such requests (i.e., an internal attribution).
    a) Such self-attribution serves to increase the likelihood that they will agree to a similar, more substantial request.
    b) Research into the foot-in-the-door technique has concentrated on understanding how specific incentives (e.g., cents-off coupons of varying amounts) ultimately influence consumer attitudes and subsequent purchase behavior.
    c) It appears that different size incentives create different degrees of internal attribution that, in turn, lead to different amounts of attitude change.
    d) It is not the biggest incentive that is most likely to lead to positive attitude change.
    e) What seems most effective is a moderate incentive, one that is just big enough to stimulate initial purchase of the brand but still small enough to encourage consumers to internalize their positive usage experience and allow a positive attitude change to occur.

> *****Use Key Term **foot-in-the-door technique** *Here; Use Learning Objective #10 Here*****

Attributions Toward Others

1. Every time a person asks "Why?" about a statement or action of another or "others"—a family member, a friend, a salesperson, a direct marketer, a shipping company— *attribution toward others* theory is relevant.

Attributions Toward Things

1. It is in the area of judging product performance that consumers are most likely to form product *attributions toward things*.
2. Specifically, they want to find out why a product meets or does not meet their expectations.
    a) In this regard, they could attribute the product's successful performance (or failure) to the product itself, to themselves, to other people or situations, or to some combination of these factors.

How We Test Our Attributions

1. Individuals acquire conviction about particular observations by acting like "naive scientists," that is, by collecting additional information in an attempt to confirm (or disconfirm) prior inferences.
2. In collecting such information, consumers often use the following:
   a) Distinctiveness—The consumer attributes an action to a particular product or person if the action occurs when the product (or person) is present and does not occur in its absence.
   b) Consistency over time—Whenever the person or product is present, the consumer's inference or reaction must be the same, or nearly so.
   c) Consistency over modality—The inference or reaction must be the same, even when the situation in which it occurs varies.
   d) Consensus—The action is perceived in the same way by other consumers.

> *****Use Key Terms** attributions toward others and attributions toward things
> *Here; Use Learning Objective #11 Here*****

DISCUSSION QUESTIONS

1. Explain how situational factors are likely to influence the degree of consistency between attitudes and behavior.

Although attitudes may be relatively consistent with behavior, they are influenced by situational factors, such as time, place, and social environment. A person's attitudes may lead to one kind of behavior in one situation and a different behavior in a different time and place. For example, a person may have a strong preference for one brand but purchase a brand that is on "special" because of having to economize.

2. Because attitudes are learned predispositions to respond, why don't marketers and consumer researchers just measure purchase behavior and forget attitudes?

Knowledge of attitudes is valuable because attitudes can be used to predict behavior before it occurs. In addition, attitudes have several components, such as perceptions, evaluations, and intentions. By knowing the strength of these components, we can plan marketing strategies designed to affect these components. Therefore, measurement of behavior does not provide guidance for strategy development in the way that attitude measurement does.

3. Explain a person's attitude toward visiting Disney World in terms of the tricomponent attitude model.

The first component of the tricomponent attitude model consists of a person's *cognitions*; that is, the knowledge and perceptions that are acquired by a combination of direct experience with the attitude-object and related information. In the case of

Disney World, this component reflects the person's knowledge of the various theme parks, hotels, prices, and activities, as well as his or her beliefs about Disney. A consumer's emotions or feelings about a particular product or brand constitute the *affective* component of an attitude. A person's positive feelings about Disney ads might lead him/her to conclude that visiting Disney World will be a positive, pleasant, and good experience. *Conation*, the final component of the tricomponent attitude model, is concerned with the likelihood or tendency that an individual will undertake a specific action or behave in a particular way with regard to the attitude-object. In the context of visiting Disney World, this component reflects a person's intention to visit the resort in the foreseeable future.

4. **How can the marketer of a "nicotine patch" (a device which assists individuals to quit smoking) use the theory of trying to segment its market? Using this theory, identify two segments that the marketer should target and propose product positioning approaches to be directed at each of the two segments.**

The *theory of trying* is designed to account for the many cases (including consumption situations) where the action or outcome is not certain, but instead reflects the consumer's attempts to consume. According to this theory, a person who attempts to quit smoking combines personal impediments (i.e., liking the act of smoking) and environmental impediments (i.e., situations where others smoke) that might prevent the desired action or outcome from occurring. The model also proposes that the frequency of past trying, that is, the consumer's prior experience with trying to quit smoking, impacts on both intention-to-try and on actually trying the nicotine patch. One segment for the nicotine patch are individuals who would adopt the product in order to overcome personal and/or environmental impediments to quitting smoking. To these consumers, the product should be positioned as a mechanism to overcome these impediments. Another segment are smokers who have tried to quit and failed. To them, the product should be positioned as a mechanism that is likely to succeed where many other methods had failed.

5. **Explain how the product manager of a breakfast cereal might change consumer attitudes toward the company's brand by (a) changing beliefs about the brand, (b) changing beliefs about competing brands, (c) changing the relative evaluation of attributes, and (d) adding an attribute.**

(a) *Changing brand beliefs* is the most common advertising appeal. If this approach is used, the cereal ads should tell consumers that the product has more vitamins and fiber and/or less sugar than competing brands. (b) The use of *comparative advertising* illustrating the brand's superiority over other brands, along key product attributes, will effectively convey this message to consumers. (c) The marketer may also stress the importance of fiber in one's diet (i.e., change the *relative evaluation of an attribute*) and, simultaneously, stress the cereal brand's high fiber content, thus appealing to consumers whose primary concerns are health and nutrition. (d) Also, the marketer can *add an attribute* by stressing the previously ignored fiber content and by putting more fiber (or even creating a new "extra fiber" version) in the cereal.

6. **The Department of Transportation of a large city is planning an advertising campaign that encourages people to switch from private cars to mass transit. Give examples how the department can use the following strategies to change commuters' attitudes: (a) changing the basic motivational function, (b) changing beliefs about public transportation, (c) using self-perception theory, and (d) using cognitive dissonance.**

(a) The *functional approach* will entail changing beliefs regarding mass transit along one or more of the basic motivational functions of attitudes; appealing to the knowledge function by showing how one might get to work faster by using mass transit rather than a private car. (b) According to the *assimilation contrast theory*, the Department of Transportation must be careful to avoid overkill or overselling their case. The users of private cars will assimilate (accept) only moderate changes between the mode of transportation they presently use and the mode they are encouraged to use (i.e., mass transit). If the change suggested by the mass transit ads is too extreme, the contrast will result in the rejection of mass transit as a transportation alternative. (c) The Department of Transportation can show the positive environmental outcomes of using mass transit, and position it as an ecologically sound transportation mode. According to *self-perception theory*, many people are likely to make inferences from the behavior portrayed in the ads (i.e., using mass transit helps the environment) and begin to like the object advertised. Also, many consumers may begin to view using mass transit as a chance to personally contribute toward improving the environment (i.e., internal attribution). (d) According to *cognitive dissonance theory*, the Department of Transportation should first induce behavior because a favorable attitude toward mass transit will follow. Thus, the ads for mass transit should be designed to induce behavior and encourage people to try mass transit by, for example, offering them free rides over a period of time. The department should reinforce this initial experience by providing good, dependable service as well as follow-up contacts (e.g., mail and phone) which include asking first-time riders for comments, thus making them feel important, involved, and comfortable about the experience. Cognitive dissonance theory predicts that an initial, effectively reinforced experience with mass transit will result in a favorable attitude toward this service and continued use of mass transit.

7. **The Saturn Corporation is faced with the problem that many consumers perceive compact and mid-size American cars to be of poorer quality than comparable Japanese cars. Assuming that Saturn produces cars that are of equal or better quality than Japanese cars, how can the company persuade consumers of this fact?**

Saturn may choose to alter one of the components of the *attitude-toward-object model*. If this approach is used, the company's advertisements should be aimed at changing the beliefs that the Japanese cars are superior; *comparative advertising* is likely to be a highly effective strategy. Another approach is to create initial *cognitive imbalance* in the minds of consumers by utilizing a highly credible source (i.e., a celebrity spokesperson) as an endorser for the American product. Such advertising will create conflicting thoughts about the car in the minds of consumers and, in their quest to achieve cognitive consistency. If this is done, they will form more positive attitudes toward Saturn.

8. Should the marketer of a popular computer graphics program prefer consumers to make internal or external attributions? Explain your answer.

Internal and external attribution indicates whether consumers assign the cause for successful or unsuccessful experiences with a product, to themselves, or to the product. For example, if consumers use *external attribution* to explain a good experience with a computer program, they "explain" the success as a result of the software package itself. Likewise, a poor experience would be blamed on the product. Although it seems that marketers would like to see their products given credit for consumers' satisfaction, it is actually a greater benefit if consumers use *internal attributions* to explain a successful experience with a product. If consumers see themselves as skillful users of the computer graphics program rather than the users of an idiot-proof product, their self-image improves with respect to that behavior and they are more likely to repeat it. Consider the benefits—greater enjoyment of the product and greater self-esteem leads to greater product usage and greater engagement in positive word-of-mouth.

9. A college student has just purchased a new personal computer. What factors might cause the student to experience postpurchase dissonance? How might the student try to overcome it? How can the retailer who sold the computer help reduce the student's dissonance? How can the computer's manufacturer help?

Although attitudes may be relatively consistent with behavior, they are influenced by situational factors, such as time, place, and social environment. A person's attitudes may lead to one kind of behavior in one situation and a different behavior in a different time and place. For example, a person may have a strong preference for one brand but purchase a brand that is on "special" because of having to economize. *Postpurchase dissonance* is likely to occur here because a personal computer is an expensive product where many brands and models are available, and many of the brands that were not selected by the student have some unique features. After the purchase, the student may be exposed to ads depicting other brands with more features and more extensive software than the computer he or she selected. In order to reduce postpurchase dissonance, the student might seek out advertisements that support his or her choice (i.e., ads for the brand purchased), talk with satisfied brand owners and users and, maybe even join a club or a users group of that computer brand. The manufacturer should help reduce postpurchase dissonance by using advertising which includes messages reassuring purchasers that they made the "right" choice, offering strong, comprehensive warranties, and providing a toll-free user-information hotline. The retailer can help by backing the manufacturer's warranty with a service contract and by mailing buyer's information about new software packages for the computer when such products become available.

EXERCISES

1. **Find two print ads, one illustrating the use of the affective component and the other illustrating the cognitive component. Discuss each ad in the context of the tricomponent model. In your view, why has each marketer taken the approach it did in each of these ads?**

Instructor's Discussion

This assignment is designed to demonstrate that sometimes marketers try to form an overall favorable evaluation (i.e., appealing to the affective component) without reference to particular attributes or features, although at other times they provide detailed information that is organized around specific product or service benefits (i.e., appealing to the cognitive component).

2. **What sources influenced your attitudes about this course before classes started? Has your initial attitude changed since the course started? If so, how?**

Instructor's Discussion

The sources of influence in attitude formation are: (a) personal experience with the product or service; (b) advertisements for various brands. (c) group influences (e.g., family, friends, word-of-mouth); (d) data from objective sources (e.g., *Consumer Reports*); (e) publicity in the media; and (f) information/advice provided by salespersons.

In the case of a college course, students are likely to cite word-of-mouth and course evaluations by former students (if such scores are available and published) as the primary sources in attitude formation. More interesting discussion will develop when students talk about changes in their initial attitudes toward the course and the reasons for such changes.

3. **Describe a situation in which you acquired an attitude toward a new product through exposure to an advertisement for that product. Describe a situation where you formed an attitude toward a product or brand on the basis of personal influence.**

Instructor's Discussion

Students' answers will vary. Their response regarding advertising influence should include several elements: (a) the advertising medium involved, (b) an indication whether the attitude was positive or negative, (c) whether the advertisement was noticed as a result of passive (e.g., TV) or active (e.g., magazine) learning, or (d) whether the exposure led to actual purchase of the item or to further information search.

The answer regarding attitude formation through personal influence should include: (a) the degree of personal involvement with the purchase, (b) the type of the personal source and its importance to the receiver, (c) the perceived credibility of the personal source (e.g., a friend) versus that of impersonal sources (e.g., ads in the media), (d) whether the attitude was positive or negative, and (e) whether the exposure led to actual purchase of the item or to search for more information about the new product.

4. Find advertisements that illustrate each of the four motivational functions of attitudes. Distinguish between ads that are designed to reinforce an existing attitude and those aimed at changing an attitude.

Instructor's Discussion

The ad for the *utilitarian function* should stress the product's usage-related benefits (e.g., durable shoes). The *ego defensive function* should reinforce the consumer's self-concept and protect it from feelings of doubt (e.g., personal care products which offer the consumer reassurance and the likelihood of approval by others). The *value-expression function* shows how the product is consistent with the person's values and lifestyles (e.g., advertising a fine, expensive fountain pen as an instrument of self expression). An ad using the *knowledge function* should indicate the brand's advantages over competitive brands (e.g., a bar graph showing the comparative levels of saturated fat in several brands of butter).

5. Think back to the time when you were selecting a college. Did you experience dissonance immediately after you made a decision? Why or why not? If you did experience dissonance, how did you resolve it?

Instructor's Discussion

Selecting a college is a personal, extensive, high-involvement decision which often results in postpurchase dissonance. Thus, most students probably experienced dissonance immediately after choosing a college; an interesting class discussion will develop when students compare their dissonance reduction processes.

S.T.A.R. PROJECTS

Ethical Issues in Consumer Behavior

S.T.A.R. Project #1

The Tellus Institute (www.tellus.org) is sponsored by foundations, government agencies, multilateral organizations, non-governmental organizations, and business. The primary mission of this institute is aid our country in navigating the transition toward ways of producing, consuming, and living that bequeath a sustainable world to future generations. Just exactly what does that noble goal mean? It means that business, industry, and other organizations that have influence in our country should adopt policies of environmental stewardship and provide for equitable development of resources and talents. The Tellus Institute conducts a diverse program of research, consulting, and communication to meet these ends.

    a. Visit the Tellus Institute Web site. Write a one-page paper that describes how this organization seeks to influence attitudes and opinions.

    b. What consumer and business ethics issues seem to be most important to this organization?

    c. Do organizations such as Tellus advance the cause of business ethics? Explain.

Instructor's Discussion

The Tellus Institute is an interesting story. After students acquaint themselves with the historical data, discussion about areas of environmental stewardship and the attitudes necessary to move in this direction should be possible. Discussion can also focus on how organizations such as this aid the fostering and advancement of consumer and business ethics. Of particular interest will be the Tellus *Business and Sustainability Group.* Students from diverse backgrounds should find this information interesting and pertinent to the study of attitudes.

S.T.A.R. Project #2

Got Milk? This famous advertising campaign by the Milk Producers organization is betting that you do. With the growing number of drink alternatives (especially for youth), however, milk has had a tough time maintaining market share. Are you supportive of people drinking milk? If so or if not, this says something about your attitude toward this product. Pursue the following exercises to learn more about how attitudes toward milk and milk drinking can be an excellent way to learn about consumer attitudes and attitude formulation (for information on the Got Milk? campaign see [www.gotmilk.com]).

    a. Attitudes have four properties. How could the Got Milk? campaign use these properties to influence attitudes toward the product?

    b. What ethical issues must the Got Milk? campaign be aware of when attempting to influence consumption of milk? Would these issues be different for other drink producers? If so, how?

    c. After examining Table 8-1, how might situations affect attitudes toward drinking milk?

    d. Using the *attitude-toward-the-ad model,* describe how the Got Milk? campaign attempts to influence attitudes. Is the approach ethical? Explain.

Instructor's Discussion

The Got Milk? campaign is an excellent way for students to discuss the pros and cons of milk drinking and the attitudes associated with each. Milk is a product that everyone knows about and has experienced. The exercise also hopes to assist students in understanding the ethical responsibilities of products such as milk. The exercise will also give students the opportunity to utilize Table 8-1 and review the *attitude-toward-the-ad model.* Encourage students to bring Got Milk? ads to class to assist with visualizing the exercise.

Small Group Projects

S.T.A.R. Project #3
The DVD movie format is rapidly replacing the VHS movie format as the format of choice in the United States. Notice the changes with respect to inventory mix the next time you are in your favorite movie rental store. Capitalizing on this trend, Netflix (www.netflix.com) has created a business model wherein the movie-watching consumer can order DVD movies via their computer, receive the movies in the mail (with no shipping charges), and return them through the mail after viewing. Sound simple? Netflix is betting that you will say "yes." With over 13,500 titles (classic to new releases), shipping within 1–3 days, no late fees, no driving, no lines, and no hassles Netflix offers a viable alternative to today's time constrained consumer. Why doesn't everyone use this new form of movie rental service? Have your group investigate this very issue.

    a. Using the tricomponent attitude model shown in Figure 8-2, have your group examine the attitudes that may be affecting the movie rental consumer.

    b. Have part of your group write a position paper supporting the traditional movie rental business model and include suggestions for influencing consumer attitudes in the future. Have another part of your group write a position paper supporting the Netflix business model and include suggestions for influencing consumer attitudes in the future.

    c. As a group, evaluate the two papers and reach consensus on which is the superior approach.

Instructor's Discussion

This exercise gives students the opportunity to work in an area that is a student favorite—movies. The two business models are easy to understand. The attitudes behind usage are not, however. Students can use themselves as test subjects. The three questions in the exercise should provide ample opportunity to explore the issue. The Web site can be brought up in class to enhance discussion.

S.T.A.R. Project #4
Opinions are formed from attitudes and beliefs. Part of the opinion process is the comparison of something. Have your group go to Epinions.com (www.epinions.com) to explore how comparisons are made in a variety of product fields. Divide the group into smaller groups and examine the rankings for the products and services found on the Epinions Web site (your group is free to pick subject evaluation areas). After this is done, relate how attitudes influence such ranking and comparison processes. Which attitude model(s) would be useful in making comparisons and formulating rankings such as those shown on this Web site? How might attitudes (opinions) change once that a viewer has examined the rankings and comparisons? What bias might be present in this evaluation system? Have your group prepare a summary report that summarizes your group's findings.

Epinions.com has a wealth of information. This group exercise is a good one to see how comparison and evaluation processes work and how these processes might impact attitudes. For example, let us say that a student did not know much about DVD players. He or she reads that a particular RCA player is ranked number one by 60 percent of respondents to the Epinions.com site. The student then has a positive attitude toward this player. What might be wrong with this evaluation method? First, how many evaluations were done, under what circumstances, were purchases made, how authentic were the evaluators, etc. Several of the attitude models can be used.

Using the Internet to Study Consumer Behavior

S.T.A.R. Project #5
Some marketing firms work toward forming attitudes in the minds of their consumers. Others work toward changing those attitudes. Strategies for attitude change is an extremely interesting subject, especially, if you consider how many attitudes might need to be changed to persuade a brand loyal consumer to switch brands. A perfect example of this is the ongoing struggle between Campbell's Soup (www.campbellsoup.com) and industry rival Progresso Soup (www.progressosoup.com). Your assignment is to visit both Web sites and make a list of attitude change strategies being employed by both companies. Evaluate the success of each. Which competitor seems to be most adept with respect to change? Comment.

Instructor's Discussion

The rivalry between Campbell's and Progresso is well known. Progresso has labeled Campbell's as watery and consisting of small portions. Campbell's has labeled Progresso as too spicy and too expensive. Both claims are built on fact and fiction. Students should review the section in the text on **Strategies of Attitude Change** before attempting this exercise. The Web sites will provide several examples that match well with these strategies. Who is winning the war? This is not clear, however, Campbell's has developed a new bigger-portion line that mimics the Progresso products.

S.T.A.R. Project #6
One of the multiattribute attitude models described in the chapter is the attitude-toward-object model. To learn more about how to apply this model, undertake the following interactive Web-based exercise. Go to the Nike Web site at www.nike.com and create your own tennis shoe. To do this use the "usa homepage," then "nike iD create," then follow the directions for creating your own tennis shoe (and, yes, if you create it, they will build it). Once you have accomplished this feat, write a short analysis paper that compares attitudes you have formed through this experience (attitude-toward-object) versus attitudes you already had toward Nike and Nike products. Comment on the differences you observe between your attitudes (before and after) toward Nike. Lastly, comment on how allowing consumers to customize products might influence attitudes.

<u>Instructor's Discussion</u>

The interactive Nike project is an excellent way to not only have fun and be creative but to illustrate how attitudes toward objects (especially through identification and potential ownership) can change through involvement. Even those students that do not particularly like Nike or Nike products often have an attitude change after the shoe creation process is complete. Additionally, one can readily observe the ease of navigation and observation associated with the Nike Web site as opposed to a rival like Reebok (www.reebok.com). Does this affect attitudes? Probably so.

CASES

Case One: It's Raining, So I'll Order Soup

Possible answers might include the notion that attitudes are learned, and that part of our relationship with comfort foods may stem from observing family members and friends during our childhood. Like many attitudes, "attitudes toward food items" tend to be *situation-specific*. We may also associate a particular food with a special event in our lives (e.g., "When our team won, Dad always took us to Baskin Robbins for ice cream"). Another line of reasoning might be that the attitude-toward-object-model could be responsible for the belief many consumers have that a way to "reward" oneself on a cold day is to have a cup or bowl of hot soup.

Case Two: Domino's for Pizza – Not Exactly!

Clearly, when students think "chicken" and fast food, they think about KFC and perhaps also the chicken sandwiches offered by Wendy's, McDonald's, or Burger King. It's when they think about pizza that they think about Domino's. By offering Buffalo Chicken Kickers™, however, Domino's is trying to create an association in the consumer's mind between itself and chicken. It then hopes that after purchasing this chicken menu item as a "side" with the order of a pizza, consumers will be willing to accept, down the road, Domino's offering whole chicken breast menu items. More specifically, the "foot-in-the-door" concept implies that consumers would look at their prior behavior—that they purchased Buffalo Chicken Kickers™—and conclude that they are open to purchasing other chicken items from Domino's (i.e., whole chicken breasts).

CHAPTER 9

Communication and Consumer Behavior

LEARNING OBJECTIVES

After studying this chapter students should be able to:
1. Define communication by enumerating the five elements of the communication process.
2. Elaborate the bases of credibility for a communication source.
3. Outline the factors affecting the target audience's reception of a communication.
4. Describe the feedback process in communication.
5. Explain the elements of a persuasive communications strategy.
6. Define and discuss the elements of a message strategy.
7. Discuss involvement theory.
8. Discuss the central elements of message presentation and their implications for marketers.
9. Argue for or against the use of advertising appeals outlined in the text.

CHAPTER SUMMARY

This chapter has described how the consumer receives and is influenced by marketing communications. There are five basic components of communication: the sender, the receiver, the medium, the message, and some form of feedback (the receiver's response). In the communications process, the sender encodes the message using words, pictures, symbols, or spokespersons, and sends it through a selected channel (or medium). The receiver decodes (interprets) the message based on personal characteristics and experiences and responds (or does not respond) based on such factors as selective exposure, selective perception, comprehension, and psychological noise.

There are two types of communications: interpersonal and impersonal (or mass) communications. Interpersonal communications occur on a personal level between two or more people and may be verbal or nonverbal, formal or informal. In mass communications, there is no direct contact between source and receiver. Interpersonal communications take place in person, by telephone, by mail, or by e-mail; mass communications occur through such impersonal media as television, radio, newspapers, and magazines. Feedback is an essential component of all communications because it provides the sender with some notion as to whether and how well the message has been received.

The credibility of the source, a vital element in message persuasiveness, often is based on the source's perceived intentions. Informal sources and neutral or editorial sources are considered to be highly objective and, thus, highly credible. The credibility of a commercial source is more problematic, and usually is based on a composite evaluation of its reputation, expertise, and knowledge, the medium, the retail channel, and the company spokespersons.

Media selection depends on the product, the audience, and the advertising objectives of the campaign. Each medium has advantages and shortcomings that must be weighed in the selection of media for an advertising campaign.

The manner in which a message is presented influences its impact. For example, one-sided messages are more effective in some situations and with some audiences; two-sided messages are more effective with others. High-involvement products (i.e., those with great relevance to a consumer segment) are best advertised through the central route to persuasion, which encourages active cognitive effort. Low-involvement products are best promoted through peripheral cues, such as background scenery, music, or celebrity spokespersons.

Emotional appeals frequently used in advertising include fear, humor, and sexual appeals. When sexual themes are relevant to the product, they can be very effective; when used solely as attention-getters, they rarely achieve brand recall. Audience participation is a very effective communications strategy because it encourages internalization of the advertising message. Future research is needed to identify the many product, audience, and situational variables that mediate the effects of message order and presentation in persuading consumers to buy.

CHAPTER OUTLINE

INTRODUCTION

1. Communication is the unique tool that marketers use to persuade consumers to act in a desired way.
2. Communication takes many forms: it can be *verbal* (either written or spoken), *visual* (an illustration, a picture, a product demonstration, a frown), or a combination of the two.
   a) It can also be symbolic—represented, say, by a high price, premium packaging, or a memorable logo—and convey special meaning that the marketer wants to impart.
3. Communication can evoke emotions that put consumers in a more receptive frame of mind, and it can encourage purchases that help consumers solve problems or avoid negative outcomes.
4. In short, communication is the bridge between marketers and consumers, and between consumers and their sociocultural environments.

COMPONENTS OF COMMUNICATION

1. Most marketers would agree that communication is the *transmission of a message from a sender to a receiver via a medium (or channel) of transmission.*
2. An essential component of communication is *feedback*, which alerts the sender as to whether the intended message was, in fact, received.

*****Use Learning Objective #1 Here; Use Figure 9-1 Here*****

The Sender

1. The sender is the initiator of the communication and can be a formal or informal source.
2. A *formal communications source* might be the organization communicating the message.
3. An *informal communications source* might be a parent or a friend who gives product information or advice.
4. Informal *word-of-mouth communication* tends to be highly persuasive.

> *****Use Key Terms* **formal communications source, informal communications source, and word-of-mouth communication** *Here; Use Learning Objective #1 Here; Use Discussion Question #3 Here*****

The Receiver

1. The receiver is the targeted prospect or a customer.
2. There are also *intermediary* audiences for a message, such as wholesalers, distributors, and retailers who receive trade.
3. There are also *unintended* audiences, which include everyone who is exposed to the message, whether or not they are specifically targeted by the source.

> *****Use Learning Objective #1 Here*****

The Medium

1. The medium is the channel or way the message is communicated.
2. It can be an *impersonal communications channel*, such as a mass medium like a newspaper or television program.
3. It can be an *interpersonal communications channel*—an informal conversation between two friends—or a formal conversation between a salesperson and a customer.
4. Mass media are generally classified as *print* (e.g., newspapers, magazines, billboards), *broadcast* (radio, television), or *electronic* (primarily the Internet).
   a) Most marketers encourage consumers to "visit" their Web site to find out more about the product or service being advertised.
   b) New modes of interactive communication that permit the audiences of mass media to provide direct feedback are beginning to blur the distinction between interpersonal and impersonal communication.
   c) *Direct marketers*, using a type of interactive marketing, use databases to seek individual responses from print, electronic, and *direct mail*.

> *****Use Key Terms* **impersonal and interpersonal communications channel, direct marketers, and direct mail** *Here; Use Learning Objective #1 Here; Use Discussion Question #1 Here*****

The Message

1. The message can be a *verbal* message, spoken or written, and usually can contain more specific product information than a nonverbal message.
2. Or, it can be a *nonverbal* message in the form of symbolic communication.
3. Nonverbal communication takes place in interpersonal channels as well as in impersonal channels.

*****Use Key Terms **verbal and nonverbal communication** Here; Use Learning Objective #1 Here; Use Figure 9-2 Here*****

The Feedback

1. Feedback is an essential component of both interpersonal and impersonal communications.
2. Prompt feedback permits the sender to reinforce, to change, or to modify the message to ensure that it is understood in the intended way.
3. Generally, it is easier to obtain feedback (both verbal and nonverbal) from interpersonal communications than impersonal communications.

*****Use Learning Objective #1 Here; Use Discussion Question #1 Here*****

THE COMMUNICATIONS PROCESS

1. In general, a company's marketing communications are designed to make the consumer aware of the product, induce purchase or commitment, create a positive attitude toward the product, give the product a symbolic meaning, or show how it can solve the consumer's problem better than a competitive product (or service) can.

The Message Initiator (Source)

1. The source (initiator) must encode the message in such a way that its meaning is interpreted by the targeted audience in precisely the intended way.
2. *Encoding* can be done through words, pictures, symbols, spokespersons, and special channels.
3. *Publicity* is usually the result of public relations efforts and tends to be more believable because its commercial origins and intent are not readily apparent.

*****Use Key Terms **encoding and publicity** Here*****

Credibility

1. The *credibility of the source* affects the *decoding* of the message.
2. The perceived honesty and objectivity of the source contributes to his/her credibility.

a) If the source is well respected and highly thought of by the intended audience, the message is much more likely to be believed, and vise-versa.

2. Credibility is built on several factors, foremost of which are the intentions of the source.

   a) If the receiver perceives any type of personal gain for the message sponsor as a result of the proposed action or advice, the message itself becomes suspect.

3. *Credibility of informal sources* is built on the perception that they have nothing to gain from their recommendation.

   a) An *opinion leader* is an example of a credible informal source.

   b) Individuals who experience postpurchase dissonance often try to alleviate their uncertainty by convincing others to make similar purchases.

*****Use Key Terms decoding and opinion leader Here; Use Learning Objective #2 Here; Use Discussion Question #3 Here*****

---

4. *Credibility of formal sources* is built on intention, reputation, expertise, and knowledge.

   a) Such formal sources as neutral rating services or editorial sources have greater credibility than commercial sources.

   b) Consumers judge commercial sources based on their past performance, the kind and quality of service, the quality and image of products offered, and their position in the community.

   c) Firms with well-established reputations generally have an easier time selling their products than do firms with lesser reputations.

   d) Furthermore, a quality image permits a company to experiment more freely in many more areas of marketing than would otherwise be considered prudent, such as self-standing retail outlets, new price levels, and innovative promotional techniques.

   e) *Institutional advertising* is designed to promote a favorable company image rather than to promote specific products.

   f) Many companies sponsor special entertainment and sports events to enhance their image and credibility with their target audiences.

*****Use Key Term institutional advertising Here; Use Learning Objective #2 Here; Use Discussion Question #3 Here*****

---

5. Credibility of spokespersons and endorsers—the spokesperson that gives the product message is often perceived as the source.

   a) Therefore, his/her reputation is extremely important.

6. Key findings of research on spokespersons and endorsers indicate that:

   a) Marketers who use celebrities to give testimonials or endorse products must be sure that the specific wording of the endorsement lies within the recognized competence of the spokesperson.

      i) When consumer comprehension is low, receivers rely on the spokesperson's credibility in forming attitudes toward the product.

      ii) When comprehension (and thus systematic information processing) is high, the expertise of the source has far less impact on a receiver's attitudes in interpersonal communications.

b) The synergy between the endorser and the type of product or service advertised is an important factor.

c) Endorsers who have demographic characteristics that are similar to those of the target audience are viewed as more credible and persuasive than those that do not.

d) The endorser's credibility is not a substitute for corporate credibility.

e) Marketers who use celebrities to give testimonials or endorse products must be sure that the specific wording of the endorsement lies within the recognized competence of the spokesperson.

7. Consumer confidence in a salesperson is created in diverse ways.

8. The reputation of the retailer who sells the product has a major influence on message credibility.

9. Message credibility—the reputation of the retailer who sells the product has a major influence of message credibility.

a) The reputation of the medium that carries the advertisement also enhances the credibility of the advertiser.

b) There is no single answer as to which medium has the most credibility, especially at a time when new forms of media and traditional media in new forms are emerging.

c) The consumer's previous experience with the product or the retailer has a major impact on the credibility of the message.

10. Effects of time on source credibility—the sleeper effect.

a) The persuasive effects of high-credibility sources do not endure over time.

b) Although a high-credibility source is initially more influential than a low-credibility source, research suggests that both positive and negative credibility effects tend to disappear after six weeks or so.

c) This phenomenon has been termed the *sleeper effect*—consumers simply forget the source of the message faster than they forget the message itself.

d) Reintroduction of a similar message by the source, however, serves to jog the audience's memory, and the original effect remanifests itself.

*****Use Key Term sleeper effect Here; Use Learning Objective #2 Here; Use Discussion Question #3 and #4 Here*****

The Target Audience (Receivers)

1. Receivers decode the messages they receive on the basis of their personal experience and personal characteristics.

*****Use Learning Objective #3 Here*****

Personal Characteristics and Comprehension

1. The amount of meaning derived from the message is the result of the message characteristics, the receiver's opportunity and ability to process the message, and the receiver's motivation.

2. One's personal characteristics, demographics, sociocultural memberships, and lifestyle are key determinants of message interpretation.

3. Perception is based on expectations, motivation, and past experience.

<u>Involvement and Congruency</u>

1. A person's level of involvement determines how much attention is paid to the message and how carefully it is decoded.

<u>Mood</u>

1. A consumer's mood (e.g., cheerfulness, unhappiness) affects the way in which an advertisement is perceived, recalled, and acted upon.
2. The consumer's mood often is influenced by the context in which the advertising message appears (e.g., the adjacent TV program or newspaper story) and the content of the ad itself; these in turn affect the consumer's evaluation and recall of the message.

<u>Barriers to Communication</u>

1. Consumers selectively perceive advertising messages.
   a) They tend to ignore advertisements that have no special interest or relevance to them.
   b) TV remote controls offer viewers the ability to "wander" among program offerings with ease (often referred to as grazing).
   c) Some marketers try to overcome *channel surfing* during commercials by *roadblocking*, i.e., playing the same commercial simultaneously on competing channels.
2. The VCR created problems for television advertisers by enabling viewers to fast-forward, or zip through commercials on prerecorded programs.

<u>Psychological Noise</u>

1. Things that impair reception of a message, such as competing advertising messages or distracting thoughts are called ***psychological noise***.
2. The best way for a sender to overcome psychological noise is to:
   a) Repeat exposure to the message.
   b) Use contrast.
   c) Use teasers.
   d) Place ads in specialized media

> *****Use Key Term** psychological noise *Here; Use Learning Objective #3 Here; Use Discussion Question #2 Here*****

Feedback—The Receiver's Response

1. The ultimate test of marketing communications is the receiver's response.
   a) Only through *feedback* can the sender determine if and how well the message has been received.
2. An advantage of interpersonal communication is the ability to obtain immediate feedback.
   a) It permits rapid adjustment of the message.
   b) This adaptability is what makes personal selling so effective.
3. Feedback is also important for *impersonal* or mass communication because of its expense.

a) The organization that initiates the message needs some method for determining whether its mass communication is being received by the intended audience, understood in the intended way, and successful in achieving the intended objectives.
4. Unlike interpersonal communications, mass communications feedback is rarely direct; instead, it is usually inferred.
   a) Receivers buy (or do not buy) the advertised product; they renew (or do not renew) their magazine subscriptions, etc.
5. Another type of feedback that companies seek from mass audiences is the degree of customer satisfaction or dissatisfaction with a product purchase.

*****Use Key Term **feedback** *Here; Use Learning Objective #4 Here; Use Figure 9-3 Here*****

Advertising Effectiveness Research

1. Advertisers often try to gauge the effectiveness of their messages by conducting audience research.
2. When feedback indicates that the audience does not note or miscomprehends the ad, an alert sponsor modifies or revises the message.
3. Mass communications feedback does not have the timeliness of interpersonal feedback.
   a) An important feedback mechanism for food and other packaged goods is based on the Universal Product Code (UPC) that is tied to computerized cash registers.
4. Generally, persuasion effects are measured through exposure, attention, interpretation, and recall.

*****Use Table 9-1 Here*****

DESIGNING PERSUASIVE COMMUNICATIONS

Communications Strategy

1. The sponsor must first establish the primary communications objectives, which might be awareness, promoting sales, encouraging certain practices, etc.
2. For a long time, the cognitive models were used to describe the communications process.
3. Today, other models are gaining popularity.
   a) One example is a model based on the key factors of perception, experience, and memory.

*****Use Table 7-1 (previously presented in Chapter 7) Here; Use Figure 9-4 Here; Use Learning Objective #5 Here*****

Target Audience

1. Selection of the appropriate audience is key.
   a) It is essential that the sponsor segment the audience into groups that are homogeneous in terms of some relevant characteristic.
   b) This enables the marketer to create specific messages for each target group and run them in specific media that are seen or heard by each target group.
2. There is a need for an umbrella message for all audiences from which they spin off specific messages for targeted segments.
3. Many organizations use public relations professionals to help them maintain a positive corporate image.

*****Use Learning Objective #5 Here*****

Media Strategy

1. First, the sponsor should develop a *consumer profile* of the target market.
2. Next, a medium with an appropriate *audience profile* needs to be selected.
3. Before selecting a specific medium, the advertiser needs to select a general media category that will enhance the message.
4. Once marketers have identified the appropriate media category, they can then choose the specific medium (or media) in that category that reaches their intended audiences.

*****Use Key Term consumer profile and audience profile Here; Use Learning Objective #5 Here; Use Table 9-2 Here; Use Discussion Question #5 Here; Use Exercise #2 Here*****

Message Strategies

1. The message is the thought, idea, attitude, image, or other information that the sender wishes to convey to the intended audience.
2. Senders must recognize what they are trying to say and their audiences' characteristics so they can encode the message appropriately.
3. Nonverbal stimuli, such as photographs or illustrations, are commonly used to add meaning or to reinforce message arguments.

*****Use Learning Objective #6 Here; Use Table 9-3 Here; Use Discussion Question #5 Here*****

Involvement Theory

1. Involvement theory suggests that individuals are more likely to devote active cognitive effort to evaluating the pros and cons of a product in a high-involvement purchase situation, and more likely to focus on peripheral message cues in a low-involvement situation.

2. This led to the *Elaboration Likelihood Model (ELM)* that proposes that, for high-involvement products, marketers should follow the **central route to persuasion**; that is, they should present advertisements with strong, well-documented, issue-relevant arguments that encourage cognitive processing.
3. When involvement is low, marketers should follow the **peripheral route to persuasion** by emphasizing noncontent visual or symbolic features material that provide the consumer with pleasant, indirect associations with the product and provoke favorable inferences about its merits.

> *****Use Key Terms* **central route to persuasion and peripheral route to persuasion** *Here;*
> *Use Figure 9-5 Here; Use Learning Objective #7 Here; Use Exercise #4 Here*****

Message Structure and Presentation

1. Some of the decisions that marketers must make in designing the message include the use of *resonance, positive or negative message framing, one-sided or two-sided messages, comparative advertising,* and the *order of presentation.*
2. *Advertising resonance* is defined as wordplay, often used to create a double meaning, used in combination with a relevant picture.
   a) Using insights provided by semiotics, researchers have found that by manipulating the resonance in an ad, they can improve consumer attitudes toward the ad and the brand, and unaided recall of advertising headlines.

> *****Use Key Term* **advertising resonance** *Here; Use Figure 9-6 Here*****

3. Should a marketer stress the benefits to be gained by using a specific product (*positive message framing*), or the benefits to be lost by not using the product (*negative message framing*)?
   a) Research suggests that the appropriate message-framing decision depends on the target audience's level of involvement with the product category.

> *****Use Key Terms* **positive and negative message framing** *Here; Use Exercise #3 Here*****

4. *One-sided messages* tell consumers only the good points (benefits).
   a) This is most effectively used when the target audience has previously used the advertiser's products.
5. *Two-sided messages* tell consumers both good (benefits) and bad (disadvantages) points of the product.
   a) These are most effectively used when the target audience uses a competitor's products.

> *****Use Key Terms* **one-sided and two-sided messages** *Here; Use Exercise #1 and #3 Here; Use Figure 9-7 Here*****

6. *Comparative advertising* claims product superiority over one or more explicitly named or identified competitors.
   a) Comparative advertising is useful in product positioning, target market selection, and brand positioning strategies that stress the differential advantage of the "underdog" product over leading brands.
   b) A downside to comparative ads may be that they assist recall of the competitor's brand at the expense of the advertised brand.
   c) Positively comparative ads were found to elicit higher levels of processing activity (high-involvement), had better recall than noncomparative ads, and were perceived as more relevant.

*****Use Key Term* comparative advertising *Here; Use Discussion Question #6 Here; Use Figure 9-8A, 9-8B, and 9-9 Here*****

7. Order effects—communications researchers have found that the *order* in which a message is presented affects audience receptivity.
   a) On television, the position of a commercial in a commercial pod can be critical.
   b) The commercials shown first are recalled best, those in the middle the least.
   c) There is also evidence to suggest that television commercials that interrupt an exciting or suspenseful part of a program tend to have lower recall than those presented during a less gripping moment.
   d) When just two competing messages are presented, one after the other, the evidence as to which position is more effective is somewhat conflicting.
   e) Magazine publishers recognize the impact of order effects by charging more for ads on the front, back, and inside covers of magazines than for the inside magazine pages, because of their greater visibility and recall.
   f) Order is also important in listing product benefits within an ad.
   g) If audience interest is low, the most important point should be made first to attract attention.
   h) If interest is high, however, it is not necessary to pique curiosity, and so product benefits can be arranged in ascending order, with the most important point mentioned last.
   i) When both favorable information and unfavorable information are to be presented (e.g., in an annual stockholders' report), placing the favorable material first often produces greater tolerance for the unfavorable news.
   j) It also produces greater acceptance and better understanding of the total message.

*****Use Key Term* order *Here*****

8. *Repetition*—is an important factor in learning.
   a) It is not surprising that repetition, or frequency of the ad, affects persuasion, ad recall, brand name recall, and brand preferences.
   b) It also increases the likelihood that the brand will be included in the consumer's *consideration set*.
   c) One study found that multiple message exposures gave consumers more opportunity to internalize product attributes, to develop more or stronger cue associations, more positive attitudes, and increased willingness to resist competitive counterpersuasion efforts.

<u>Advertising Appeals</u>

1. *Factual and emotional appeal* effectiveness varies with the circumstance and the audience.
   a) Reason-why appeals are more effective in persuading educated audiences.
   b) Emotional appeals are more effective in persuading less educated audiences.
2. Fear Appeals—some researchers have found a negative relationship between the intensity of fear appeals and their ability to persuade.
   a) The mention of possible harmful effects of a product category or usage situation causes negative attitudes toward the product.
   b) Some researchers have found a positive relationship between fear and persuasiveness.
   c) When the audience focuses on controlling the danger rather than the fear, there is an acceptance of the message.
   d) There is some indication that the mention of possible harmful effects of using a product category although proclaiming the benefits of the advertised product results in negative attitudes toward the product itself.

*****Use Learning Objective #9 Here*****

3. Humor—a significant portion of ads use humor because marketers believe it increases ad effectiveness.
   a) Humor should be used selectively because there are so many qualifying conditions to its effectiveness.
   b) Audience characteristics have a significant impact.

*****Use Learning Objective #9 Here; Use Table 9-4 Here*****

4. Abrasive advertising—they work because of the sleeper effect as only the brand name and the persuasive message are retained over time.
   a) All of us have at one time or another been repelled by so-called agony commercials, which depict in diagrammatic detail the internal and intestinal effects of heartburn, indigestion, clogged sinus cavities, hammer-induced headaches, and the like.
   b) Nevertheless, pharmaceutical companies often run such commercials with great success because they appeal to a certain segment of the population that suffers from ailments that are not visible, and which therefore elicit little sympathy from family and friends.

*****Use Learning Objective #9 Here*****

5. Sex in advertising—there is more daring sexual imagery, extending far beyond the traditional product categories of fashion and fragrance, into such categories as shampoo, beer, cars, and resorts.

a) A study that examined the effects of sexual advertising appeals on cognitive processing and communication effectiveness found that sexual appeals interfere with message comprehension, particularly when there is substantial information to be processed.

b) It also found that more product-related thinking occurs in response to nonsexual appeals, and that visual sexual elements in the ad are more likely to be processed than the verbal content, drawing cognitive processing away from product or message evaluation.

c) These and other findings support the theory that sexual advertising appeals often detract from the processing of message content.

d) There are strong indications that the type of interest that sex evokes often stops exactly where it started—with sex.

e) Some researchers have concluded that nudity may negatively impact the product message.

f) The advertiser may be giving up persuasiveness to achieve "stopping power."

g) One thread seems to run through all the research findings regarding sex in advertising:

h) The advertiser must be sure that the product, the ad, the target audience, and the use of sexual themes and elements all work together.

*****Use Learning Objective #9 Here; Use Exercise #2 Here; Use Figure 9-11 Here*****

---

6. Audience participation—the provision of feedback changes the communications process from one-way to two-way communication.

a) This is important to senders, because it enables them to determine whether and how well communication has taken place.

b) It also is important to receivers, because it enables them to participate, to be involved, to experience in some way the message itself.

c) Although participation is easily accomplished in interpersonal situations and drives the interactivity of cyber communications, it takes a great deal of ingenuity to achieve in impersonal communications.

*****Use Learning Objective #5 and #9 Here; Use Figure 9-12 Here*****

DISCUSSION QUESTIONS

1. Explain the differences between feedback from interpersonal communications and feedback from impersonal communications. How can the marketer obtain and use each kind of feedback?

Interpersonal communication enables the sender to obtain immediate feedback. In personal selling situations, for example, the salesperson can obtain immediate verbal and nonverbal reactions from the prospect, which enable him or her to modify, repeat, or explain in greater detail the sales message. In *impersonal communication*, feedback is somewhat delayed. Return coupons, requests for more information, sales figures, and brand awareness surveys are all methods of feedback as to the effectiveness of the marketing message. A marketer who plans to use a survey to assess the effectiveness of a communications campaign must take a similar survey prior to the campaign, in order to obtain "benchmark" figures against which to compare the campaign's results. As in interpersonal communications, unfavorable feedback indicates that the communication campaign should be revised.

2. List and discuss the effects of psychological barriers on the communications process. What strategies can a marketer use to overcome psychological noise?

Among the psychological barriers that serve to impede receipt of mass communications are selective exposure and selective attention. Both of these selectivity "filters" are part of a body of knowledge known as consistency or balance theory, which postulates that individuals seek information that is consistent with their needs, interests, and attitudes, and avoid information that is not. Most consumers are bombarded daily with more messages than any one person could possibly comprehend; this clutter of competing commercial messages constitutes psychological noise. To preserve their sanity, individuals subconsciously direct their attention to those messages that are in their realm of interest or experience, and ignore those that are not. In a marketing context, people selectively perceive information about products or services in which they are interested or which relate to their lifestyles, and they ignore information concerning products in which they have no interest. Thus, marketers must effectively position their products by communicating to consumers how these offerings meet their needs better than their competition. Many ads show how particular brands are related to particular lifestyles while trying to establish lasting brand images, which stand out within the advertising clutter and lead to brand loyalty on the part of consumers.

3. List and discuss factors that determine the credibility of formal communications sources of product information. What factors influence the perceived credibility of an informal communications source?

Informal sources such as friends, neighbors, and relatives have a strong influence on receiver's behavior because they are perceived as having nothing to gain from a product transaction they recommend. Among formal sources, neutral rating services or editorial sources have greater credibility than commercial sources because of the likelihood that they are more objective in their product assessments. When the intentions of a source are clearly profit making, then reputation, expertise, and knowledge become important factors in message credibility. The credibility of commercial messages is often based on the composite evaluation of the reputation of the company sending the message, the retail outlet that carries the product, the medium that carries the message, and the company spokesperson (the actor or sales representative who delivers the message).

4. What are the implications of the sleeper effect for the selection of spokespersons and the scheduling of advertising messages?

The persuasive effects of high-credibility sources do not endure over time. Though a high-credibility source is initially more influential than a low-credibility source, research suggests that both positive and negative credibility effects tend to disappear after six weeks or so. This phenomenon has been termed the *sleeper effect*. Consumers simply forget the source of the message filter, then they forget the message itself. Reintroduction of the message by the source, however, serves to jog the audience's memory and the original effect remanifests itself—that is, the high-credibility source remains more persuasive than the low-credibility source. The implication for marketers who use high-credibility spokespersons is that they must rerun the ad or commercial regularly in order to maintain its persuasiveness.

5. Should marketers use more body copy than artwork in print ads? Explain your answer.

The *central and peripheral routes persuasion theory* suggests that individuals are more likely to devote active cognitive effort to evaluating the pros and cons of a product in a high-involvement situation, and more likely to focus on peripheral message cues in a low-involvement situation. Thus, for high-involvement products, marketers should follow the central route to persuasion; that is, they should present advertisements with strong, well-documented, issue-relevant arguments that encourage cognitive processing (i.e., body copy/verbal information). When involvement is low, marketers should follow the peripheral route to persuasion by emphasizing such non-content message elements as artwork, background scenery, music, or celebrity spokespersons. Such highly visual or symbolic cues provide the consumer with pleasant, indirect associations with the product, and provoke favorable inferences about its merits.

6. For what kinds of audiences would you consider using comparative advertising? Why?

Comparative advertising should be used if the audience is critical or unfriendly (e.g., if it uses competitive products), if it is well educated, or if it is likely to hear opposing product claims from competing marketers. A friendly audience (e.g., one which uses the advertiser's products), tends to be favorably predisposed to the marketer's message and screens out opposing arguments from competitors. Therefore, advertising which reinforces brand loyalty, rather than comparative messages, should be aimed at friendly audiences.

EXERCISES

1. Bring two advertisements to class: one illustrating a one-sided message and one a two-sided message. Which of the measures discussed in the chapter would you use to evaluate the effectiveness of each ad? Explain your answers.

Instructor's Discussion

A one-sided (or supportive) message is often used with audiences who are friendly (e.g., who are brand loyal to the product being advertised), who are not highly educated, and who are not likely to hear negative comments about the product. Two-sided (or refutation) messages are often used in advertisements for products that are characterized by intense competition, such as cars, soft drinks, and headache remedies. A two-sided message provides audiences with counter-arguments when they hear competing ads and thus serves to inoculate them against a competing marketer's claims. Two-sided ads tend to be more credible and more appealing to highly educated audiences.

2. **Find one example of each of the following two advertising appeals: fear and sex. One example must be a print ad and the other a TV commercial. Analyze the placement of each advertisement in the medium, in which it appeared according to the media selection criteria, presented in Table 9-2.**

Instructor's Discussion

Students' analysis will vary widely. There should be some gender differences in perceptions. This may be an opportunity to help each gender understand how the other perceives advertising. This exercise is designed to illustrate how marketers utilize the advertising appeals discussed in the text.

3. **Watch one hour of TV on a single channel during prime time and tape the broadcast. Immediately after watching the broadcast, list all the commercials you can recall seeing. For each commercial, identify (a) the message framing approach used and (b) whether the message was one-sided or two-sided. Compare your list with the actual taped broadcast. Explain any discrepancies between your recollections and the actual broadcast on the basis of concepts discussed in this chapter.**

Instructor's Discussion

This exercise is designed to illustrate the affect of message framing and one-sided versus two-sided messages on the recall and persuasive abilities of advertising messages. Have students videotape the hour they watch. Have someone other than the viewer record the commercials, his or her products, content, etc., to measure the level of recall in the viewer.

4. **For three of the commercials you watched in the preceding exercise, identify whether the marketer used the central or peripheral route to persuasion. Explain your answer and speculate on why the marketer chose the approach it used to advertise the product or service.**

Instructor's Discussion

This exercise illustrates the use of involvement theory in message presentation.

S.T.A.R. PROJECTS

Ethical Issues in Consumer Behavior

S.T.A.R. Project #1
One of the most important aspects of consumer communication, whether it is impersonal or interpersonal, is that it be built on an ethical pillar. Company after company in the early twenty-first century faced ethical dilemmas with respect to public communications and disclosures. Some fared well with their dilemmas and some did not. Worldcom, Andersen, Enron, Dynegy, and Bridgestone-Firestone were among those that faced their communication and ethics

problems poorly. To learn more about these classic difficulties visit the Colorado State University E-business Ethics Center Web site at www.e-businessethics.com. Once there observe the several company stories found on the Web site's Corporate Ethics Crisis link. Pick one company and investigate its difficulties with respect to consumer communication difficulties. Report your findings. Comment on what the company in question did right and what they did wrong. How do you feel about what you read?

Instructor's Discussion

The Web site is an excellent resource site for contemporary business ethics issues. The resource links are up-to-date and full of information. Additionally, special features of the Web site include information about codes of conduct, ethics centers, organizational citizenship, government citizenship, a gray matters ethics game, and surveys on ethics.

S.T.A.R. Project #2

The credibility of the message initiator (source) is an important aspect of an effective communication process. The credibility of the source affects the decoding of the message. When the spokesperson for a marketer's message is a celebrity or an endorser, the credibility as well as the acceptability of the message is affected. Obviously, because of the power that a celebrity (or endorser) has to impact acceptance, ethics can be an important factor in these message forms. Using the facts about spokespersons and endorsers contained in the chapter, find one ad that displays what you perceive to be good ethical behavior by a spokesperson or celebrity endorser. Find one ad that displays what you perceive to be poor ethical behavior by a spokesperson or celebrity endorser. Explain your categorization and comment on the ethical behavior involved. In the case of the poor ethical behavior, how could the situation be corrected?

Instructor's Discussion

The chapter presents a very interesting discussion about credibility of a message source and then refines this discussion by explaining the unique role of the spokesperson or endorser. The findings from the body of research in this area are interesting and noteworthy. Students should review this material before undertaking the assignment. Pick a few ad examples to show to the class and have the students that picked the ads explain the rationale for the picks.

Small Group Projects

S.T.A.R. Project #3

Feedback is an important aspect of effective communication. Prompt feedback permits the sender to reinforce, to change, or to modify the message to ensure that it is understood in the intended way. The Internet provides an excellent way to provide almost instantaneous feedback to the communicator. Your group's assignment is to review the process of feedback by undertaking an interesting experiment. A current popular collegiate Web site is Hot or Not (see www.hotornot.com). This Web site has been featured in *People*, *Newsweek*, *Time*, and *USA Today*. The Web site is simple in its makeup. Interested males and females submit a digital picture of themselves to the Web site and visitors to the Web site vote on whether the person is attractive (hot or not). A running counter lets the viewer know how many other people have voted on the featured person and what the overall rating score is. The voting is not scientific but it is fun. Have your group review this process for its feedback value. How could it be improved? What are biases that might be involved? How could the males and females who score low improve their scores using effective communication principles?

Instructor's Discussion

This Web site may not be for everyone, however, most students seem to have fun admiring and poking fun at their peers. Beyond the fun, the Web site does illustrate how that effective communication may be worth more than just a pretty or handsome face. For example, students may observe that the picture itself and the setting of the picture may be more important to achieving a high score than the face that is in the picture. See how many communication principles can be associated with this exercise.

S.T.A.R. Project #4

One the best sources of credibility evaluation with respect to products and services is *Consumer Reports*. This impartial organization rates products and services and reports these findings to the consuming public. The analysis of the products and services under investigation is detailed, often scientific, and lengthy. Many consumers, whether they subscribe to the *Consumer Reports* magazine or not, frequently use the organization's findings in assessing potential purchases. Your group's assignment is to go to the *Consumer Reports* Web page (see www.consumerreports.com). Pick a product or service category and investigate the credibility of the product or service. Write a short report about your findings. Next, go to a store that carries or supplies the product or service. Evaluate the product or service in the store environment the way a consumer normally would (i.e., talk to a sales or service person, observe, read, listen, etc.). Compare the two different approaches to gaining information about the product or service. Write a short evaluation of what you have done and what you have learned.

Instructor's Discussion

This exercise affords the group an opportunity to examine one of the best sources of consumer information—*Consumer Reports*. Additionally, the students are required to use their own observational skills to make comparisons, judgments, and evaluations. This experience will help the students with material found in later chapters of the text and with any assigned term projects.

Using the Internet to Study Consumer Behavior

S.T.A.R. Project #5

Two of the best advertising effectiveness research agencies are A.C. Nielsen (see www.acnielsen.com) and MediaMark (see www.mediamark.com). Each of these organizations has their own approach to analyzing the communication effectiveness of advertising. Go to both of the Web sites, review the material that you find, and write a brief summary of the services provided by the two organizations. Next, pick an area of consumer or advertising research that interests you. See which of the organizations provides the best information to research your chosen subject. Comment on what you found.

These two Web sites provide a wealth of information to the students. If the students are creative and probe the Web site services to their fullest, they will find that a great amount of research information or links to information is available (even for the non-client). These Web sites can be used for future research.

S.T.A.R. Project #6

Are you ready to go shopping but don't want to make the shopping trip? Well, mySimon (see www.mysimon.com) has just the answer for you. Shop from your own computer and avoid the hassles normally associated with the shopping experience. mySimon is what is called a shopping bot. The service has product comparisons, ratings, prices, and sources for all kinds of products and services. Your assignment is tryout mySimon. Pick a product and allow the shopping bot to do the shopping for you. Once the shopping process has been completed, evaluate the experience and compare this experience to the normal shopping trip. Comment on differences, similarities, and results. What did you learn about communication and consumer behavior through this experience?

Instructor's Discussion

There are many shopping bots, however, this service is one of the best. Students should be able to navigate the site with ease. Be sure to ask students to compare this service with the normal shopping trip. If the shopping bot experience receives high marks, ask students if they plan to use the service. If they do not, probe for the reasons. Many students will find that they are creatures of habit and simply do not want to leave their comfort zones. How might a marketer deal with this?

CASES

Case One: The Growing Interactivity of Standard Television

Question 1—Answer:

The feedback to Websites like TWop is much greater in terms of quantity and speed and viewable by anyone, not just the recipients of a conventional fan letter (the producers or "star" of the show). Moreover, postings to TWop evolve into intricate thematic "threads" that allow many different people to build upon one another's comments—much like the dynamics of a focus group. Like traditional television prior to the Internet, a fan letter is a unidirectional, usually one shot-communication without follow up. Internet postings allow users to have a virtual two-way conversation with replies and further replies, all nearly instantaneous. Sites such as TWop provide television producers with the opportunity to monitor their audiences and, should they choose, react to those audiences. Although professional Hollywood screen writers are likely to take the myriad posts of ordinary viewers with a grain of salt, it would seem foolish to ignore them completely. Furthermore, those who post comments about such shows are likely to be those who care most about them. Such a demographic group is not likely to be easily discernable through other communication methods and may hold unique marketing opportunities for future programming.

Question 2—Answer:

The Nielsen rating system and "posting" are similar in that both reflect viewer attention to a specific program and can, to a certain extent, be considered a measure of success (or failure) for a given program or episode. The Nielsen rating system and "posting" are different in that posting reflects a *nonrandomized, self-selected* sample of viewing audience and requires that sample to do something active beyond simply viewing a program (i.e., they must visit a Web site, read a certain amount about a program, and compose a short text message with their input). The Nielsen rating system and "postings" also differ qualitatively in that the Nielsen rating system merely measures the number of viewers who had their televisions tuned to a particular program. Posts do not provide a statistically accurate measure of overall viewer attention, but do provide *content* regarding viewers' opinions beyond simply whether they tuned in or not.

Case Two: Target Audience

Question 1—Answer:

Producers of television and movies do what will make them the most money. If television advertisers are willing to pay much more money for shows that reach the 18–34 year old age group, television producers will accommodate them. When advertisers decide their target audience might not be 18–34 year olds after all, television producers can be expected to adapt quickly to whatever new "target audience" is perceived. The real question is, why do advertisers prefer to reach a younger, less affluent market with generally less disposable income than, say, the 35–65 year old market?

Question 2—Answer:

Much of the "target audience" hype appears to rest on a complex sociological and cultural bias in favor of youth and a fear of aging. To be associated with any older age bracket is seemingly universally feared—remember GM's "this is not your father's Oldsmobile" campaign. GM retired the Oldsmobile brand shortly after that campaign. There is also the theory that older consumers have relatively fewer years of consuming left. Thus, although Cadillac may sell surprisingly well among those over sixty, GM worries about who will be buying their Cadillacs in 10 or 20 years. Such long-range professed concerns are atypical of American businesses, which are almost universally focused on short-term results.

CHAPTER 10

Reference Groups and Family Influences

LEARNING OBJECTIVES

After studying this chapter students should be able to:
1. Define a group.
2. Understand the power of reference groups on consumer behavior.
3. Identify six consumer-relevant groups.
4. List and explain the factors that determine reference group influence.
5. Describe the five types of reference groups.
6. Explain the major forms of reference group appeals.
7. Discuss how the family has changed.
8. Explain the role of the family in the consumer socialization of individuals.
9. List and describe the three major functions of the family.
10. Describe the relationship between family decision-making and consumption-related roles.
11. Contrast the traditional family life cycle and the nontraditional family life cycle.

SUMMARY

Almost all individuals regularly interact with other people who directly or indirectly influence their purchase decisions. Thus, the study of groups and their impact on the individuals is of great importance to marketers concerned with influencing consumer behavior.

Consumer reference groups are groups that serve as frames of reference for individuals in their purchase decisions. Examples of reference groups include (1) friendship groups, (2) shopping groups, (3) work groups, (4) virtual groups or communities, and (5) consumer-action groups. Reference groups that influence general values or behavior are called normative reference groups; those that influence specific attitudes are called comparative reference groups. The concept of consumer reference groups has been broadened to include groups with which consumers have no direct face-to-face contact, such as celebrities, political figures, and social classes.

The credibility, attractiveness, and power of the reference group affect the degree of influence it has. Reference group appeals are used very effectively by some advertisers in promoting their goods and services because they subtly induce the prospective consumer to identify with the pictured user of the product.

The five types of reference group appeals most commonly used in marketing are celebrities, experts, the common man, the executive and employee spokesperson, and the trade spokes-character. Celebrities are used to give testimonials or endorsements as actors or as company spokespersons. Experts may be recognized experts in the product category or actors playing the part of experts (such as an automobile mechanic). The common-man approach is designed to show that individuals who are just like the prospect are satisfied with the advertised product. Increasingly, firms are using their top executives as spokespersons because their appearance in company advertisements seems to imply that someone at the top is watching over the consumer's interest.

For many consumers their family is the primary reference group for many attitudes and behaviors. The family is the prime target market for most products and product categories. As the most basic membership group, *families* are defined as two or more persons related by blood, marriage, or adoption that reside together. There are three types of families: married couples, nuclear families, and extended families. Socialization is a core function of the family. Other functions of the family are the provision of economic and emotional support and the pursuit of a suitable lifestyle for its members.

The members of a family assume specific roles in their everyday functioning; such roles or tasks extend to the realm of consumer purchase decisions. Key consumer-related roles of family members include influencers, gatekeepers, deciders, buyers, preparers, users, maintainers, and disposers. A family's decision-making style often is influenced by its lifestyle, roles, and cultural factors.

The majority of consumer studies classify family consumption decisions as husband-dominated, wife-dominated, joint, or autonomic decisions. The extent and nature of husband-wife influence in family decisions depends, in part, on the specific product or service and selected cultural influences.

Classification of families by stage in the family life cycle (FLC) provides valuable insights into family consumption-related behavior. The traditional FLC begins with bachelorhood, moves on to marriage, then to an expanding family, to a contracting family, and to an end with the death of a spouse. Dynamic sociodemographic changes in society have resulted in many nontraditional stages that a family or nonfamily household might pass through (such as childless couples, couples marrying later in life, single parents, unmarried couples, or single-person households). These nontraditional stages are becoming increasingly important to marketers in terms of specific market niches.

CHAPTER OUTLINE

INTRODUCTION

1. Most individuals interact with other people on a daily basis, especially with members of their own families.
2. The family commonly provides the opportunity for product exposure and trial and imparts consumption values to its members.

WHAT IS A GROUP?

1. A *group* is two or more people who interact to accomplish either individual or mutual goals.
    a) This broad definition covers everything from intimate groups to formal work groups.
    b) Included in this definition, too, is a kind of "one-sided grouping" in which an individual consumer observes the appearance or actions of others who unknowingly serve as consumption-related role models.
2. Sometimes groups are classified by membership status.
    a) A group to which a person either belongs or would qualify for membership is called a *membership group*.
3. There are also groups in which an individual is not likely to receive membership, despite acting like a member by adopting the group's values, attitudes, and behavior—this is considered to be *symbolic groups*.

> *****Use Key Terms* group and symbolic groups *Here; Use Learning Objective #1 Here; Use Discussion Question #1 Here*****

UNDERSTANDING THE POWER OF REFERENCE GROUPS

1. A *reference group* is any person or group that serves as a point of comparison (or reference) for an individual in forming either general or specific values, attitudes, or a specific guide for behavior.
    a) They help us understand the impact of other people on an individual's consumption beliefs, attitudes, and behavior.
    b) It helps marketers choose their methodology to affect desired changes in consumer behavior.
2. From a marketing perspective, *reference groups* are groups that serve as *frames of reference* for individuals in their purchase or consumption decisions.
3. Reference groups that influence general or broadly defined values or behavior are called *normative reference groups*.
4. Reference groups that serve as benchmarks for specific or narrowly defined attitudes or behavior are called *comparative reference groups*.
    a) A comparative reference group might be a neighboring family whose lifestyle appears to be admirable and worthy of imitation.
5. Normative reference groups influence the development of a basic code of behavior.
6. Comparative reference groups influence the expression of specific consumer attitudes and behavior.

> *****Use Key Terms* reference group, normative reference group, and comparative reference group *Here; Use Learning Objective #2 Here; Use Discussion Question #1 Here*****

210

A Broadened Perspective on Reference Groups

1. The meaning of "reference group" has changed over the years.
   a) Originally, reference groups were narrowly defined to include only those groups with which a person interacted on a direct basis.
   b) The concept gradually has broadened to include both direct and indirect individual or group influences.
2. *Indirect reference groups* consist of those individuals or groups with whom a person does not have direct face-to-face contact, such as movie stars, sports heroes, political leaders, TV personalities, or even a well-dressed and interesting looking person on a street corner.
3. References a person might use in evaluating his or her own general or specific attitudes or behavior vary.

*****Use Key Term* indirect reference group *Here; Use Learning Objective #3 Here; Use Discussion Question #1 Here; Use Figure 10-1 Here*****

Factors That Affect Reference Group Influence

1. The degree of influence that a reference group exerts on an individual's behavior usually depends on the nature of the individual and the product and on specific social factors.

*****Use Learning Objective #4 Here; Use Table 10-1 Here*****

Information and Experience

1. An individual who has firsthand experience with a product or service, or can easily obtain full information about it, is less likely to be influenced by the advice or example of others.
   a) A person who has little or no experience with a product or service and does not expect to have access to objective information about it (e.g., a person who believes that relevant advertising may be misleading or deceptive) is more likely to seek out the advice or example of others.

*****Use Learning Objective #4 Here*****

Credibility, Attractiveness, and Power of the Reference Group

1. A reference group that is perceived as credible, attractive, or powerful can induce consumer attitude and behavior change.
2. When primarily concerned with the acceptance or approval of others they like, with whom they identify, or who offer them status or other benefits, consumers are likely to adopt their product, brand, or other behavioral characteristics.
3. When consumers are primarily concerned with the power that a person or group can exert over them, they might choose products or services that conform to the norms of that person or group in order to avoid ridicule or punishment.

4. Unlike other reference groups, however, *power groups* are not as likely to cause attitude change.
   a) Individuals may conform to the behavior of a powerful person or group but are not as likely to experience a change in their own attitudes.
5. Different reference groups may influence the beliefs, attitudes, and behavior of an individual at different points in time or under different circumstances.

*****Use Learning Objective #4 Here*****

Conspicuousness of the Product

1. A *visually conspicuous* product is one that will stand out and be noticed.
2. A *verbally conspicuous product* may be highly interesting, or it may be easily described to others.
3. Products that are especially conspicuous and status revealing (a new automobile, fashion clothing, sleek laptop computer, or home furniture) are most likely to be purchased with an eye to the reactions of relevant others.

*****Use Learning Objective #4 Here*****

Reference Groups and Consumer Conformity

1. Marketers may have divergent goals with regard to **consumer conformity**.
2. The ability of reference groups to change consumer attitudes and behavior by encouraging conformity is subject to the group's ability to:
   a) Inform or make the individual aware of a specific product or brand.
   b) Provide the individual with the opportunity to compare his or her own thinking with the attitudes and behavior of the group.
   c) Influence the individual to adopt attitudes and behavior that are consistent with the norms of the group.
   d) Legitimize the decision to use the same products as the group.
3. A nonconformity appeal is also possible but requires a shift in attitudes or behavior.

*****Use Key Term **consumer conformity** Here; Use Learning Objective #4 Here; Use Discussion Question #1 Here*****

SELECTED CONSUMER-RELATED REFERENCE GROUPS

1. Five specific reference groups are considered because they give us a kind of cross-section of the types of groups that influence consumers' attitudes and behavior. They are:
   a) Friendship groups.
   b) Shopping groups.
   c) Work groups.
   d) Virtual groups or communities.

e) Consumer-action groups.

*****Use Learning Objective #5 Here; Use Exercise #1 Here*****

Friendship Groups

1. Friendship groups are classified as *informal groups* because they are usually unstructured and lack specific authority levels.
2. Seeking and maintaining friendships is a basic drive of most people.
3. The opinions and preferences of friends are an important influence in determining the products or brands a consumer ultimately selects.

*****Use Key Term informal group Here; Use Learning Objective #5 Here; Use Exercise #1 Here*****

Shopping Groups

1. Two or more people who shop together can be called a *shopping group*.
   a) The motivations range from primarily social to reducing risk.
   b) A special form of a shopping group is the in-home shopping party.
      i) Early purchasers tend to create a bandwagon effect.
      ii) Undecided guests often overcome a reluctance to buy when they see their friends make positive purchase decisions.
      iii) Furthermore, some of the guests may feel obliged to buy because they are in the home of the sponsoring host or hostess.

*****Use Key Term shopping group Here; Use Learning Objective #5 Here*****

Work Groups

1. Both the formal work group and the informal friendship/work group have potential for influencing consumer behavior.
2. The *formal work group* consists of individuals who work together as part of a team and, thus, have the opportunity to influence each other's consumption-related attitudes and actions.
3. Members of informal work groups may influence the consumption behavior of other members during coffee or lunch breaks or after-hours meetings.
4. Recognizing that work groups influence consumers' brand choices and that most women now work outside the home, firms are redirecting their sales efforts to the workplace rather than the home.

*****Use Learning Objective #5 Here; Use Exercise #1 Here*****

Virtual Groups or Communities

1. Thanks to computers and the Internet, we are witnessing the beginnings of a new type of group—virtual groups or communities.
2. While fifty years ago the definition of a community stressed the notion of geographic proximity and face-to-face relationships, today's communities are much more broadly defined as sets of "social relations among people."
   a) These communities provide their members with access to an extensive amount of information and/or fellowship and social interaction covering an extremely wide range of topics and issues.
3. The anonymity of the Internet gives its users the freedom to express whatever views they wish, and to also benefit from savoring the views of others.
   a) Because of this anonymity, Internet users can say things to others that they would not say in face-to-face interactions.
4. Communicating over the Internet permits people to explore the boundaries of their personalities.

Brand Communities

1. The next step in the evolution of communities will be brand communities.
2. An illustration would be Jeep owners.

*****Use Learning Objective #5 Here*****

Consumer-Action Groups

1. A *consumer-action group*—has emerged in response to the consumerist movement.
   a) They can be divided into two broad categories.
      i) Those that organize to correct a specific consumer abuse and then disband.
      ii) And, those that organize to address broader, more pervasive, problem areas and operate over an extended or indefinite period of time.
2. The overriding objective of many consumer-action groups is to bring sufficient pressure to bear on selected members of the business community to make them correct perceived consumer abuses.

*****Use Key Term consumer-action group Here; Use Learning Objective #5 Here; Use Exercise #1 Here*****

CELEBRITIES AND OTHER REFERENCE GROUP APPEALS

1. Celebrities and other similar reference group appeals are used very effectively by advertisers to communicate with their markets.
2. Celebrities can be a powerful force in creating interest or actions with regard to purchasing or using selected goods and services.

3. Identification may be based on admiration (e.g., of an athlete), on aspiration (of a celebrity or a way of life), on empathy (with a person or a situation), or on recognition (of a person real or stereotypical, or of a situation).
4. Five major types of reference group appeals in common marketing usage are:
    a) Celebrity appeals.
    b) Expert appeals.
    c) Common man appeals.
    d) Executive and employee appeals.
    e) Trade or spokes-character appeals.
5. These appeals, as well as less frequently employed appeals, are often operationalized in the form of testimonials or endorsements.
    a) In the case of the common man, they may be presented as *slice-of-life commercials*.

> *****Use Learning Objective #6 Here; Use Discussion Question #2 and #3 Here; Use Exercise #2 Here*****

Celebrities

1. Celebrities have a very common type of reference group appeal.
2. They represent an idealization of life that most people imagine that they would love to live.
3. Advertisers spend enormous sums of money to have celebrities promote their products with the expectation that the reading or viewing audience will react positively to the celebrity's association with their products.
4. A firm has the choice of using the celebrity in different ways:
    a) *Testimonials*—if the celebrity has personally used the product.
    b) *Endorsement*—celebrity adds his/her name to products which he/she may be an expert with or not.
    c) *Actor* or *Spokesperson*—the celebrity represents the product over time in a variety of media and in personal appearances.
5. *Celebrity credibility* is a powerful influence.
    a) It is based on the audience's perception of the celebrity's expertise and trustworthiness.
6. Not all companies use celebrities because they aren't convinced they are worth the money.

> *****Use Key Terms testimonial, endorsement, actor, spokesperson, and celebrity credibility Here; Use Learning Objective #6 Here; Use Discussion Question #2 and #3 Here; Use Figure 10-2 Here; Use Table 10-2 and 10-3 Here; Use Exercise #2 Here*****

The Expert

1. A type of reference group appeal used by marketers is the *expert*—a person who, because of his or her occupation, training, or experience, can help the consumer evaluate the product being promoted.

> *****Use Learning Objective #6 Here; Use Figure 10-3 Here*****

The Common Man

1. A reference group appeal of based on testimonials of satisfied customers is called the *common-man approach*.
    a) It demonstrates that someone just like the customer is satisfied with the product or service.
    b) These commercials are of described as being *slice-of-life* commercials.
        i)   Families are often depicted in "real-life" situations in commercials.

*****Use Learning Objective #6 Here; Use Figure 10-4 Here*****

The Executive and Employee Spokesperson

1. This form of advertising has grown more popular over the last twenty years and is the result of the success of highly innovative executive spokespersons.
2. Like the celebrity, the executive spokesperson is admired by the general population because of his/her achievements and the status implicitly conferred on business leaders in the United States.
3. A variation of this is the use of a lower level manager or front-line employee who speaks directly to the consuming public.

*****Use Learning Objective #6 Here*****

Trade or Spokes-Characters

1. The trade or spokes-character and the cartoon character serve as quasi-celebrity endorsers.
2. This person represents the idealized image and dispenses important product information.
3. This category of "person" is largely exclusive to a specific product or product-line.

*****Use Learning Objective #6 Here; Use Figure 10-5 Here*****

Other Reference Group Appeals

1. There are other forms of reference group appeals, such as the respected retailer or the editorial content of special-interest magazines.
2. *Seals of approval* and objective product ratings can also serve as potential endorsements.

*****Use Learning Objective #6 Here*****

THE FAMILY IS A CONCEPT IN FLUX

1. The *family* is a basic concept in society but is not easy to define because family composition and structure, as well as the roles played by family members, are almost always in transition.
2. Traditionally, the *family* is defined as two or more persons related by blood, marriage, or adoption who reside together.
   a) About 68.5 percent of the just over 105.5 million households are families.
3. Although *families* sometimes are referred to as *households*, not all households are families.
4. Within the context of consumer behavior, households and families usually are treated as synonymous.
5. In most Western societies, three types of families dominate: the married couple, the nuclear family, and the extended family. Types include:
   a) The married couple—a husband and wife, is the simplest structure.
   b) The *nuclear family*—a husband and wife and one or more children. This is still commonplace.
   c) The *extended family*—a husband, wife, one or more children, and at least one grandparent. At one time this was the norm, but geographic mobility has reduced its presence.
   d) A fourth form, the *single-parent family*—one parent and at least one child—is growing due to divorce, separation, and out-of-wedlock births.
6. The predominant form of the family is largely influenced by the culture within which the families exist.

*****Use Key Terms family, families, households, nuclear family, extended family, and single-parent family Here; Use Learning Objective #7 Here*****

The Changing U.S. Family

1. Important demographic changes reflect the dynamic nature of the family.
2. There is no doubt that the "typical" or "traditional" family household has changed.
   a) Today, the most common type of household in the United States is "not married, no children" with 32 percent of the total of households.
   b) In 1972, 73 percent of children lived with two parents. That number is only 51 percent in 1998.
3. Attitudes with respect to children and child-rearing have also been changing.

*****Use Learning Objective #7 Here; Use Figure 10-6 Here; Use Table 10-4 Here*****

SOCIALIZATION OF FAMILY MEMBERS

1. The *socialization of family members* is a central family function.
2. In the case of young children, this process includes imparting to children the basic values and modes of behavior consistent with the culture.

a) These generally include moral and religious principles, interpersonal skills, dress and grooming standards, appropriate manners and speech, and the selection of suitable educational and occupational or career goals.

3. Marketers frequently target parents who are looking for assistance in the task of socializing their children.

a) To this end, marketers are sensitive to the fact that the socialization of young children provides an opportunity to establish a foundation on which later experiences continue to build throughout life.

*****Use Key Term socialization of family members Here; Use Learning Objective #8 Here; Use Figure 10-7 Here; Use Table 10-5 Here; Use Exercise #4 Here*****

Consumer Socialization of Children

1. The aspect of childhood socialization that is particularly relevant to the study of consumer behavior is *consumer socialization*, which is defined as the process by which children acquire the skills, knowledge, and attitudes necessary to function as consumers.

2. A variety of studies have focused on how children develop consumption skills.

a) Many preadolescent children acquire their *consumer behavior norms* through observation of their parents and older siblings who function as role models and sources of cues for basic consumption learning.

b) In contrast, adolescents and teenagers are likely to look to their friends for models of acceptable consumption behavior.

3. Shared shopping experiences (i.e., co-shopping when mother and child shop together) also give children the opportunity to acquire in-store shopping skills.

a) Co-shopping is a way of spending time with one's children while at the same time accomplishing a necessary task.

4. Consumer socialization also serves as a tool by which parents influence other aspects of the socialization process.

a) For instance, parents frequently use the promise or reward of material goods as a device to modify or control a child's behavior.

b) According to research, adolescents reported that their parents frequently used the promise of chocolate candy as a means of controlling their behavior (e.g., getting them to complete homework or to clean their rooms).

*****Use Key Term consumer socialization Here; Use Learning Objective #8 Here; Use Figure 10-8 Here; Use Discussion Question #4 Here; Use Exercise #4 Here*****

Adult Consumer Socialization

1. Socialization begins in early childhood and extends throughout a person's entire life.

*****Use Learning Objective #8 Here; Use Exercise #4 Here*****

Intergenerational Socialization

1. It is common for product or brand loyalty or preference to be passed from one generation to another, sometimes up to three or four generations.

*****Use Learning Objective #8 Here; Use Figure 10-9 Here; Use Exercise #4 Here*****

OTHER FUNCTIONS OF THE FAMILY

1. Other basic functions include economic well-being, emotional support, and suitable family lifestyles.

*****Use Learning Objective #9 Here*****

Economic Well-Being

1. Providing financial means to its dependents is unquestionably a basic family function.
2. How the family divides its responsibilities for providing economic well-being has changed considerably during the past twenty-five years.
   a) No longer are the traditional roles of husband as economic provider and wife as homemaker and child-rearer still valid.
   b) It is very common for married women with children in the United States and other industrial countries to be employed outside the home and for their husbands to share household responsibilities.
   c) More than 70 percent of women in United States who are over the age of 18 claim that it is more difficult to be a mother now than it was 20 or 30 years ago.
3. The economic role of children also has changed.
   a) Today, although many teenage children work, they rarely assist the family financially.
   b) Teenagers are expected to pay for their own amusements; others contribute to the costs of their formal education and prepare themselves to be financially independent.

*****Use Learning Objective #9 Here; Use Figure 10-10 Here*****

Emotional Support

1. The provision of emotional nourishment (including love, affection, and intimacy) to its members is an important core function of the contemporary family.
2. The family provides support and encouragement and assists its members in coping with decision making and personal or social problems.
3. If the family cannot provide adequate assistance when it is needed, it may turn to a counselor, psychologist or other helping professional as an alternative.

*****Use Learning Objective #9 Here*****

Suitable Family Lifestyles

1. Another important family function in terms of consumer behavior is the establishment of a suitable *lifestyle* for the family.
2. Upbringing, experience, and the personal and jointly held goals of the spouses determine the importance placed on education or career, on reading, television viewing, the learning of computer skills, the frequency and quality of dining out, and on the selection of other entertainment and recreational activities.
3. Family lifestyle commitments, including the allocation of time is greatly influencing consumption patterns.

*****Use Learning Objective #9 Here; Use Figure 10-11 Here*****

FAMILY DECISION MAKING AND CONSUMPTION-RELATIED ROLES

1. Marketers most frequently examine the attitudes and behavior of the one family member whom they believe to be the major *decision maker*.
2. Sometimes they also examine the attitudes and behavior of the person most likely to be the primary user of the product or service.

*****Use Learning Objective #10 Here*****

Key Family Consumption Roles

1. For a family to function as a cohesive unit, various tasks must be carried out by one or more family members.
2. In a dynamic society, family-related duties are constantly changing.
   a) We can identify eight distinct roles in the *family decision-making process,* however.
   b) The number and identity of the family members who fill these roles vary from family to family and from product to product.
3. The eight roles in the family decision-making process include:
   a) Influencers—family member(s) who provide information to other members about a product or service.
   b) Gatekeepers—family member(s) who control the flow of information about a product or service into the family.
   c) Deciders—family member(s) with the power to determine unilaterally or jointly whether to shop for, purchase, use, consume, or dispose of a specific product or service.
   d) Buyers—family member(s) who make the actual purchase of a particular product or service.
   e) Preparers—family member(s) who transform the product into a form suitable for consumption by other family members.
   f) Users—family member(s) who use or consume a particular product or service.
   g) Maintainers—family member(s) who service or repair the product so that it will provide continued satisfaction.
   h) Disposers—family member(s) who initiate or carry out the disposal or discontinuation of a particular product or service.

*****Use Learning Objective #10 Here; Use Discussion Question #5 Here; Use Exercise #3 Here; Use Table 10-6 and 10-7 Here*****

Dynamics of Husband-Wife Decision Making

1. Marketers are interested in the relative amount of influence that a husband and a wife have when it comes to family consumption choices.
2. Family consumption decisions can be classified as:
   a) *Husband dominated.*
   b) *Wife dominated.*
   c) *Joint*—equal or syncratic.
   d) *Autonomic*—solitary or unilateral.
3. The relative influence of a husband and wife on a particular consumer decision depends in part on the product and service category.
   a) It changes over time.
4. Husband-wife decision-making also appears to be related to cultural influence.
   a) In the People's Republic of China there were substantially fewer "joint" decisions and more "husband-dominated" decisions for many household purchases than among Chinese in the United States.
   b) In another recent cross-cultural study, husband-wife decision-making was studied among three groups: Asian-Indians living in India, Asian-Indians living in the United States, and American nationals.
      i) Results show a decrease in husband-dominated decisions and an increase in wife-dominated decisions, going from Asian-Indians in India, to Asian-Indians in the United States, to American nationals.

*****Use Key Terms husband dominated, wife dominated, joint, and autonomic *Here; Use Learning Objective #10 Here; Use Figure 10-12 Here*****

THE FAMILY LIFE CYCLE

1. Sociologists and consumer researchers have long been attracted to the concept of the *family life cycle (FLC)* as a means of depicting what was once a rather steady and predictable series of stages that most families progressed through.
2. The current decline in the percentage of families that progress through a traditional FLC (to be explored shortly) seems to be caused by a host of societal factors including:
   a) Increasing divorce rate.
   b) The explosive number of out-of-wedlock births.
   c) The 35-year decline in the number of extended families as many young families moved to advance their job and career opportunities.
3. FLC analysis enables marketers to segment families in terms of a series of stages spanning the life course of a family unit.

4. The FLC is a composite variable created by systematically combining such commonly used demographic variables as marital status, size of family, age of family members (focusing on the age of the oldest or youngest child), and employment status of the head of household.
5. The ages of the parents and the relative amount of disposable income usually are inferred from the stage in the family life cycle.
6. The text divides the treatment of the FLC concept into two sections.
    a) The first section considers the traditional FLC schema.
    b) The alternative FLC stages, including increasingly important nontraditional family structures are considered separately.

*****Use Key Term **family life cycle (FLC)** *Here; Use Learning Objective #11 Here*****

Traditional Family Life Cycle

1. *Traditional family life cycle* models have five basic stages.
    a) Stage I—Bachelorhood. Young single adult living apart from parents.
    b) Stage II—Honeymooners. Young married couple.
    c) Stage III—Parenthood. Married couple with at least one child living at home.
    d) Stage IV—Postparenthood. An older married couple with no children living at home.
    e) Stage V—Dissolution. One surviving spouse.

*****Use Key Term **traditional family life cycle** *Here*****

Stage I—Bachelorhood

1. The first FLC stage consists of young single men and women who have established households apart from their parents.
2. Most members of this FLC stage are fully employed, many are college or graduate students who have left their parents' homes.
3. Young single adults are apt to spend their incomes on rent, basic home furnishings, the purchase and maintenance of automobiles, travel and entertainment, and clothing and accessories.
4. It is relatively easy to reach this segment because many special-interest publications target singles.
5. Marriage marks the transition from the bachelorhood stage to the honeymooner stage.

*****Use Figure 10-13 Here*****

Stage II—Honeymooners

1. The honeymoon stage starts immediately after the marriage vows are taken and generally continues until the arrival of the couple's first child.
2. This FLC stage serves as a period of adjustment to married life.

3. These couples have available a combined income that often permits a lifestyle that provides them with the opportunities of more indulgent purchasing of possessions or allows them to save or invest their extra income.
4. Honeymooners have considerable start-up expenses when establishing a new home (major and minor appliances, bedroom and living room furniture, carpeting, drapes, dishes, and a host of utensils and accessory items).
   a) Also important as sources of new product information are the so-called shelter magazines, such as *Better Homes and Gardens* and *Metropolitan Home*.

Stage III—Parenthood

1. When a couple has its first child, the honeymoon is considered over.
2. The parenthood stage (sometimes called the full-nest stage) usually extends over more than a 20-year period.
   a) Because of its long duration, this stage can be divided into shorter phases.
      i) Preschool phase.
      ii) Elementary school phase.
      iii) High school phase.
      iv) College phase.
3. Throughout these parenthood phases, the interrelationships of family members and the structure of the family gradually change and the financial resources of the family change significantly.
4. Many magazines cater to the information and entertainment needs of parents and children.

Stage IV—Postparenthood

1. Postparenthood, when all the children have left home, is traumatic for some parents and liberating for others.
2. This so-called empty-nest stage signifies for many parents almost a "rebirth," a time for doing all the things they could not do while the children were at home and they had to worry about soaring educational expenses.
3. For the mother, it is a time to further her education, to enter or reenter the job market, to seek new interests.
4. For the father, it is a time to indulge in new hobbies.
5. For both, it is the time to travel, to entertain, perhaps to refurnish their home, or to sell it in favor of a new home or condominium.
6. Married couples tend to be most comfortable financially.
7. Many empty nesters retire although they are still in good health.
8. Older consumers tend to use television as an important source of information and entertainment.
   a) They favor programs that provide the opportunity to "keep up with what's happening," especially news and public affairs programs.

*****Use Figure 10-14 Here*****

<u>Stage V—Dissolution</u>

Dissolution of the basic family unit occurs with the death of one spouse. The surviving spouse (usually the wife) often tends to follow a more economical lifestyle. Many surviving spouses seek each other out for companionship; others enter into second (or third and even fourth) marriages.

<u>Marketing and the Traditional FLC</u>

1. It is possible to trace how the FLC concept impacts a single product or service over time.

*****Use Learning Objective #11 Here; Use Discussion Question #6 Here; Use Exercise #5 Here; Use Table 10-8 Here*****

<u>Modifications to the FLC</u>

1. The traditional FLC model has lost some of its ability to represent the current stages a family passes through.
2. The underlying sociodemographic forces that drive this expanded FLC model include divorce and later marriages, with and without the presence of children.
3. Although somewhat greater reality is provided by this modified FLC model, it only recognizes families that started in marriage, ignoring such single-parent households as unwed mothers and single persons who adopt a child.

*****Use Learning Objective #11 Here; Use Figure 10-15 Here*****

<u>Nontraditional FLC Stages</u>

1. Nontraditional FLC stages that are derived from the dynamic sociodemographic forces operating during the past 25 or so years.
2. These nontraditional stages include not only family households but also nonfamily households: those consisting of a single individual and those consisting of two or more unrelated individuals.
3. Nearly 30 percent of all households are currently nonfamily households (i.e., men or women living alone or with another person as an unmarried couple).

*****Use Discussion Question #7 Here; Use Table 10-9 Here*****

<u>Consumption in Nontraditional Families</u>

1. When households undergo status changes they become attractive targets for many marketers.
2. In another sphere, the substantial increase in dual-income households (i.e., working wives and the subset of working mothers) has also tended to muddy the lifestyle assumptions implicit in the traditional FLC.

3. The side-by-side existence of traditional and nontraditional FLC stages is another example of our reoccurring observation that the contemporary marketplace is complex in its diversity, and it is a challenge to segment and serve.

*****Use Learning Objective #11 Here; Use Discussion Question #8 Here; Use Exercise #5 Here*****

DISCUSSION QUESTIONS

1. **As a marketing consultant, you have been asked to evaluate a new promotional campaign for a large retail chain. The campaign strategy is aimed at increasing group shopping. What recommendations would you make?**

The promotion of *group shopping* is important to retailers because some studies showed that individuals shopping with others often tend to buy more than originally planned, whereas individuals shopping alone are likely to deviate little from their original purchase plans. Shopping groups also tend to cover more territory in the store than individual shoppers, and thus have greater exposure to merchandise. Shopping with others also provides an element of social fun, reduces the risk that a purchase decision will be socially unacceptable, and, in instances where none of the members have information about the quality or features of the product under consideration, members may feel more confident with a collective decision. All these elements can be incorporated into a promotional campaign aimed at increasing group shopping.

2. **Many celebrities who are considered to be persuasive role models often appear in TV beer commercials. Does the use of such celebrities in beer advertising constitute an unethical marketing practice? Discuss.**

Before discussing the question, poll students on paper as to how many consume beer and how much—one beer a week, one per day, etc. Keep this data until after the discussion. You may find personal experience with beer and consumption levels have a direct relationship to students' views of the ethical nature of the problem. In many cases, the use of a celebrity does not necessarily increase consumption of the product because the celebrity serves primarily to get attention, create awareness, and enhance advertising recall. Among teenagers, however, using a celebrity may imply social approval and, in the case of beer, a product for which significant potential for excessive use exists, it may encourage them to drink more. Because it is often impossible to ensure that only adults (and not teenagers) are exposed to many beer ads, using a celebrity in beer advertising definitely constitutes an ethical issue, and marketers must carefully evaluate the social implications of using celebrities in beer ads. Promote a lively discussion among students.

3. **You are the marketing vice-president for a large soft drink company. Your company's advertising agency is in the process of negotiating a contract to employ a superstar female singer to promote your product. Discuss the reference group factors that you would raise before the celebrity is hired.**

225

Generally, consumers judge the credibility of a celebrity endorsement in terms of the celebrity's perceived expertise in the specific product category and her general trustworthiness. Before the celebrity is hired, the company and its advertising agency must evaluate her image and behavior off stage, and the impact it is likely to have on the company's name. This is a particularly important issue because a celebrity involved in a controversy (e.g., an arrest for drugs, a highly publicized divorce, performing in a sexually-explicit music video, or being accused of sexually deviant behavior) is likely to have an adverse impact on the reputation of the company that uses the celebrity to endorse a product.

4. **How does the family influence the socialization of children? What role does television play in consumer socialization?**

The family influences the consumer socialization of its children by imparting values, beliefs, attitudes and modes of behavior that relate to consumption through either direct instruction of children, or indirectly as children imitate the behavior of other family members. It was found that TV commercials have great influence on children. Thus, television advertising conveys consumption-related values and is part of the consumer socialization of children. This role of TV is important to both marketers and legislators because of the sometimes rather fine distinction between what constitutes effective marketing and potentially harmful influence on children.

5. **As a marketing consultant, you were retained by the Walt Disney Company to design a study investigating how families make vacation decisions. Who, within the family, would you interview? What kind of questions would you ask? How would you assess the relative power of each family member in making vacation-related decisions?**

As Disney's marketing consultant, you must identify the distinct roles in the family decision-making process regarding vacations. You should identify and interview both the influencers and deciders regarding vacation decisions. It is likely that you would have to interview both parents and children. The questions asked should be designed to reveal the relative influence of the various family members regarding the many factors involved in a typical family's decision to visit Disney World. These factors include; the time of year during which the vacation is taken, the length of the vacation, the amount of money to be spent.

6. **Which of the five stages of the traditional family life cycle constitute the most lucrative segment(s) for the following products and services: (a) telephone party lines, (b) a Club Med vacation, (c) Domino's pizza, (d) compact disc players, (e) mutual funds, and (f) motor homes? Explain your answers.**

Students should segment the markets for these products in the context of the information presented on the five basic stages of the FLC, and propose appropriate strategies to market these products to the chosen target markets. For each stage of the FLC, the students should evaluate the purchase likelihood of each of the six products and services by applying a ranking scale ranging from 1 = very low purchase probability, to 5 = very high probability.

7. **As the marketing manager of a high-quality, fairly expensive line of frozen dinners, how would you use the non-family household information listed in Table 10-9 to segment the market and position your product?**

See Table 10-9 first. The emphasis here would be on dual-income families and childless couples. The timesaving aspects, ease of preparation, etc., would be key factors for busy dual-career couples or childless couples spending their time doing things other than cooking.

8. **A domestic airline's frequent flyer program states that award tickets are transferable only to family members. As an airline executive charged with reevaluating this policy, how would you use the census data listed in Table 10-10 to decide whether or not to change the present policy?**

This question requires the students to analyze the data represented in Table 10-10 and draw justifiable conclusions.

EXERCISES

1. **Prepare a list of formal and informal groups to which you belong and give examples of purchases for which each served as a reference group. In which of the groups you listed is the pressure to conform the greatest? Why?**

Instructor's Discussion

Answers will certainly vary, but a number of similarities in students' answers may appear. The list of formal groups is likely to be smaller than the list of informal groups. Students are likely to mention their friends, classmates, dormitory partners, and coworkers as informal groups to which they belong. Their formal groups might include structured university activities, such as student government, a fraternity or sorority, or a student club. Students are likely to mention visible products and purchases, or perceived social risk, as examples of consumption situations where reference group influence was particularly important. The instructor should use this opportunity to point out how reference groups influence varies according to the type of product purchased.

2. **With a paper and pencil, spend one hour watching a network television channel during prime time. Record the total number of commercials that aired. For each commercial using a celebrity endorser, record the celebrity's name, the product or service advertised, and whether the celebrity was used in a testimonial, as an endorser, an actor, or a spokesperson.**

Instructor's Discussion

A variation that gives you more control and accuracy would be to make a videotape of commercials and show it in class. Watching a variety of programs, the students will come up with a good selection of commercials; it is also likely that many students will list the same often-shown commercials. During the classroom discussion, the instructor and students should classify each of the often-shown commercials depicting celebrities into one of the categories listed in the question.

3. **Think of a recent major purchase your family has made. Analyze the roles performed by the various family members in terms of the following consumption roles: influencers, gatekeepers, deciders, buyers, preparers, users, maintainers, and disposers.**

Instructor's Discussion

This exercise will illustrate the wide variation of roles that family members play in the family consumption decision-making process.

4. **Select three product categories and compare the brands you prefer to those your parents prefer. To what extent are the preferences similar? Discuss the similarities in the context of consumer socialization.**

Instructor's Discussion

This exercise is designed to illustrate the concept of consumer socialization which is defined as the process by which children acquire the skills, knowledge, and attitudes necessary to function as consumers.

5. **Identify one traditional family and one nontraditional family (or household) featured in a TV sitcom or series. (The two families/households can be featured in the same or in different television shows). Classify the traditional group into one stage of the traditional FLC. Classify the nontraditional group into one of the categories described in Table 10-4. Select two characters of the same gender and approximate age, one from each group, and compare their consumption behavior (such as clothes, furniture, stated or implied attitudes toward spending money).**

Instructor's Discussion

Many TV sitcoms depict nontraditional families or households; the contrast between the two characters selected by the student will illustrate the diversity of American households and families.

S.T.A.R. PROJECTS

Ethical Issues in Consumer Behavior

S.T.A.R. Project #1

The opening ad to this chapter features one of Dannon yogurt's new products—Danimals. For complete look at this new line see www.dannon.com. Notice the headline provided in the chapter opening ad—"Get them started on the road to healthy snacking." Do you see any ethical difficulties with this approach? What if the Danimals container showed the character saying "Buy me, please. I want to go home with you"? Consider the ethics involved in both of the above questions and write a brief policy statement for Dannon that would give the company direction with respect to its communication contact and responsibility to its customers and their children.

Instructor's Discussion

The Dannon issue is not an easy one. In the first case, even though promoting snacks or disguising snacks under cloak of health may questionable, nothing has been done wrong ethically. At least that would be the view of the company. In the second case, a different issue arises. Having cartoon characters ask children (or their parents) to buy them and take them home creates ethical difficulties. Why? Children are endeared to cartoon characters and, thereby, are heavily influenced by them. All may not feel this way. Promote a discussion. Read the best policy statements to the class.

S.T.A.R. Project #2

The National Beverage Company (see www.nationalbeverage.com) makes the popular Shasta and Faygo drinks. The company also produces water products, juices, and specialty drinks such as VooDoo Rain (similar to Mountain Dew). The company has provided low cost alternatives to store brands and more heavily advertised national brands (such as Coca-Cola and Pepsi-Cola) for a number of years. The Shasta brand is especially popular with cost-conscious moms. Assume that National Beverage is considering product line expansion to include a wine cooler product. The product will be named Shasta Cooler—"Shasta with a punch!" The rationale behind the move is to capitalize on the popular Shasta name, expand into the rapidly growing wine cooler field, and to increase profits. Assume the company believes that this spin-off brand will also be popular with cost conscious consumers. Evaluate the possibility of this line expansion from an ethical perspective. Considering what you have learned about groups and the family, make a decision for the company. Be sure to explain your position and describe any modifications that you might feel are necessary.

Instructor's Discussion

Students should see that, although adding the wine cooler product might be an opportunity for the company, confusion with the popular family-oriented product is bound to occur. Is this right or wrong? Will the product's name and slogan be the main issue? Have students discuss and comment. Be sure to discuss the responsibilities that company's owe to their customers.

Small Group Projects

S.T.A.R. Project #3

The modern grocery store has undergone some dramatic changes that have mirrored the demographic changes that have occurred in our society over the last ten to fifteen years. Family units, singles, and relationships between couples have changed and are continuing to change. Your group assignment is to go to a local grocery store and observe the product categories on the grocery shelves. Consider product line mixes and any perceived changes from a few years ago. For example, which is more dominant, single-serving items or multiple-serving items? Assess what you see. Next, interview a store manager and get his or her impressions on the changing grocery customer. Match this material to the information provided in the chapter. Write a short paper that summarizes your observations, your interview, and your discoveries.

Instructor's Discussion

This is a good project to help the group master observation and assessment. The group will find that many changes have occurred in the grocery store. How does information technology assist the grocery store in tracking changes (e.g., bar codes)? Read the best of the papers to the class and discuss the perceived changes. Do the changes match the information provided in the chapter?

S.T.A.R. Project #4

As indicated in the chapter, thanks to computers and the Internet, we are witnessing the emergence of a new type of group—virtual groups or communities. A popular form of this type of group or community is one where knowledge is exchanged. The knowledge community or chat room may soon be the primary clearinghouse for information on the Web. Your group's assignment is to investigate online knowledge communities by visiting the following Web sites that provide tools for knowledge community construction: (a) PeopleLink at www.peoplelink.com and Participate.com at www.participate.com. PeopleLink will set up, host, and manage online forums. Participate.com provides hosting, consulting, training, marketing, and even moderators who can keep knowledge discussions jumping. Your group should write a short evaluation paper that outlines the activities of these two sites, list primary features and costs of service, and evaluate what you perceive to be the future of knowledge communities as groups (use whatever resources necessary to make this evaluation).

Instructor's Discussion

The knowledge community is truly a unique form of virtual group. Experts believe it is a group format that will receive increasing attention. Students should have fun exploring this issue. Be sure that groups report their evaluations and findings. For additional knowledge community Web sites see Infopop at www.infopop.com, SiteScape at www.sitescape.com, Coolboard at www.coolboard.com, eRoom Technology at www.eroom.com, and Multex.com at www.multex.com.

Using the Internet to Study Consumer Behavior

S.T.A.R. Project #5
Ask any bride what the major problem with holding her wedding was and she will probably respond, "the planning and all the tension it brought." As experts in human behavior studied this problem, a simple solution was derived—have someone else do the planning and bear the tension. Today, this is all possible (with a minimal cost) by using the Internet. Many brides-to-be have been trilled to discover that such Web sites as Bride.com (www.bride.com) and the Wedding Channel (www.weddingchannel.com) take the burden off of their beautiful shoulders and place it where it should be—with the experts. Does the process work? Your assignment is to see. In other words, plan your own wedding using the sites above. Once you have made the attempt, write a short evaluation paper that describes your experience. What connections did the merchants involved attempt to make with you as a potential consumer? What do you perceive to be the principle value of such sites? What problems did you encounter? What other services besides wedding planning could such sites undertake?

Instructor's Discussion

Yes, even males find this assignment interesting. Students can begin the assignment by listing all the advantages to using such services. Follow with disadvantages. How do the two lists compare? Do such services have a role to play in other events? Could funerals, moving, child birthing, choosing a college, picking a mate, or other tension events be aided through such sites? Students normally have fun discussing this subject. As I have discovered, it is not unusual for a bride-to-be to plan her whole wedding in such a manner. Would there be a cultural stigma associated with such a bold move? Think about it.

S.T.A.R. Project #6
One of the most important reference groups that we all encounter is the friendship group. This was especially true when we were children. One Web site that specializes fostering the friendship group is the PBS Kids site (see www.pbskids.org). This colorful Web site has games, adventures, information, and mechanisms by which even the most distant child may be made to feel part of a larger group. PBS programming stresses the global child. Their Web site does the same thing. Your assignment is to visit the PBS Kids Web site and evaluate it as a reference group mechanism or vehicle for enhancing the friendship group. How would this site influence children? How does the Web site aid the child in making choices? Does the Web site avoid commercialism that is so common to other child-oriented Web sites? If so, how? Be sure to be specific with your comments.

Instructor's Discussion

The PBS Kids Web site is an excellent site to compare against other child sites such as Disney, Sesame Street, or Warner Bros. Even though the students are no longer children, have them evaluate the Web site with respect to the services provided for children and friendship groups. How does the Web site appeal to this unique reference group? What responsibilities must the site shoulder? How good of a job is it doing? Discussion should follow.

CASES

Case One: Child-Free, Not Childless

1. Although not being part of the "traditional" Family Life Cycle, they do constitute an important nontraditional FLC stage, as Figure 10-17 in the chapter shows. They are not part of any stage that involves children, either in or out of the home (e.g., empty nesters).

2. Clearly, child-free couples do not spend money on disposable diapers, baby toys, and so on. They do tend to spend significantly more on entertainment, food, and dining out, and are also big spenders when it comes to liquor, clothing, pets, and generally buying themselves "stuff."

Case Two: Who Is Harley Earl?

1. Because automobiles are highly conspicuous products (people are seen and associated with what they drive), automobiles are very strongly associated with reference group influence. Mr. Earl is being used as an "expert" endorser for Buick automobiles. It is probably expected that the actor portraying Mr. Earl will be able to get the message across that today, as in the past, Buick automobiles are styled in a way that the consumer can "love."

2. The actor playing Mr. Earl is depicted as an "expert" and an automotive visionary, whereas Tiger Woods is being used as a "sports celebrity." In either case, however, the purpose is to sell more automobiles (more Buick automobiles).

CHAPTER 11

Social Class and Consumer Behavior

LEARNING OBJECTIVES

After studying this chapter students should be able to:
1. Distinguish between and define social class and social status.
2. List and briefly discuss the variations in the number and types of social-class categories.
3. Explain the three broad measures of social class.
4. Identify the single variable indexes that are used to measure social class.
5. Discuss the use of composite-variable indexes to measure social class.
6. Comment on social class profiles as a way of distinguishing between social classes.
7. Articulate a definition of social mobility and its practical consequences for marketers.
8. Explain geodemographic clustering and the service—PRIZM—that identifies factors necessary for the clustering.
9. Distinguish the affluent consumer and their importance to marketers.
10. Describe the middle-class consumer and relevant marketing ramifications.
11. Describe the downscale consumer and relevant marketing ramifications.
12. Describe the new techno class consumer and marketing strategies appropriate to reaching him/her.
13. Discuss several specific applications of social class information to consumer behavior.

CHAPTER SUMMARY

Social stratification, the division of members of a society into a hierarchy of distinct social classes, exists in all societies and cultures. Social class usually is defined by the amount of status that members of a specific class possess in relation to members of other classes. Social class membership often serves as a frame of reference (a reference group) for the development of consumer attitudes and behavior.

The measurement of social class is concerned with classifying individuals into social class groupings. These groupings are of particular value to marketers, who use social classification as an effective means of identifying and segmenting target markets. There are three basic methods for measuring social class: subjective measurement, reputational measurement, and objective measurement. Subjective measures rely on an individual's self-perception; reputational measures rely on an individual's perceptions of others; and objective measures use specific socioeconomic measures, either alone (as a single variable index) or in combination with others (as a composite-variable index). Composite-variable indexes, such as the Index of Status Characteristics and the Socioeconomic Status Score, combine a number of socioeconomic factors to form one overall measure of social class standing.

Class structures range from two-class to nine-class systems. A frequently used classification system consists of six classes: upper-upper, lower-upper, upper-middle, lower-middle, upper-lower, and lower-lower. Profiles of these classes indicate that the socioeconomic differences between classes are reflected in differences in attitudes, in leisure activities, and in consumption habits. This is why segmentation by social class is of special interest to marketers.

In recent years, some marketers have turned to geodemographic clustering as an alternative to a strict social class typology. Geodemographic clustering is a technique that combines geographic and socioeconomic factors to locate concentrations of consumers with particular characteristics. Particular attention currently is being directed to affluent consumers, who represent the fastest-growing segment in our population; however, some marketers are finding it extremely profitable to cater to the needs of nonaffluent consumers.

Research has revealed social class differences in clothing habits, home decoration, and leisure activities, as well as saving, spending, and credit habits. Thus, astute marketers tailor specific product and promotional strategies to each social-class target segment.

CHAPTER OUTLINE

INTRODUCTION

1. Some form of class structure or social stratification has existed in all societies throughout the history of human existence.
2. In contemporary societies, an indication of the presence of social classes is the common reality that people who are better educated or have more prestigious occupations like physicians and lawyers often are more highly valued than those who are truck drivers and farm hands.
   a) This is so, even though all four occupations are necessary for a society's well-being.
   b) Moreover, a wide range of differences in values, attitudes, and behavior exists among members of different social classes.

WHAT IS SOCIAL CLASS?

1. Although *social class* can be thought of as a continuum range of social positions on which each member of society can be placed, researchers have preferred to divide the continuum into a small number of specific social classes, or *strata*.
2. *Social class* is defined as the division of members of a society into a hierarchy of distinct status classes, so that members of each class have relatively the same status, and members of all other classes have either more or less status.

*****Use Key Term **social class** *Here; Use Learning Objective #1 Here*****

Social Class and Social Status

1. Researchers define each social class by the amount of status (*social status*) the members of that class have in comparison to members of other social classes.

2. In social class research (sometimes called *social stratification*), status is frequently thought of as the relative rankings of members of each social class in terms of specific status factors. Examples include:
   a) Relative wealth—amount of economic assets.
   b) Power—degree of personal choice.
   c) Prestige—the degree of recognition received from others.
3. To secure an understanding of how status operates within the minds of consumers, researchers have explored the idea of *social comparison theory*.
   a) The idea is that individuals quite normally compare their own material possessions with those owned by others in order to determine their relative social standing.
   b) Status is often defined in terms of purchasing power.
   c) A related concept is *status consumption*—the process by which consumers endeavor to increase their social standing through conspicuous consumption or possessions.
4. Other theories aside, status is often defined in terms of convenient demographic variables:
   a) Family income.
   b) Occupational status.
   c) Educational attainment.

***

*****Use Key Term* social status *Here; Use Learning Objective #1 Here; Use Discussion Question #3 Here; Use Table 11-1 Here*****

Social Class is Hierarchical and a Natural Form of Segmentation

1. Social class categories are usually ranked in a hierarchy ranging from low to high status.
   a) Thus, members of a specific social class perceive members of other social classes as having either more or less status than they do.
   b) Within this context, social class membership serves consumers as a frame of reference (i.e., a reference group) for the development of their attitudes and behavior.
2. The hierarchical aspect of social class is important to marketers.
3. Consumers may purchase certain products because these products are favored by members of their own or a higher social class (e.g., a fine French Champagne), and consumers may avoid other products because they perceive the products to be "lower-class" products (e.g., a digital readout wristwatch as a dress watch).
4. The classification of society's members into a small number of social classes has also enabled researchers to note the existence of shared values, attitudes, and behavioral patterns among members within each social class and differing values, attitudes, and behavior *between* social classes.

Social Class Categories

1. Little agreement exists among sociologists on how many distinct class divisions are necessary to adequately describe the class structure of the United States.
   a) The choice of how many separate classes to use depends on the amount of detail that the researcher believes is necessary to explain adequately the attitudes or behavior under study.

2. Marketers are interested in the social class structures of communities that are potential markets for their products and in the specific social class level of their potential customers.

*****Use Learning Objective #2 Here; Use Table 11-2 and 11-3 Here; Use Figure 11-1 Here*****

THE MEASUREMENT OF SOCIAL CLASS

1. There is no general agreement as to how to measure social class.
2. The result is a wide variety of measurement techniques, which may be classified into *subjective measures*, *reputational measures*, and *objective measures*.

*****Use Key Terms subjective measures, reputational measures, and objective measures Here; Use Learning Objective #3 Here; Use Discussion Question #1 Here*****

Subjective Measures

1. In the subjective approach to measuring social class, individuals are asked to estimate their own social class positions.
   a) The resulting classification of social class membership is based on the participants' self-perceptions or self-images.
   b) Social class is treated as a "personal" phenomenon, one that reflects an individual's sense of belonging or identification with others.
   c) This feeling of social-group membership is often referred to as *class consciousness*.
2. Subjective measures of social class membership tend to produce an overabundance of people who classify themselves as middle class.
   a) Moreover, it is likely that the subjective perception of one's social class membership, as a reflection of one's self-image, is related to product usage and consumption preferences.

*****Use Key Term class consciousness Here; Use Learning Objective #3 Here*****

Reputational Measures

1. In this form, selected community informants make initial judgments concerning the social class membership of others within the community, rather than themselves.
   a) This gives researchers a better understanding of the specific class structures of the communities being studied.
   b) Consumer researchers, however, are more concerned with understanding markets and consumers than social structure.
   c) This method is often considered impractical.

*****Use Learning Objective #3 Here*****

Objective Measures

1. Objective measures consist of selected demographic or socioeconomic variables concerning the individual(s) under study.
   a) These are measured through questionnaires of factual questions.
   b) The most frequently used questions are about occupation, amount of income, and education.
   c) Sometimes geodemographic data in the form of zip codes and residence-neighborhood information is added.
2. Socioeconomic measures of social class are important when segmenting the market. Marketers match the socioeconomic profiles of their target audience with the audience profiles of selected media.
3. Marketing managers who have developed socioeconomic profiles of their target markets can locate these markets (i.e., identify and measure them) by studying the socioeconomic data periodically issued by the United States Bureau of the Census and numerous commercial geodemographic data services.
4. Socioeconomic audience profiles are regularly developed and routinely made available to potential advertisers by most of the mass media.
   a) These objective measures of social class fall into two basic categories, single variable and composite variable.

*****Use Learning Objective #3 Here; Use Discussion Question #1 Here; Use Table 11-4 and 11-5 Here; Use Exercise #2 Here*****

Single-Variable Indexes

1. A *single-variable index* uses only one socioeconomic variable to evaluate social class membership. Four examples follow:
   a) Occupation—occupation is a widely accepted and probably the best documented measure of social class, because it reflects occupational status.
      i) The importance of occupation as a social class indicator is dramatized by the frequency with which people ask others they meet for the first time, "What do you do for a living?"
      ii) More important, marketers frequently think in terms of specific occupations when defining a target market for their products.
      iii) It appears that business executives and professionals who are self-employed or entrepreneurs are substantially more likely to be very wealthy than their counterparts who work for someone else.

*****Use Key Term single-variable index Here; Use Learning Objective #4 Here; Use Discussion Question #4 Here; Use Exercise #1 Here; Use Table 11-6 Here*****

   b) Education—the level of a person's formal education is another commonly accepted approximation of social class standing.
      i) Generally speaking, the more education a person has, the more likely it is that the person is well paid.

*****Use Learning Objective #4 Here; Use Discussion Question #4 Here; Use Table 11-7 Here*****

    c) Income—researchers who favor income as a measure of social class use either *amount* or *source* of income.
       i) Although income is a popular estimate of social class standing, not all consumer researchers agree that it is an appropriate index of social class.
      ii) Some argue that a blue-collar automobile mechanic and a white-collar assistant bank manager may both earn $53,000 a year, yet because of (or as a reflection of) social class differences, each will spend that income in a different way.
     iii) Further substantiating the importance of consumers' personal values, rather than amount of income, is the observation that affluence may be more a function of attitude or behavior than of income level.

*****Use Learning Objective #4 Here; Use Discussion Question #2, #3, and #4 Here; Use Table 11-8 Here*****

    d) Other Variables—quality of neighborhood and dollar value of residence are rarely used as sole measures of social class.
       i) They are, however, used informally to support or verify social class membership assigned on the basis of occupational status or income.
      ii) Finally, possessions have been used by sociologists as an index of social class.
         a) The best-known and most elaborate rating scheme for evaluating possessions is *Chapin's Social Status Scale,* which focuses on the presence of certain items of furniture and accessories in the living room and the condition of the room.

*****Use Key Term Chapin's Social Status Scale Here; Use Learning Objective #4 Here; Use Discussion Question #1 Here; Use Figure 11-2 Here*****

Composite-Variable Indexes

1. *Composite-variable indexes* systematically combine a number of socioeconomic variables to evaluate social class membership.
    a) They seem to better reflect social class complexity than single element indicators.
2. Two of the more important composite indexes are:
    a) *Index of Status Characteristics*—the Warner Index of Status Characteristics—(ISC)—is a classic composite measure of social class that weighs occupation, source of income, house type, and dwelling area.
    b) *Socioeconomic Status Scores*—the United States Bureau of Census developed the Socioeconomic Status Score (SES) that combines the socioeconomic variables of occupation, family income, and educational attainment.

*****Use Key Terms composite-variable indexes, Index of Status Characteristics, and Socioeconomic Status Scores Here; Use Learning Objective #3 and #5 Here; Use Discussion Question #1 and #2 Here*****

LIFESTYLE PROFILES OF THE SOCIAL CLASSES

1. Consumer research has found evidence that within each of the social classes, there is a constellation of a specific lifestyle factors (shared beliefs, attitudes, activities, and behaviors) that distinguish members of a social class from members of other social classes.
2. People in any class may possess values, attitudes, and behavioral patterns that are a hybrid of two or more classes.

*****Use Learning Objective #6 Here; Use Exercise #2 and #3 Here; Use Table 11-9 Here*****

China: Pursuing a Middle-Class Lifestyle

1. In recent years, established marketers from all over the world have singled out China as a highly desirable growth market for their brands.
2. The wealthiest 20 percent of urban Chinese households (about 80 million) constitutes a highly attractive market.
   a) The "little rich" include those with about $3,200 in income.
   b) The "yuppies" include those with about $9,500 in income.
   c) The two middle-class segments tend to differ more in terms of their consumption patterns than in terms of their attitudes, lifestyles and media behavior.

*****Use Table 11-10 and 11-11 Here*****

SOCIAL CLASS MOBILITY

1. Individuals can move either up or down in social class standing from the class position held by their parents.
2. Most Americans think of *upward mobility.*
   a) This results in the upper classes being the reference group for many ambitious men and women in America.
   b) Recognizing these aspirations, marketers frequently incorporate higher-class symbols into their advertising.
3. Social class mobility also contributes to products and services filtering down from a higher level to a lower one.

*****Use Key Term upward mobility Here; Use Learning Objective #7 Here; Use Figure 11-3 Here*****

Some Signs of Downward Mobility

1. There are signs of some *downward mobility*.
2. Young adults will find it very difficult to "do better" than their parents, and may not do as well as their mothers and fathers.

*****Use Key Term* downward mobility *Here; Use Learning Objective #7 Here*****

GEODEMOGRAPHIC CLUSTERING

1. Traditional social class measures have been enhanced by the linkage of geographic and socioeconomic consumer data to create more powerful *geodemographic clusters*.
2. One popular clustering service is *PRIZM*.
   a) This service assigns every one of the U.S. micro neighborhoods (zip + 4 areas) to one of 62 PRIZM clusters.
   b) These are collapsed into 15 groups.
   c) Marketers can superimpose these geodemographic clusters onto product and service usage data, media exposure data, and lifestyle data to create a sharply defined picture of their target markets.

*****Use Key Terms* geodemographic clusters and PRIZM *Here; Use Learning Objective #8 Here; Use Discussion Question #5 Here; Use Table 11-12 and 11-13 Here*****

THE AFFLUENT CONSUMER

1. Affluent households are an attractive marketing target because of their disproportionately high amount of discretionary income.
2. For over 25 years, Mendelsohn Media Research has conducted an annual study of the *affluent market*—currently defined in terms of three affluent segments:
   a) Those with household incomes of $75,000 to $99,999 per year—the "least affluent."
   b) Those with incomes of $100,000 to $199,999 per year—the "medium affluent."
   c) Those with incomes of $200,000 or more per year—the "most affluent."
3. Although the affluent market consists of only 25 percent of all households, this upscale market consumes more in several categories than the nonaffluent market.
4. The average household income for these consumers is $139,000, and 62 percent are employed in either a professional or managerial capacity.
5. Still further, a growing subcategory of the affluent are *millionaires*.
   a) Currently, more than 3 million American households have a net worth of more than $1 million.

*****Use Key Term* affluent market *Here; Use Learning Objective #9 Here; Use Discussion Question #6, #7, and #8 Here; Use Figure 11-4 and 11-5 Here*****

The Media Exposure of the Affluent Consumer

1. Those homes with an income of more than $75,000 a year view less TV than less affluent households.
2. They read 6.1 different publications, listen to 12.5 hours of weekday radio, and watch 24.7 hours of TV per week.
    a) 92 percent subscribe to cable TV.

> *****Use Learning Objective #9 Here; Use Discussion Question #8 Here; Use Table 11-5 (previously used) and 11-14 Here*****

Segmenting the Affluent Market

1. The affluent market is not one single market.
    a) Affluent consumers do not share the same lifestyles.
2. In an effort to isolate distinct segments, Mediamark Research, Inc. has developed the following affluent market-segmentation scheme for the *Upper Deck* consumers (the top 10 percent of households in terms of incomes):
    a) Well-feathered nests—households that have at least one high-income earner and children present. (38 percent of the Upper Deck).
    b) No strings attached—households that have at least one high-income earner and no children. (35 percent of the Upper Deck).
    c) Nanny's in charge—households that have two or more earners, neither earning high incomes, and children present. (9 percent of the Upper Deck).
    d) Two careers—households that have two or more earners, neither earning high incomes and no children present. (11 percent of the Upper Deck).
    e) The good life—households that have a high degree of affluence with no person employed, or with the head-of-household not employed. (7 percent of the Upper Deck)
3. An untapped market is the rural affluent. Categories include:
    a) Suburban transplants—those who move to the country but still commute to high-paying urban jobs.
    b) Equity-rich suburban expatriates—sell homes for a huge profit, buy less expensive homes in small towns, live off the difference.
    c) City folks with country homes—wealthy snowbirds and vacationers.
    d) Wealthy landowners—wealthy farmers and other natives who make a comfortable living off the land.

> *****Use Learning Objective #9 Here; Use Discussion Question #7 and #8 Here*****

MIDDLE-CLASS CONSUMERS

1. It is not easy to define the borders of what is meant by "middle class."
2. Though other measures are possible (such as those earning between $25,000 and $75,000) the upper boundary of being middle class is about $85,000.

3. For many marketers "middle class" can be thought of as including households that range from lower-middle to middle-middle class.
4. Because technological and luxury products are becoming more affordable to this class, it is even more difficult to define "middle class."
5. There is mounting evidence that the "middle class" is disappearing in America.
6. This is not true in other countries where the middle class is increasing.

*****Use Learning Objective #10 Here; Use Table 11-15 Here*****

THE WORKING CLASS AND OTHER NONAFFLUENT CONSUMERS

1. Although many marketers go after the affluent, the size and income of the nonaffluent group make them an important target market.
2. Lower-income, or *downscale*, consumers are households earning $30,000 or less.
3. Downscale consumers are more brand loyal than wealthier consumers because they can less afford to make mistakes in switching to unfamiliar brands.

*****Use Key Term downscale Here; Use Learning Objective #11 Here; Use Discussion Question #7 and #8 Here; Use Figure 11-4 and 11-5 Here*****

THE ARRIVAL OF THE "TECHNO-CLASS"

1. Techno is a new basis of class standing
   a) The degree of literacy, familiarity, and competency with technology, especially computers and the Internet sets the standard for this class.
2. Those who are unfamiliar or lack computer skills are being referred to as "technological underclassed."
3. These extraordinary stories of entrepreneurial and technological accomplishments, when coupled with a general sense of not wanting to be left out of the "sweep of computer technology" have propelled parents to seek out computer training for their children, even their infant children.
4. Fifty-five-year-old professionals, who were initially reluctant to "learn computers," are now seeking "personal computer training."
5. Consumers throughout the world have come to believe that it is critical to acquire a functional understanding of computers in order to ensure that they do not become obsolete, or hinder themselves socially or professionally.
6. It appears that those without necessary computer skills will increasingly find themselves to be "underclassed" and "disadvantaged."

*****Use Learning Objective #12 Here*****

The Geek Status

1. The increasingly positive image of geeks has made them and their lifestyles the target of marketers' messages designed to appeal to their appetite for novel technological products.

*****Use Learning Objective #12 Here*****

SELECTED CONSUMER BEHAVIOR APPLICATIONS OF SOCIAL CLASS

Clothing, Fashion, and Shopping

1. Most people dress to fit their self-images, which include their perceptions of their own social class membership.
2. Members of specific social classes differ in terms of what they consider fashionable or in good taste.
   a) Lower middle-class consumers have a strong preference for T-shirts, caps, and other clothing that offer an *external point of identification*.
   b) Upper-class consumers are likely to buy clothing that is free from such supporting associations.
      i) Upper-class consumers also seek clothing with a more subtle look.
3. Social class is also an important variable in determining where a consumer shops.

*****Use Learning Objective #13 Here; Use Table 11-16 Here*****

The Pursuit of Leisure

1. Social class membership is also closely related to the choice of recreational and leisure-time activities.
   a) Upper-class consumers are likely to attend the theater and concerts, to play bridge, and to attend college football games.
   b) Lower-class consumers tend to be avid television watchers and fishing enthusiasts, and they enjoy drive-in movies and baseball games.
2. Over the past decade or so, however, a number of changes are increasingly being observed that point to a further blurring of social-class lines with regard to leisure interests.

*****Use Learning Objective #13 Here; Use Figure 11-7 Here*****

Saving, Spending, and Credit

1. Saving, spending, and credit card usage all seem to be related to social class standing.
2. Upper-class consumers are more future-oriented and confident of their financial acumen; they are more willing to invest in insurance, stocks, and real estate.
3. In comparison, lower-class consumers are generally more concerned with immediate gratification; when they do save, they are primarily interested in safety and security.

Social Class and Communication

1. Social class groupings differ in terms of their media habits and in how they transmit and receive communications.
2. When it comes to describing their world, lower-class consumers tend to portray it in rather personal and concrete terms, although middle-class consumers are able to describe their experiences from a number of different perspectives.
3. Such variations in response indicate that middle-class consumers have a broader or more general view of the world, although lower-class consumers tend to have a narrow or personal view, seeing the world through their own immediate experiences.
4. Regional differences in terminology, choice of words and phrases, and patterns of usage also tend to increase as we move down the social class ladder.
5. Selective exposure to various types of mass media differs by social class.
   a) Higher social class members tend to prefer current events and drama, although lower-class individuals tend to prefer soap operas, quiz shows, and situation comedies.
   b) Higher-class consumers tend to have greater exposure to magazines and newspapers than do their lower-class counterparts.
   c) Lower-class consumers are likely to have greater exposure to publications that dramatize romance and the lifestyles of movie and television celebrities.

DISCUSSION QUESTIONS

1. **Marketing researchers generally use the objective method to measure social class, rather than the subjective or reputational methods. Why is the objective method preferred by researchers?**

The *objective method* is often preferred because: a) The objective approach is based on consumers' responses to one or more factual questions about socioeconomic items (e.g., occupation, income, education) which can be easily included in most self-administered marketing research questionnaires. b) Most media have socioeconomic profiles of their audiences; therefore, objective measures are useful for matching media audiences and target markets. c) Because the subjective method relies on self-perception, it tends to produce an overabundance of people who classify themselves as "middle class" or "don't know." d) The *reputational method* relies on an informed participant to make judgments concerning the social class membership of others and, therefore, it is limited to small community studies. On the other hand, a marketing research study that utilizes a sample drawn from a large population is generally required to yield the kind of findings needed for formulating marketing strategies.

2. **Under what circumstances would you expect income to be a better predictor of consumer behavior than a composite measure of social class (e.g., based on income, education, and occupation)? When would you expect the composite social class measure to be superior?**

Whether income alone or a composite measure of social class is a better predictor of consumer behavior is likely to depend on what dimension of consumer behavior is being predicted. For acquisitive behavior (i.e., buying or not buying a product), income alone has been found to be a better predictor. For more expressive behavior (i.e., frequency of use, how the product is used), however, composite variable indexes have been found to be better predictors.

3. **Describe the correlation between social status or prestige and income. Which is a more useful segmentation variable? Discuss.**

Status is frequently thought of as the relative rankings of members of each social class in terms of specific status factors. For example, relative wealth (amount of economic assets), power (the degree of personal choice or influence over others), and prestige (the degree of recognition received from others), are three factors frequently employed when estimating social class. When considering consumer behavior and marketing research, status is most often defined in terms of one or more of the following convenient demographic (socioeconomic) variables: family income, occupational status, and educational attainment. These socioeconomic variables, as expressions of status, are commonly used by marketing practitioners to measure social class. There is a strong positive correlation between educational attainment and household income, and because it is strongly related to the amount of status a person has, income is a popular estimate of social class standing; however, not all consumer researchers agree that income is an appropriate index of social class. How people decide to spend their incomes reflects different values, and it is the difference in values that is an important discriminator of social class between people, not the amount of income they earn. Indeed, there is a growing belief that affluence may be more a function of attitude or behavior than of income level.

4. **Which status-related variable—occupation, education, or income—is the most appropriate segmentation base for: (a) expensive vacations, (b) opera subscriptions, (c) People magazine subscriptions, (d) fat-free foods, (e) personal computers, (f) pocket-size cellular telephones, and (g) health clubs?**

Occupation is the most appropriate segmentation base for personal computers and cellular telephones because these products reflect a person's career and profession. Education should be used to segment markets for opera and magazine subscriptions and for products and services that are related to physical health (e.g., fat-free foods, health clubs) because such purchases reflect a person's educational attainment. Expensive vacations (e.g., flying to Europe on the Concord or winter weekend trips to an island with a warm climate) are non-necessity, luxurious activities that only individuals with very high incomes can afford.

5. **Consider the Rolex watch, which has a retail price range starting at about $2,000 for a stainless steel model to thousands of dollars for a solid gold model. How might the Rolex company use geodemographic clustering in its marketing efforts?**

First, Rolex should identify the socioeconomic characteristics of the buyers of its product line. A service such as PRIZM could be used to pinpoint the geographic areas in the United States where such individuals reside. The firm should then make sure that its products are sold by retailers in those areas, and advertise them in the local media and national periodicals that offer local editions to the selected areas.

6. **How would you use the research evidence on affluent households presented in this chapter to segment the market for: (a) home exercise equipment, (b) vacations, and (c) banking services?**

Affluent United States households constitute an especially attractive target segment because its members have incomes that provide them with a disproportionately larger share of all discretionary income—"the little extras" that allow the purchase of luxury cruises, foreign sports cars, time-sharing, ski resort condos, and fine jewelry. Affluent consumers are a promising target market for home exercise equipment and for vacations because they are heavy purchasers of many types of equipment for the home and heavy users of travel-related services (e.g., frequent-flyer programs, rented cars). And, because affluent households have greater incomes, they require more extensive and sophisticated banking services. The marketers of the products and services listed in the question should segment affluent consumers according to their lifestyles and income levels and use these segmentation frameworks to target them.

7. **How can a marketer use knowledge of consumer behavior to develop financial services for affluent consumers? For "downscale" consumers?**

The differences in financial needs between these two groups are critical to the marketers targeting them. Thus, marketers of such services as automobile and home improvement loans, noninterest-bearing checking accounts, and life insurance should understand the modest lifestyles of their customers and appropriately depict them in advertising. On the other hand, marketers of gold credit cards, mutual funds, brokerage accounts, and home-equity loans should target mostly upscale consumers because the data indicates that these individuals have a need for such services.

8. **You are the owner of two furniture stores, one catering to upper-middle class consumers and the other to lower-class consumers. How do social class differences influence each store's: (a) product lines and styles, (b) advertising media selection, (c) the copy and communication style used in the ads, and (d) payment policies?**

(a) Product lines and styles; the furniture directed at the upper-middle class should be distinctive, highly styled, modern, and with an artistic quality. The furniture directed at the lower-class should be traditional, sturdy, comfortable, and highly utilitarian. (b) Upper-middle-class consumers regard their homes as symbols of achievements and sources of status and prestige. They place symbolic value on furniture, and advertising directed at them should stress a total home environment as a means of self-expression. Lower-class consumers seek respectability and conformity to norms, and promotion directed at them should focus on the practical and utilitarian aspects of furniture. (c) Social classes vary in terms of how they transmit and receive communications. Thus, lower-class members portray their world in rather personal and concrete terms, and the advertising copy directed at them should be simple, straightforward and should describe immediate experiences. Upper-middle-class people generally describe their experiences from a number of different perspectives, and the promotion directed at them should be designed to create a "total" experience, atmosphere, or feel. (d) Because some lower-class consumers may not have the total sum required for a purchase, the store should offer deposit lay-away and installment payment plans. The retailer should also recognize that members of the lower social classes tend to use their credit cards for installment payments, although members of higher social classes pay their credit card bills in full each month. Thus, an in-store sales appeal of "buy now and pay later" is likely to lure lower-class consumers into buying. In the case of upper-middle-class patrons, an in-store offer of a lower price for payment with cash or personal check rather that a credit card (made possible by the fact that the merchant does not have to pay credit card company fees during such purchases) is an effective payment policy.

EXERCISES

1. **Copy the list of occupations in Table 11-6 and ask students majoring in areas other than marketing (both business and nonbusiness) to rank the relative prestige of these occupations. Are any differences in the rankings related to the students' majors? Explain.**

Instructor's Discussion

Table 11-6 presents findings from a continuing survey that estimates the relative honesty and perceived ethical standards that people assign to many basic occupational titles. Because this ranking is based more on perceived societal prestige than on status or wealth, not all of the occupations toward the top half of the table earn greater incomes and/or require more formal education than those toward the bottom half. In reality, however, a close association exists between occupational status, income, and education. This exercise is designed to illustrate that different members of the same society, who share similar values, may still rank various occupations differently, especially when such rating is based on honesty and ethical standards.

2. **Find three print ads in one of the publications listed in Table 11-5. Using the social class characteristics listed in Table 11-9, identify the social class targeted by each ad and evaluate the effectiveness of the advertising appeals used.**

Instructor's Discussion

This exercise will demonstrate that various publications are targeted at different social classes, and that the advertisements in these publications reflect the audiences' sociodemographic characteristics and consumption patterns.

3. **Select two households featured in two different TV series or sitcoms. Classify each household into one of the social classes discussed in the text, and analyze its lifestyle and consumption behavior.**

Instructor's Discussion

This exercise is designed to show that TV programs often target specific social classes. The instructor should choose the programs. It might even be best if you videotaped the program and showed it in class.

S.T.A.R. PROJECTS

Ethical Issues in Consumer Behavior

S.T.A.R. Project #1
The chapter examines social status (social stratification) in terms of the relative rankings of members of each social class in terms of specific status factors. Designer clothing could certainly be one of these factors. Whether one is young or old, prestige clothing ("the clothes make the man [or woman]") is an overt symbol of one's social class (possessions). Right or wrong, we do measure people by their dress. Your assignment is to investigate this process. During your investigation also review the ethics used by the fashion, designer, or prestige clothing manufacturers in attracting customers. After you have reviewed secondary material on the problem at hand, write a short paper that describes what you have learned.

Instructor's Discussion

Students generally have opinions about fashion or prestige clothing. Start the discussion by reviewing the high price of such clothing and how upscale and downscale consumers view such clothing. Encourage students to bring in ads, supply Web sites, or summarize secondary material on this issue.

S.T.A.R. Project #2
American Demographics magazine is an excellent source for information about the American consumer, his or her habits, and trends or changes being experienced by the U.S. consumer market. This publication, like some government publications, is constantly collecting infor-

mation about us. Your assignment is to go to the *American Demographics* Web site at www.americandemographics.com and find a story that would involve social class issues within the U.S. market. Be sure the story not only describes market behavior but also examines a business ethics question. The question could be in the area of promotion, data collection, purchasing of products, pricing, or any one of many other ethical areas. Typical stories on the Web site involve the census, social groups, gender issues, and American sub-groups such as targeting baby boomers. Once you have read your story, summarize it and report back to the class on your findings. Remember to stress an ethical issue that impacts consumer behavior in your summary.

Instructor's Discussion

American Demographics (though an expensive publication) is an excellent Web source of information about consumer issues. By surveying the Web site students will learn how to use the resource and how to investigate information provided by this source. Choose one or two of the summaries for in-class discussion.

Small Group Projects

S.T.A.R. Project #3
As described in the chapter, geodemographic clustering is a unique way to group consumers. The PRIZM method developed by Claritas (see www.claritas.com) is a unique way to study consumers based on such socioeconomic and demographic factors as education, income, occupation, family life cycle, ethnicity, housing, and urbanization. Your group should review the material found in Table 11-12 and 11-13. Next, learn about the PRIZM method via the Claritas Web site. Write a short summary report that discusses the validity of geodemographic clustering as a research technique, the value of PRIZM, and the future of this form of research. Present your findings to the class.

Instructor's Discussion

This project affords the student teams an excellent opportunity to learn more about geodemographic clustering and the PRIZM method. Students should also be able to see that the data provided in the Tables is indeed a good way to explore social group data. Teams usually approach this assignment from different directions, therefore, discussion usually increases overall class understanding and knowledge.

S.T.A.R. Project #4
One of the hottest sports sweeping the country is wrestling—that's right wrestling. What was at one time considered to be a lower-class entertainment event has gone prime time. How does a sport (and some would question whether it is a sport or merely hype) such as this become popular with upper and middle classes? To learn more, have your group investigate the World Wrestling Entertainment Web site at www.wwe.com. From this visit, determine how this sport attempts to appeal to all social classes. Be specific in your assessment. What can you determine about the demographics of someone that enjoys and attends this sport? Where did you find such

information? How could the information you found be used by promoters of the sport? Write a summary report of your group's findings.

<u>Instructor's Discussion</u>

Wrestling is not for everyone. The chief demographic today, however, is young males 18–30 who enjoy extreme sports (and extreme action or violence). The WWE certainly caters to this group. Through live events and televised matches, fans are paying really big money to see what wrestling has to offer. These fans are also not necessarily the same fans that are attracted to traditional sports such as football, basketball, or baseball. This project should produce a lively discussion and match well to the material found at the end of the chapter on social class application.

Using the Internet to Study Consumer Behavior

S.T.A.R. Project #5
Increasingly, one of the ways for the time-conscious parent to save shopping time is to use the Internet for toy purchases for their children. Toy retailers have found that an up-to-date and user-friendly Web site is an excellent way to extend markets and outreach to customers. In general, a toy retailer's Web site is as extensive as their in-store offerings. Nothing can quite match the excitement and atmosphere of an in-store shopping visit (especially at Christmas time), however. Toys-R-Us (see www.toysrus.com) and FAO Schwartz (see www.fao.com) take two distinctly different approaches to Web merchandising of their products. Assuming that you were the merchandising manager for a locally independent toy store, indicate what you would take from both (either) of the above toy store Web sites to build an effective Web site for your store given that your intent was to reach and market to upscale consumers who were willing to pay a little more for a lot more in the way of toys and toy services. Write a short report detailing your Web strategy to reach these consumers. Be sure to detail what might make the upscale toy consumer different from those found in other market categories and how your Web site expects to meet those needs.

<u>Instructor's Discussion</u>

The student should be able to learn a great deal by visiting the two suggested Web sites. It is obvious that FAO Schwartz appeals to upscale consumers. Toys-R-Us, however, has also been successful in appealing to upscale consumers. Students should notice that Toys-R-Us has also formed an alliance with Amazon.com to extend its reach to toy consumers. Would such an alliance be useful in reaching this segment? What evidence could be presented in affirmative? Select the best student responses and have them presented in class.

S.T.A.R. Project #6
Two firms that seem to have successfully targeted the upscale consumer are Sharper Image (see www.sharperimage.com) and London-based Harrod's (see www.harrods.com). Sharper Image specializes in cutting-edge electronics and gadgets that cannot be found in traditional electronics retailers. Harrod's is a department store that even James Bond would find appealing (in fact, he has on several occasions). After reviewing the above Web sites, decide which company is best

positioned to also appeal to (a) middle class consumers and (b) downscale consumers. Write a short report that details your rationale and provides suggestions for how each could improve Web facilities to expand their market to these secondary consuming groups. Would expansion be a good idea for both (either) of the two firms? Explain.

<u>Instructor's Discussion</u>

The students will find ample evidence of the appeals to the upscale consumer on the two Web sites. Deciding how to go after the (a) middle class consumer and (b) downscale consumer will not be as easy. The first temptation is to say that because Harrod's is a department store it will be in a better position to appeal to the secondary groups. Sharper Image, however, has found that it can promote many of the products carried in its store (on its Web site) through late-night TV and home shopping channels—both traditional secondary market channels. Pick the most creative two or three papers and have them presented in class. Both of the exercises in this section should be appropriate for discussion of the upscale and downscale markets. See references found in the **Notes** section at the end of the chapter for additional guidance on these two markets. For detail, see Notes #10, #27, #31, #34, #36, and #48.

CASES

Case One: Make Mine Top Loading

Chapter 11 provides Figures and Tables (e.g., Table 11-14 and Figure 11-5) and relates household income to specific magazines and/or types of magazines. Any of the magazines read by high income households, as long as they have a female focus (e.g., Vanity Fair, not GQ), would seem to be acceptable as an answer.

Case Two: Do They Still Make Plastic Slipcovers?

Although student responses may vary, one answer to the question is that the upper lower class and the lower middle class are most likely to be plastic slipcover purchasers. The social class suggested by students must be one that has the income to purchase new furniture, because it is highly unlikely that a consumer goes out and purchases plastic slipcovers for existing or pre-owned ("used") furniture. In addition, there may be a small subsegment of individuals in the upper social classes that spend large sums of money on sofas and chairs, and may want them to be protected. *The Wall Street Journal* article notes that although "Manhattanites don't understand it," many immigrants to America, who aren't wealthy, want to protect their new couches and chairs when they purchase them. The article also speaks of a wealthy 36-year-old woman who spent $1,200 for each of her dining room chairs, and then purchased plastic slipcovers to protect them from her husband, children, and pets.

CHAPTER 12

The Influence of Culture on Consumer Behavior

LEARNING OBJECTIVES

After studying this chapter students should be able to:
1. Explain culture and how it is acquired.
2. Discuss how culture is learned.
3. Describe how culture may be measured and examined.
4. Outline American core values.
5. Explain why core values are not an entirely American phenomenon.

CHAPTER SUMMARY

The study of culture is the study of all aspects of a society. It is the language, knowledge, laws, and customs that give that society its distinctive character and personality. In the context of consumer behavior, culture is defined as the sum total of learned beliefs, values, and customs that serve to regulate the consumer behavior of members of a particular society. Beliefs and values are guides for consumer behavior; customs are unusual and accepted ways of behaving.

The impact of culture is so natural and ingrained that its influence on behavior is rarely noted. Yet culture offers order, direction, and guidance to members of society in all phases of human problem solving. Culture is dynamic, and gradually and continually evolves to meet the needs of society.

Culture is learned as part of social experience. Children acquire from their environment a set of beliefs, values, and customs that constitute culture (i.e., they are encultured). These are acquired through formal learning, informal learning, and technical learning. Advertising enhances formal learning by reinforcing desired modes of behavior and expectations; it enhances informal learning by providing models for behavior.

Culture is communicated to members of the society through a common language and through commonly shared symbols. Because the human mind has the ability to absorb and process symbolic communication, marketers can successfully promote both tangible and intangible products and product concepts to consumers through mass media.

All the elements of the marketing mix serve to communicate symbolically with the audience. Products project an image of their own; so does promotion. Price and retail outlets symbolically convey images concerning the quality of the product.

The elements of culture are transmitted by three pervasive social situations: the family, the church, and the school. A fourth social institution that plays a major role in the transmission of culture is the mass media, both through editorial content and through advertising.

Wide ranges of measurement techniques are used to study culture. The range includes projective techniques, attitude measurement methods, field observation, participant observation, content analysis, and value measurement survey techniques.

A number of core values of the American people are relevant to the study of consumer behavior. These include achievement and success, activity, efficiency and practicality, progress, material comfort, individualism, freedom, conformity, humanitarianism, youthfulness, and fitness and health.

Because each of these values varies in importance to the members of our society, each provides an effective basis for segmenting consumer markets.

CHAPTER OUTLINE

INTRODUCTION

1. The study of culture is a challenging undertaking because its primary focus is on the broadest component of social behavior in an entire society.
2. In contrast to the psychologist, who is principally concerned with the study of individual behavior, or the sociologist, who is concerned with the study of groups, the anthropologist is primarily interested in identifying the very fabric of society itself.

WHAT IS CULTURE?

1. Given the broad and pervasive nature of **culture**, its study generally requires a detailed examination of the character of the total society, including such factors as language, knowledge, laws, religions, food customs, music, art, technology, work patterns, products, and other artifacts that give a society its distinctive flavor.
2. In a sense, culture is a society's personality. For this reason, it is not easy to define its boundaries.
3. *Culture* is the sum total of learned beliefs, values, and customs that serve to direct the consumer behavior of members of a particular society.
4. *Beliefs* consist of the very large number of mental or verbal statements that reflect a person's particular knowledge and assessment of something.
5. *Values* also are beliefs, however, values differ from other beliefs because they must meet the following criteria:
    a) They are relatively few in number,
    b) They serve as a guide for culturally appropriate behavior,
    c) They are enduring or difficult to change,
    d) They are not tied to specific objects or situations, and
    e) They are widely accepted by the members of a society.
6. In a broad sense, both values and beliefs are mental images that affect a wide range of specific attitudes that, in turn, influence the way a person is likely to respond in a specific situation.

7. *Customs* are overt modes of behavior that constitute culturally approved or acceptable ways of behaving in specific situations.
   a) Customs consist of everyday or routine behavior.
   b) Although beliefs and values are guides for behavior, customs are usual and acceptable ways of behaving.

*****Use Key Term culture *Here; Use Learning Objective #1 Here; Use Discussion Question #1 Here; Use Exercise #3 Here*****

THE INVISIBLE HAND OF CULTURE

1. The impact of culture is so natural and automatic that its influence on behavior is usually taken for granted.
2. Often, it is only when we are exposed to people with different cultural values or customs that we become aware of how culture has molded our own behavior.
3. Consumers both view themselves in the context of their culture and react to their environment based upon the cultural framework that they bring to that experience. Each individual perceives the world through his or her own cultural lens.

*****Use Learning Objective #1 Here*****

CULTURE SATISFIES NEEDS

1. Culture exists to satisfy the needs of people within a society.
   a) It offers order, direction, and guidance in all phases of human problem solving by providing tried and true methods of satisfying physiological, personal, and social needs.
   b) Similarly, culture also provides insights as to suitable dress for specific occasions (e.g., what to wear around the house, what to wear to school, what to wear to work, what to wear to church, what to wear at a fast food restaurant, or a movie theater).
2. Cultural beliefs, values, and customs continue to be followed as long as they yield satisfaction.
3. In a cultural context, when a product is no longer acceptable because its related value or custom does not adequately satisfy human needs, it must be modified.

*****Use Learning Objective #1 Here; Use Discussion Question #1 Here; Use Exercise #3 Here*****

CULTURE IS LEARNED

1. At an early age we begin to acquire from our social environment a set of beliefs, values, and customs that make up our culture.

2. For children, the learning of these acceptable cultural values and customs is reinforced by the process of playing with their toys.
   a) As children play, they act out and rehearse important cultural lessons and situations.

*****Use Learning Objective #1 and #2 Here*****

How Culture Is Learned

1. There are three distinct forms of learning:
   a) *Formal learning*—adults and older siblings teach a young family member "how to behave."
   b) *Informal learning*—a child learns primarily by imitating the behavior of selected others.
   c) *Technical learning*—teachers instruct the child in an educational environment as to what, how, and why it should be done.
2. It seems that advertising can influence all three forms of learning.
   a) It most influences informal learning by providing models.
3. The repetition of advertising messages creates and reinforces cultural beliefs and values.

*****Use Learning Objective #1 and #2 Here; Use Discussion Question #2 Here; Use Figure 12-1 Here*****

Enculturation and Acculturation

1. The learning of one's own culture is known as *enculturation*.
2. The learning of a new or foreign culture is known as *acculturation*.

*****Use Key Terms acculturation and enculturation Here; Use Learning Objective #1 and #2 Here*****

Language and Symbols

1. To acquire a common culture, the members of a society must be able to communicate with each other through a common language.
   a) Without a common language, shared meaning could not exist and true communication would not take place.
2. Basically, the symbolic nature of human language sets it apart from all other animal communication.
3. A *symbol* is anything that stands for something else.
   a) Symbols may have several, even contradictory, meanings.
   b) Marketers use symbols to convey desired product images or characteristics.
4. Price and channels of distribution are also significant symbols of the marketer and the marketer's product.
   a) The type of store where the product is sold is also an important symbol of quality.

*****Use Key Term symbol Here; Use Learning Objective #1 and #2 Here; Use Exercise #1 and #4 Here; Use Figure 12-2 Here*****

Ritual

1. A *ritual* is a type of symbolic activity consisting of a series of steps occurring in a fixed sequence and repeated over time.
2. Rituals extend over the human life cycle from birth to death.
   a) They can be public or private.
   b) It is often formal and scripted—i.e., proper conduct is prescribed.
3. Important to marketers, rituals tend to be replete with ritual artifacts (products) that are associated with, or somehow enhance, performance of the ritual.
4. *Ritualistic behavior* is any behavior that is made into a ritual.

*****Use Key Term ritual Here; Use Learning Objective #1 and #2 Here; Use Exercise #2 Here; Use Figure 12-3 Here; Use Table 12-1 and 12-2 Here*****

Culture Is Shared

1. To be considered a cultural characteristic, a particular belief, value, or practice must be shared by a significant portion of the society.
2. Culture is often viewed as group *customs*.
3. Various social institutions transmit the elements of culture and make sharing of culture a reality.
   a) *Family*—the primary agent for enculturation, teaches consumer-related values and skills.
   b) *Educational institutions*—charged with imparting basic learning skills, history, patriotism, citizenship, and the technical training needed to prepare people for significant roles within society.
   c) *Houses of worship*—provide religious consciousness, spiritual guidance, and moral training.
   d) *Mass media*—is a fourth and often overlooked transmitter of culture.
      i) It disseminates information about products, ideas, and causes.
      ii) We have daily exposure to advertising, and through those ads, receive cultural information.

*****Use Learning Objective #1 and #2 Here*****

CULTURE IS DYNAMIC

1. Culture continually evolves; therefore, the marketer must carefully monitor the sociocultural environment in order to market an existing product more effectively or to develop promising new products.

a)   This is not easy because many factors are likely to produce cultural changes within a given society.
2.   The changing nature of culture means that marketers have to consistently reconsider:
   a)   *Why* consumers are now doing what they do.
   b)   *Who* are the purchasers and the users of their products?
   c)   *When* they do their shopping.
   d)   *How* and *where* they can be reached by the media.
   e)   *What* new product and service needs are emerging?

*****Use Learning Objective #1 Here; Use Table 12-3 Here*****

THE MEASUREMENT OF CULTURE

1.   There are a variety of measures of culture; projective tests, attitude measurement techniques, as well as content analysis, consumer fieldwork, and value measurement instruments.

*****Use Learning Objective #3 Here*****

Content Analysis

1.   ***Content analysis*** focuses on the content of verbal, written, and pictorial communications.
   a)   It is a relatively objective means for determining social and cultural changes within a specific society.
   b)   It is useful to marketers and public policy makers interested in comparing advertising claims of competitors within a specific industry.

*****Use Key Term content analysis Here; Use Learning Objective #3 Here; Use Exercise #4 Here*****

Consumer Fieldwork

1.   When examining a specific society, anthropologists frequently immerse themselves in the environment under study through ***consumer fieldwork***.
2.   Researchers are likely to select a small sample of people from a particular society and carefully observe their behavior.
3.   ***Field observation*** has a number of distinct characteristics:
   a)   It takes place within a natural environment.
   b)   It is performed sometimes without the subjects' awareness.
   c)   It focuses on observation of behavior.
4.   Instead of just observing behavior, researchers sometimes become ***participant-observers***.
   a)   They become active members of the environment they are studying.
5.   Another form of fieldwork, depth interviews and focus-group sessions, are also quite often employed by marketers to get a first look at an emerging social or cultural change.

6. In the relatively informal atmosphere of focus group discussions, consumers are apt to reveal attitudes or behavior that may signal a shift in values that, in turn, may affect the long-run market acceptance of a product or service.

*****Use Key Terms **consumer fieldwork, field observation, and participant-observers** Here; Use Learning Objective #3 Here****

Value Measurement Survey Instruments

1. Anthropologists have traditionally observed behavior and inferred dominant or underlying values.
   a) Recently there has been a gradual shift to directly measuring values.
2. *Value instruments*—ask people how they feel about such basic personal and social concepts as freedom, comfort, national security, and peace.
3. A variety of popular value instruments have been used in research:
   a) The Rokeach Value Survey.
   b) List of Values.
   c) Values and Lifestyles—VALS.
4. The **Rokeach Value Survey** is a self-administered value inventory, which is divided into two parts.
   a) Part one consists of 18 *terminal value items*, designed to measure the relative importance of end-states of existence (personal goals).
   b) Part two consists of 18 *instrumental value items*, designed to measure the basic approaches an individual might take to reach end-state values.
5. The LOV is a related instrument.
   a) Its scale asks consumers to identify their two most important values from a nine-value list.

*****Use Key Term **Rokeach Value Survey** Here; Use Learning Objective #3 Here; Use Discussion Question #3 Here; Use Table 12-4 Here*****

AMERICAN CORE VALUES

1. Identification of *core values* is a very difficult task for several reasons.
   a) The United States is a very diverse country consisting of a variety of *subcultures*, each of which interprets and responds to society's basic beliefs and values in its own specific way.
   b) Also, rapid technological change has occurred in the United States, and in itself makes it difficult to monitor changes in cultural values.
   c) Finally, the existence of contradictory values in American society is somewhat confusing.
2. When selecting specific core values researchers are guided by three principles:
   a) The value must be pervasive—accepted and used by a significant portion of the American people,

b) The value must be enduring—influencing the actions of Americans over an extended period of time.

c) The value must be consumer-related—providing insights that help marketing people understand the consumption actions of the American people.

> *******Use Key Terms core values and subcultures *Here; Use Learning Objective #4 Here; Use Discussion Question #4 Here; Use Exercise #3 Here********

Achievement and Success

1. These values have historical roots in the traditional Protestant work ethic, which considers work to be spiritually healthy.
   a) Furthermore, research shows the achievement orientation is closely associated with the technical development and economic growth of the American society.
2. Individuals who consider a sense of accomplishment to be an important personal value tend to be achievers who strive hard for success.
   a) Although closely related, achievement and success are different.
      i) *Achievement* is its own direct reward—it is satisfying to the achiever.
      ii) *Success* implies an extrinsic reward—financial or status improvements.

> *******Use Learning Objective #4 Here; Use Discussion Question #4 Here; Use Figure 12-4 Here********

Activity

1. Americans feel is it important to be *active* or *involved*.
2. Keeping busy is widely accepted as a healthy and even necessary part of the American lifestyle.
   a) This can have both a positive and negative effect on products.

> *******Use Learning Objective #4 Here; Use Discussion Question #4 Here********

Efficiency and Practicality

1. In terms of *efficiency*, Americans admire anything that saves time and effort.
2. In terms of *practicality*, Americans are generally receptive to any new product that makes tasks easier and can help solve problems.
3. Americans also attach great importance to time and punctuality.
4. Americans seem to be convinced that "time waits for no one," which is reflected in their habitual attention to being prompt.
5. Americans place a great deal of importance on getting there first, on the value of time itself; on the notion that time is money, on the importance of not wasting time, and on identifying "more" time.
6. The frequency with which Americans look at their watches, and the importance attached to having an accurate timepiece, tend to support the American value of punctuality.

***** *Use Learning Objective #4 Here; Use Discussion Question #4 Here; Use Figure 12-5 Here* *****

Progress

1. *Progress* is linked to the values reviewed earlier and the central belief that people can always improve themselves—that tomorrow will be better than today.
2. Progress often means the acceptance of change—new products designed to fulfill previously under- or unsatisfied needs.

***** *Use Learning Objective #4 Here; Use Discussion Question #4 Here; Use Figure 12-6 Here* *****

Material Comfort

1. To most Americans, *material comfort* signifies the attainment of the good life.
2. It is a *relative* view; satisfaction with the amount of material goods comes in terms of how they compare to others.

***** *Use Learning Objective #4 Here; Use Discussion Question #4 Here* *****

Individualism

1. Americans want to be themselves.
   a) Self-reliance, self-interest, self-confidence, self-esteem, and self-fulfillment are all expressions of individualism.
2. Consumer appeals frequently take the form of reinforcing the consumers' sense of identity with products that both reflect and emphasize that identity.

***** *Use Learning Objective #4 Here; Use Discussion Question #4 Here* *****

Freedom

1. To the marketer, *freedom of choice* means the opportunity to choose from a wide range of alternatives.
2. This preference is reflected in the large number of competitive brands and product variations that can be found on the shelves of the modern supermarket or department store.

***** *Use Learning Objective #4 Here; Use Discussion Question #4 Here; Use Figure 12-7 Here* *****

External Conformity

1. *External conformity* is a necessary process by which the individual adapts to society.
2. Conformity takes the form of standardized goods and services.

3. The availability of a wide choice of standardized products allows the consumer to be:
   a) Individualistic—selecting products that close friends do not have.
   b) Conforming—purchasing products similar to those their friends do have.
      i) There is a ping-pong relationship between these two values.
      ii) The more individualistic Americans are, the more they create patterns or trends to conform to, perhaps only in smaller numbers.

*****Use Learning Objective #4 Here; Use Discussion Question #4 Here*****

Humanitarianism

1. Americans tend to be charitable and willing to come to the aid of people less fortunate.
2. Many companies try to appeal to consumers by emphasizing their concern for environmental and social issues.

*****Use Learning Objective #4 Here; Use Discussion Question #4 Here; Use Table 12-5 Here*****

Youthfulness

1. Americans tend to place an almost sacred value on appearing young.
2. This should not be confused with youth.
   a) *Youthfulness* is looking and acting young regardless of chronological age.
3. A great deal of advertising is directed to creating a sense of urgency about retaining one's youth and fearing aging.

*****Use Learning Objective #4 Here; Use Discussion Question #4 Here; Use Figure 12-8 Here*****

Fitness and Health

1. Americans' preoccupation with *fitness and health* has emerged as a core value.
2. This value has manifested itself in a number of ways, including tennis, racquetball, and jogging, and the continued increases in sales of vitamins.
3. Fitness and health are becoming lifestyle choices for many consumers.
4. Although there is no denying the fitness and healthy living trend in American society, there is evidence that consumers find it difficult "to be good."
5. Many Americans are unwilling to compromise on flavor for health benefits, with the result being a kind of reverse trend toward full-flavored, rich foods.

*****Use Learning Objective #4 Here; Use Discussion Question #4 Here; Use Figure 12-9 Here; Use Exercise #3 Here*****

Core Values Not an American Phenomenon

1. Cultural values are not all unique or originally American.
   a) Some were borrowed, particularly from European society.

*****Use Learning Objective #5 Here*****

DISCUSSION QUESTIONS

1. **Distinguish among beliefs, values, and customs. Illustrate how the clothing a person wears at different times or for different occasions is influenced by customs.**

   Beliefs consist of the very large number of mental or verbal statements that reflect a person's particular knowledge and assessment of something. *Values* are also beliefs, however, values differ from other beliefs because they must meet certain criteria: (a) they are relatively few in number, (b) they serve as a guide for culturally appropriate behavior, (c) they are enduring or difficult to change, (d) they are not tied to specific objects or situations, and (e) they are widely accepted by the members of a society. *Customs* are overt modes of behavior that constitute culturally approved or acceptable ways of behaving in specific situations. Students' answers on clothing will vary based on their experiences. Listen for sexist or ethnic stereotyping as students share their opinions.

2. **A manufacturer of fat-free granola bars is considering targeting school-age children by positioning its product as a healthy, nutritious snack food. How can an understanding of the three forms of cultural learning be used in developing an effective strategy to target the intended market?**

   Anthropologists have identified three distinct forms of cultural learning; *formal learning*, in which adults and older siblings teach a young family member how to behave, *informal learning*, in which a child learns primarily by imitating the behavior of selected others, family, friends, TV heroes; and *technical learning*, in which teachers instruct the child in an educational environment about what should be done, how it should be done, and why it should be done. A marketer might target the child's parents with informative/educational advertising so that they would tell their child the food is acceptable. They might use superhero role models from TV programs, enjoying the snack food and showing how it helps them defeat the bad guys. The marketer might use scenario or slice-of-life commercials to show the child how to use the product.

3. **The Citrus Growers of America are planning a promotional campaign to encourage the drinking of orange and grapefruit juices in situations where many consumers normally consume soft drinks. Using the Rokeach Value Survey Instrument (Table 12-4), identify relevant cultural, consumption-specific, and product-specific values for citrus juices as an alternative to soft drinks. What are the implications of these values for an advertising campaign designed to increase the consumption of citrus juices?**

The instructor should stress that there are links between cultural, consumption-specific, and product-specific values. The attitudes and values toward soft drinks and citrus juices are culturally derived, and given the popularity and diverse usage of soft drinks, the Citrus Growers of America are going to have difficulty luring consumers away from them. The Citrus Growers of America organization must convey the notion that the product-specific values of drinking citrus juices are congruent with consumption-specific and cultural values. Thus, the association should consider the links between culture and consumption of juices and soft drinks; some of these possible links are:

Cultural Values	Consumption-Specific Values	Product-Specific Values
*An exciting and active life	*physical health *well being	*natural drink *the vitamins in the juice *nutritional content
*Freedom	*self identity *nonconformity	*be different from the crowd *citrus juices are not only for breakfast
*Pleasure	*enjoying life	*refreshing taste *cool
*Friendship others	*being with others	*drink juices in the company of others

4. **For each of the products and activities listed below:**
   a. **Identify the core values most relevant to their purchase and use.**
   b. **Determine whether these values encourage or discourage use or ownership.**
   c. **Determine whether these core values are shifting, and if so, in what direction. The products and activities are:**
      1. **Donating money to charities**
      2. **Donating blood**
      3. **Compact disc players**
      4. **Telephone answering machines**
      5. **Toothpaste**
      6. **Diet soft drinks**
      7. **Foreign travel**
      8. **Suntan lotion**
      9. **Cellular phones**
      10. **Interactive TV home-shopping services**
      11. **Fat-free foods**
      12. **Products in recyclable packaging**

The following chart can be used as a guide for the classroom discussion. Instructors are encouraged to add products and services to the list, and invite students to do the same.

Product or Activity	Core Value(s)	Encourages or Discourages	Direction of Shift
Donating money to charities	Humanitarianism	Encourages	No shift
Donating blood	Humanitarianism	Encourages	No shift
Compact disc players	Efficiency, Practicality Material Comfort	Encourages	No shift
Phone answering machine	Efficiency, Practicality	Encourages	Up
Toothpaste	External Conformity	Encourages	No shift
Diet soft drink	Fitness and Health; External Conformity	Encourages Encourages	Up No shift
Foreign travel	Individualism; Freedom	Encourages Encourages	Up Up
Suntan lotions	Youthfulness; Fitness and Health	Encourages Encourages	Up Up
Cellular phones	Efficiency, Practicality	Encourages	Up
Interactive TV home shopping	Efficiency, Practicality Progress	Encourages	Up
Fat-free foods	Fitness and Health	Encourages	Up
Recyclable packaging	Ecological concern	Encourages	Up

EXERCISES

1. **Identify a singer or singing group whose music you like and discuss the symbolic function of the clothes that person (or group) wears.**

Instructor's Discussion

This exercise will illustrate how nonverbal symbols communicate cultural values. Depending on your current taste in music you might want to pick a couple of students to be the monitors of the accuracy of the students' analysis. Or, videotape selected presentations on MTV or the like, show the clips in class, and have the students comment.

2. **Think of various routines in your everyday life (such as grooming or food preparation). Identify one ritual and describe it. In your view, is this ritual shared by others? If so, to what extent? What are the implications of your ritualistic behavior to the marketer(s) of the product(s) you use during your routine?**

<u>Instructor's Discussion</u>

Prepare to share a couple of your own or family rituals to prime the pump. Students' responses will vary based on their backgrounds. This can be an exercise that provides students insights into how others live.

3a. **Summarize an episode of a weekly television series that you watched recently. Describe how the program transmitted cultural beliefs, values, and customs.**

b. **Select and describe three commercials that were broadcast during the program mentioned in 3a. Do these commercials create or reflect cultural values? Explain your answer.**

<u>Instructor's Discussion</u>

In advance of the class, the professor should assign a TV program that all students must watch and analyze. The discussion of the programs' content and commercials provides an excellent illustration of utilizing content analysis to explore cultural beliefs, values, and customs.

4a. **Find two different advertisements for deodorants in two magazines that are targeted to different audiences. Content-analyze the written and pictorial aspects of each ad, utilizing any core values discussed in this chapter. How are these values portrayed to the target audiences?**

b. **Identify symbols used in these ads and discuss their effectiveness in conveying the desired product image or characteristics.**

<u>Instructor's Discussion</u>

This exercise provides students with an opportunity to identify the presence of cultural values in advertising and analyze the ways that manufacturers of various brands within the same product category often employ different cultural values in their promotional efforts.

<u>**S.TA.R. PROJECTS**</u>

Ethical Issues in Consumer Behavior

S.T.A.R. Project #1
Do a search of popular magazines that carry a number of clothing and consumer products ads. Select magazines that are clearly targeting an Anglo market, an African-American market, and a Hispanic market. Compare the ads in the different magazines for similarities and differences. How are the beliefs, values, and customs of the three American-cultural groups different and/or similar? What different symbols are used to convey messages within the different magazines? Are the predominant color schemes different? Once the preceding analysis is completed, comment on any ethical issues that you have observed during your research. Write a short paper that summarizes your findings.

Instructor's Discussion

This exercise asks students to review contemporary magazines and use these publications to observe cultural differences between the three primary ethnic subcultures in our society. Pick the best of the short papers and discuss the results with the class. Especially focus on any discovered ethical issues.

S.T.A.R. Project #2
Review the material found in the chapter and in Table 12-6 on American Core Values. As you read about the general features and relevance to consumer behavior of the American Core Values, consider the ethical responsibility that marketers must have when directing promotional efforts toward these values. Write a short paper that expresses what you perceive these ethical responsibilities to be. You may pick a particular company or product to use as an example or may discuss the issues generally. Be sure to consider using illustrations (advertisements) of your thoughts or position.

Instructor's Discussion

The primary purpose of this exercise is to get students to review material in the chapter on American Core Values. The exercise will give them the opportunity to once again review the material found in Table 12-6. Additionally, the exercise asks students to consider the values in light of ethical responsibility. For example, individualism (free speech) may give one the right of expression but it does not guarantee racism, bigotry, or harmful actions toward others. Or consider that although material comfort is great, everyone cannot afford this. What problems might be encountered by those that feel slighted by promotions that stress material acquisition?

<u>Small Group Projects</u>

S.T.A.R. Project #3
The learning of one's own culture is called enculturation. How do we learn this culture? Members of society learn a great deal through communication in a common language. Your group's assignment is to examine three different age groups with respect to communication.

Examine children (aged 5–8), teens (aged 13–16), and young adults (aged 19–22) with respect to their slang language and symbols that convey messages. Devise a table that describes at least ten (10) language or symbols for communication illustrations for each group. Write a short paper that discusses what you have done and conclusions on the differences and similarities found. Present the information in class.

Instructor's Discussion

This exercise asks students to review three stages that they should have some familiarity with because each has pasted through these stages or is currently in the last stage. Slang language is an interesting cultural expression because it not only identifies age groups but ethnic formations as well. Put the best of these lists on the board and discuss how marketers might use this information.

S.T.A.R. Project #4

"We all live in tribes." Well, maybe not all of us, but those on the hit CBS TV series Survivor certainly do (see www.cbs.com). Your group's assignment is to examine tribal (ritual) behavior and its impact on consumer behavior. Begin the assignment by examining the Survivor TV show's history found on the CBS Web site. Next, do secondary research on tribal behavior (rituals). For example, review rituals in the military, sports, fraternities, sororities, clubs, and organizations and how these rituals are transferred to consumptive behavior. Once this has been completed, write a short position paper that summarizes your findings and indicates what you have learned about the relationship between tribal (ritual) behavior and consumer behavior.

Instructor's Discussion

Most students really enjoy considering tribes and rituals. After reviewing the material in the chapter, most will have a good basis on which to build this project. By going to the CBS Web site, students can trace the history of the survivor series by going to the "select a show" feature and scrolling to the Survivor series.

Using the Internet to Study Consumer Behavior

S.T.A.R. Project #5

Advertising symbols are important ways that companies communicate with consumers. We all know the logos for Kellogg's, Chevrolet, and IBM. Your assignment in this question is to play a symbols game and see how you score. Mr. Joey Katzen has developed an excellent symbols recognition game to be found at www.joeykatzen.com/alpha. The *Retail Alphabet Game* takes letters (symbols) from well-known retail names or phrases and asks you to identify them. This trivia game helps us to understand how important symbols and names are to the marketing and communication effort. Play the game and tell us how you scored. What did you miss? What did you get right? What conclusions can you draw about your ability to recognize symbols? Write a short paper that expresses your thoughts.

The game is fun and informative. The students can play historical versions of the game at no cost. Mr. Katzen only charges for the most recent version. The Web site is also an excellent download site. Have fun with this one.

S.T.A.R. Project #6

One of the easiest ways to examine one's values is to observe how they dress. Specifically, jewelry says a lot about the man or woman. Your assignment is to find four (4) wrist watch Web sites and review the products found on these Web sites. Taking the American Core Values discussed in the chapter (see Table 12-6), write a short paper about how the companies you investigated appeal to American Core Values. Be sure to include examples to illustrate your feelings. Lastly, comment on how the opening Web pages of the sampled sites set the stage for value transmission to the consumer. What specific devices are used by the site marketers?

Instructor's Discussion

Students will find several illustrations in the chapter that can be used to begin the search (such as Citizen and Rolex). Students should next carefully examine Table 12-6 and the values included. Does the wrist watch appeal to the efficiency and practically value or the individualism value? Be sure that students are clear as to their conclusions. This subject is an easy one to discuss in class. Try pulling up several Web sites to illustrate.

CASES

Case One: Eat and Run

Considering the discussion in Chapter 12 of American Core Values, it would seem that these meals "on the go" are consistent with existing values. In particular, such American core values as "activity" and "efficiency" and "practicality" point to a "value-environment" that would suggest the acceptance of such a product. One might also argue that "fitness and health" (especially for a Yogurt product fortified with vitamins) and "freedom" (i.e., "freedom of choice") might also be applicable core values.

Case Two: Make My Rent-A-Car "Personal"

Because Enterprise rents so many different types of vehicles, the customer has the freedom of choice to select the exact type of vehicle he or she needs for the specific occasion at hand. This might be a minivan for a family vacation, or a convertible for a summer's day drive in the country. It might also be beneficial to bring up the issue of segmentation in the class discussion, because Enterprise has targeted the consumer (i.e., nonbusiness) segment of the rent-a-car market.

CHAPTER 13

Subcultures and Consumer Behavior

LEARNING OBJECTIVES

After studying this chapter students should be able to:
1. Define subculture.
2. Discuss the methods used for defining and segmenting the various subcultures in America.
3. Outline the geographic impact of nationality subcultures.
4. Explain the importance of the prominent religious subcultures.
5. Identify the consequence of regional and geographic subcultures.
6. Identify the major racial subcultures.
7. Define and discuss the Generation Y, Generation X, baby boomers, and the older consumer markets.
8. Describe the relationship of sex roles and consumer behavior.
9. Discuss how marketers segment the Working Woman market.

SUMMARY

Subcultural analysis enables marketers to segment their markets to meet the specific needs, motivations, perceptions, and attitudes shared by members of a specific subcultural group. A subculture is a distinct cultural group that exists as an identifiable segment within a larger, more complex society. Its members possess beliefs, values, and customs that set them apart from other members of the same society; at the same time, they hold to the dominant beliefs of the overall society. Major subcultural categories in this country include nationality, religion, geographic location, race, age, and sex. Each of these can be broken down into smaller segments that can be reached through special copy appeals and selective media choices. In some cases (such as the elderly consumer), product characteristics can be tailored to the specialized needs of the market segment. Because all subcultural groups, the marketer must determine for the product category how specific subcultural memberships interact to influence the consumer's purchase decisions.

CHAPTER OUTLINE

INTRODUCTION

1. Culture has a potent influence on all consumer behavior.
2. Individuals are brought up to follow the beliefs, values, and customs of their society and to avoid behavior that is judged "unacceptable" or considered taboo.
   a) In addition to segmenting in terms of cultural factors, marketers also segment overall societies into smaller subgroups (subcultures) that consist of people who are similar in terms of their ethnic origin, their customs, and/or the ways they behave.

b) These subcultures provide important marketing opportunities for astute marketing strategists.

3. The subcultural divisions discussed are based on a variety of sociocultural and demographic variables, such as nationality, religion, geographic locality, race, age, sex, even working status.

WHAT IS SUBCULTURE?

1. Members of specific *subcultures* possess beliefs, values, and customs that set them apart from other members of the same society.

2. *Subculture* is defined as being a distinct cultural group that exists as an identifiable segment within a larger, more complex society.

*****Use Key Term** subculture *Here; Use Learning Objective #1 Here*****

---

3. A cultural profile of a society or nation is a composite of two elements:
   a) The unique beliefs, values, and customs subscribed to by its members.
   b) The central or core cultural themes shared by the majority of the population, regardless of specific subcultural memberships.

4. Each subculture has its own unique traits.

5. Subcultural analysis enables the marketing manager to focus on sizable and natural market segments.
   a) When carrying out such analyses, the marketer must determine whether the beliefs, values, and customs shared by members of a specific subgroup make them desirable candidates for special marketing attention.

*****Use Discussion Question #1 and #2 Here; Use Table 13-1 Here; Use Figure 13-1 and 13-2 Here; Use Exercise #1 Here*****

NATIONALITY SUBCULTURES

1. For many people, *nationality* is an important subcultural reference that guides what they value and what they buy.

2. Although most U.S. citizens are born in the United States, some still retain a pride and identification with the language and customs of their ancestors.
   a) This identification can manifest itself in consumption behavior.

3. When it comes to consumer behavior, ancestral pride is manifested most strongly in the consumption of ethnic foods, in travel to their "homeland," and in the purchase of numerous cultural artifacts.

4. A good illustration of the importance of ethnic origin as a subcultural market segment is the *Hispanic American subculture*.

*****Use Key Terms** nationality and Hispanic American subculture *Here; Use Learning Objective #2 Here*****

Hispanic Subcultures

1. Hispanic Americans represent almost 12 percent of the United States population (35.5 million people, with buying power of $452 billion).
2. Hispanic Americans are younger (the median age of Hispanics is about 10 years younger than the median age of non-Hispanic whites), they are members of larger families, and they are more likely to live in an "extended family" household—consisting of several generations of family members.
   a) Not only are Hispanic households more likely than black or non-Hispanic white families to contain children, Hispanics spend more time caring for their children.
3. With the number of Hispanic Americans expected to grow to over 38 million by the year 2005, this subculture is anticipated to comprise the largest minority in the United States by that time.
4. The ten metro areas with the largest Hispanic populations are also home to 58 percent of the Hispanic population of the United States.
5. There are 12 Hispanic subgroups now identified in the United States.
   a) The three largest Hispanic subcultural groups consist of Mexican-Americans (about 64 percent of total Hispanic-Americans), Puerto Ricans (approximately 10 percent of the total), and Cubans (about 4 percent of the total).
   b) These subcultures are heavily concentrated geographically, with more than 70 percent of their members residing in California, Texas, New York, and Florida; Los Angeles, alone, is home to one-fifth of the Hispanic population of the United States.
   c) Although more than 60 percent of all Mexican-Americans (the largest Hispanic group) were born in the United States, 72 percent of Cuban-Americans were born in Cuba.

Understanding Hispanic Consumer Behavior

1. Hispanic and Anglo consumers differ in terms of a variety of important buyer behavior variables.
2. Hispanic subculture is dynamic and evolving.
   a) More and more Hispanics are food shopping in non-Hispanic supermarkets, for example.
   b) They appear to be in the process of acculturation.

*****Use Table 13-2 Here*****

Defining and Segmenting the Hispanic Market

1. The Hispanic market (in addition to using self-identification and degree of identification segmentation) might be segmented by using a combination of the country of origin and geographic concentration in the United States.
2. Language provides still another basis for segmenting the Hispanic-American market, even though there are significant variations regarding their language preferences.
3. Hispanics seem to prefer media in the first language they learned to speak.
4. There is also some evidence that "Hispanic assimilation is a myth."

a) Second and third generation Hispanics in the United States, people who are completely bilingual and who speak English without a trace of an accent, are big viewers of Spanish-language television.

b) And this fact seems to hold true regardless of the Hispanic household's income.

5. Each of the major Hispanic subcultural groups appears to have some distinct beliefs, values, and customs; thus, a marketing strategy that may be successful with Puerto Ricans in New York might fail with Cubans in Miami.

6. Finally, the Hispanic market may be segmented in terms of the degree of acculturation to the dominant American cultural values, customs, artifacts, and rituals.

*****Use Learning Objective #2 and #3 Here; Use Table 13-3 Here; Use Figure 13-3 and 13-4 Here*****

RELIGIOUS SUBCULTURES

1. The United States has more than 200 different organized *religious subcultures*.
   a) Of this number, Protestant denominations, Roman Catholicism, and Judaism are the principle organized religious faiths.
2. Consumer behavior is commonly directly affected by religion in terms of products that are *symbolically* and *ritualistically* associated with the celebration of various religious holidays.
3. Religious requirements or practices sometimes take on an expanded meaning beyond their original purpose.
4. Targeting specific religious groups with specially designed marketing programs can be very profitable.

*****Use Key Term religious subculture Here; Use Learning Objective #2 and #4 Here; Use Figure 13-5 Here*****

GEOGRAPHIC AND REGIONAL SUBCULTURES

1. The United States is a large country, one that enjoys a wide range of climatic and geographic conditions.
2. It is only natural that many Americans have a sense of *regional* identification and use this identification as a way of describing others (e.g., "He is a true New Englander").
3. There are regional differences in consumption behavior, especially when it comes to food and drink.
   a) Regional differences also include brand preferences.

*****Use Key Term regional Here; Use Learning Objective #3 Here*****

4. Consumer research studies document regional differences in consumption patterns.
   a) This distinction helps redefine local markets in terms of specific urban lifestyle.

*****Use Learning Objective #2, #3, and #5 Here; Use Discussion Question #2 Here; Use Table 13-5, 13-6, and 13-7 Here*****

RACIAL SUBCULTURES

1. The major *racial subcultures* in the United States are Caucasian, African American, Asian American, and American Indian.
   a) The majority of research has focused on the difference between African American and Caucasian consumers and only recently turned to Asian Americans.

*****Use Key Term racial subcultures Here*****

The African American Consumer

1. Consisting of about 36 million people, *African American consumers* currently constitute the largest racial minority in the United States (almost 13 percent of the population).
   a) Purchasing power estimated to be $572 billion.
2. This important subcultural grouping is frequently portrayed as a single, undifferentiated "African American market," consisting of consumers who have a uniform set of consumer needs.
   a) In reality it consists of numerous subgroups, each with distinctive backgrounds, needs, interests, and opinions.

*****Use Key Term African American consumers Here; Use Learning Objective #6 Here*****

Consumer Behavior Characteristics of African American Consumers

1. There are meaningful differences in terms of product preferences and brand purchase patterns.
2. African American consumers tend to prefer popular or leading brands, are brand loyal, and are unlikely to purchase private-label and generic products.
3. Almost two-thirds of African-Americans are willing to pay more to get "the best."
4. Some meaningful differences exist among Anglo white, African American, and Hispanic American consumers in the purchase, ownership, and use of a diverse group of products.

*****Use Table 13-8 Here*****

Reaching the African American Audience

1. Traditionally, marketers have subscribed to one of two distinct marketing strategies.
   a) Some have followed the policy of running all their advertising in general mass media in the belief that African Americans have the same media habits as whites.

b) Others have followed the policy of running additional advertising in selected media directed exclusively to African Americans.

c) Both strategies may be appropriate in specific situations and for specific product categories.

    i) For products of very broad appeal (e.g., aspirin or toothpaste), it is possible that the mass media (primarily television) may effectively reach all relevant consumers, including African American and white.

    ii) For other products (e.g., personal grooming products or food products), marketers may find that mass media do not communicate effectively with the African American market.

2. African Americans have cultural values subtly different from the U.S. population as a whole.

3. Many marketers supplement their general advertising with advertisements in magazines, newspapers, and other media directed specifically to African Americans.

4. In recent years, major advertisers targeting the African American market have increasingly used the specialized services of African American advertising agencies.

*****Use Discussion Question #3 Here; Use Learning Objective #2 and #6 Here; Use Table 13-9 Here*****

Asian American Consumers

1. The *Asian American* population (primarily Chinese, Filipinos, Japanese, Asian Indians, Koreans, and Vietnamese) is currently about 12 million in size and is the fastest-growing American minority (on a percentage basis).

2. It is expected that immigration should push the Asian American population to 13 million by 2005, which represents a gain of almost 54 percent since 1990.

3. The current Asian American market, which represents close to 4 percent of the United States population.

4. Because Asian Americans are largely family-oriented, highly industrious, and strongly driven to achieve a middle-class lifestyle, they are an attractive market for increasing numbers of marketers.

5. About 60 percent of Asian Americans have incomes of at least $60,000 and about 50 percent hold professional positions.

*****Use Key Term Asian American Here; Use Learning Objective #6 Here*****

Where Are the Asian Americans?

1. Asian Americans are largely urban people, who are presently concentrated in and around a small number of large American cities.

    a) About half of Asian Americans live in greater Los Angeles, San Francisco, and New York.

2. Marketers can be misled by the urban numbers displayed by this segment. Many Asian Americans live in the suburbs.

Understanding the Asian-American Consumer

1. Local newspapers and weekly news magazines frequently portray the accomplishments of Asian Americans, who have shown themselves to be hardworking, very family-oriented, and strivers for excellence in educational pursuits (for themselves and their children).
    a) Supporting this profile, United States Census Bureau data reveal that more Asian Americans, on a per-capita basis, own their own businesses than non-Asian American minorities.
    b) Those who do not own their own businesses are largely in professional, technical, or managerial occupations.
    c) They also tend to be better educated and more computer literate than the general population.
    d) Additionally, many Asian Americans are young and live a good part of their lives in multi-income households.

Asian Americans as Consumers

1. The buying power of Asian Americans amount to about $254 billion annually.
    a) They value quality and are willing to pay for it.
    b) This population segment tends to be loyal customers.
    c) The segment is frequently more male-oriented when it comes to consumption decisions.
    d) The segment is attracted to retailers who make it known that they welcome Asian American patronage.
2. It is important to remember that Asian Americans are really drawn from diverse cultural backgrounds.
    a) Vietnamese Americans are more likely to follow the traditional model wherein the man makes the decision for large purchases, whereas Chinese American husbands and wives are more likely to share in the decision-making process.
3. The use of Asian American models in advertising is effective in reaching this market segment.

*****Use Learning Objective #2 and #6 Here; Use Discussion Question #4 Here; Use Table 13-10 Here*****

AGE SUBCULTURES

1. Four *age subculture* segments have been singled out for discussion (*Generation Y, Generation X, baby boomers,* and *seniors*) because their distinctive lifestyles qualify them for consideration as subcultural groups.

*****Use Key Terms age subculture, Generation Y, Generation X, baby boomers, and seniors Here; Use Learning Objective #2 Here*****

The Generation Y Market

1. This age cohort (a cohort is a group of individuals born over a relatively short and continuous period of time) includes the approximately 71 million Americans born between the years 1977 and 1994 (i.e., the children of the baby boomers).
   a) This cohort is also known as the "echo boomers" or the "millennium generation."
   b) This group is often described as being pragmatic, savvy, socially and environmentally aware, and open to new experiences.

Appealing to Generation Y

1. The teen segment of Generation Y spends over $150 billion annually and influences purchases by their parents of several times this amount.
2. They have grown up in a media-saturated environment and tend to be aware of "marketing hype."
3. This group has shifted some of its TV viewing time to the Internet.

*****Use Learning Objective #2 and #7 Here; Use Figure 13-6 Here; Use Exercise #3 Here*****

The Generation X Market

1. This group (Xers, busters, or slackers) consists of approximately 46 million 23- to 37-year-olds who spend about $125 billion yearly.
2. They do not like labels, are cynical, and do not want to be singled out and marketed to.
3. They are in no rush to marry, start a family, or work excessive hours to earn high salaries.
   a) Job satisfaction is typically much more important than salary.
   b) It is more important to enjoy life and to have a lifestyle that provides freedom and flexibility.

Appealing to Generation X

1. Members of Generation X often pride themselves on their sophistication.
2. Not necessarily materialistic, they do purchase good brand names but not necessarily designer labels.
3. They want to be recognized by marketers as a group in their own right.
4. One key for marketers appears to be sincerity.
5. Baby boomer media does not work with Generation X members.
   a) Xers are the MTV generation.
   b) The Fox network claims that 38 percent of its viewers are in this age group.

*****Use Learning Objective #2 and #7 Here; Use Discussion Question #5 Here; Use Exercise #2 and #3 Here*****

The Baby Boomer Market

1. They are especially attractive because:
   a) They are largest age category alive today.
   b) They make important consumer purchase decisions.
   c) They contain a small subsegment of trendsetting consumers—Yuppies—who influence the consumer tastes of other age segments of society.

Who are the Baby-Boomers?

1. This segment was born between 1946 and 1964, aged mid-30s to mid-50s.
2. They represent 40 percent of the adult population and comprise 50 percent of all people in professional and managerial occupations and more than one-half of those with at least a college degree.

*****Use Figure 13-7 Here*****

Consumer Characteristics of Baby Boomers

1. Baby boomers tend to be motivated consumers.
2. They enjoy buying for themselves, for their homes or apartments, and for others—they are consumption-oriented.
3. Yuppies are by far the most sought-after subgroup of baby boomers.
   a) Although only 5 percent of the population, they generally are well off financially, well educated, and in enviable professional or managerial careers.
   b) They often are associated with status brand names.

*****Use Learning Objective #2 and #7 Here; Use Discussion Question #5 Here; Use Exercise #2 and #3 Here; Use Table 13-11 Here; Use Figure 13-8 Here*****

Older Consumer

1. America is aging; the number of elderly consumers is growing twice as fast as the overall U. S. population.
2. People over age 50 comprise fully one-third of the adult U.S. market.
3. Some people think of older consumers as:
   a) The annual discretionary income of this group amounts to half of all the nation's discretionary income.
   b) This group controls 70 percent of the nation's wealth, which now amounts to about $70 trillion.

Defining "Older" in Older Consumer

1. Driving the growth of the elderly population are three factors:
   a) The declining birthrate.
   b) The aging of the huge baby boomer segment.

    c)   Improved medical diagnoses and treatment.
2. In the United States, "old age" is officially assumed to begin with a person's 65th birthday (i.e., when the individual qualifies for full Social Security and Medicare).
    a)   People who are 60 years old, however, tend to view themselves as being 15 years younger than their chronological age.
3. Research consistently suggests that people's perceptions of their ages are more important in determining behavior than their chronological ages (i.e., the number of years lived).
4. In fact, people may at the same time have a number of different perceived or **cognitive ages**.
    a)   Elderly consumers perceive themselves to be younger than their chronological ages on four perceived age dimensions: *feel age* (how old they feel); *look age* (how old they look); *do age* (how involved they are in activities favored by members of a specific age group); and *interest age* (how similar their interests are to those of members of a specific age group).

*****Use Key Term* **cognitive ages** *Here*****

Segmenting the Elderly Market

1. The elderly are not homogeneous.
2. One consumer gerontologist has suggested that the elderly are more diverse in interests, opinions, and actions than other segments of the adult population.
3. One relatively simple segmentation scheme partitions the elderly into three chronological age categories:
    a)   The young-old (65 to 74 years of age).
    b)   The old (those 75 to 84).
    c)   The old-old (those 85 years of age and older).
4. The elderly can also be segmented in terms of motivations and *quality-of-life orientation*.

*****Use Learning Objective #2 Here; Use Table 13-12 Here*****

Cyberseniors

1. One should not stereotype seniors as being technologically deficient.
2. There are more Internet users over the age of 50 than under the age of 20.
3. The attraction of the Internet to seniors seems to be based on its communication ability.
4. There appears to be a relationship between the amount of time an older adult spends on the Internet and his or her out-of-home mobility.

Marketing to the Older Consumer

1. Older consumers do want to be marketed to, but only for the "right" kinds of products and services and using the "right" advertising presentation.

*****Use Learning Objective #2 and #7 Here; Use Discussion Question #6 and #7 Here; Use Exercise #3 and #4 Here*****

SEX AS A SUBCULTURE

1. Because sex roles have an important cultural component, it is quite fitting to examine **gender** as a subcultural group.

*****Use Key Term gender Here; Use Learning Objective #2 Here*****

Sex Roles and Consumer Behavior

1. In American society, for instance, aggressiveness and competitiveness often were considered traditional *masculine traits*; neatness, tactfulness, gentleness, and talkativeness were considered traditional *feminine traits*.
2. In terms of role differences, women have historically been cast as homemakers with responsibility for child-care and men as the providers or breadwinners.
3. Marketers are increasingly appealing to consumers' broader vision of gender-related role options.

*****Use Learning Objective #8 Here*****

Consumer Products and Sex Roles

1. Within every society, it is quite common to find products that are either exclusively or strongly associated with the members of one sex.
2. In the United States for most products, the **sex role** link has either diminished or disappeared; for others, the prohibition still lingers.
3. An interesting product category with regard to the blurring of a gender appeal is men's fragrances.

*****Use Key Term sex role Here; Use Learning Objective #8 Here; Use Table 13-13 Here*****

The Working Woman

1. Marketers' interest in the **working woman** is increasing.
2. Marketers recognize this is becoming a large market—65 million strong.
3. Forty percent of all business travelers today are women.

Segmenting the Working Woman Market

1. Marketers have developed categories that differentiate the motivations of working and nonworking women and have divided the female population into four segments.
    a) Stay-at-home housewives.
    b) Plan-to-work housewives.
    c) Just-a-job working women.
    d) Career-oriented working women.

2. Twenty-five percent of all working women bring home a paycheck that is larger than their husbands.
   a) Ten years ago it was only 17 percent.
3. Working women spend less time shopping than nonworking women.
   a) They accomplish this "time economy" by shopping less often and by being brand- and store-loyal.
4. Working women also are likely to shop during evening hours and on the weekend, as well as to buy through direct-mail catalogs.

*****Use Learning Objective #2 and #9 Here*****

SUBCULTURAL INTERACTION

1. All consumers are simultaneously members of more than one subcultural segment; this can be viewed as *subcultural interaction*.
2. Marketers should strive to understand how multiple subcultural memberships interact to influence target consumers' relevant consumption behavior.
3. Promotional strategy should not be limited to a single subcultural membership.

*****Use Key Term subcultural interaction Here*****

DISCUSSION QUESTIONS

1. **Why is subcultural analysis especially significant in a country such as the United States?**

The United States is becoming an increasingly diverse society. Subcultures based on nationality, religion, geographic location, race, age, and sex, provide markets with exciting opportunities and numerous pitfalls to negotiate in their promotional strategies. By the year 2050 minorities may account for 47 percent of the economy. American companies will increasingly target advertising at these groups.

2. **Discuss the importance of subcultural segmentation to marketers of food products. Identify a food product for which the marketing mix should be regionalized. Explain why and how the marketing mix should be varied across geographic areas of the United States.**

Subcultures are identifiable groups within a society and as such, constitute "natural" segmentation variables. In the United States, people belong to many subcultural groups that influence the consumption of food products. For example: (a) nationality influences the consumption of many ethnic foods; (b) religion places restrictions on eating certain foods; and (c) different geographic regions have different food tastes and customs, (e.g., grits in the South and the general popularity of Mexican food in the West and Southwest). As illustrated in the answer to the previous question, the United States is increasingly becoming ethnically diverse, and many marketers are targeting nationality/ethnic subcultures.

3. **How can marketers of the following products use the material presented in this chapter to develop promotional campaigns designed to increase market share among African American, Hispanic, and Asian American consumers? The products are: (a) compact disc players, (b) ready-to-eat cereals, and (c) designer jeans.**

The marketers of the products listed in the question should consider the following data in targeting African American, Hispanic American, and Asian Americans:

Targeting African Americans: The segmentation of the African American market has largely been approached in terms of social class—they tend to be strongly middle-class in their values. They tend to prefer leading brands, are brand loyal, and unlikely to purchase private-label and generic products (see Table 13-8). Some marketers have been running all their advertising in the general mass media in the belief that African Americans have the same media habits as Caucasians, although others have followed the policy of running additional advertising in selected media directed exclusively to African Americans.

Targeting Hispanic Americans: Hispanic Americans represent a growing portion of the U.S. population, and although sharing a common language, consist of separate subcultural markets corresponding to different countries of origin—Mexico, Puerto Rico, and Cuba, etc. Almost 50 percent of Hispanic Americans live in the suburbs. Presently, the biggest Latino suburbs are in southern California, but Latino suburbs are also growing quickly in Florida and southern Texas. Generally, suburban Hispanics have higher per capita incomes than their central-city counterparts and constitute an increasingly lucrative market segment. (See Tables 13-2 for characteristics.)

Targeting Asian Americans: Presently, Asian Americans are the fastest growing minority group, almost 40 percent of today's immigrants to America come from Asia. Asian Americans are composed of several distinct subcultures. Presently, most live in Hawaii and California, but New York, Philadelphia, and Washington D.C. also have large Asian populations. Asian Americans are family-oriented, strongly driven to achieve middle-class lifestyle, and as such, highly industrious and entrepreneurial. They are the minority group with the highest percentage of self-employment and tend to be better educated and more computer-literate than the general population. Marketers are just beginning to understand the complexity of this segment. For example, targeting Asian Americans with promotions designed to stimulate short-term sales (e.g., coupons) is a poor approach because these consumers are interested in building long-term brand relationships that often result in intense brand loyalty. Thus, it is not enough to promote products to them; a marketer must establish a relationship. It also appears that Asian Americans are comfortable with being bilingual; in a recent survey, the majority of the Asian American respondents said that they spoke English all the time at work, but more than half chose to be interviewed in their native language. Advertising to Asian Americans represents a challenge. For example: (a) they view comparative advertising as rude; (b) American humor often does not translate well into their subculture; (c) an ad designed to appeal to Koreans failed because it used a Chinese model;

and (d) Chinese consumers complained about the sexual innuendo of corks popping out of champagne bottles featured in bank New Year holiday TV ads targeted at them.

4. **Asian Americans are a small proportion of the total United States population. Why are they an important market segment? How can a marketer of personal computers effectively target Asian Americans?**

Use the information under Question 3.

5. **Sony is introducing a new 27-inch TV with a picture-in-picture feature. How should the company position and advertise the product to (a) Generation X consumers and (b) affluent baby boomers?**

Student response will very likely differ significantly from the instructor's. Prepare your own answers and then when appropriate compare them to the students' and use the exercise to demonstrate the difference in perception across generations. For Generation-Xers, marketers should emphasize ease of use and quality-of-life in a laid-back manner. Emphasize the brand name, but do not place a premium price on the product. With baby boomers, personalize the product, offer convenience, and competitive pricing.

6. **In view of the anticipated growth of the over-50 market, a leading cosmetics company is re-evaluating the marketing strategy for its best-selling moisturizing face cream for women. Should the company market the product to younger (under-50) as well as older women? Would it be wiser to develop a new brand and formula for consumers over 50 rather than target both age groups with one product? Explain your answer.**

A moisturizer face cream is a product that should probably be positioned in a way depicting the target consumer's perceived or cognitive age rather than the individual's chronological age. Because most older consumers feel and consider themselves younger than their chronological ages, developing a new brand and formula for over-50 consumers is unlikely to be successful. Research suggests that people's perception of their ages is more important in determining behavior than their chronological age. Elderly consumers perceive themselves to be younger than their chronological age on four perceived age dimensions: (a) feel-age—how old they feel, (b) look-age—how old they look, (c) do-age—how involved they are in activities favored by members of a specific age group, and (d) interest-age—how similar their interests are to those of members of a specific age group. Therefore, the company should not design a new brand specifically for older consumers and continue marketing the existing brand to younger as well as older women. This may prove to be a complex endeavor, however, and the company must ensure that none of the advertising messages and appeals directed at older women alienates the under-50 users of the product.

7. **Marketers realize that people of the same age often exhibit very different lifestyles. Using the evidence presented in this chapter, discuss how developers of retirement housing can use older Americans' lifestyles to more effectively segment their markets.**

Marketers of retirement housing should be careful to avoid falling into the myths of the elderly market. Similar to other market segments, the elderly market is not homogeneous. Some argue their interests, etc., are even more diverse than other markets. One simple segmentation scheme partitions the elderly into three chronological age categories: (a) young-old—65 to 74 years old—tend to have health and money, (b) old—75 to 84 years old, and (c) old-old—85+ usually require various specialized housing and medical services.

8a. **How should marketers promote products and services to working women? What appeals should they use? Explain.**
  b. **As the owner of a Saturn automobile dealership, what kinds of marketing strategies would you use to target working women?**

The marketer avoids high-pressure sales approaches and stress sincere, polite, and helpful salespeople. When it comes to the features a woman seeks in a new car, emphasize safety and reliability more. Address product design. For example: (1) recognizing that men and women are generally not the same height, car makers are replacing the front "bench-type" seat with split seats which the driver and passenger can adjust independently; (2) lumbar support was built into seat backs to make them more comfortable for pregnant women (they also relieve back strain for men); (3) buttons are spaced farther apart to accommodate females' long fingernails (and, also, men with big fingers); (4) power steering was originally developed for women, recognizing that they have less strength than men (this feature is also preferred by men, and especially many older consumers); and (5) reinforced side-door impact beams, child safety locks, and integrated child seats are features developed to appeal specifically to women.

EXERCISES

1. **Using one of the subculture categories listed in Table 13-1, identify a group that can be regarded as a subculture within your university or college. (a) Describe the norms, values, and behaviors of the subculture's members. (b) Interview five members of that subculture regarding attitudes toward the use credit cards. (c) What are the implications of your findings for marketing credit cards to the group you selected?**

Instructor's Discussion

The answer to this exercise provides an interesting foundation for a class discussion. If students select one of the subcultures described in the text, their findings should be compared with the book's information and used to formulate a strategy for a credit card company targeting the subculture chosen.

2. **Interview one baby boomer and one Generation X consumer regarding the purchase of a car. Prepare a report on the difference in attitudes between the two individuals. Do your findings support the text's discussion of the differences between boomers and busters? Explain.**

Instructor's Discussion

This exercise is designed to illustrate the differences in the values of two generations. The professor should compare the students' observations to the information presented in the answer to Discussion Question 5.

3. **Many of your perceptions regarding price versus value are likely to be different than those of your parents or grandparents. Researchers attribute such differences to cohort effects, which are based on the premise that consumption patterns are determined early in life. Therefore, individuals who had experienced different economic, political and cultural environments during their youth are likely to be different types of consumers as adults. Describe instances in which your parents or grandparents disagreed with or criticized purchases you had made. Describe the cohort effects that explain each party's position during these disagreements.**

Instructor's Discussion

This exercise is designed to demonstrate that individuals who had experienced similar economic, political, and cultural environments during their youth share a common generational personality in their present consumption habits. For example, older consumers who formed their values while trying to earn a living during the Great Depression (i.e., people 65 and over) are likely to be highly price-conscious. On the other hand, people whose expectations about life were formed during World War II (i.e., persons 50–64 years old) feel much more comfortable about spending because their expectations were exceeded during the post-war recovery, and they were pleasantly surprised by the economic success that many of them presently enjoy.

4. **Find two good and two bad examples of advertising directed toward elderly consumers. To what degree are these ads stereotypical? Do they depict the concept of perceived age? How could these ads be improved by applying some of the chapter's guidelines for advertising to elderly consumers?**

Instructor's Discussion

The professor should provide examples for the students to analyze using the information contained in the text. A recent review of successful marketing to older consumers indicates that these individuals respond well to messages that stress autonomy, altruism, personal growth, and revitalization. Furthermore, marketers targeting this group must recognize that, compared with young adults, mature adults are less influenced by peers, more introspective, more sensitive to the context of messages, more flexible, more individualistic, less price sensitive, determine values in more complex ways, and are whole-picture oriented (rather than detail oriented).

S.T.A.R. PROJECTS

Ethical Issues in Consumer Behavior

S.T.A.R. Project #1

Some Web sites attract a wide spectrum of visitors. Such a Web site is Women.com (see www.women.com). This intriguing site focuses on a variety of female issues. Everything from fashion and decorating tips to women's rights is addressed on Women.com. Your assignment is to review the site and then list five (5) women's issues that are impacted by good ethical behavior by marketers. Next, cite the specific ethical behavior that is associated with the issue you addressed. Lastly, indicate (in your opinion) how the issues are faring with respect to advancement of positive ethical behavior.

Instructor's Discussion

The students should be able to easily identify issues that are linked to good ethical practice and behavior. For example, women's health, child rearing, and relationship management would be a good place to start a discussion. Have students meet in small groups to discuss their findings and opinions.

S.T.A.R. Project #2

The United States is a nation of many religions. This nation was founded on each citizen's right to express religious beliefs and to live with religious freedom even if that freedom meant to have no religion at all. "In God We Trust" is a great part of our heritage. In recent years, however, organized religion and religious teaching has suffered some setbacks because of the nation's fundamental desire to separate church and state. For example, prayer is no longer appropriate in schools or in certain governmental gatherings. Has this shift affected our culture? Your assignment is to study the religious subculture section of the chapter. Write a short position paper that outlines how marketers should ethically appeal to this subculture. What is appropriate and what is not? Is a religious appeal by marketers appropriate at all? Comment on these issues.

Instructor's Discussion

Nothing gets one's attention more than discussions about religion or sex. We all have opinions about each. This assignment asks students to consider the religious subculture as a viable marketing segment. The chapter provides ample illustrations of how appeals are made by marketers to this subculture. The assignment asks students to consider the ethics of such approaches. Because of the inflammatory nature of this area, be sure to carefully control discussion to avoid hurting someone's feelings or positions.

Small Group Projects

S.T.A.R. Project #3

Action, action, action! Those words would be appropriate to the National Organization of Women (N.O.W.) (see www.now.org). N.O.W. has supporters and detractors. No matter how you look at this organization you have to respect its dedication to women's causes. Others, however, believe that a less direct approach to women's issues is more appropriate. Many of these see Cosmopolitan magazine as a better spokesperson for female positions. Your group's assignment is to do a comparison between how N.O.W. and Cosmopolitan magazine (see www.cosmopolitan.com) approach women's issues. Many believe that the two organizations are on the opposite end of the spectrum from one another. Your group should construct a method to compare the two organizations. Once this is done, write a short position paper that describes which of the two organizations does a better job of addressing women's issues. Which organization does a better job of marketing to the female subculture? Explain your rationale.

Instructor's Discussion

Talk about differences—N.O.W. and Cosmo are often miles apart. Though female students may not be closely aligned with either organization, both organizations are interesting studies. Both are marketing dynamos (though N.O.W might not like to admit it). Students can examine each organization through stances on political protest, women's rights, women's relationships, and women's purchasing. Be careful to control discussion as some (even males) may have very pronounced feelings about either or both of these organizations.

S.T.A.R. Project #4

One of the best ways to see how marketers use culture and subculture as vehicles for marketing efforts is to study how products, brands, and promotional messages are designed for and directed toward these two concepts. Your group's assignment is to review the research material available on Brandweek (see www.brandweek.com), Adweek (see www.adweek.com), and Mediaweek (see www.mediaweek.com). Once you have examined the material contained in these three Web sites describe three (3) ways marketing efforts are directed toward (a) culture and (b) subculture. To be more specific, pick two of the subcultures described in the text to use as examples in the (b) part of the assignment. Summarize your findings in a short descriptive paper.

Instructor's Discussion

The three Web sites contain a vast amount of information about branding, promotion, and media application with respect to product distribution. Students are free to choose any of the described subcultures for examples. Normally, age, gender, and ethnicity are the easiest to apply. The Web sites carry stories about each of these subcultures on almost a constant basis. You may wish to assign particular subcultures to the various groups to ensure diversity for learning purposes. Lastly, these are excellent Web sites to bring up using your LCD in class. Because all of the publications are linked, it makes it easy to move from one publication to another to discuss topics and applications.

Using the Internet to Study Consumer Behavior

S.T.A.R. Project #5

One of the easiest ways to study marketing's relationship to racial subcultures is to use the Internet. Recent statistics indicate that African American and Hispanic Americans are using the Web in increasing numbers. Therefore, marketing efforts via the Web are increasing for both of these two groups. Your assignment is to take one (1) of the following Web sites and examine how the Web site is making marketing appeals to its particular racial subculture. Specifically, describe the chosen site's marketing activities, how the site attempts to build relationships with viewers, and how the site might impact a viewer's consumptive behavior. Pick from these Web sites: Black Entertainment Network (see www.bet.com); Ebony magazine (see www.ebony.com); Univision (see www.univision.com); or, Telemundo (see www.telemundo.com). Write a short summary paper about your findings and thoughts.

Instructor's Discussion

Most students will pick one of the two African American Web sites because the Hispanic Web sites are in Spanish only. Whichever site is chosen, the students' learning experience should be enhanced. Another good idea is to ask minority students to comment on Web sites that do a better job of reaching their racial group. This query usually produces a variety of specific racial Web sites that can be discussed by the entire class. Most will find these sites to be interesting.

S.T.A.R. Project #6

Of all the racial subcultures, the Asian Americans seem to have embraced the Web most completely. According to statistics and information provided in the chapter, the Asian American group is technologically astute, earns the highest income of all the major racial minorities, and is the most educated. Your assignment is to explore this racial subculture by visiting Asian Avenue (see www.asianavenue.com). Though joining the Web site is a requirement for visitation, a screen name and e-mail address is all that is required. Once you have done this, match the information you find (for example, ads, products, and information) with the information provided in the chapter about this group. Write a short descriptive paper that combines the data from both of these two information sources and produce a new profile of the Asian American consumer.

Instructor's Discussion

This assignment will help the student to update the information found in the chapter. As with the assignment that was directed toward the African American and Hispanic American racial subculture, ask students from the Asian American for Web sites that are oriented toward their particular racial group.

CASES

Case One: Subculture By Satellite

Marketers, via DBS systems, now have access to ethnic markets, and can do so on a national scale. An advertisement placed on a Mandarin language channel, for example, could reach Chinese-Americans regardless of whether they live in New York, San Francisco, or some small town in Mississippi. DBS, therefore, can provide an economically viable way for a marketer to target a specific ethnic market.

Case Two: Avon's Anew Ultimate

1. This mini case is designed to get students thinking about the concept of cognitive age. Because there are various components of cognitive age (e.g., *do* age, *interest* age, *feel* age, and *look* age), it is *look* age that is likely to be the most relevant specific cognitive age that relates to a product like Avon's Anew Ultimate. Research on cognitive age has continuously revealed that *look* age is most similar (closest in estimate) to the consumer's chronological age (i.e., his or her "birth age"), whereas for the other cognitive age components, cognitive age is younger than chronological age. In terms of creating messages for mature adult audiences, an almost universal goal is to appear younger or more youthful. This is especially true in Western countries where youth tends to be valued and thought of as a positive ideal.

In terms of the portrait of the New-Age Elderly consumer presented in Chapter 13, it is noteworthy that a generally younger overall cognitive age is associated with being a New-Age older consumer—a segment of the overall older or mature market that tends to be forward thinking in their attitudes and actions.

2. Some student's might also point out that the $30 price for a small jar might restrict the purchase of the product to more affluent consumers. Others might counter-argue, however, that the extensive amount of value placed on youthfulness might drive nonaffluent consumers to also seek out and purchase this product. Moreover, the discussion of the older consumer in Chapter 13 does point up that there is a significant affluent subsegment of the older consumer market.

The instructor might wish to introduce a discussion of gender. It is anticipated that Avon will exclusively target this product to females. The question is: "What about males?" Would they respond to such a product? Also, would young women (20 years of age) be interested in such a product if it were stressed that early use would retard the skin aging process?

CHAPTER 14

Cross-Cultural Consumer Behavior: An International Perspective

LEARNING OBJECTIVES

After studying this chapter students should be able to:
1. Explain the reasons for and importance of becoming multinational for the American corporation.
2. Discuss the importance of cross-cultural consumer analysis.
3. Describe the process of acculturation.
4. Outline alternative multinational strategies.
5. Conduct an initial assessment of the multinational strategies used by corporations.
6. Describe cross-cultural psychographic segmentation.
7. Review the major marketing mistakes made by multinational corporations.

SUMMARY

With so much diversity present among the members of just one nation (as in the United States), it is easy to appreciate that numerous larger differences may exist between citizens of different nations having different cultures, values, beliefs, and languages. If international marketers are to satisfy the needs of consumers in potentially very distinct markets effectively, they must understand the relevant similarities and differences that exist between the peoples of the countries they decide to target.

When consumers make purchase decisions, they seem to take into consideration the countries of origin of the brands that they are assessing. Consumers frequently have specific attitudes or even preferences for products made in particular countries. These country of origin effects influence how consumers rate quality, and sometimes, which brands they will ultimately select.

As increasing numbers of consumers from all over the world come in contact with the material goods and lifestyles of people living in other countries and as the number of middle-class consumers grows in developing countries, marketers are eager to locate these new customers and to offer them their products. The rapidly expanding middle class in countries of Asia, South American and Eastern Europe possess relatively substantial buying power because their incomes are largely discretionary (for necessities like housing and medical care are often provided by the state, at little or no cost).

For some international marketers, acculturation is a dual process: First, they must learn everything that is relevant to the product and product category in the society in which they plan to market, then they must persuade the members of that society to break with their traditional ways of doing things to adopt the new product. The more similar a foreign target market is to a marketer's home market, the easier the process of acculturation. Conversely, the more different a foreign target market is, the more difficult the process of acculturation.

Some of the problems involved in cross-cultural analysis include differences in language, consumption patterns, needs, product usage, economic and social conditions, marketing conditions, and market research opportunities. There is an urgent need for more systematic and conceptual cross-cultural analyses of the psychological, social, and cultural characteristics concerning the consumption habits of foreign consumers. Such analyses would identify increased marketing opportunities that would benefit both international marketers and their targeted consumers.

CHAPTER OUTLINE

THE IMPERATIVE TO BE MULTINATIONAL

1. Today the issue is generally not whether to market a brand in other countries but rather how to do it (e.g., the same product, the same "global" advertising campaign, or "tailored" products and localized ads for each country).
2. This challenge has been given special meaning by the efforts of the *European Union* (EU) to forming a single market.
   a) It is unclear whether this diverse market will be transformed into a single market of homogeneous "Euroconsumers" with the same or very similar wants and needs.
   b) Many people hope that the introduction of the "euro" as a common currency among a number of EU members will help shape Europe into a huge, powerful, single market.
3. The *North American Free Trade Agreement* (NAFTA), which currently consists of the United States, Canada, and Mexico, provides free-market access to 400 million consumers.
4. The emerging Association of Southeast Asian Nations (ASEAN), consisting of Indonesia, Singapore, Thailand, the Philippines, Malaysia, Brunei, and Vietnam, is another important economic alliance that offers marketers new global markets.
   a) The members of this group have formed the ASEAN Free Trade Area (AFTA) to promote regional trade.
5. Many firms are developing strategies to take advantage of these and other emerging economic opportunities.
6. Firms are selling their products worldwide for a variety of reasons.
   a) Overseas markets represent the single most important opportunity for future growth as home markets reach maturity.
   b) Consumers all over the world are increasingly eager to try "foreign" products that are popular in different and far-off places.

*****Use Key Terms* **European Union** and **North American Free Trade Agreement** *Here; Use Learning Objective #1 Here; Use Discussion Question #1 and #2 Here; Use Exercise #1 Here; Use Table 14-1 Here*****

Acquiring Exposure to Other Cultures

1. How consumers in one culture secure exposure to the goods of other people living in other cultures is an important part of consumer behavior.

2. A portion of consumers' exposure to different cultures tends to come about through consumers' own initiatives—their travel, their living and working in foreign countries, or even their immigration to a different country.
3. Consumers often obtain a "taste" of different cultures from contact with foreign movies, theater, art and artifact, and, most certainly, exposure to unfamiliar and different products.
   a) Within this context, international marketing provides a form of "culture transfer."

*****Use Learning Objective #1 Here; Use Discussion Question #2 Here; Use Exercise #1 Here*****

Country-of-Origin Effects

1. Researchers have shown that consumers use their knowledge of where products are made in the evaluation of their purchase options.
2. Such a country-of-origin effect seems to come about because consumers are often aware that a particular firm- or brand-name is associated with a particular country.
3. Consumers tend to have an attitude or even a preference when it comes to a particular product being made in a particular country.
   a) This attitude might be positive, negative, or neutral.
   b) In addition, some research evidence shows that some consumers may refrain from purchasing products from particular countries due to animosity.

*****Use Learning Objective #1 Here; Use Discussion Question #2 Here; Use Figure 14-1 Here*****

CROSS-CULTURAL CONSUMER ANALYSIS

1. *Cross-cultural consumer analysis* is defined as the effort to determine to what extent the consumers of two or more nations are similar or different.
   a) In a broader context it might include a comparison of subcultural groups within a single country.

*****Use Key Term cross-cultural consumer analysis Here; Use Learning Objective #2 Here; Use Discussion Question #4 Here*****

Similarities and Differences Among People

1. A major objective of cross-cultural consumer analysis is to determine how consumers in two or more societies are similar and how they are different.
2. Such an understanding of the similarities and differences that exist between nations is critical to the multinational marketer, who must devise appropriate strategies to reach consumers in specific foreign markets.
3. The greater the similarity between nations, the more feasible it is to use relatively similar strategies in each nation.

a) On the other hand, if the cultural beliefs, values, and customs of specific target countries are found to differ widely, then a highly *individualized* marketing strategy is indicated for each country.

4. A firm's success in marketing a product or service in a number of foreign countries is likely to be influenced by how similar the beliefs, values, and customs are that govern the use of the product in the various countries.

*****Use Learning Objective #2 Here; Use Discussion Question #3 Here; Use Figure 14-2 Here; Use Table 14-2 Here; Use Exercise #2 and #3 Here*****

Time Effects

1. The pace of life differs from one nation to another.
   a) The average children's birthday party in the United States lasts approximately two hours.
   b) Brazilians are willing to wait a little more than two hours for a late arriver to show up at a birthday party.
2. How time is spent on the job is also an issue that varies from country to country.
   a) In the United States., about 80 percent of work time is spent on the task, and perhaps 20 percent is used for social activities.
   b) But in countries like India and Nepal, the balance is closer to 50 percent on each; and in Japan, social time, such as having tea with peers in the middle of the day, is considered to be a part of work.
3. Research on pace of life in 31 countries (basing overall pace on how long pedestrians take to walk 60 feet, the minutes it takes a postal clerk to complete a stamp-purchase transaction, and the accuracy of public clocks) reveals substantial cross-cultural differences.
   a) Switzerland has the fastest pace of life; Mexico has the slowest pace of life.

*****Use Learning Objective #2 Here; Use Discussion Question #3 Here; Use Table 14-3 Here*****

The Growing Global Middle Class

1. The growing middle class in developing countries is a phenomenon that is very attractive to global marketers.
2. The news media has given considerable coverage to the idea that the rapidly expanding middle class in countries of Asia, South America, and Eastern Europe is based on the reality that although per capita income may be low, there is nevertheless considerable buying power in a country like China, where $1,500 of income is largely discretionary income.
3. Although a growing middle class may provide a market for products like Big Macs and fries, it should always be remembered that the same product might have different meanings in different countries.
   a) A U.S. consumer wants his or her "fast food" to be fast, a Korean consumer is more likely to view a meal as a social or family-related experience.
4. Regulations in different countries may preclude the use of some of the marketing practices that a firm employs in the United States.

*****Use Learning Objective #2 Here*****

Acculturation Is a Needed Marketing Viewpoint

1. Many marketers make a strategic error when contemplating an international expansion, thinking that if domestic consumers like it, international consumers will like it.
2. Marketers need to go through an acculturation process, learning everything that is relevant to their product usage in the foreign countries in which they plan to operate.
3. Cross-cultural *acculturation* is a dual process for marketers.
   a) First, marketers must thoroughly orient themselves to the values, beliefs, and customs of the new society.
   b) Second, marketers must persuade the members of that society to break with their own traditions.
4. A social marketing effort designed to encourage consumers in developing nations to secure polio vaccinations for their children would require a two-step acculturation process.
   a) First, the marketer must obtain an in-depth picture of a society's present attitudes and customs with regard to preventive medicine and related concepts.
   b) Then, the marketer must devise promotional strategies that will convince the members of a target market to have their children vaccinated, even if doing so requires a change in current attitudes.

*****Use Key Term acculturation Here; Use Exercise #3 and #4 Here*****

Distinctive Characteristics of Cross-Cultural Analysis

1. It is often difficult for a company planning to do business in foreign countries to undertake *cross-cultural consumer research*.
2. In many countries there is a limited amount of information regarding consumer and market statistics.

*****Use Key Term cross-cultural consumer research Here; Use Learning Objective #2 and #3 Here; Use Discussion Question #4 and #8 Here*****

Applying Research Techniques

1. Although domestic research methods are useful in foreign countries, language and word usage often differ from nation to nation causing some difficulties.
2. To avoid research measurement problems consumer researchers should familiarize themselves with the research services in the countries where they are evaluating markets.

*****Use Learning Objective #2 Here; Use Discussion Question #8 and #11 Here; Use Table 14-4 Here*****

ALTERNATIVE MULTINATIONAL STRATEGIES: GLOBAL VERSUS LOCAL

1. Marketers are arguing for one of two approaches.
    a) One, the world markets are becoming more similar, and therefore standardized marketing strategies is appropriate.
    b) Or two, that the variations among nations are too great for a standardized marketing strategy.
2. The challenge is deciding whether to use *shared needs and values* as a segmentation strategy or to use *national borders* as a segmentation strategy.

> *****Use Learning Objective #4 Here; Use Discussion Question #5 and #6 Here*****

Favoring a "World Brand"

1. *World brands* are those products that are manufactured, packaged, and positioned the same way regardless of the country in which they are sold.
2. Marketers of products with a wide or almost mass-market appeal have embraced a world branding strategy.
    a) Still other marketers selectively use a world branding strategy.

> *****Use Key Term world brand Here; Use Learning Objective #4 Here; Use Discussion Question #5, #6, and #7 Here; Use Figure 14-3 Here*****

Adaptive Global Marketing

1. Some firms embrace a strategy that adapts their advertising messages to the specific values of particular cultures because they feel that the world brand concept may be going too far.
    a) In some cases the differences are sufficient to make localized advertising more appropriate than a global approach.
    b) Some marketers feel that the world-brand concept goes too far.
    c) Sometimes marketers need to use a mixture.
2. In taking such an adaptive approach, global advertisers with knowledge of cross-cultural differences can tailor their supplemental messages more effectively to suit individual local markets.
3. It is also important to note that consumers in different countries of the world have vastly different amounts of exposure to advertisements.

> *****Use Learning Objective #4 Here; Use Discussion Question #5 and #6 Here*****

Frameworks for Assessing Multinational Strategies

1. *Multinational* marketers face the challenge of creating marketing and advertising programs capable of communicating with a diversity of target markets.
    a) These frameworks enable international marketers to assess the positions their products enjoy in specific foreign markets.

2. A firm might decide either to standardize or localize its product and either standardize or localize its communications program.

3. The four possibilities that this decision framework considers range from a company incorporating a **global strategy** (i.e., standardizing both product and communications program) to developing a completely **local strategy** (i.e., customizing both the product and communications program) for each unique market.

    a) In the middle there are two mixed strategies.

4. Another orientation for assessing whether to use a global versus local marketing strategy concentrates on a high-tech to high-touch continuum.

    a) **Product standardization** appears to be most successful for high-involvement products that approach either end of the high-tech/high-touch continuum.

    b) When marketing high-tech products abroad, it is important to note that many industrialized nations lag far behind the United States in computer usage.

*****Use Key Terms* multinational, global strategy, local strategy, and product standardization *Here; Use Learning Objective #4 and #5 Here; Use Discussion Question #6, #7, and #10 Here; Use Exercise #4 Here; Use Table 14-5, 14-6, and 14-7 Here*****

CROSS-CULTURAL PSYCHOGRAPHIC SEGMENTATION

1. Although worldwide consumers may be similar in many ways, any differences in attitudes or behavior can be crucial in determining satisfaction and may provide an opportunity for segmenting consumers in terms of cultural differences.

    a) This problem has resulted in the need for **cross-cultural psychographic segmentation**.

2. Some firms might attempt to establish a global branding strategy, whereas others would design an individual or local marketing strategy.

    a) "The only ultimate truth possible is that humans are both deeply the same and obviously different….."

3. This book is based on the same thesis.

    a) If we believe in tailoring marketing strategies to specific segments of the American market; it follows then that we also believe in tailoring marketing strategies to the needs—psychological, social, cultural, and functional—of specific foreign segments.

4. Global psychographic research often reveals cultural differences of great importance to marketers.

*****Use Key Term* cross-cultural psychographic segmentation *Here; Use Learning Objective #6 Here; Use Discussion Question #9 and #10 Here; Use Table 14-8 Here*****

MARKETING MISTAKES: A FAILURE TO UNDERSTAND DIFFERENCES

1. In most cases, the gamble for marketers in international marketing is not knowing whether the product, the promotional appeal, the pricing policy, or the retail channels that are effective in one country will work in other countries and in trying to determine what specific changes should be made to ensure acceptance in each foreign market.

*****Use Learning Objective #7 Here; Use Discussion Question #11 Here; Use Exercise #3 Here*****

Product Problems

1. International marketers frequently neglect to modify their products to meet local customs and tastes.
2. American marketers, selling food products in Japan, frequently learn the hard way (through poor sales performance) that they must alter traditional product characteristics.
3. To avoid problems, marketers must ascertain in advance whether the physical characteristics of their products will be acceptable to the new market.
4. Color is also a critical variable in international marketing, because the same color often has different meanings in different cultures.
   a) For example, consider the color blue.
      i) In Holland, it stands for warmth; in Iran, it represents death; in Sweden, it connotes coldness; in India, it means purity.

*****Use Learning Objective #7 Here; Use Discussion Question #11 Here*****

Promotional Problems

1. When communicating with consumers in different parts of the world, the promotional message must be consistent with the language and customs of the particular target society.
2. The Seven-Up, Inc.'s highly successful "Uncola" theme, developed for the U. S. market, was considered inappropriate for many foreign markets because it did not translate well into other languages.
3. Product names and promotional phrases can also cause considerable problems for international marketers.
   a) The word "clock" in Chinese sounds like the word "death."

*****Use Learning Objective #7 Here; Use Discussion Question #11 Here*****

Pricing and Distribution Problems

1. International marketers must adjust their pricing and distribution policies to meet local economic conditions and customs.
   a) For instance, in many developing nations, small-sized product packages often are a necessity because consumers cannot afford the cash outlay required for the larger sizes popular in the United States and other affluent countries.
2. It should also be remembered that what American's view as "low-cost" might not be viewed similarly in other countries.
   a) U.S. fast food franchises that operate in Mexico, such as Burger King, Wendy's, and McDonalds, are all considered upscale to the Mexican consumer.
3. Japan's traditional distribution system differs from the United States in that a close, complex relationship exists among the larger Japanese manufacturers and their distributors and retailers.
4. Marketers must vary their distribution channels by nation.

*****Use Learning Objective #7 Here; Use Discussion Question #11 Here*****

DISCUSSION QUESTIONS

1. **Will the elimination of trade barriers among the countries of the European Union change consumer behavior in these countries? How can U. S. companies take advantage of the economic opportunities emerging in Europe?**

It is unlikely that the highly diverse European market will be transformed into a single market of homogeneous needs and wants. Therefore, American companies should take advantage of the elimination of trade barriers in Europe by buying European companies that produce brands that are widely recognized by European consumers. Then, the American firms should use their technology and marketing skills to improve the products made by their European subsidiaries, extend these product lines, and market these goods to consumers in Western as well as Eastern Europe. American companies should also take notice that some European companies are following similar strategies and that the competition for Europe's customers is becoming more aggressive.

2. **With all the problems facing companies that go global, why are so many companies choosing to expand internationally? What are the advantages of expanding beyond the domestic market?**

American companies are increasingly deriving the majority of their sales and profits from overseas operations. For example, 64 percent of Coke's total sales and over 40 percent of Procter & Gamble's total sales are derived from international sales. The reasons for companies expanding internationally include; taking advantage of emerging markets, escaping recessions in the United States, keeping up with or escaping competition, taking advantage of liberal tax laws, disposing of inventories of older products, extending the life cycles of products which had reached their peaks in the United States, and trying to establish a global image. Some companies may choose to "go global" because they would like to keep up with technology or test their products in foreign markets first.

3. Are the cultures of the world becoming more similar or more different? Discuss.

This question provides a vehicle for an interesting class discussion. Marketers are arguing both sides of the issue. Some see an increase in a people's distinctive tastes and standards based on nationalism, regionalism, or culture. Others see the influence of media and pop culture as blending cultures and blurring national boundaries. Your authors argue that the cultures of the world are not becoming more similar. In spite of this fact, it is apparent that America's pop culture, that is, our movies, TV shows, and pop music, is popular all around the globe. Will recent world events and conflicts change this popularity?

4. What is cross-cultural consumer analysis? How can a multinational company use cross-cultural research to design each factor in its marketing mix? Illustrate your answer with examples.

Cross-cultural consumer analysis is defined as the effort to determine to what extent the consumers of two or more nations are similar or different. Such an analysis provides marketers with an understanding of the differences and similarities in psychological, social, cultural, and environmental factors, and permits the design of effective marketing strategies for each of the specific countries involved. Table 14-2 shows what multinational marketers found when they studied Chinese and American cultures. Table 14-3, presents a summary of research pace of life differences.

5. What are the advantages and disadvantages of global promotional strategies?

The major advantage of a global promotional strategy is cost savings across the board in designing and implementing a marketing mix. Thus, the manufacturer of Aramis, a well-established brand of men's fragrance sold in more than 120 countries, has been running a worldwide advertising campaign depicting a blurred form of a hurrying businessman that prevents the viewer from fully identifying the model's ethnic group, and Gillette uses a global approach (i.e., the same ads running in different countries/languages) for its Sensor Shaving System. Although local marketing strategies are clearly more expensive and complex than global ones, in many cases, differences between the needs and wants of consumers in different countries are strong enough to preclude the use of global promotional approaches. Thus, McDonald's localizes its advertising to consumers in different countries, and Procter & Gamble and Colgate-Palmolive create different versions of their products as well as localized promotions in targeting world-wide consumers.

6. Should Head & Shoulders shampoo be sold worldwide with the same formulation? In the same package? With the same advertising theme? Explain your answers.

Product standardization works best with high-involvement products that approach either end of the high-tech/high-touch continuum. Low involvement products in the mid-range of high-tech/high-touch continuum are best as local brands using market-by-market executions. Procter & Gamble has four brands that are marketed under the same name worldwide (Camay soap, Crest toothpaste, Head & Shoulders shampoo, and Pampers diapers), but the formulas, package sizes, and scents of each product vary from country to country. The company believes that globally standardized products are not desirable. Although Colgate-Palmolive sells Palmolive soap in 43 countries, at one time the company marketed it in 9 different shapes, 22 fragrances, and 17 packages. Although the brand was offered on a global basis, the soap's many different versions did not allow Colgate-Palmolive to enjoy the efficiencies of global advertising and manufacturing. The firm implemented a program to move toward a global brand by conducting research with consumer-user groups. Consequently, Palmolive soap was re-launched with only 3 shapes, 7 fragrances, and 3 packages. Table 14-6 and 14-7 present two frameworks that may be used to evaluate the degree of global standardization feasible for a particular product or service.

7a. If you wanted to name a new product that would be acceptable to consumers throughout the world, what cultural factors would you consider?

Multinational firms have had some difficulty in using the domestic brand names of their products in foreign markets. Some of the key questions that a multinational firm must ask itself with respect to naming its new products in other countries are: Is the name easily translated? Does the name have the same positive connotation in various languages? Would an obviously "American" name add or detract from the product's image? Does the name imply a specific use that might not be congruent with usage patterns in other cultures?

b. What factors might inhibit an attempt by Apple to position a new laptop computer as a world brand?

Although some American products are positioned as world brands (e.g., Coca Cola, Marlboro), Apple might be blocked by language differences that would mean changes in keyboards, word processing software, power source differences, and differences in telephone communication systems for transmission of information via computer. In Asia, long commutes on public transportation are typical, and business people need laptops. The commutes are not nearly as long in Europe and more often involve personal vehicles rather than public transportation.

8. An American company is introducing a line of canned soups in Poland. (a) How should the company use cross-cultural research? (b) Should the company use the same marketing mix it uses in the United States to target Polish consumers? (c) Which, if any, marketing mix components should be designed specifically for marketing canned soups in Poland? Explain your answers.

Among the formerly Communist countries, Poland's growing economy probably represents the most promising market for Western consumer goods. The American company must take note of the following factors, however, that represent both opportunities and barriers for marketing canned soups in Poland. (1) Although Poles consume a lot of soup, 98 percent of Polish soups are homemade. Thus the company must introduce varieties that resemble homemade soups and carefully position them. (2) As Poland's economy continues to grow, women will continue joining the workforce. Thus, advertising canned soups to working women looking for convenience represents a marketing opportunity. (3) Polish consumers often purchase foods in small stores and tend to rely on the advice of storekeepers. Thus, the company must make a special effort to gain the support of shop owners so that these merchants will stock the product in their stores and recommend it to consumers. (4) Many Poles still associate mass media with Communist propaganda. Thus, a huge advertising blitz on TV is unlikely to be effective. (5) Some English on the label and an advertising theme stating that the product is sold throughout the world are good strategies to use in Poland because its citizens aspire to disassociate themselves from Communism and the "Eastern European" label. (6) Poles regard free samples with suspicion because they figure that if the product is free, something is wrong with it.

9. **Mercedes-Benz, a German car manufacturer, is using cross-cultural psychographic segmentation to develop marketing campaigns for a new two-seater sports car model directed at consumers in different countries. How should the company market the car in the United States? How should it market the car in Japan?**

Students' answers will vary. They may need to do some outside research on Japan in order to answer this question. Global psychographic research often reveals cultural differences of great importance to marketers. Table 14-8 presents a brief description of six global market segments. Table 14-9 shows worldwide cohorts. Although not all Asian these segments and cohorts show the kinds of differences marketers need to be sensitive to in their cross-cultural marketing efforts.

10. **What advice would you give to an American retailer who wants to sell women's clothing in Japan?**

Again, students' answers will vary. This question could be used to create a class assignment helping students familiarize themselves with a major Asian market. The American retailer should utilize cross-cultural analysis to study the Japanese in designing the marketing strategies aimed at Japanese consumers. In addition, the American company should consider language differences, and other socioeconomic psychographic information. The marketer should be careful to avoid typical product promotion, price, and distribution problems that sometimes plague cross-cultural marketing.

11. **Select two of the marketing mistakes discussed in the text. Discuss how these mistakes could have been avoided if the companies involved had adequately researched some of the issues listed in Table 14-4.**

The purpose of this question is to demonstrate how the lack of cross-cultural analysis often leads to blunders in international marketing.

EXERCISES

1. **Have you ever traveled outside the United States? If so, please identify some differences in values, behavior, and consumption patterns you noted between people in a country you visited and Americans.**

Instructor's Discussion

Responses to this exercise will vary based on the sophistication of your students. Its purpose is to lead the students to conduct small-scale, firsthand cross-cultural analysis. Help students to think and not make stereotypical, superficial observations. You can also rent a current foreign film on video, watch it, and note places where these behaviors are demonstrated. Then show selected clips of the film and have the students notice the differences depicted in the film.

2. **Interview a student from another culture about his or her use of (a) credit cards, (b) fast-food restaurants, (c) shampoo, and (d) sneakers. Compare your consumption behavior to that of the person you interviewed and discuss any similarities and differences you found.**

Instructor's Discussion

Prepare students with a caution. Some international students will be offended by this kind of questioning. A variation on this exercise would be for you to bring into class and interview selected international students or faculty and have the students take notes. This exercise is designed to illustrate to students the importance of cross-cultural consumer analysis and the need to adapt marketing programs to the values, customs, and needs of consumers in various countries.

3. **Much has been written about the problems at Euro Disney, the Walt Disney Company's theme park and resort complex, which opened in France in April 1992. These difficulties were largely attributed to Disney's lack of understanding of European (particularly French) culture, and the company's failure to modify its American theme park concept to fit the preferences and customs of European visitors. Discuss how the Walt Disney Company could have used input from cross-cultural analysis in better designing and operating Euro Disney, using a computerized literature search about Euro Disney from your school's library.**

Instructor's Discussion

The problems facing Euro Disney and the reasons behind them are summarized in a recent case available from the Harvard Business School entitled "Euro Disney: The First 100 Days" (# 9-693-013).

4. **Select one of the following countries: Mexico, Brazil, Germany, Italy, Israel, Kuwait, Japan, or Australia. Assume that a significant number of people in the country you chose would like to visit the United States and have the financial means to do so. Now, imagine you are a consultant for your state's tourism agency and you have been charged with developing a promotional strategy to attract tourists from the country you chose. Conduct a computerized literature search of the databases in your school's library and select and read several articles about the lifestyles, customs, and consumption behavior of people in the country you chose. Prepare an analysis of the articles and, on the basis of what you read, develop a promotional strategy designed to persuade tourists from that country to visit your state.**

Instructor's Discussion

This exercise utilizes the analysis of secondary data in studying the values and lifestyles of consumers in another culture.

S.T.A.R. PROJECTS

Ethical Issues in Consumer Behavior

S.T.A.R. Project #1
Probably no trade arrangements have had bigger impacts on the United States in recent years than the initiation of North American Free Trade Agreement (NAFTA) or the creation of the European Union (EU). Your assignment is to pick one of these two major trade arrangements or agreements and conduct secondary research on the ethical statements, areas, or arrangements that impact consumers found within your chosen agreement or arrangement. For example, does your chosen trade arrangement or agreement have an ethics statement? If so, what does it mandate for signatories? How are consumers treated within the framework of the trade arrangement or agreement (what recourse with respect to complaints do consumers have)? Write a short summary paper outlining your findings.

Instructor's Discussion

The best place to start to accomplish this assignment is to review the material found in the chapter. Next, library or Internet sources can be used to explore NAFTA or the EU. Students should remember that current periodicals such as *Business Week* or *Fortune* often carry articles about NAFTA or the EU. Pick one or two of the best student summaries and read the material to the class or have the student authors describe their findings. Use this as a springboard to more complete discussion of the ethical issues found in either or both of these trade arrangements or agreements.

S.T.A.R. Project #2
Assume that you are the marketing manager for a food products company that has just developed a new frozen "French fry" product. This new "French fry" product comes in small microwavable pouches and is noted for its crispiness. The product has been test marketed in New England and has shown favorable results. Your task is to attempt to sell the product idea to Canadian

consumers. This might be a difficult task because of Canadian resistance to some United States products. The decision, however, has been made to go forward. Write a short position and strategy paper that outlines how you would attempt to introduce the product into Canada. Remember that English and French speaking Canadians might receive the product differently. Be sure to identify in your paper any cultural or ethical issues that must be addressed by such an introduction. Lastly, evaluate the likelihood of success of the product in the Canadian market. Explain your conclusions.

Instructor's Discussion

Description of the product was kept to a minimum on purpose. In this way students can create their own product by making assumptions. Encourage them to do so. Students can research the Canadian market by using the library or the Internet. Students should certainly comment on Canadian resistance to becoming Americanized. Students should also see that a product such as this might not be popular in the French Canadian markets because the descriptor "French fry" might be offensive. How could the company overcome this difficulty? In the English speaking Canadian market, "French fries" might also be referred to as "chips." Would this be a problem? What stigma might be associated with a microwavable product (i.e., would it be limp or soggy?)? This project is a good one to use for discussion with respect to product introductions.

Small Group Projects

S.T.A.R. Project #3
In this chapter, your group's assignment is to go on a magazine fact-finding mission. Using the six segments described in Table 14-6, look for foreign magazines (or magazines directed toward foreign consumers) in your university or college library. Find ads that would seem to appeal to each of the designated market segments described in the Table. Photocopy the ads and match them to the segments. Provide a short rationale that explains and justifies your choices. Write a short report that summaries your research, findings, and conclusions. Discuss your work and ads with the class.

Instructor's Discussion

It might be a wise idea to read the associated material in the chapter before beginning this project. Note the source of material for Table 14-6. Please remind students not to tear out magazine ads, photocopying is relatively easy to do. Have a discussion wherein all groups can share their findings and conclusions. Be sure to conclude the discussion with a summary of how foreign ads are different from United States ads.

S.T.A.R. Project #4
Your group should research two to three companies that are reportedly doing an excellent job of recognizing the various cross-cultural similarities and differences among the consumers of different societies. Your group should focus on company marketing strategies. What marketing strategies have these companies employed in order to meet the needs of the consumers in these foreign cultures? How do these marketing strategies differ from the marketing strategies used for the American culture? Select at least one company that has been unsuccessful at recognizing

cross-cultural similarities and differences. What did this company do wrong? What could this company have done better in order to be successful in its attempt? (Note: Coca Cola could qualify for both categories. Their early attempts at cross-cultural marketing were disastrous, especially in Asia. Now they are one of the premier international marketers.)

Instructor's Discussion

As an instructor, you can select the companies for the students or allow them to be creative with their own selection. Remember to have them explain or justify their picks. The focus of this assignment is on how companies recognize and deal with cross-cultural similarities and differences. Students should reference the material in the chapter before beginning this assignment. If students have a difficult time getting started, recommend that the section on Marketing Mistakes be read.

Using the Internet to Study Consumer Behavior

S.T.A.R. Project #5
How would you like to plan your own cruise to an exotic foreign port or island paradise? Carnival Cruise Line (see www.carnival.com) is betting that just such a dream is one that you would like to realize. Carnival, a leader in the foreign travel and cruise industry, has constructed a Web site that allows the aspiring traveler to become his or her own travel agent. Your assignment is to plan and tentatively book your own cruise. You will be able to do so without commitment. As you plan your cruise make note of the consumer decisions that you must reach, the ease or difficulty in doing this, and choices that are allowed. Once you have completed the process, write a short report that summarizes your experience. Was the Web site an aid to your booking objective? What were the Web site's strong and weak points? How could it be improved? What did you learn about booking travel online? As a consumer, would you use this method if you were doing it for real?

Instructor's Discussion

Nothing is quite as much fun as booking a dream vacation (especially if money is no object). Students will be exposed to a consumer-friendly Web site that has been evaluated as one of the best. To extend this project, the instructor might select some of the other cruise Web sites and create a comparison for Carnival. Or, the instructor might invite a travel agent to speak to the class about the advantages of using a travel agent over self-booking or Web site booking.

S.T.A.R. Project #6
At any given time the world is in turmoil somewhere. This turmoil often impacts global business and commerce. If business and commerce are affected, consumers are also affected. Your assignment is to use the Internet to research how global events impact global consumers. A good place to start your Internet search is to review the latest stories and headlines found on either CNN (see www.cnn.com) or *U. S. News and World Report* (see www.usnews.com). Other sources can be used, however, these two news-oriented Web sites do an adequate job of reporting global events and consumer issues that are impacted by world events. For example, does war in the Middle-East impact gasoline prices or automobile sales? Does disagreement

304

among members of the United Nations (especially the powerful members) hurt trade and consumer purchasing? Are American consumers welcomed around the world if anti-Americanism is high? Write a summary report about your findings and conclusions.

<u>Instructor's Discussion</u>

Students are free to be creative with this assignment. As was indicated in the assignment, world events are constantly changing and these events impact consumers and consumption. Each student should create his or her own illustrations. These illustrations should be supported by world events and secondary material. Have a discussion that involves not only contemporary news stories but the human side as well. International students can usually provide good insight into this area. The only real danger of this assignment is that it might degrade to a political discussion rather than one that centers on consumers and consumption. Watch this danger and keep students focused and on track.

CASES

Case One: Starbucks

Student answers should vary, but may include the creation of a world brand, the use of adaptive global marketing (e.g., selling Green Tea in Asia), and/or product standardization (e.g., selling the same blend of coffee worldwide), to cite a few possible responses. Additionally, students may want to discuss the fact that citizens of other nations may not be able to afford the equivalent of U.S. $3.00 for a cup of coffee, or that overseas consumers might prefer that their coffee have a different taste (e.g., stronger, milder, sweeter, etc.).

Case Two: Baby-Sitting by Cell Phone

1.   The service should potentially be equally successful in any and all of the three cities mentioned. Each has a large middle class, a large number of dual-income families, and parents wanting to make sure that their children are safe. Cell phone ownership, however, is higher in Hong Kong than in the other cities.

2.   Although parents in any and all parts of the globe want their offspring to be safe, different cultures exhibit different preferences with respect to food products, food textures, and food tastes. Bottom line, it is generally more difficult for a food product to be accepted cross-culturally than a technology like a new cellular phone service.

CHAPTER 15

Consumer Influence and the Diffusion of Innovations

LEARNING OBJECTIVES

After studying this chapter students should be able to:
1. Define opinion leadership and explain the dynamics of the opinion leadership process.
2. Describe viral marketing.
3. Describe the dynamics of the opinion leadership process.
4. Describe the motivations of opinion leaders and opinion receivers.
5. Explain the four basic measurement techniques for measuring opinion leadership.
6. Profile the opinion leader.
7. Profile a market maven and its importance.
8. Discuss how the situational environment, the interpersonal flow, and the multistep flow affect opinion leadership.
9. Describe how opinion leaders can be created.
10. Describe the diffusion process including the four approaches for defining a new product.
11. Identify the five characteristics that influence diffusion.
12. Outline the channels of communication available to assist the diffusion process.
13. Explain the importance of time and three interrelated elements of time to diffusion.
14. Discuss the five stages in the consumer adoption process.
15. Profile the consumer innovator.
16. List and explain the personality traits of the consumer innovator.

SUMMARY

Opinion leadership is the process by which one person (the opinion leader) informally influences the actions or attitudes of others, who may be opinion seekers or merely opinion recipients. Opinion receivers perceive the opinion leader as a highly credible, objective source of product information who can help reduce their search time and perceived risk. Opinion leaders, in turn, are motivated to give information or advice to others in part because doing so enhances their own status and self-image and because such advice tends to reduce any postpurchase dissonance that they may have. Other motives include product involvement, "other" involvement, and message involvement.

Market researchers identify opinion leaders by such methods as self-designation, key informants, the sociometric method, and the objective method. Studies of opinion leadership indicate that this phenomenon tends to be product-specific; that is, individuals "specialize" in a product or product category in which they are highly interested. An opinion leader for one product category may be an opinion receiver for another.

Generally, opinion leaders are gregarious, self-confident, innovative people who like to talk. Additionally, they may feel differentiated from others and choose to act differently (or public individuation). They acquire information about their areas of interest through avid readership of special-interest magazines and by means of new-product trials. Their interests often overlap adjacent product areas; thus, their opinion leadership may extend into related areas. The market maven is an intensive case of such a person. These consumers possess a wide range of information about many different types of products, retail outlets, and other dimensions of markets. They both initiate discussions with other consumers and respond to requests for market information over a wide range of products and services. Market mavens are also distinguishable from other opinion leaders, because their influence stems not so much from product experience but from a more general knowledge or market expertise that leads them to an early awareness of a wide array of new products and services.

The opinion leadership process usually takes place among friends, neighbors, and work associates who have frequent physical proximity and, thus, have ample opportunity to hold informal product-related conversations. These conversations usually occur naturally in the context of the product-category usage.

The two-step flow of communication theory highlights the role of interpersonal influence in the transmission of information from the mass media to the population at large. This theory provides the foundation for a revised multistep flow of communication model, which takes into account the fact that information and influence often are two-way processes and that opinion leaders both influence and are influenced by opinion receivers.

Marketers recognize the strategic value of segmenting their audiences into opinion leaders and opinion receivers for their product categories. When marketers can direct their promotional efforts to the more influential segments of their markets, these individuals will transmit this information to those who seek product advice. Marketers try to both simulate and stimulate opinion leadership. They have also found that they can create opinion leaders for their products by taking socially involved or influential people and deliberately increasing their enthusiasm for a product category.

The diffusion process and the adoption process are two closely related concepts concerned with the acceptance of new products by consumers. The diffusion process is a macro process that focuses on the spread of an innovation (a new product, service, or idea) from its source to the consuming public. The adoption process is a micro process that examines the stages through which an individual consumer passes when making a decision to accept or reject a new product.

The definition of the term *innovation* can be firm-oriented (new to the firm), product-oriented (a continuous innovation, a dynamically continuous innovation, or a discontinuous innovation), market-oriented (how long the product has been on the market or an arbitrary percentage of the potential target market that has purchased it), or consumer oriented (new to the consumer). Market-oriented definitions of innovation are most useful to consumer researchers in the study of the diffusion and adoption of new products.

Five product characteristics influence the consumer's acceptance of a new product: relative advantage, compatibility, complexity, trialability, and observability (or communicability).

Diffusion researchers are concerned with two aspects of communication—the channels through which word of a new product is spread to the consuming public and the types of messages that influence the adoption or rejection of new products. Diffusion is always examined in the context of a specific social system, such as a target market, a community, a region, or even a nation.

Time is an integral consideration in the diffusion process. Researchers are concerned with the amount of purchase time required for an individual consumer to adopt or reject a new product, with the rate of adoption, and with the identification of sequential adopters. The five-adopter categories are innovators, early adopters, early majority, late majority, and laggards.

Marketing strategists try to control the rate of adoption through their new product pricing policies. Marketers who wish to penetrate the market to achieve market leadership try to achieve wide adoption as quickly as possible by using low prices. Those who wish to recoup their developmental costs quickly use a skimming pricing policy but lengthen the adoption process.

The traditional adoption process model describes five stages through which an individual consumer passes to arrive at the decision to adopt or reject new product: awareness, interest, evaluation, trial, and adoption. To make it more realistic, an enhanced model is suggested as one that considers the possibility of a pre-existing need or problem, the likelihood that some form of evaluation might occur through the entire process, and that even after adoption there will be postadoption or purchase evaluation that might either strengthen the commitment or alternatively lead to discontinuation.

New-product marketers are vitally concerned with identifying the consumer innovator so that they may direct their promotional campaigns to the people who are most likely to try new products, adopt them, and influence others. Consumer research has identified a number of consumer-related characteristics, including: product interest, opinion leadership, personality factors, purchase and consumption traits, media habits, social characteristics, and demographic variables that distinguish consumer innovators from later adopters. These serve as useful variables in the segmentation of markets for new product introductions.

CHAPTER OUTLINE

WHAT IS OPINION LEADERSHIP?

1. Perhaps the most important thing for marketers to understand about word of mouth (personal influence) is its huge potential economic impact.
2. *Opinion leadership* (or word-of-mouth communications) is the process by which one person (the opinion leader) informally influences the actions or attitudes of others, who may be opinion seekers or merely opinion recipients.
3. The key characteristic of the influence is that it is interpersonal and informal and takes place between two or more people, *none of whom represents a commercial selling source that would gain directly from the sale of something.*

4. One of the parties in a word-of-mouth encounter usually offers advice or information about a product or service, such as which of several brands is best, or how a particular product may be used.
   a) This person is the *opinion leader* and may become an *opinion receiver*.
   b) Individuals who actively seek information and advice about products are sometimes called *opinion seekers*.
   c) The terms opinion receiver and opinion recipient will be used interchangeably.
5. Most studies of opinion leadership are concerned with the measurement of the behavioral impact that opinion leaders have on the consumption habits of others.
6. Influentials, opinion leaders are:
   a) Almost four times more likely than others to be asked about political and government issues, as well as how to handle teens.
   b) Three times more likely to be asked about computers or investments; and
   c) Twice as likely to be asked about health issues and restaurants.
7. When an information seeker knows little about a particular product or service, a strong-tie source will be sought.
8. When the consumer has some prior knowledge of the subject area, then a weak-tie source is acceptable.

*****Use Key Terms opinion leadership, opinion leader, opinion receiver, and opinion seekers Here; Use Learning Objective #1 Here*****

Word of Mouth in Today's *Always in Contact* World

1. Today, many people find themselves, by choice, to be "always" available to friends, family, and business associates.
2. An interesting phenomenon of the increased use of cell phones is the generation of younger users (consumers) who are the "thumb generation" because they use their thumbs to manipulate the functions on their cell phones. Does this make them unique?

*****Use Table 15-1 Here*****

Viral Marketing

1. Also known as "buzz marketing," "wildfire marketing," "avalanche marketing," or any one of a dozen other names, *viral marketing* describes any strategy that encourages individuals to pass on a marketing message to others, creating the potential for exponential growth in the message's exposure and influence.
2. Viral marketing is the marriage of e-mail and word of mouth.
3. It is called "viral" because it allows a message to spread like a virus.

*****Use Table 15-2 Here; Use Learning Objective #2 Here*****

DYNAMICS OF THE OPINION LEADERSHIP PROCESS

1. Opinion leadership as a process is a very dynamic and powerful consumer force.
   a) As informal communication sources, opinion leaders are remarkably effective at influencing consumers in their product-related decisions.

Credibility

1. Opinion leaders are highly credible sources of information, because they usually are perceived as objective concerning the product or service information or advice they dispense.
   a) Their intentions are perceived as being in the best interests of the opinion recipients.

*****Use Discussion Question #1 Here*****

Positive and Negative Product Information

1. Information provided by marketers is invariably favorable to the product and/or brand.
2. The very fact that opinion leaders provide both favorable and unfavorable information adds to their credibility.

*****Use Figure 15-1 Here; Use Exercise #2 Here*****

Information and Advice

1. Opinion leaders are the source of both information and advice.
   a) They may simply talk about their *experience* with a product, *relate* what they know about a product, or, more aggressively, *advise* others to buy or to avoid a specific product.
2. The kinds of product or service information that opinion leaders are likely to transmit include:
   a) Which of several brands is best.
   b) How to best use a specific product.
   c) Where to shop.
   d) Who provides the best service.

*****Use Figure 15-2 Here; Use Discussion Question #1 Here*****

Opinion Leadership Is Category-Specific

1. Opinion leadership tends to be *category-specific*; that is, opinion leaders often "specialize" in certain product categories about which they offer information and advice.
2. When other product categories are discussed, however, they are just as likely to reverse their roles and become opinion receivers.

Opinion Leadership Is a Two-Way Street

1. Consumers who are opinion leaders in one product-related situation may become opinion receivers in another situation, even for the same product.
2. An opinion leader may also be influenced by an opinion receiver as the result of a product-related conversation.

> *****Use Learning Objective #3 Here; Use Discussion Question #2 Here; Use Exercise #1 Here*****

THE MOTIVATION BEHIND OPINION LEADERSHIP

The Needs of Opinion Leaders

1. Motivation theory suggests that people may provide information or advice to others to satisfy some basic need of their own.
   a) Opinion leaders may be unaware of their own underlying motives.
   b) Opinion leaders may simply be trying to reduce their own postpurchase dissonance.
2. The information or advice that an opinion leader dispenses may provide all types of tangential personal benefits, it may confer attention, imply some type of status, grant superiority, demonstrate awareness and expertise, and give the feeling of possessing inside information and the satisfaction of "converting" less adventurous souls.
3. In addition to *self-involvement*, the opinion leader may also be motivated by product involvement, social involvement, and message involvement.
4. Opinion leaders who are motivated by product involvement may find themselves so pleased or so disappointed with a product that they simply must tell others about it.
5. Those who are motivated by social involvement need to share product-related experiences.
   a) Individuals who are bombarded with advertising messages and slogans tend to discuss them and the products they are designed to sell.

> *****Use Learning Objective #4 Here; Use Discussion Question #2 Here; Use Exercise #1 and #2 Here*****

The Needs of Opinion Receivers

1. Opinion receivers satisfy a variety of needs by engaging in product-related conversations.
   a) First, they obtain new-product or new-usage information.
   b) Second, they reduce their perceived risk by receiving firsthand knowledge from a user about a specific product or brand.
   c) Third, they reduce the search time entailed in the identification of a needed product or service.
   d) Moreover, opinion receivers can be certain of receiving the approval of the opinion leader.
2. Research reveals that women and men differ with respect to the types of products and services they are likely to seek advice about.

*****Use Learning Objective #4 Here; Use Table 15-3 Here; Use Exercise #1 Here*****

Purchase Pals

1. Purchase pals serve as information sources that actually accompany consumers on shopping trips.
2. Although purchase pals were used only 9 percent of the time for grocery items, they were used 25 percent of the time for purchases of electronic equipment.
3. Male purchase pals are more likely to be used as sources of product category expertise, product information, and retail store and price information.
4. Female purchase pals are more often used for moral support and to increase confidence in the buyer's decisions.

Surrogate Buyers Versus Opinion Leaders

1. There are instances in which surrogate buyers replace opinion leaders in this role.
2. For example, workingwomen are increasingly turning to wardrobe consultants for help in purchasing business attire, most new drugs start out requiring a doctor's prescription, and many service providers make decisions for their clients.

*****Use Table 15-4 Here*****

MEASUREMENT OF OPINION LEADERSHIP

1. In measuring opinion leadership, the researcher has a choice of four basic measurement techniques:
   a) The self-designating method.
   b) The sociometric method.
   c) The key informant method.
   d) The objective method.

*****Use Learning Objective #5 Here; Use Discussion Question #3 Here*****

2. In the self-designating method, respondents are asked to evaluate the extent to which they have provided others with information about a product category or specific brand or have otherwise influenced the purchase decisions of others.
   a) The self-designating technique is used more often than other methods for measuring opinion leadership because consumer researchers find it easy to include in market research questionnaires.
   b) Because this method relies on the respondent's self-evaluation, however, it may be open to bias.
3. The sociometric method measures the person-to-person informal communication of consumers concerning products or product categories.
   a) Respondents are asked to identify:

  i) The specific individuals (if any) to whom they provided advice or information about the product or brand under study.

  ii) The specific individuals (if any) who provided them with advice or information about the product or brand under study.

 b) Individuals designated by the primary respondent are tentatively classified as opinion leaders.

 c) This approach has useful applications to the study of consumer behavior.

 d) Any intact community provides an opportunity to measure and evaluate the flow of word-of-mouth communications concerning a new product and its subsequent impact on product trial.

4. A key informant is a person who is keenly aware or knowledgeable about the nature of social communications among members of a specific group.

 a) The key informant is asked to identify those individuals in the group who are most likely to be opinion leaders.

 b) The key informant does not have to be a member of the group under study.

 c) This research method is relatively inexpensive, because it requires that only one individual or at most several individuals be intensively interviewed, whereas the self-designating and sociometric methods require that a consumer sample or entire community be interviewed.

 d) The key informant method, however, is generally not used by marketers because of the difficulties inherent in identifying an individual who can objectively identify opinion leaders in a relevant consumer group.

 e) The key informant method would seem to be of greatest potential use in the study of industrial or institutional opinion leadership.

5. The objective method is much like a "controlled experiment"—it involves placing new products or new product information with selected individuals and then tracing the resulting "Web" of interpersonal communication concerning the relevant product(s).

> *****Use Learning Objective #5 Here; Use Discussion Question #3 Here; Use Table 15-5 Here; Use Figure 15-3 Here*****

A PROFILE OF THE OPINION LEADER

1. Just who are opinion leaders?

 a) Marketers have long sought answers to this question.

 b) If they are able to identify the relevant opinion leaders for their products, they can design marketing messages that encourage them to communicate with and influence the consumption behavior of others.

2. Consumer researchers have attempted to develop a realistic profile of the opinion leader.

 a) They reveal a keen sense of knowledge and interest in the particular product or service area, and they are likely to be consumer innovators.

 b) They also demonstrate a greater willingness to talk about the product, service, or topic; they are more self-confident; and they are more outgoing.

3. Within the context of a specific subject area, opinion leaders receive more information via nonpersonal sources and are considered by members of their groups to have expertise in their area of influence.
4. Mass media exposure or habits—opinion leaders are likely to read special-interest publications devoted to the specific topic or product category in which they "specialize."
    a) The opinion leader tends to have greater exposure to media specifically relevant to his or her area of interest than the nonleader.
    b) Mass and targeted (special-interest) media like to point out the impact that their particular audience has on influencing the tastes and buying behavior of others.

*****Use Learning Objective #6 Here; Use Table 15-6 Here*****

FREQUENCY AND OVERLAP OF OPINION LEADERSHIP

1. Opinion leadership is not a rare phenomenon.
    a) More than one-third of the people studied in a consumer research project are classified as opinion leaders with respect to some self-selected product category.
2. Do opinion leaders in one product category tend to be opinion leaders in other product categories?
    a) The answer comes from *opinion leadership overlap* research.
    b) Opinion leadership tends to overlap across certain combinations of interest areas.
    c) Overlap is likely to be highest among product categories that involve similar interests.
3. *Market maven*—these consumers possess a wide range of information about many different types of products, retail outlets, and other dimensions of markets.
    a) They both initiate discussions with other consumers and respond to requests for market information.
    b) Although they appear to fit the profile of opinion leaders in that they have high levels of brand awareness and tend to try more brands, unlike opinion leaders their influence extends beyond the realm of high-involvement products.
    c) Market mavens are also distinguishable from other opinion leaders because their influence stems not so much from product experience but from a more general knowledge or *market expertise* that leads them to an early awareness of a wide array of new products and services.

*****Use Key Term **market maven** Here; Use Learning Objective #7 Here; Use Discussion Question #4 Here*****

THE SITUATIONAL ENVIRONMENT OF OPINION LEADERSHIP

1. Product discussions generally occur within relevant situational contexts (e.g., when a specific product or a similar product is used or serves as an outgrowth of a more general discussion that touches on the product category).

2. Opinion leaders and opinion receivers often are friends, neighbors, or work associates, for existing friendships provide numerous opportunities for conversation concerning product-related topics.
3. Close physical proximity is likely to increase the occurrences of product-related conversations.

*****Use Learning Objective #8 Here*****

THE INTERPERSONAL FLOW OF COMMUNICATION

1. A classic study of voting behavior concluded that ideas often flow from radio and print media to opinion leaders and from them to the general public.
2. This so-called *two-step flow of communication theory* portrays opinion leaders as direct receivers of information from impersonal mass-media sources, which in turn transmit (and interpret) this information to the masses.
3. This theory views the opinion leader as a middleman between the impersonal mass media and the majority of society.

*****Use Key Term **two-step flow of communication theory** Here; Use Learning Objective #8 Here; Use Figure 15-4 Here*****

Multistep Flow of Communication Theory

1. A more comprehensive model of the interpersonal flow of communication depicts the transmission of information from the media as a multistep flow.
2. The revised model takes into account the fact that information and influence often are two-way processes in which opinion leaders both influence and are influenced by opinion receivers.
   a) This is presented as an illustration of the *multi-step flow of communication theory*.

*****Use Key Term **multi-step flow of communication theory** Here; Use Learning Objective #8 Here; Use Figure 15-5 Here*****

OPINION LEADERSHIP AND THE FIRM'S MARKETING STRATEGY

1. Marketers have long been aware of the power that opinion leadership exerts on consumers' preferences and actual purchase behavior.
2. Many marketers look for an opportunity to encourage word-of-mouth communications and other favorable informal conversations.
3. New product designers take advantage of the effectiveness of word-of-mouth communication by deliberately designing products to have word-of-mouth potential.
   a) A new product should give customers something to talk about.

315

4. Proof of the power of word-of-mouth is the cases in which critics hate a movie and the viewing public like it and tell their friends.
   a) In instances where informal word of mouth does not spontaneously emerge from the uniqueness of the product or its marketing strategy, some marketers have deliberately attempted to stimulate or to simulate opinion leadership.

Programs Designed to Stimulate Opinion Leadership

1. Advertising and promotional programs designed to persuade consumers to "tell your friends how much you like our product" are one way in which marketers encourage consumer discussions of their products or services.
2. The objective of a promotional strategy of stimulation is to run advertisements or a direct marketing program that is sufficiently interesting and informative to provoke consumers into discussing the benefits of the product with others.

Advertisements Simulating Opinion Leadership

1. A firm's advertisements can also be designed to simulate product discussions by portraying people in the act of informal communication.

*****Use Exercise #2 Here*****

Word-of-Mouth May Be Uncontrollable

1. Informal communication is difficult to control.
2. Negative comments, frequently in the form of rumors that are untrue, can sweep through the marketplace to the detriment of a product.
3. Indeed, a study by the White House Office of Consumer Affairs found that 90 percent or more of unhappy customers would not do business again with the company that is the source of their dissatisfaction.
   a) Each dissatisfied customer will share his or her grievance with at least nine other people, and 13 percent of unhappy customers will tell more than 20 people about the negative experience.
4. Some common rumor themes are:
   a) The product was produced under unsanitary conditions.
   b) The product contained an unwholesome or culturally unacceptable ingredient.
   c) The product functioned as an undesirable depressant or stimulant.
   d) The product included a cancer-causing element or agent.
   e) The firm was owned or influenced by an unfriendly or misguided foreign country, governmental agency, or religious cult.
5. Some marketers have used toll-free telephone numbers in an attempt to head off negative word-of-mouth, displaying an 800 number prominently on their products' labels.
6. A particularly challenging form of "negative" word-of-mouth can be generated today over the Internet, when a dissatisfied consumer decides to post his or her story on a bulletin board for all to see.

Creation of Opinion Leaders

1. Marketing strategists agree that promotional efforts would be significantly improved if they could segment their markets into opinion leaders and opinion receivers.
2. Some researchers have suggested that it might be more fruitful to "create" product-specific opinion leaders.
3. In one classic study, a group of socially influential high school students (class presidents and sports captains) were asked to become members of a panel that would rate newly released records.
   a) As part of their responsibilities, panel participants were encouraged to discuss their record choices with friends.
   b) This study suggests that product-specific opinion leaders can be created by taking socially involved or influential people and deliberately increasing their enthusiasm for a product category.

*****Use Learning Objective #9 Here*****

DIFFUSION OF INNOVATIONS

1. Consumer acceptance of new products and services is studied from the research perspective known as the *diffusion of innovations*.
   a) This diffusion requires an understanding of two related processes:
      i) *Diffusion process*.
      ii) *Adoption process*.
2. Diffusion is a macro process concerned with the spread of a new product (an innovation) from its source to the consuming public.
3. Adoption is a micro process that focuses on the stages through which an individual consumer passes when deciding to accept or reject a new product.
4. In addition to an examination of these two interrelated processes, the chapter presents a profile of *consumer innovators*.

*****Use Key Terms diffusion of innovations, diffusion process, adoption process, and consumer innovations Here; Use Learning Objective #10 Here*****

THE DIFFUSION PROCESS

1. The diffusion process is concerned with how innovations spread, and how they are assimilated within a market.
2. Diffusion is the process by which the acceptance of an innovation is spread by communication to members of a social system over a period of time.
3. There are four elements to the definition:
   a) The innovation.
   b) The channel of communication.
   c) The social system.

d) Time.

Use Learning Objective #10 Here; Use Exercise #3 Here**

The Innovation

1. There is no universally accepted definition of the terms product *innovation* or new product.
2. There are four approaches to defining a new product or a new service:
   a) Firm-oriented.
   b) Product-oriented.
   c) Market-oriented.
   d) Consumer-oriented.

Use Key Term** innovation Here; Use Learning Objective #10 Here; Use Exercise #3 Here**

Firm-Oriented Definitions

1. A *firm-oriented* approach treats the newness of a product from the perspective of the company producing or marketing it.
2. When the product is "new" to the company, it is considered new.
   a) This ignores whether or not the product is actually new to the marketplace.
3. This definition is not very useful when the goal is to understand consumer acceptance of a new product.

Product-Oriented Definitions

1. This approach focuses on the features of the product itself, and the effects these features are likely to have on consumers' established usage patterns.
2. There are three types of product innovations:
   a) *Continuous innovation*, which is the least disruptive to consumer patterns.
   b) *Dynamically continuous innovation*, which, although not altering established behavior patterns, is somewhat more disruptive.
   c) *Discontinuous innovation*, which requires consumers to adopt new behavior patterns.

Use Key Terms** continuous innovation, dynamically continuous innovation, and discontinuous innovation Here; Use Figure 15-7 Here; Use Exercise #3 Here**

Market-Oriented Definitions

1. This approach judges the newness of a product in terms of how much exposure consumers have to the new product.
2. There are two ways of looking at this orientation:
   a) The product could be considered to be new if it has been purchased by only a small percentage of the potential market.

b) The product could be considered to be new if it has been on the market for a relatively short period of time.
c) These are both subjective measurements because the research has to establish the degree of market penetration involved.

Consumer-Oriented Definition

1. Some market researchers favor this approach to defining an innovation.
   a) A new product is any product that a potential consumer judges to be new.
   b) The newness is based on consumer perception.
2. Although endorsed by some advertisers and marketers, it has received little systematic attention.
   a) Additionally, it should be pointed out that although this portion of the chapter deals primarily with what might be described as "purchase" innovativeness (i.e., time of adoption), a second type of innovativeness, "use-innovativeness," has been the subject of some thought and research.
3. A consumer is being *use-innovative* when he or she uses a previously adopted product in a novel or unusual way.

Product Characteristics That Influence Diffusion

1. Not all new products have equal consumer acceptance potential. As a consequence, marketers try to anticipate consumer acceptance.
2. Researchers have identified five product characteristics that seem to influence consumer acceptance of new products:
   a) *Relative advantage*—degree to which potential customers perceive a new product as superior to existing substitutes.
   b) *Compatibility*—degree to which the customer feels the new product is consistent with their present needs, values, and practices.
   c) *Complexity*—degree to which a new product is difficult to understand or use. Complexity is especially important in dealing with technological fear.
   d) *Trialability*—degree to which a new product is capable of being tried on a limited basis.
   e) *Observability*—ease with which a product's benefits or attributes can be observed, imagined, or described to potential consumers.
3. Consumer perception is the key to these characteristics.
   a) How the consumer sees the product is a valid question.

> *****Use Learning Objective #11 Here; Use Discussion Question #5 Here; Use Table 15-7 Here; Use Figure 15-8 Here*****

Resistance to Innovation

1. Seeking to answer what makes some new products almost instant successes has marketers looking at the product characteristics of an innovation.

a) Such characteristics offer clues to help determine the extent of consumer resistance, which increases when perceived relative advantage, perceived compatibility, trialability, and communicability are low, and perceived complexity is high.

2. *Innovation overload* is used to describe the situation in which the increase in information and options available to the consumer are so great that they seriously impair decision-making.

The Channels of Communication

1. How quickly an innovation spreads through a market depends on the degree of communication between marketers and consumers, as well as communication among consumers themselves.
2. A variety of new channels of communication have been developed to inform consumers of innovative products and services.
3. Interactive marketing messages, in which the consumer becomes an important part of the communication, rather than just a "passive" message recipient.
4. Many Web sites currently ask the Internet user if he or she would like to be informed about new products, discount offers, and so on, relevant to the focus of the site.

*****Use Learning Objective #10 and #12 Here; Use Exercise #3 Here*****

The Social System

1. In terms of consumer behavior, market segment, and target market are synonymous with the term *social system* in diffusion research.
2. A social system is a physical, social, or cultural environment to which people belong and within which they function.
3. The orientation of a social system, with its own special values or norms, is likely to influence the acceptance or rejection of new products.
   a) If the social system is modern in orientation, the acceptance of innovations is likely to be high.
   b) If the social system is traditional in orientation, innovations that are perceived as radical or as infringements on established custom are likely to be avoided.
4. One authority describes the characteristics of a typical modern social system in the following terms:
   a) A positive attitude toward change.
   b) An advanced technology and a skilled labor force.
   c) A general respect for education and science.
   d) An emphasis on rational and ordered causal relationships rather than on emotional ones.
   e) An outreach perspective, in which members of the system frequently interact with outsiders.
5. The key point is that a social system's orientation is the climate in which marketers must operate to gain acceptance for their new products.

*****Use Learning Objective #10 Here; Use Exercise #3 Here*****

Time

1. Time is the backbone of the diffusion process.
2. Three ways of considering time are important:
   a) The amount of purchase time.
   b) The identification of adopter categories.
   c) The rate of adoption.

*****Use Learning Objective #13 Here; Use Exercise #3 Here*****

Purchase Time

1. This form of time has been characterized as the amount of time that elapses between the consumers' initial awareness of the new product and the point at which they purchase or reject the product.
2. Purchase time is an important concept because the average time a consumer takes to adopt a new product is a predictor of the overall length of time it will take for the new product to achieve widespread adoption.

*****Use Learning Objective #13 Here; Use Table 15-8 Here*****

Adopter Categories

1. The concept of *adopter categories* involves a classification scheme that indicates where a consumer stands relative to other consumers when he or she adopts a new product.
2. Consumers are classified into five adopter categories; *innovators, early adopters, early majority, late majority,* and *laggards.*
   a) Some argue that the bell curve (see Figure 15-9) is an erroneous depiction, because it may lead to the inaccurate conclusion that 100 percent of the members of the social system under study (the target market) eventually will accept the product innovation.
   b) The *"nonadopter"* category is in accord with marketplace reality, for not all potential consumers adopt a product innovation.
3. Instead of the classic five-category adopter scheme, many consumer researchers have used other classification schemes, most of which consist of two or three categories that compare *innovators* or *early triers* with *later triers* or *nontriers.*

*****Use Key Term **adopter category** Here; Use Learning Objective #13 Here; Use Discussion Question #6 Here; Use Figure 15-9 Here; Use Table 15-9 and 15-10 Here*****

Rate of Adoption

1. The rate of adoption is concerned with how long it takes a new product or service to be adopted by members of a social system; that is, how quickly it takes a new product to be accepted by those who will ultimately adopt it.

2. In general, the diffusion of products worldwide is becoming a more rapid phenomenon.
3. The objective in marketing new products is usually to gain wide acceptance of the product as quickly as possible.
4. Marketers desire a rapid rate of product adoption to penetrate the market and quickly establish market leadership (obtain the largest share of the market) before competition takes hold.
   a) A *penetration policy* is usually accompanied by a relatively low introductory price designed to discourage competition from entering the market.
5. Rapid product adoption also demonstrates to marketing intermediaries (wholesalers and retailers) that the product is worthy of their full and continued support.
6. Under certain circumstances, marketers might prefer to avoid a rapid rate of adoption for a new product.
   a) For example, marketers who wish to use a pricing strategy that will enable them to recoup their development costs quickly might follow a *skimming policy*.

*****Use Learning Objective #10 and #13 Here; Use Discussion Question #7 and #8 Here; Use Figure 15-10 Here; Use Table 15-10 Here*****

THE ADOPTION PROCESS

1. The second major process in the diffusion of innovations is *adoption*.
2. The focus of this process is the stages through which an individual consumer passes although arriving at a decision to try or not to try or to continue using or to discontinue using a new product.

Stages in the Adoption Process

1. It is often assumed that the consumer moves through five stages in arriving at a decision to purchase or reject a new product: (1) awareness, (2) interest, (3) evaluation, (4) trial, and (5) adoption (or rejection).
2. These are called the **stages in the adoption process**.
3. Although the traditional adoption process model is insightful in its simplicity, it does not adequately reflect the full complexity of the consumer adoption process.
   a) It does not adequately acknowledge that there is quite often a need or problem-recognition stage that consumers face before acquiring an awareness of potential options or solutions.
   b) Also, the adoption process does not adequately provide for the possibility of evaluation and rejection of a new product or service after each stage, especially after trial.
   c) It does not explicitly include postadoption or postpurchase evaluation.
4. The adoption of some products and services may have minimal consequences, although the adoption of other innovations may lead to major behavioral and lifestyle changes.

*****Use Key Term stages in the adoption process Here; Use Learning Objective #14 Here; Use Figure 15-11 Here; Use Table 15-11 Here*****

The Adoption Process and Information Sources

1. The adoption process provides a framework for determining which types of information sources consumers find most important at specific decision stages.
2. The key point is that impersonal mass-media sources tend to be most valuable for creating initial product awareness.
   a) Then the relative importance of these sources declines although the relative importance of interpersonal sources increases.

*****Use Figure 15-12 Here*****

A PROFILE OF THE CONSUMER INNOVATOR

Defining the Consumer Innovator

1. Consumer innovators can be defined as the relatively small group of consumers who are the earliest purchasers of a new product.
   a) The problem with this definition is the concept "earliest."
   b) Innovators are defined as the first 2.5 percent of the social system to adopt an innovation.
2. In many marketing diffusion studies, however, the definition of the consumer innovator has been derived from the status of the new product under investigation.
   a) Other researchers have defined innovators in terms of their innovativeness, that is, their purchase of some minimum number of new products from a selected group of new products.
3. Noninnovators would be defined as those who purchase none or only one of the new fashion products.

*****Use Learning Objective #15 Here; Use Exercise #4 Here*****

Interest in the Product Category

1. Consumer innovators are much more interested than either later adopters or nonadopters in the product categories that they are among the first to purchase.
2. Consumer innovators are more likely than noninnovators to seek information concerning their specific interests from a variety of informal and mass media sources.
3. They are more likely to give greater deliberation to the purchase of new products or services in their areas of interest than noninnovators.

*****Use Learning Objective #15 Here; Use Exercise #4 Here*****

The Innovator Is an Opinion Leader

1. There is a strong tendency for consumer opinion leaders to be innovators.
2. Consumer innovators provide other consumers with information and advice about new products. Those who receive such advice frequently follow it.
3. The consumer innovator often influences the acceptance or rejection of new products.
4. When innovators are enthusiastic about a new product and encourage others to try it, the product is likely to receive broader and quicker acceptance.
5. Because motivated consumer innovators can influence the rate of acceptance or rejection of a new product, they influence its eventual success or failure.

*****Use Learning Objective #15 Here; Use Exercise #4 Here*****

Personality Traits

1. Consumer innovators generally are *less dogmatic* than noninnovators.
2. Consistent with their open-mindedness, it appears that innovative behavior is an expression of an individuals' *need for uniqueness*.
3. Still further, consumer innovators all differ from noninnovators in terms of *social character*.
4. Consumer innovators are *inner-directed*.
    a) In contrast, noninnovators are other-directed.
    b) The initial purchasers of a new line of automobiles might be inner-directed, whereas the later purchasers of the same automobile might be other-directed.
    c) This suggests that as acceptance of a product progresses from early to later adopters, a gradual shift occurs in the personality type of adopters from inner-directedness to other-directedness.
5. There also appears to be a link between *optimum stimulation level* and consumer innovativeness.
    a) Individuals who seek a lifestyle rich with novel, complex, and unusual experiences (i.e., high optimum stimulation levels) are more willing to risk trying new products, to be innovative, to seek purchase-related information, and to accept new retail facilities.
6. *Variety-seeking consumers* tend to be brand switchers and purchasers of innovative products and services.

*****Use Learning Objective #16 Here; Use Exercise #4 Here*****

Perceived Risk and Venturesomeness

1. *Perceived risk* is the degree of uncertainty or fear about the consequences of a purchase that a consumer feels when considering the purchase of a new product.
2. Research on perceived risk and the trial of new products overwhelmingly indicates that the consumer innovator is a low-risk perceiver; that is, they experience little fear of trying new products or services.
3. *Venturesomeness* is a broad-based measure of a consumer's willingness to accept the risk of purchasing new products.

a) Measures of venturesomeness have been used to evaluate a person's general values or attitudes toward trying new products.
b) A typical measurement scale might include such items as:
   i) I prefer to try a toothpaste when it first comes out, wait and learn how good it is before trying it.
   ii) When I am shopping and see a brand of paper towels I know about but have never used, I am very anxious or willing to try it, hesitant about trying it, very unwilling to try it.
   iii) I like to be among the first people to buy and use new products that are on the market (measured on a five-point "agreement" scale).
c) Venturesomeness seems to be an effective barometer of actual innovative behavior.
d) Consistent with their greater venturesomeness and lower risk perception, consumer innovators are likely to learn about innovations earlier than others.

*****Use Learning Objective #16 Here*****

Purchase and Consumption Characteristics

1. Consumer innovators are *less* brand loyal.
2. Consumer innovators are more likely to be deal-prone.
3. Consumer innovators are also likely to be heavy users of the product category in which they innovate.
   a) Specifically, they purchase larger quantities and consume more of the product than noninnovators.
4. Finally, for products like VCRs, PCs, microwave ovens, 35-mm cameras, and food processors, usage variety is likely to be a relevant dimension of new product diffusion.
5. To sum up, a positive relationship exists between innovative behavior and heavy usage.

*****Use Learning Objective #15 and #16 Here; Use Exercise #4 Here*****

Media Habits

1. Comparisons of the media habits of innovators and noninnovators across such widely diverse areas of consumption as fashion clothing and new automotive services suggest that innovators have somewhat greater total exposure to magazines than noninnovators, particularly to special-interest magazines devoted to the product category in which they innovate.
2. Consumer innovators are also less likely to watch television than noninnovators.
   a) Studies concerning the relationship between innovative behavior and exposure to other mass media, such as radio and newspapers, have been too few, and the results have been too varied to draw any useful conclusions.

*****Use Learning Objective #15 Here; Use Figure 15-13 Here; Use Exercise #4 Here*****

Social Characteristics

1. Consumer innovators are more socially accepted and socially involved than noninnovators.
   a) This greater social acceptance and involvement of consumer innovators may help explain why they function as effective opinion leaders.

*****Use Learning Objective #15 Here; Use Exercise #4 Here*****

Demographic Characteristics

1. It is reasonable to assume that the age of the consumer innovator is related to the specific product category in which he or she innovates.
   a) Research suggests that consumer innovators tend to be younger than either later adopters or noninnovators.
   b) Probably because many of the products selected for research attention are particularly attractive to younger consumers.
2. Consumer innovators have more formal education, higher personal or family incomes, and are more likely to have higher occupational status (to be professionals or hold managerial positions) than later adopters or noninnovators.

*****Use Learning Objective #15 Here; Use Discussion Question #8 Here; Use Table 15-12 Here; Use Exercise #4 Here*****

Are There Generalized Consumer Innovators?

1. Do consumer innovators in one product category tend to be consumer innovators in other product categories?
   a) The answer to this strategically important question is a guarded "No."
   b) The overlap of innovativeness across product categories, like opinion leadership, seems to be limited to product categories that are closely related to the same basic interest area.
   c) Such a pattern suggests that it is generally a good marketing strategy to target a new product to consumers who were the first to try other products in the same basic product category.
2. There is evidence that suggests that a new type of more generalized "high-tech" innovator does exist, that is, the "change leader."
   a) Such individuals tend to embrace and popularize many of the innovations that are ultimately accepted by the mainstream population.
   b) They tend to have a wide range of personal and professional contacts representing different occupational and social groups; most often, these contacts tend to be "weak ties" or acquaintances.
3. Change leaders also appear to fall into one of two distinct groups:
   a) A younger group can be characterized as being stimulation-seeking, sociable, and having high levels of fashion awareness.
   b) A middle-aged group is highly self-confident and has very high information-seeking needs.

4. Similar to change leaders, "technophiles" are individuals who purchase technologically advanced products soon after their market debut.
   a) Such individuals tend to be technically curious people.
   b) Another group responding to technology are adults who are categorized as "techthusiasts"—people who are most likely to purchase or subscribe to emerging products and services that are technologically oriented.
      i) These consumers are typically younger, better educated, and more affluent.

DISCUSSION QUESTIONS

1a. Why is an opinion leader a more credible source of product information than an advertisement for the same product?

Opinion leaders are credible sources of information because they are perceived as objective, they base their product advice on firsthand experience, and they are perceived as motivated by the best interests of the receiver, rather than for personal gain.

b. Are there any circumstances where information from advertisements is likely to be more influential than word-of-mouth?

Word-of-mouth greatly influences consumption behavior of products, which reflect group norms and are highly visible (e.g., clothing), and of products where there is highly perceived risk (e.g., stereo equipment, personal computers, cars). Advertising is likely to be more influential than word-of-mouth when consumers are not very involved with the product and when the perceived risk is low. Under such conditions, repetitive exposure to product information, through advertising, is likely to create a distinctive product image and consumer awareness that will cause the consumer to purchase the product.

2. Why would a consumer who has just purchased an expensive fax machine for home use attempt to influence the purchase behavior of others?

The purchaser of an expensive fax machine is likely to experience cognitive dissonance. To reduce such anxiety and confirm one's purchase behavior, the buyer might discuss the purchase with others, tell peers and friends how wonderful it is to have a fax machine and even try to persuade them to purchase the product. (See Table 15-3 for a complete list of the motivations of opinion leaders and receivers.)

3. A company that owns and operates health clubs across the country is opening a health club in your town. The company has retained you as its marketing research consultant and asked you to identify opinion leaders for its service. Which of the following identification methods would you recommend: the self-designating method, the sociometric method, the key-informant method, or the objective method? Explain your selection. In your answer, be sure to discuss the advantages and disadvantages of the four measurement methods as they relate to the marketing situation just described.

The self-designating method for measuring opinion leadership is most commonly used by marketers because it is the least expensive, and it lends itself to inclusion in self-administered marketing research questionnaires. Students can, however, choose any one of the four techniques, provided that have a good rationale for their selections. The benefits and limitations of each technique are summarized in Table 15-5.

4. **Do you have any "market mavens" among your friends? Describe their personality traits and behaviors. Identify a situation where a market maven has given you advice regarding a product or service, and discuss what you believe was his or her motivation for doing so.**

Answers will vary significantly among students. In any social setting, and especially in groups, such as a college campus, that consist primarily of young, single adults who are highly influenced by peers, there are likely to be market mavens; such individuals probably provide others with advice on clothes, cars, stereo equipment, travel, and health/exercise products, and services. The classroom discussion should examine how market mavens differ from other students on campus in terms of their motivations, interests, consumption-related knowledge, and shopping behavior.

5. **Describe how a manufacturer might use knowledge of the following product characteristics to speed up the acceptance of pocketsize cellular telephones:**
   a. Relative advantage
   b. Compatibility
   c. Complexity
   d. Trialability
   e. Observability

a. Relative Advantage—The degree to which potential customers perceive the pocketsize cellular phone as superior to other telephones is the product's relative advantage. Thus, the product can be positioned as a superior replacement of an older existing product—the business beeper.

b. Compatibility—The degree to which potential consumers feel a new product is consistent with their needs, values, and practices is a measure of compatibility. Thus, cellular phones should be promoted as being highly compatible with the needs of individuals holding managerial and professional jobs, who are often in transit, pressed for time, and must continually stay in touch with their offices and clients.

c. Complexity—The degree to which a new product is difficult to use. Clearly, cellular phones are rather simple to use. Generally, easy-to-use products gain wider consumer acceptance than complex innovations.

d. Trialability—The degree to which a new product can be tried on a limited basis. Enabling consumers to try cellular telephones on a limited basis is likely to speed up the diffusion rate of the new product.

e. Observability—The ease with which a product's benefits can be observed, imagined, or described to potential customers. Marketers can convey the benefits of pocket-size cellular telephones to consumers rather easily. Some consumers, however, may feel apprehensive about using the product because of recent media coverage depicting the very limited research evidence suggesting that extensive personal use of cellular phones may cause brain cancer.

6. **Toshiba has introduced a new laptop computer that weighs seven pounds, has a color screen, and a powerful processor, into which a full-size desktop screen and keyboard can be easily plugged. How can the company use the diffusion of innovations framework to develop promotional, pricing, and distribution strategies targeted to:**
   a. **Innovators**
   b. **Early adopters**
   c. **Early majority**
   d. **Late majority**
   e. **Laggards**

Adopter Category	Promotional Appeal	Distribution	Pricing
Innovators	Appeals that stress the product's newness and "snob appeal."	Selective	Skimming
Early Adopters	Factual appeals stressing the product's attributes and related benefits.	Selective	Skimming
Early Majority	"Expert" appeals and endorsements or testimonials.	Intensive	Lower prices
Late Majority	Conformity appeals (e.g., "Everyone in your profession has it, why not you?").	Intensive	A lot of competition and prices keep dropping
Laggards	Suggesting that the new product does what existing competitive products do, only better.	Intensive	As above

7. **Is the curve that describes the sequence and proportion of adopter categories among the population (Figure 15-10) similar in shape to the product life cycle curve? Explain your answer. How would you use both curves in developing a marketing strategy?**

The two curves are somewhat similar in shape because both represent the product's market position over time. The two curves, however, are not the same because the diffusion curve represents the proportion of consumers who adopted the product whereas the product life cycle traces sales. Thus, the diffusion curve fails to represent repurchases, because each consumer is counted in only one of the adopter categories. On the other hand, the product life cycle represents dollar sales, which include both initial and repeated purchases. Also, the late stages of the product life cycle often do not match the sharply declining diffusion curve, because dollar sales are unlikely to drop. At this late stage, repeat purchases are likely to be made by the product's innovators and early adopters (due to brand loyalty) as well as by laggards entering the market for the first time; such sales will be reflected in the product life cycle but not in the diffusion curve. Both curves are used differently in developing marketing strategies. The diffusion model provides important guidelines regarding marketing strategies during the new product's introduction (i.e., penetration versus skimming pricing measures, utilizing the knowledge about the five product characteristics that influence diffusion). Also, this curve illustrates how the consumer groups entering the market at various times represent distinct adopter segments to be uniquely targeted. The product life-cycle traces the life of the product within its competitive and production environments, and pinpoints the product modification, distribution, pricing, and promotional strategies that should be undertaken during the growth, maturity, and decline stages of a given product category.

8. **Sony is introducing a 27-inch TV with a built-in VCR, a picture-in-picture feature, and a feature that allows the viewer to simultaneously view frozen frames of the last signals received from 12 channels.**

  a. **What recommendations would you make to Sony regarding the initial target market for the new TV model?**

  Innovators are the initial target market for the new TV model. These consumers are venturesome, open to new ideas, eager to try new products, perceive less risk in adopting new offerings, and are more socially integrated than other consumers. In terms of personality traits, these individuals are open-minded, inner-directed, and like exciting and new concepts (i.e., high optimum stimulation level).

  b. **How would you identify the innovators for this product?**

  Sony should derive the definition of consumer innovators from the status of its new product. Thus, those consumers who purchase the new TV-model within a designated period of time following the product's introduction are defined as the "innovators." The company should study the characteristics of these consumers (including the data from the warranty cards that purchasers of the new product have filled out) and use the knowledge gained to develop marketing strategies for the introductions of other electronic innovations.

  c. **Select three (3) characteristics of the consumer innovators (as summarized in Table 15-12). Explain how Sony might use each of these characteristics to influence the adoption process and speed up the diffusion of the new product.**

  In addition to considering the characteristics discussed in the answer to b. (above), Sony should examine the purchase and consumption patterns, level of interest in the product category, media habits, and demographic characteristics of those consumers who are defined as innovators for the product. Then, Sony should continue marketing the product to consumers with similar characteristics and, gradually target those who are noninnovators/later adopters.

d. Should Sony follow a penetration or a skimming policy in introducing the product? Why?

Because the new product involves very high development costs, Sony will probably follow a skimming policy by introducing the product at a high price and targeting consumers who are willing to pay top dollar. Such an approach will enable Sony to recoup the development costs quicker. As other companies come up with TV sets that have features similar to Sony's model, however, the company must gradually lower the price in order to attract additional market segments.

EXERCISES

1. Describe two situations where you served as an opinion leader and two situations where you sought consumption-related advice/information from an opinion leader. Indicate your relationship to the persons with whom you interacted. Are the circumstances during which you engaged in word-of-mouth communications consistent with the text's material? Explain.

Instructor's Discussion

This exercise demonstrates that opinion leadership is a two-way process, and that, at different times, the same person can serve as an opinion leader or an opinion receiver/seeker. The professor can use this exercise to illustrate the superiority of the multistep flow of communication model Figure 15-3, over the two-step model Figure 15-5 in understanding the dynamics of word-of-mouth.

2a. Find ads that simulate and ads that stimulate opinion leadership and present them in class.
b. Can you think of negative rumors that you have heard recently about a company or a product? If so, present them in class.

Instructor's Discussion

a. A variation is to find ads that you think do this, present them on overhead and discuss why they do or don't stimulate opinion leadership.

b. There are several well-researched and documented cases of negative rumors starting and corporations battling them. Create a case study of one such account and use that to help students answer this portion of the question.

3. Identify a product, service, or style that was recently adopted by you and/or some of your friends. Identify what type of innovation it is, and describe its diffusion process up to this point in time. What are the characteristics of people who adopted it first? What types of people did not adopt it? What features of the product, service, or style are likely to determine its eventual success or failure?

<u>Instructor's Discussion</u>

The objective of this exercise is to demonstrate that the concepts discussed in this chapter are highly applicable to the student's own behavior and immediate social system.

4. With the advancement of digital technology, some companies plan to introduce interactive TV systems that will allow viewers to select films from video libraries and view them on demand. Among people you know, identify two who are likely to be the innovators for such a new service and construct consumer profiles using the characteristics of consumer innovators discussed in the text.

<u>Instructor's Discussion</u>

Students should draw on material from Table 15-13 and the discussion of technothusiasts.

S.TA.R. PROJECTS

Ethical Issues in Consumer Behavior

S.T.A.R. Project #1
As indicated in the chapter, one of the hottest forms of marketing that has been spurred by the Internet Age is viral or buzz marketing. This marketing technique is a way for a marketing message to spread exponentially throughout the marketplace using e-mail or other Internet formats such as chat rooms. After reading the examples from the chapter, your assignment is to find what you perceive to be a viral or buzz effort that has recently occurred. Analyze the effort for its marketing effectiveness and its adherence to sound or good business ethics. Think about the effort carefully—was anyone harmed? Was the truth told? Were facts accurate? Was this the most ethical way to transmit information about the product or service? Write a short summary report about the viral or buzz event, its impact, its effectiveness, and any ethical issues of note.

<u>Instructor's Discussion</u>

This project asks students to review the concept of viral or buzz marketing. Several publications have examined the phenomenon recently (see *Business Week* and others). For a good secondary research start see Footnote 7. at the end of the chapter. The emphasis is on whether this popular idea is ethical or whether the tendency toward excess may doom it. This project can also be combined with 2. below for a discussion of the potential for harmful word of mouth.

S.T.A.R. Project #2

The power of the Internet can be abused. Abuse is really a matter of perspective, however. For example, if a consumer or an organization were to openly criticize a company, its marketing practices, or products/services, the company could make the claim that the consumer or organization was treating it (the company) unfairly and using the cover of freedom of speech to harm its reputation and business. From the consumer's or an organization's standpoint, the criticism might be deserved and it was (is) exercising its constitutional right to complain and seek redress over some perceived wrong. The Internet has proved to be a useful vehicle for making such statements about companies. Your assignment is to research two such complaint Web sites (Web Pages That Suck at www.websitesthatsuck.com and the Stealing Home Coalition at www.homedepotsucks.com). Review the Web sites, examine the ethics of their behavior and the issues involved and then write a short position paper that takes a stance on the usefulness (or harmfulness) of such Web sites. Be sure to review the ethical issues involved.

Instructor's Discussion

This is a sensitive issue, however, the students should find the information useful and informative. One site claims to educate through its "trashing" of Web sites and the other Web site claims to be a platform for curing a wrong and environmental danger. Whether or not these claims are true, it should make for a useful discussion. This exercise can be combined with 1. above for discussion purposes.

Small Group Projects

S.T.A.R. Project #3

As a group study the diffusion of Internet services to the general public. Your group can look at the Internet as a service, or look at the main service the Internet provides. As your group examines this issue, consider what definition of innovation best fits the Internet and its service aspect and what product characteristics contribute to its diffusion. Your group should think through your own adoption process for using this service. Write a paper explaining your group's thoughts and findings.

Instructor's Discussion

This short project asks groups to examine the Internet in light of information presented in the chapter. You may modify the project if you so choose to be more specific or to include specific tools on the Internet such as search engines.

S.T.A.R. Project #4

As students you are familiar with the concept of innovations even if it is a term that is not in your normal vocabulary. Innovations impact your daily lives. Your assignment is to build on data found in the chapter and in Figure 15-7. Examine the figure. Notice the links (innovative connections) between the telephone, cell phone, and fax machine. Your assignment is build a separate connection or grid for the cell phone. Consider how cell phone technology is changing the way we live and communicate (review the chapter material on market groups that are using cell phones in unusual ways). Predict where this technology will take us next. For example, will the cell phone eventually replace the PC as our primary way of computing and reaching the Internet? Write a report that explains the connection or grid your group developed and summarize what you perceive the future holds for this innovation.

Instructor's Discussion

This project should aid the student in building on the information found in the chapter and in Figure 15-7. Be sure to save time for class discussion. Often, if one group puts their ideas on the board, other groups can quickly build on the issues.

Using the Internet to Study Consumer Behavior

S.T.A.R. Project #5

As indicated in the section entitled Diffusion of Innovations, Gillette (see www.gillette.com) has a policy that 40 percent of sales must come from products introduced within the past five years. Wouldn't it be great if all companies followed a similar doctrine and objective? Gillette has been considered to be an innovative company for almost a century. Following the policy above is one of the reasons that it has an innovative reputation. Your assignment is to go to the Gillette Web site, pick a product from the Gillette inventory, and trace how the product either has or should be diffused through our market system. Use any of the tools, ideas, or suggestions provided by the chapter to carry out your assignment. Write a short report that summarizes your attempt and findings.

Instructor's Discussion

This project is left wide-open on purpose. It should be a good gauge of what students have learned about innovation and diffusion. You may modify in any way you see fit. There is ample information on the Gillette Web site to pursue the development of any one of several products.

S.T.A.R. Project #6

The speed at which products are being introduced and being accepted or rejected is increasing because of the Internet and its ability to bring information to consumers. Using the information that you find contained in Table 15-7, find a product that you have noticed recently and perceive to be new. Examine how the Internet is being used to bring this new product to the consuming public. Which of the characteristics found in the table are relevant to the new product? What do you perceive the future of the new product to be? Have any rating services reviewed the product as yet (if so, what are the ratings?)? How will these ratings impact the product's success? Write a short report that summarizes your thoughts and findings on the new product.

Instructor's Discussion

This project is a simple way to test whether students understand the characteristics found in Table 15-7. To often the characteristics become a memorized list rather than a series of characteristics that come alive with new products and new product development.

CASES

Case One: Let the Robot Pick It Up

Class discussion should touch on each of the five product characteristics.

Relative advantage—The consumer would not have to push or pull a vacuum cleaner, which is a significant advantage.

Compatibility—It should be consistent with the consumer's present needs, which would be to get the carpet clean.

Complexity—Although it is difficult to judge this characteristic without knowing exactly how a robot vacuum would operate, it is believed that the product would not be overly complex to operate.

Trialability—It is doubtful that the product can be tried on a limited basis, and trying it in a store might not really simulate home usage. If the manufacturer were to offer a 30-day money back guarantee (similar to the one offered by a number of men's electric shaver manufacturers), however, then consumers might not let trialability serve as a barrier to purchase.

Observability—Although a robot vacuum cleaner probably will not have a great deal of social visibility (i.e., most people put their vacuum cleaners away when company comes over), it should create a great deal of "buzz" in that a purchaser would instigate a conversation with a friend, neighbor, or coworker about his or her new home robot. So the appliance will be high in communicability, if not observability.

Case Two: Selling Movie Tickets

Clearly, the purpose of the Web site is to create a "buzz" for the film, which is what viral marketing is all about. As the text notes, one aspect of viral marketing is that a message recipient is encouraged to pass along the information to others, which is, essentially, what an opinion leader does. Each movie studio hopes that movie or entertainment opinion leaders will seek out their Web sites, and then spread favorable movie related information to their friends, coworkers, neighbors, and other family members.

CHAPTER 16

Consumer Decision Making and Beyond

LEARNING OBJECTIVES

After studying this chapter students should be able to:
1. Describe a decision.
2. Enumerate the three levels of consumer decision making.
3. Explain the four models of consumer decision making discussed in the text.
4. Outline a model of consumer decision-making.
5. Discuss the three stages of consumer decision making in the process component of the decision-making model.
6. Outline the rules consumers use in decision making.
7. Discuss purchase and postpurchase behavior as part of the consumer decision process.
8. Explain consumer gifting behavior.
9. Describe the elements of the consuming and possessing process.
10. Explain the importance of relationship marketing.

SUMMARY

The consumer's decision to purchase or not to purchase a product or service is an important moment for most marketers. It can signify whether a marketing strategy has been wise, insightful, and effective, or whether it was poorly planned and missed the mark. Thus, marketers are particularly interested in the consumer's decision-making process. For a consumer to make a decision, more than one alternative must be available. (The decision not to buy is also an alternative.)

Theories of consumer decision making vary, depending on the researcher's assumptions about the nature of humankind. The various models of consumers (economic view, passive view, cognitive view, and emotional view) depict consumers and their decision-making processes in distinctly different ways.

An overview consumer decision-making model ties together the psychological, social, and cultural concepts examined in Parts II and III into an easily understood framework. This decision model has three sets of variables: input variables, process variables, and output variables.

Input variables that affect the decision-making process include commercial marketing efforts, as well as noncommercial influences from the consumer's sociocultural environment. The decision process variables are influenced by the consumer's psychological field, including the evoked set (or the brands in a particular product category considered in making a purchase choice). Taken as a whole, the psychological field influences the consumer's recognition of a need, prepurchase search for information, and evaluation of alternatives.

The output phase of the model includes the actual purchase (either trial or repeat purchase) and postpurchase evaluation. Both prepurchase and postpurchase evaluation feed back in the form of experience into the consumer's psychological field, and serve to influence future decision processing.

The process of gift exchange is an important part of consumer behavior. Various gift-giving and gift-receiving relationships are captured by the following five specific gifting classification scheme: (1) intergroup gifting (a group gives a gift to another group); (2) intercategory gifting (an individual gives a gift to a group or a group gives a gift to an individual); (3) intragroup gifting (a group gives a gift to itself or its members), (4) interpersonal gifting (an individual gives a gift to another individual), and (5) intrapersonal gifting (a self-gift).

Consumer behavior is not just making a purchase decision or the act of purchasing; it also includes the full range of experiences associated with using or consuming products and services. It also includes the sense of pleasure and satisfaction derived from possessing or collecting "things." The outputs of consumption are changes in feelings, moods, or attitudes; reinforcement of lifestyles; an enhanced sense of self, satisfaction of a consumer-related need: belonging to groups; and expressing and entertaining oneself.

Among other things, consuming includes the simple utility of using a superior product, the stress reduction of a vacation, the sense of having a "sacred" possession, and the pleasures of a hobby or a collection. Some possessions serve to assist consumers in their effort to create "personal meaning" and to maintain a sense of the past.

Relationship marketing impacts consumers' decisions and their consumption satisfaction. Firms establish relationship marketing programs (sometimes called loyalty programs) to foster usage loyalty and a commitment to their products and services. At its heart, relationship marketing is all about building trust (between the firm and its customers), and keeping promises made to consumers. Therefore, the emphasis in relationship marketing is almost always on developing long-term bonds with customers by making them feel special and by providing them with personalized services.

CHAPTER OUTLINE

INTRODUCTION

1. This chapter takes a broader perspective and examines *consumer decision making* in the context of all types of *consumption choices*, ranging from the consumption of new products to the use of old and established products.
2. It also considers consumers' decisions not as the end point, but rather as the beginning point of a consumption process.

*****Use Key Term* consumer decision making *Here*****

WHAT IS A DECISION?

1. In the most general terms, a decision is the selection of an option from two or more alternative choices.
2. If the consumer has no alternatives from which to choose and is literally forced to make a particular purchase or take a particular action (e.g., use a prescribed medication), then this does not constitute a decision and is commonly referred to as a "Hobson's choice."
   b) In actuality, no-choice purchase or consumption situations are fairly rare.

*****Use Learning Objective #1 Here; Use Table 16-1 Here*****

LEVELS OF CONSUMER DECISION MAKING

1. Not all consumer decisions receive or require the same amount of effort in the information search.
2. Researchers have identified three specific levels of consumer decision making: *extensive problem solving, limited problem solving,* and *routinized response behavior.*

*****Use Key Terms extensive problem solving, limited problem solving, and routinized response behavior Here; Use Learning Objective #2 Here; Use Discussion Question #3 Here*****

Extensive Problem Solving

1. When consumers have no established criteria for evaluating a product, or have not narrowed their choices, then they are in *extensive problem solving.*
2. At this level, the consumer needs a great deal of information to establish a set of criteria on which to judge specific brands and a correspondingly large amount of information concerning each of the brands to be considered.

*****Use Learning Objective #2 Here; Use Discussion Question #3 Here*****

Limited Problem Solving

1. At this level consumers have already established the basic criteria for evaluating the product category but haven't established preferred categories.
2. Their search for additional information is more like "fine-tuning;" they must gather additional brand information to discriminate among the various brands.

*****Use Learning Objective #2 Here; Use Discussion Question #3 Here*****

Routinized Response Behavior

1. At this level, consumers have some experience with the product category and a well-established set of criteria with which to evaluate the brands they are considering.
   a) They may search for a small amount of additional information.
2. Just how extensive a consumer's problem-solving task is depends on how well established his or her criteria for selection are, how much information he or she has about each brand being considered, and how narrow the set of brands is from which the choice will be made.
3. Routinized response behavior implies little need for additional information.

*****Use Learning Objective #2 Here; Use Discussion Question #3 Here*****

MODELS OF CONSUMERS: FOUR VIEWS OF CONSUMER DECISION MAKING

1. The term *models of consumers* refer to a general view or perspective as to how and why individuals behave as they do.
2. Four views will be examined:
   a) An *economic view*.
   b) A *passive view*.
   c) A *cognitive view*.
   d) An *emotional view*.

*****Use Learning Objective #3 Here; Use Discussion Question #1 Here*****

An Economic View

1. The consumer has often been characterized as making *rational decisions.*
   a) This model, called the *economic man* theory, has been criticized by consumer researchers for a number of reasons.
   b) To behave rationally in the economic sense, a consumer would have to:
      i) Be aware of all available product alternatives.
      ii) Be capable of correctly ranking each alternative in terms of its benefits and its disadvantages.
      iii) Be able to identify the one best alternative.
   c) This perspective is unrealistic because:
      i) People are limited by their existing skills, habits, and reflexes.
      ii) People are limited by their existing values and goals.
      iii) People are limited by the extent of their knowledge.
2. Consumers operate in an imperfect world, therefore the economic view is often rejected as too idealistic and simplistic.

*****Use Learning Objective #3 Here; Use Discussion Question #1 Here*****

A Passive View

1. The opposite of the economic view is the view of the consumer as basically submissive to the self-serving interests and promotional efforts of marketers (i.e., the *passive view*).
2. Consumers are perceived as impulsive and irrational purchasers, ready to yield to the arms and aims of marketers.
3. The principal limitation of this model is that it fails to recognize that the consumer plays an equal, if not dominant, role in many buying situations by seeking information about product alternatives and selecting the product that appears to offer the greatest satisfaction.
4. This view is largely unrealistic.

*****Use Learning Objective #3 Here; Use Discussion Question #1 Here*****

A Cognitive View

1. This view portrays the consumer as a *thinking problem solver.*
2. The cognitive model focuses on the processes by which consumers seek and evaluate information about selected brands and retail outlets.
3. Consumers are viewed as information processors, and this leads to the formulation of preferences, and ultimately, purchase intentions.
4. In contrast to the economic view, this view recognizes that the consumer is unlikely to seek all possible information, but will only seek information until he/she has what is perceived as sufficient information to make a satisfactory decision.
5. Consumers are presumed to use *heuristics*—short-cut decision rules to facilitate decision making.
   a) They also use decision rules when exposed to too much information—*information overload*.
6. This model depicts a consumer who does not have complete knowledge, and therefore cannot make perfect decisions, but who actively seeks information and attempts to make satisfactory decisions.

*****Use Key Terms **heuristics and information overload** Here; Use Learning Objective #3 Here; Use Discussion Question #1 Here; Use Exercise #1 Here; Use Figure 16-1 Here*****

An Emotional View

1. Although aware of the *emotional* or *impulsive side* of consumer decision making, marketers have preferred the economic or passive models.
2. In reality, when is comes to certain purchases or possessions, deep feelings or emotions are likely to be highly involved.
3. Possessions may also serve to preserve a sense of the past and help with transitions in times of change.

4. When a consumer makes what is basically an emotional purchase decision, less emphasis tends to be placed on searching for prepurchase information and more on the current mood or feelings.
5. Unlike an *emotion*, which is a response to a particular environment, a mood is more typically an unfocused, pre-existing state—already present at the time a consumer "experiences" an advertisement, a retail environment, a brand, or a product.
6. *Mood* is important to consumer decision making in that it impacts when consumers shop, where they shop, and whether they shop alone or with others.
    a) Some retailers attempt to create a mood for shoppers.
    b) Individuals in a positive mood recall more information about a product than those in a negative mood.

*****Use Key Term moods Here; Use Learning Objective #3 Here; Use Discussion Question #1 Here; Use Exercise #1 Here*****

A MODEL OF CONSUMER DECISION MAKING

1. The model looks at cognitive processes, problem solving, and to some degree, the emotional aspects of consumer decision making as well.
2. This is not an exhaustive review but a synthesis and coordination of relevant concepts into a whole.

*****Use Learning Objective #4 Here; Use Discussion Question #9 Here; Use Figure 16-2 Here*****

Input

1. The *input* component draws on external influences that provide information or influence a consumer's product-related values, attitudes, and behavior.

*****Use Discussion Question #2 Here*****

Marketing Inputs

1. The firm's marketing activities are a direct attempt to reach, inform, and persuade consumers to buy and use its products.
2. The impact of a firm's marketing efforts is governed by the consumer's perception of these efforts.
3. Marketers should be alert to consumer perceptions by sponsoring consumer research, rather than to rely on the intended impact of their marketing messages.

*****Use Discussion Question #2 Here*****

341

<u>Sociocultural Inputs</u>

1. *Sociocultural* inputs consist of a wide range of noncommercial influences—comments of a friend, an editorial in the newspaper, a family member, and direct noncommercial sources of information.
2. The unwritten codes of conduct communicated by culture indicate right and wrong consumption behavior.
3. The cumulative impact of each firm's marketing efforts, the influence of family, friends, and neighbors, and society's existing code of behavior are all likely to affect the how and what of consumer purchases.

*****Use Discussion Question #2 Here; Use Learning Objective #4 Here; Use Figure 16-2 Here*****

Process

1. The *process* component of the model is concerned with how consumers make decisions.
2. *Psychological field*—represents the internal influences—motivation, perception, learning, personality, and attitudes—that affect consumers' decision-making processes.
3. The consumer decision consists of three states: ***need recognition***, ***prepurchase search***, and ***evaluation of alternatives***.

*****Use Key Terms need recognition, prepurchase search, and evaluation of alternatives Here; Use Learning Objective #5 Here; Use Figure 16-2 Here*****

<u>Need Recognition</u>

1. *Recognition of a need* occurs when a consumer is faced with a problem.
2. Among consumers there seem to be two different problem recognition styles.
   a) *Actual state types*—consumers who perceive that they have a problem when a product fails to perform satisfactorily.
   b) *Desired state types*—the desire for something new may trigger the decision process.

*****Use Learning Objective #5 Here; Use Exercise #2 Here*****

<u>Prepurchase Search</u>

1. *Prepurchase search* begins when a consumer perceives a need that might be satisfied by the purchase and consumption of a product.
   a) The consumer usually searches his or her memory first.
   b) If no experience is present then he/she may engage in an extensive search of the outside environment.
   c) Past experience is considered an internal source of information.
      i) The greater the relevance of past experience, the less of an external search.
      ii) The degree of perceived risk can also influence this stage.

iii) High risk situations will lead to complex information gathering, low-risk, simple search and evaluation.
2. The act of "shopping" is an important form of external information.
   a) According to a recent consumer study there is a big difference between men and women in terms of their response to shopping.
   b) In addition to gender differences, research reveals that price considerations can also play a role in determining the extent of the search process.
3. An examination of the external search effort associated with the purchase of different product categories (e.g., TVs, VCRs, or personal computers) found that, as the amount of total search effort increased, consumer attitudes toward shopping became more positive, and more time was made available for shopping.
   a) The less consumers know about a product category and the more important the purchase is to them, the more time they will make available and the more extensive their prepurchase search activity is likely to be.
4. The Internet has had a great impact on prepurchase search.
   a) Web sites can provide consumers with much of the information they need about the products and services they are considering.
5. How much information a consumer will gather also depends on various situational factors.

*****Use Discussion Question #4 Here; Use Learning Objective #5 Here; Use Table 16-2 and 16-3 Here*****

Evaluation of Alternatives

1. When evaluating potential alternatives, consumers tend to use two types of information:
   a) A "list" of brands (the evoked set).
   b) The criteria they will use to evaluate each brand.
2. Evoked set—*evoked set* refers to the specific brands the consumer considers in making a purchase in a particular product category.
   a) The *inept set* consists of brands the consumer excludes from purchase consideration as unacceptable.
   b) The *inert set* is those brands to which the consumer is indifferent because they are perceived as having no advantage.
   c) The evoked set consists of the small number of brands the consumer is familiar with, remembers, and finds acceptable.
3. The five terminal positions in the model that do not end in purchase would appear to have perceptual problems. For example:
   a) Brands may be unknown because of the consumer's selective exposure to advertising media and selective perception of advertising stimuli.
   b) Brands may be unacceptable because of poor qualities or attributes or inappropriate positioning in either advertising or product characteristics.
   c) Brands may be perceived as not having any special benefits and are regarded indifferently by the consumer.
   d) Brands may be overlooked because they have not been clearly positioned or sharply targeted at the consumer market segment under study.

e) Brands may not be selected because they are perceived by consumers as unable to satisfy perceived needs as fully as the brand that is chosen.
4. The implication for marketers is that promotional techniques should be designed to impart a more favorable, perhaps more relevant product image to the target consumer.

*****Use Key Terms** evoked set, inept set, and inert set *Here; Use Table 16-4 Here; Use Figure 16-3 Here; Use Exercise #3 and #4 Here*****

5. Criteria used for evaluation brands—the criteria consumers' use for evaluating brands are usually expressed in terms of important product attributes.
   a) When a company knows that consumers will be evaluating alternatives, they sometimes advertise in a way that recommends the criteria that consumers should use in assessing product or service options.
   b) Research shows that when consumers discuss such "right products," there is little or no mention of price; brand names are not often top-of-mind; items often reflect personality characteristics or childhood experiences; and it is often "love at first sight."

*****Use Table 16-4 and 16-5 Here; Use Figure 16-4 Here; Use Exercise #3 Here; Use Discussion Question #5 Here*****

6. Consumer decision rules—consumer decision rules are referred to as *heuristics, decision strategies,* and *information-processing strategies,* and are procedures used by consumers to facilitate brand choices.
   a) These rules reduce the burden of decision making.
   b) ***Compensatory decision rules***—a consumer evaluates brand options in terms of each relevant attribute and computes a weighted or summated score for each brand.
      i) The computed score reflects the brand's relative merit as a potential purchase choice.
      ii) The assumption is that the consumer will choose the brand with the highest score.
      iii) A unique feature of a compensatory decision rule is that it allows a positive evaluation of a brand on one attribute to balance out a negative evaluation on some other attribute.
   c) ***Noncompensatory decision rules*** do not allow consumers to balance positive evaluations of a brand on one attribute against a negative evaluation on some other attribute. Forms include:
      i) ***Conjunctive decision rule***—the consumer establishes a minimally acceptable level that is established as a cutoff point for each attribute.
         a) If any particular brand falls below the cutoff point on any one attribute, the brand is eliminated from consideration.
      ii) ***Disjunctive rule***—this rule mirrors the conjunctive rule.
         a) The consumer establishes a minimally acceptable level as a cutoff point for each attribute.
         b) In this case if a brand alternative meets or exceeds the cutoff established for any one attribute, however, it is accepted.

iii) *Lexicographic decision rule*—the consumer first ranks the attributes in terms of perceived relevance or importance.

    a)   The consumer then compares the various brand alternatives in terms of the single attribute that is considered most important.

    b)   If one brand scores sufficiently high on this top-ranked attribute, it is selected, and the process ends.

    c)   The highest-ranked attribute may reveal something about the individual's consumer orientation.

7. A variety of decision rules appear common. Nine out of ten shoppers who go to the store for frequently purchased items have a specific shopping strategy for saving money.

    a) Practical loyalists—look for ways to save on those brands and products that they would buy anyway.

    b) Bottom-Line Price Shoppers—buy the lowest-priced item, with little or no regard for brand.

    c) Opportunistic Switchers—use coupons or sales to decide among brands and products that fall within their evoked set.

    d) Deal Hunters—look for the best "bargain" and are not brand-loyal.

8. A synthesized decision rule, the ***affect referral decision rule***, is the simplest, and is the consumer remembering past evaluations from his/her evoked set and selecting the brand with the highest perceived overall rating.

*****Use Key Terms** compensatory decision rules, noncompensatory decision rules, conjunctive decision rule, disjunctive rule, lexicographic decision rule, and affect referral decision rule *Here; Use Learning Objective #6 Here; Use Table 16-5, 16-6, and 16-7 Here; Use Exercise #3 Here; Use Discussion Question #5 Here*****

---

9. Going online to secure assistance in decision making—for the past several years researchers have been examining how using the Internet has impacted the way consumers make decisions.

    a) Three factors that have been researched are:

        i)   *Task complexity* (number of alternatives and amount of information available for each alternative).

        ii) *Information organization* (presentation, format, and content).

        iii) *Time constraint* (more or less time to decide).

*****Use Table 16-8 Here*****

---

10. Lifestyles as a consumer decision strategy—an individual's or family's decisions to be committed to a particular lifestyle impacts their consumer behavior.

    a) Research suggests that 15 percent of Baby Boomers will be seeking a simpler lifestyle.

11. Incomplete information and noncomparable alternatives—in many situations consumers face incomplete information. They cope with this missing information in a number of ways.

    a) They may delay decision making until the missing information is available.

    b) They may ignore the missing information and work with available information.

c) Consumers may change their decision-making strategy to accommodate the missing information.

d) Consumers may infer or construct the missing information.

e) Consumers may conclude that none of their choices offer sufficient benefits to warrant purchase.

f) Sometimes consumers use decision rules to compare dissimilar alternatives.

12. A series of decisions—a purchase can involve a number of decisions rather than a single decision.

13. Decision rules and marketing strategy—an understanding of which decision rules consumers apply in selecting a particular product or service is useful to marketers concerned with formulating a promotional program.

14. Consumption vision—a study found the attitudes and search behavior of a vision, "a mental picture or visual image of specific usage outcomes and/or consumption consequences."

a) Such visions allow consumers to imagine or vicariously participate in the consumption of the product or service prior to making an actual decision.

*****Use Learning Objective #4 and #5 Here*****

OUTPUT

1. The output portion of the consumer decision-making model concerns two closely associated kinds of postdecision activity: *purchase behavior* and *postpurchase evaluation*.

2. The objective of both activities is to increase the consumer's satisfaction with his or her purchase.

*****Use Key Terms purchase behavior and postpurchase evaluation Here; Use Learning Objective #7 Here*****

Purchase Behavior

1. Consumers make three types of purchases: *trial purchases*, *repeat purchases*, and *long-term commitment purchases*.

a) Trial is the exploratory phase of purchase behavior in which consumers attempt to evaluate a product through direct use.

i) When a trial is satisfactory, consumers are likely to repeat the purchase.

b) Repeat purchase behavior is similar to brand loyalty.

i) A repeat purchase usually signifies that the product meets with the consumer's approval and that the consumer is willing to use it again and in larger quantities.

ii) This form is closely related to *brand loyalty*.

c) Trial is not always feasible, such as with big-ticket items and durable goods. In that case the consumer moves from evaluation directly to long-term commitment.

*****Use Learning Objective #7 Here*****

Postpurchase Evaluation

1. As consumers use a product, they evaluate its performance in light of their own expectations.
2. There are three possible outcomes of such evaluation.
   a) Actual performance matches the standard, leading to a neutral feeling.
   b) *Positive disconfirmation* when the performance exceeds the standard.
   c) *Negative disconfirmation* when the performance is below the standard.
3. An important aspect of the purchase process is reducing *postpurchase cognitive dissonance,* when consumers try to reassure themselves that their choice was a wise one.
4. The degree of postpurchase analysis relates to the importance of the product decision and the experience acquired in using the product.
5. The consumer's postpurchase evaluation feeds back as experience to the consumer's psychological field and serves to influence future related decisions.

*****Use Learning Objective #4 and #7 Here; Use Discussion Question #6, #7, and #8 Here; Use Exercise #5 Here*****

CONSUMER GIFTING BEHAVIOR

1. The amount of money spent and feelings generated by gifts make them an interesting part of consumer behavior.
2. *Gifting behavior* is the process of gift exchange that takes place between a giver and receiver.
   a) It includes gifts given to (and received from) others and gifts to oneself, or *self-gifts*.
3. Gifting is symbolic communication with implicit and explicit meanings.
4. One of the models of gifting reveals the following five gifting subdivisions:
   a) Intergroup gifting.
   b) Intercategory gifting.
   c) Intragroup gifting.
   d) Interpersonal gifting.
   e) Intrapersonal gifting.
5. Intergroup gifting occurs when one group exchanges gifts with another.
6. Intercategory gifting is an individual giving a group a gift, or a group giving an individual a gift.
7. An intragroup gift is a gift that a group gives itself.
8. Interpersonal gifts occur between two individuals.
9. An intrapersonal gift is a self-gift.

*****Use Key Terms gifting behavior and self-gifts Here; Use Learning Objective #8 Here; Use Table 16-9, 16-10, 16-11, 16-12, and 16-13 Here*****

BEYOND THE DECISION: CONSUMING AND POSSESSING

1. Historically consumer behavior studies have focused on the product, service, or brand choices.
2. We now see that the experience of possessing, collecting, or consuming things contributes to consumer satisfaction and overall quality of life.
3. Consumer choices might be viewed at the beginning of the *consumption process* rather than at the end.
   a) The choice or purchase decision is the input of the process.
   b) The input stage includes a consumption set and a consumption style.
   c) The process stage consists of using, possessing, collecting, and disposing of things and experiences.
   d) The output stage would include changes in feelings, attitudes, and behaviors, as well as reinforcement of a lifestyle.

*****Use Key Term* consumption process *Here; Use Learning Objective #9 Here; Use Figure 16-5 Here*****

Products Have Special Meaning and Memories

1. Consuming is a diverse and complex process.
2. It includes utility of a product, the psychological use of the product, memories, etc.
3. As a consequence, some possessions create personal meaning for consumers and/or help them maintain a sense of the past.
4. Some people maintain their identity after major changes in their life by linking to their past.

*****Use Learning Objective #9 Here*****

Relationship Marketing

1. Many firms are pursuing *relationship marketing* in order to build loyal usage and a commitment to their company's products and services.
   a) It is built on trust that grows from keeping promises.
2. The goal of relationship marketing is to build strong, lasting relationships with a core group of customers.
3. The emphasis is on developing long-term bonds, making consumers feel good about the company, and giving the consumer some kind of personal connection to the business.
4. A review of the composition of 66 consumer relationship marketing programs revealed three elements shared by more than 50 percent of the programs.
   a) Fostering ongoing communication with customers (73 percent of the programs).
   b) Furnishing loyalty by building extras like upgrades and other perks (68 percent of the programs).
   c) Stimulating a sense of belonging by providing a "club membership" format (50 percent of the programs).

5. Like personal relationships between individuals who are willing to do favors for each other, "relationship" marketers offer loyal customers special services, discounts, increased communications, and attention beyond the core product or service, without expecting an immediate payback.
   a) A new form of relationship marketing has resulted as Internet usage has increased. The term used on the Internet is "permission marketing."
6. Although direct marketing, sales promotion, and general advertising may be used as part of a relationship marketing strategy, relationship marketing stresses long-term commitment to the individual customer.
7. Ultimately, it is to a firm's advantage to develop long-term relationships with existing customers, because it is easier and less expensive to make an additional sale to an existing customer than to make a new sale to a new consumer.
8. Research indicates that consumers today are less loyal than in the past, due to six major forces:
   a) The abundance of choice.
   b) Availability of information.
   c) Entitlement (consumers repeatedly ask "What have you done for me lately?").
   d) Commoditization (most products/services appear to be similar—nothing stands out).
   e) Insecurity (consumer financial problems reduce loyalty).
   f) Time scarcity (not enough time to be loyal).

> *******Use Key Term relationship marketing *Here; Use Learning Objective #10 Here; Use Figure 16-6 and 16-7 Here; Use Table 16-14 Here********

DISCUSSION QUESTIONS

1. Compare and contrast the economic, passive, cognitive, and emotional models of consumer decision making.

The *economic view* portrays consumers as making rational decisions. Clearly, this model is not characteristic of most consumption situations because consumers are rarely aware and knowledgeable of all the product alternatives in any given situation, and of all the features and benefits of the product offerings they can choose from. Thus, they are often unable to make rational decisions. The *passive view* depicts the consumer as basically submissive to the self-serving interests and promotional efforts of marketers. Consumers are perceived as impulsive and irrational purchasers, ready to yield to the arms and aims of marketers. The *cognitive view* depicts consumers as problem solvers where they cognitively process information, seek out products and services that fulfill their needs, form preferences, make choices, and engage in postpurchase evaluations of their selections. Such decision making is characteristic of consumption situations where consumers are highly involved with purchases and experience high levels of perceived risk. The *emotional view* states that consumers often have deep emotions or feelings regarding many purchases. This is typical of consumption situations where consumers place more emphasis on their current moods and feelings and less emphasis on prepurchase information. In such cases, a product is bought on an impulse

—on a whim—or because the buyer is emotionally driven. Emotional advertising appeals include stressing nostalgia, fantasy, and being "seduced" by the product.

2. **What kinds of marketing and sociocultural inputs would influence the purchase of: (a) a TV with a built-in VCR, (b) a concentrated liquid laundry detergent, and (c) fat-free ice cream? Explain your answers.**

Students' answers will vary. Students should see *marketing inputs* as the firm's marketing efforts to reach, inform, and persuade consumers to buy and use its products. These inputs take the form of specific marketing-mix strategies that consist of the product itself (including its package, size, and guarantees); mass-media advertising, direct marketing, personal selling, and other promotional efforts; pricing policy; and the selection of distribution channels to move the product from the manufacturer to the consumer. *Sociocultural inputs* consist of a wide range of noncommercial influences, the comments of a friend, an editorial in the newspaper, usage by a family member or an article in *Consumer Reports*. The influences of social class, culture, and subculture, though less tangible, are important input factors that are internalized and affect how consumers evaluate and ultimately adopt (or reject) products. Unlike the firm's marketing efforts, sociocultural inputs do not necessarily support the purchase or consumption of a specific product, but may influence consumers to avoid a product.

3. **Define extensive problem solving, limited problem solving, and routinized response behavior. What are the differences among the three decision-making approaches? What type of decision process would you expect most consumers to follow in their first purchase of a new product or brand in each of the following areas: (a) chewing gum, (b) sugar, (c) men's aftershave lotion, (d) carpeting, (e) paper towels, (f) a cellular telephone, and (g) a luxury car? Explain your answers.**

Again students' answers will vary. They should demonstrate a clear understanding of the three decision frameworks. Extensive problem solving—the consumer has no pre-established criteria to evaluate the product category or brands. The consumer has not narrowed the brand alternatives into an evoked set. Limited problem solving—the consumer has established basic criteria for evaluating the product category or brand. The consumer has no clear preferences among the brands in his or her evoked set. Routinized response behavior—the consumer has some experience with the product category. The consumer has established criteria with which to evaluate brands in his or her evoked set. Also, little or no additional information is needed to make a brand choice. The strategies which one might expect consumers to follow in their first purchase of a new product or brand clearly depend on how involved they are with the purchase. Because involvement is consumer-related rather than product-related, there are no standardized answers to the second part of this question. Here are some suggestions: (a) chewing gum—limited problem solving; (b) sugar—routinized response behavior; (c) men's aftershave lotion—limited problem solving; (d) carpeting—extensive problem solving; (e) paper towels—routinized response behavior; (f) a cellular telephone—extensive problem solving; and (g) a luxury car—extensive problem solving.

4a. Identify three different products that you believe require reasonably intensive prepurchase search by a consumer. Then, using Table 16-2 as a guide, identify the specific characteristics of these products that make intensive prepurchase search likely.

b. For each of the products that you listed, identify the perceived risks that a consumer is likely to experience prior to purchase. Discuss how the marketers of these products can reduce these perceived risks.

Students' answers to this question will demonstrate that products requiring intensive prepurchase search are ones with high consumer involvement and high perceived risk, and are also likely to be expensive and infrequently purchased (e.g., cars, personal computers, stereo systems).

5. Let's assume that this coming summer you are planning to spend a month touring Europe and are, therefore, in need of a good 35mm camera. (a) Develop a list of product attributes that you will use as the purchase criteria in evaluating various 35mm cameras. (b) Distinguish the differences that would occur in your decision process if you were to employ compensatory versus noncompensatory decision rules.

Students' answers will probably focus on personal criteria and fail to apply the text content. Be prepared to lead the students to relate their process and the decision-making process described in the text. For example, when using a compensatory decision rule, you would evaluate each brand in your evoked set in terms of the intrinsic product features or attributes that you believe to be important. For instance, if your criteria for this camera include compactness, ease of picture taking, and high picture-quality, a compensatory decision would require you to evaluate each brand in terms of all three criteria in order to arrive at a final choice. In using a noncompensatory decision rule, you would evaluate each camera brand in terms of a single relevant criterion. For instance, if you feel that picture quality is the most important criterion for selecting a camera, you would purchase the brand believed to deliver the highest quality photographic results.

6. How can a marketer of very light, very powerful laptop computers use its knowledge of customers' expectations in designing a marketing strategy?

The marketer should be aware of what the consumer expects from the laptop computer because if the product fails to operate as the consumer expects it to, he or she might return it, not buy products under that brand name again, and spread unfavorable word-of-mouth about the company. The promotion for the computer must not build up unrealistic expectations about the product by promising, for example, an easy-to-use product (because virtually all personal computers are complex products and users must spend a considerable amount of time learning how to operate them properly). The positioning approach used must be designed to deliver benefits that are congruent with those consumer needs and expectations uncovered by research studies.

7. **How do consumers reduce postpurchase dissonance? How can marketers provide positive reinforcement to consumers after the purchase in order to reduce their dissonance?**

Marketing strategies to reduce postpurchase dissonance include: (a) ads which reassure buyers that they made the right choice; (b) reassuring messages and text within the instruction manuals; (c) extensive warranties, guarantees, and service; (d) a mechanism to obtain further information about the product (e.g., an 800 number, a corporate service center); (e) postpurchase contacts with buyers by mail or phone (e.g., a "welcome back" postcard mailed by a travel agent to a client returning from a vacation that was arranged by the same travel agent).

8. **The Gillette Company, which produces the highly successful Sensor shaving blade, has recently introduced a clear gel antiperspirant and deodorant for men. Identify the perceived risks associated with the purchase of this new product and outline a strategy designed to reduce these perceived risks during the product's introduction.**

Because Gillette is a well-known company, consumers have little to worry about wasting time and money (i.e., little or no financial and time loss risks) or buying a product that will not work properly (i.e., no functional or physical risks). Therefore, Gillette's promotional messages for the new product should capitalize on the firm's image of quality, an image that was strongly reinforced by the success of the Sensor blade, by depicting the firm as a marketer of a complete line of men's grooming products and toiletries. Gillette already has an extensive marketing network and should use it to promote and distribute the new product. Indeed, ads for the new antiperspirant mentioned the Sensor by name, and the packages of this well-established shaving blade included coupons for, and free trial-size samples of, the company's new men's grooming products (an apparent utilization of stimulus generalization).

9. **Albert Einstein once wrote that "the whole of science is nothing more than a refinement of everyday thinking." Do you think that this quote applies to the development of the consumer decision-making model presented in Figure 16-2?**

Students' answers will vary widely. Help them to see that the model presented in Figure 16-2 ties together many of the ideas on consumer decision making and consumption behavior discussed throughout the book. It does not presume to provide an exhaustive picture of the complexities of consumer decision making. Rather, it is designed to synthesize and coordinate relevant concepts into a significant whole. The model includes input into consumer decision making, the process of the decision, and its output. Thus, this model is congruent with Einstein's view.

EXERCISES

1. **Find two print advertisements: one that illustrates the cognitive model of consumer decision making and one that illustrates the emotional model. Explain your choices. In your view, why did the marketers choose the approaches depicted in the advertisements?**

Instructor's Discussion

The objective of this exercise is to illustrate that the different views of consumer decision making are often depicted in advertising. Help the students identify the elements of the advertisement that would tap into the information process of the cognitive process. Require students to identify the emotive and mood elements of the emotional appeal.

2. **Describe the need recognition process that took place before you purchased your last can of soft drink. How did it differ from the process that preceded the purchase of a new pair of sneakers? What role, if any, did advertising play in your need recognition?**

Instructor's Discussion

Answers will vary by student. Have students focus on how their need for a soft drink arose. Did the student simply realize that he/she was thirsty, was it the act of eating, or did some input, an ad, or comment from a friend arouse the need? In a case of a new pair of sneakers, the student's problem recognition might have been caused by the wearing down of an old pair, by an ad for a new, more advanced or more fashionable brand, and/or by the fact that peers were switching to a new type or brand of sneakers. Because sneakers are a highly visible product, a marketer can arouse the need for the product by showing how it helps the wearer to gain approval and prestige among peers. Some students might also point out that an ad depicting a sports celebrity wearing a particular pair of sneakers can trigger the need for the product.

3. **List the colleges that you considered when choosing which college or university to attend, and the criteria that you used to evaluate them. Describe how you acquired information on the different colleges along with the different attributes that were important to you and how you made your decision. Be sure to specify whether you used compensatory or noncompensatory decision rules.**

Instructor's Discussion

Students' answers will vary from extensive information searchers to choosing because of convenience or parental direction. This exercise will demonstrate the complexities of prepurchase search during a high-involvement decision bearing a high degree of personal relevance and commitment. It may also show what was a high involvement decision for some was low involvement for others. Was risk a factor?

4. **Select one of the following product categories: (a) compact disc players, (b) fast-food restaurants, and (c) shampoo, and: (1) write down the brands that constitute your evoked set, (2) identify brands that are not part of your evoked set, and (3) discuss how the brands included in your evoked set differ from those that are not included in terms of important attributes.**

Instructor's Discussion

Answers will vary among students. Help the students explore why brands were included and excluded from their evoked set. Generally, those brands not included in the evoked set are the ones that are perceived as being of lower quality, having fewer features, being less stylish, and being less heavily promoted. Discuss the implications for marketers.

5. **Select a newspaper or magazine advertisement that attempts: (a) to provide the consumer with a decision strategy to follow in making a purchase decision, or (b) to reduce the perceived risk(s) associated with a purchase. Evaluate the effectiveness of the ad you selected.**

Instructor's Discussion

This exercise is designed to illustrate how two of the concepts described in this chapter are utilized in advertisements.

S.TA.R. PROJECTS

Ethical Issues in Consumer Behavior

S.T.A.R. Project #1
As a consumer behavior expert for a nationwide clothing manufacturer you have been asked to address a consortium of Better Business Bureaus via a nationwide interactive TV/Satellite hookup. When you arrive at the TV studio where the broadcast will occur you learn that the sponsors have also invited a speaker from Ralph Nader's consumer organization to address the same audience. This speaker will contend that consumers should use an economic view in consumption decisions. Your presentation was to assert that consumers primarily use a cognitive view in making their decisions. As the unannounced "debate" begins, your fellow speaker labels your company as being one that dupes consumers through mass media advertising and plays on the consumers' emotions and passivity (addiction to mass media for information) to sell products. Considering the response and the ethics of what was just done, formulate a response to support your position with respect to the cognitive view of consumer decision making. How could you ethically come out of this "debate" on top?

Instructor's Discussion

This scenario asks students to consider their actions when placed in a difficult role. First, the debate was unannounced and, therefore, preparation for a debate would be minimal. Second, the speaker that students would be matched against has an aggressive agenda. Lead students through a response format. Should they attack, be submissive, be explanatory, take the high road, or refuse to participate? This might be good training for the unexpected encounter.

S.T.A.R. Project #2

Examine Figure 16-2. Notice the three main sections—input, process, and output. Where within the model would the greatest potential for ethical dilemmas lie? Where within the model would be the place where the opportunity to excel in good ethical behavior would be greatest? How could a company use this model to guide its ethical behavior toward consumers? Explain your thoughts.

Instructor's Discussion

This question is intended to make students think as they answer the last series of questions in the text. Use an open forum to get student ideas. Encourage creativity. Remind students that good ethical behavior is not inconsistent with excellence in understanding consumer behavior.

Small Group Projects

S.T.A.R. Project #3

Your group's assignment is to pick a product category such as personal computers, clothing, cars, or recreation. Using your chosen category, chart, outline, or diagram how consumers make purchase decisions in the chosen area. Focus on need recognition, prepurchase search, and evaluation of alternatives. Lastly, your group should pick a "reporter" to summarize your group's findings for the entire class.

Instructor's Discussion

This assignment is a good summary for the group experience and the basic substance of the course and text. Add product categories for a large class to ensure that every group has a separate discussion area. Use this as a basis for discussion on how the product and its importance to the consumer effects the way they make decisions.

S.T.A.R. Project #4

Your group's assignment is to explain the levels of consumer decision making. Review the material in the text on extensive problem solving, limited problem solving, and routinized response behavior. In order to explain the levels, construct examples that differ from those presented in the text. Next, show how your examples could become one of the other forms. What would need to change in the purchase environment for the change(s) to occur? How would this change (changes) impact the strategic decision making of the manufacturer(s) of your product example(s)? Write a short summary report that outlines your group's findings. Discuss your findings with other class members. Note the similarities and differences with other groups.

Instructor's Discussion

This project will aid the groups to summarize the consumer behavior process shown in the text and give further reinforcement to learning associated with the levels of consumer decision making. Pick the best examples and have student groups discuss their examples in class.

Using the Internet to Study Consumer Behavior

S.T.A.R. Project #5

Review Table 16-2 before beginning this assignment. Your task is to go on a prepurchase search via the Internet. The product category is up to you. You can either search for a product via the Internet that you will eventually purchase in a store or the search can be for a product that would be purchased online. Once you have completed your prepurchase search, list the factors that impacted your search. How do these factors match to those listed in Table 16-2? Is the Internet a good way to search for products? Comment. Lastly, write a summary report about your experience and whether you thought it was beneficial or not. Be sure to describe your successes and failures encountered during the search process.

Instructor's Discussion

This assignment asks students to use the Internet to do a prepurchase search and then to comment on their experiences. The assignment also affords students the opportunity to review the situational factors shown in Table 16-2. Pick a few students to discuss their experiences while on their search. Try picking one student who has never searched for products via the Internet (yes, there will be some) and one student who is an experienced Internet searcher and shopper. Contrast the information provided by these two students.

S.T.A.R. Project #6

Consumer decision rules, even though you use them everyday, are often difficult to understand. Before beginning this assignment, review the consumer decision rules found in the chapter. Once this is done, examine the illustrations provided in Table 16-7 as a way of summarizing the various rules. Your assignment is to design your own new BMW (see the design feature at www.bmw.com). As you design your new car, consider the decision rules that are impacting and formulating your decisions. Once you have designed your new car, download a picture of the car and list all the features you have included in your ideal car (another download feature of the Web site). Write a short summary report that describes what you did, what decision rules you used, and how these rules influenced your overall decision process. Discuss your efforts with the class. Show your new car.

Instructor's Discussion

This assignment lets students have some fun designing their own luxury car and at the same time learn about decision rules. As students complete the assignment be sure to have them show their new car, explain what decision rules were used, and how the rules influenced their decision making process. The results are often surprising.

CASES

Case One: Making Paper Obsolete

Because a number of Tablet PC models are really laptop PCs offering a touch screen that can be written on, product attributes are likely to be similar to those for a standard laptop, such as processing speed, type and size of display, amount of memory, hard disk size, and so on.

Case Two: A Really Big Zippo

Considering the cult status of the original Zippo lighter, it would seem that the Zipper Multi-Purpose Lighter has a good chance to be a commercial success. In addition to men purchasing the item as a self-gift, spouses may also purchase it as a gift for one another because of its ease-of-use and childproof feature. Additionally, there are likely to be consumers who would prefer purchasing a quality item with a lifetime warranty to an inexpensive plastic disposable product. At its relatively modest retail selling price, it may also prove to be a "hot" seller at holiday time.